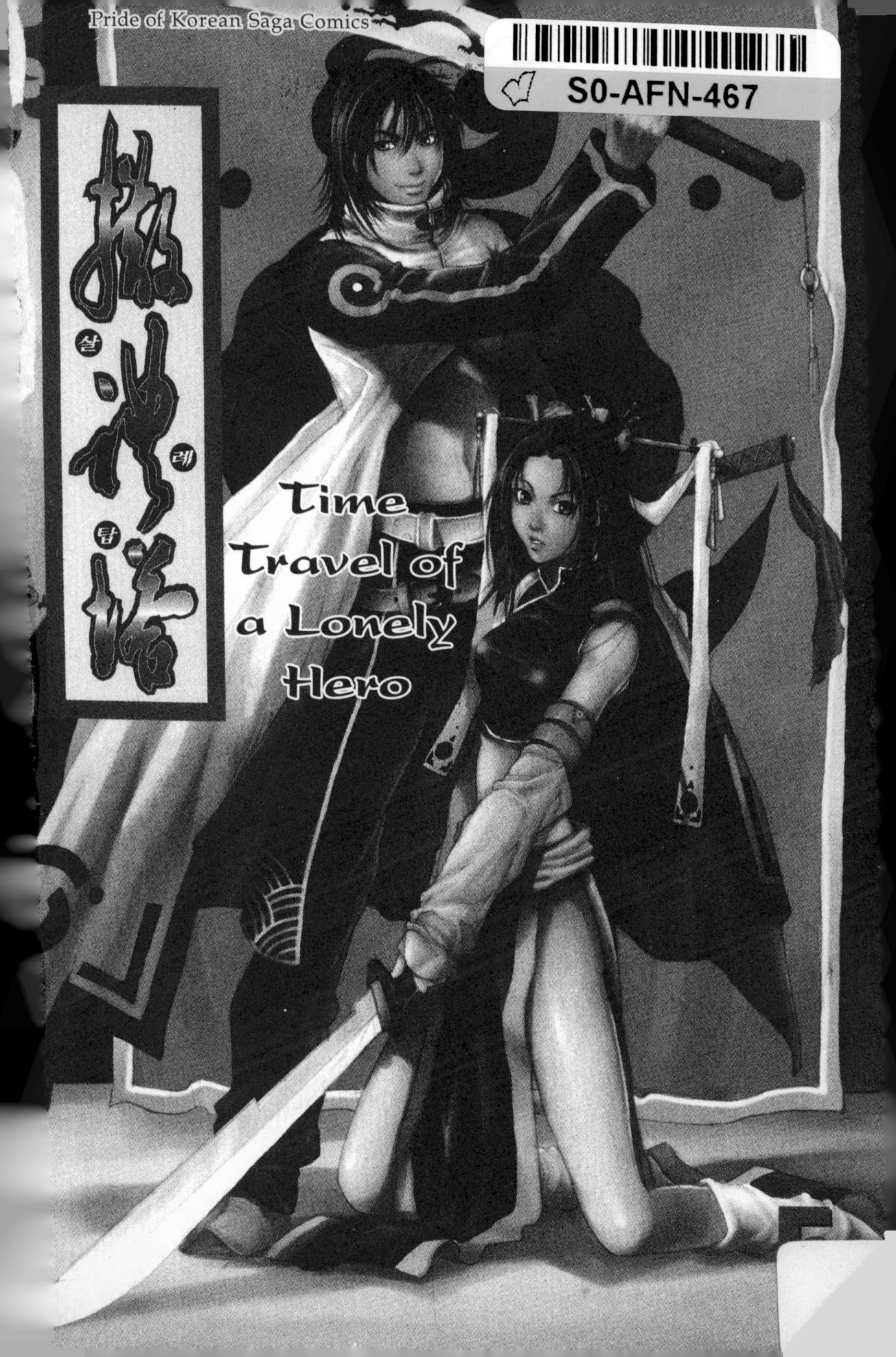
Pride of Korean Saga Comics
살
례
탑
Time Travel of a Lonely Hero

Threads of Time Vol. 5
created by Mi Young Noh

Translation - Jihae Hong
English Adaptation - Brandon Montclare
Retouch and Lettering - Deron Bennet
Production Artist - Vicente Rivera, Jr.
Cover Design - Kyle Plummer

Editor - Luis Reyes
Digital Imaging Manager - Chris Buford
Pre-Press Manager - Antonio DePietro
Production Managers - Jennifer Miller and Mutsumi Miyazaki
Art Director - Matt Alford
Managing Editor - Jill Freshney
VP of Production - Ron Klamert
Editor-in-Chief - Mike Kiley
President and C.O.O. - John Parker
Publisher and C.E.O. - Stuart Levy

A **TOKYOPOP** Manga

TOKYOPOP Inc.
5900 Wilshire Blvd. Suite 2000
Los Angeles, CA 90036

E-mail: info@TOKYOPOP.com
Come visit us online at www.TOKYOPOP.com

ISBN: 1-59532-036-9

First TOKYOPOP printing: May 2005
10 9 8 7 6 5 4 3 2 1
Printed in the USA

Threads of Time

Volume 5

By
Mi Young Noh

HAMBURG // LONDON // LOS ANGELES // TOKYO

Threads of Time
TOKYOPOP
Mi Young Noh 1

Threads of Time Vol. 1

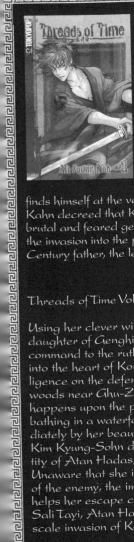

High school kendo champion Moon Bin Kim suffers from a recurring nightmare in which he lives as Sa Kyung Kim, the son of a prominent warrior family in 13th Century Korea (Koryo). After a freak accident at the school swimming pool Moon Bin falls into a coma, but his modern-day personality resurfaces in the distant past when Sa Kyung revives miraculously after years of unconsciousness. As if being displaced in medieval Koryo isn't enough, Moon Bin finds himself at the very brink of war. From his deathbed Genghis Kahn decreed that Koryo should be conquered. Sali Tayi, the most brutal and feared general of the Mongol army, is appointed to lead the invasion into the peninsula. Opposing him is Moon Bin's 13th Century father, the legendary warlord Kim Kyung-Sohn.

Threads of Time Vol. 2

Using her clever wiles and substantial might, the stunning granddaughter of Genghis Kahn, Atan Hadas, is made second-in-command to the ruthless Sali Tayi. Her first mission is to be sent into the heart of Koryo to gather intelligence on the defensive forces. In the woods near Ghu-Zhu Palace, Moon Bin happens upon the princess while she is bathing in a waterfall, and is smitten immediately by her beauty. At the same time, Kim Kyung-Sohn discovers the true identity of Atan Hadas, and orders her arrest. Unaware that she is a princess and a spy of the enemy, the impetuous Moon Bin helps her escape capture. Returning to Sali Tayi, Atan Hadas learns that a full-scale invasion of Koryo has begun.

Threads of Time
TOKYOPOP
Mi Young Noh 2

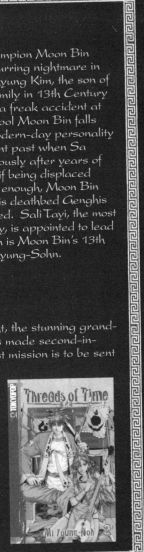

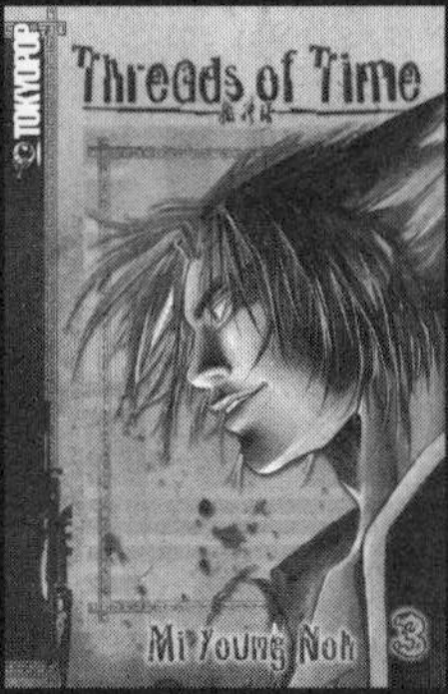
Threads of Time
TOKYOPOP
Mi Young Noh 3

Threads of Time Vol. 3

In an all-out assault the Mongol army ravages the northern towns and outposts of the land. With their howling warcries, the invaders cut a bloody swath toward Ghu-Zhu Palace, the stronghold of Koryo's defense. General Sali Tayi offers Koryo an ultimatum: surrender to the devastating ferocity of the Mongol army or go to war with it. With his valor unmoved by the Mongol's threats, Kim Kyung-Sohn upholds a remarkable resistance. Despite facing overwhelming enemy forces, the Koryo palace weathers the storm of a vicious Mongol siege. On the field of battle, the two commanders engage one another in personal combat and Kim Kyung-Sohn astonishingly perseveres—keeping the hopes of a successful resistance alive for one more day.

Threads of Time Vol. 4

Having had both his body and his pride injured, Sali Tayi vows to deliver death to not only Kim Kyung-Sohn, but to his entire family as well. Locating the defenseless village of Keh Kung, the crazed Mongol general orders the rape and massacre of his opponent's household. Witnessing the brutality of her fellow soldiers, Atan Hadas begins to doubt the glorified honors of the Koryo conquest. Walking again in the woods outside Keh Kung, she is reunited with the equally pensive Moon Bin. Seeking to repay Moon Bin for his earlier assistance, Atan Hadas warns of the slaughter and counsels that he should flee the land and save himself. Unable to abandon his 13th Century family, Moon Bin returns to his home to find that everything he knew in this new reality has been destroyed...

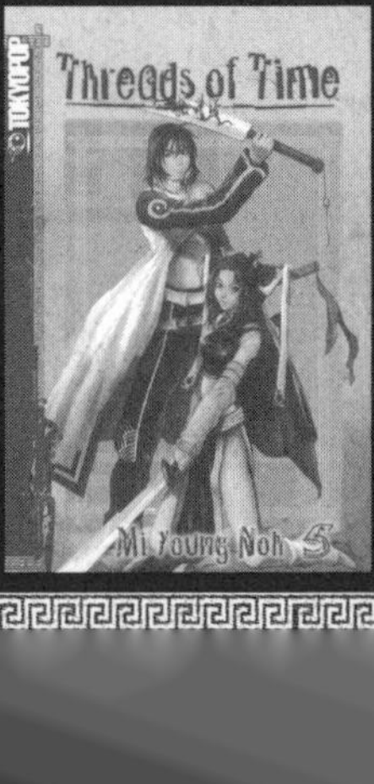
Threads of Time
TOKYOPOP
Mi Young Noh

contents

Threads of Time

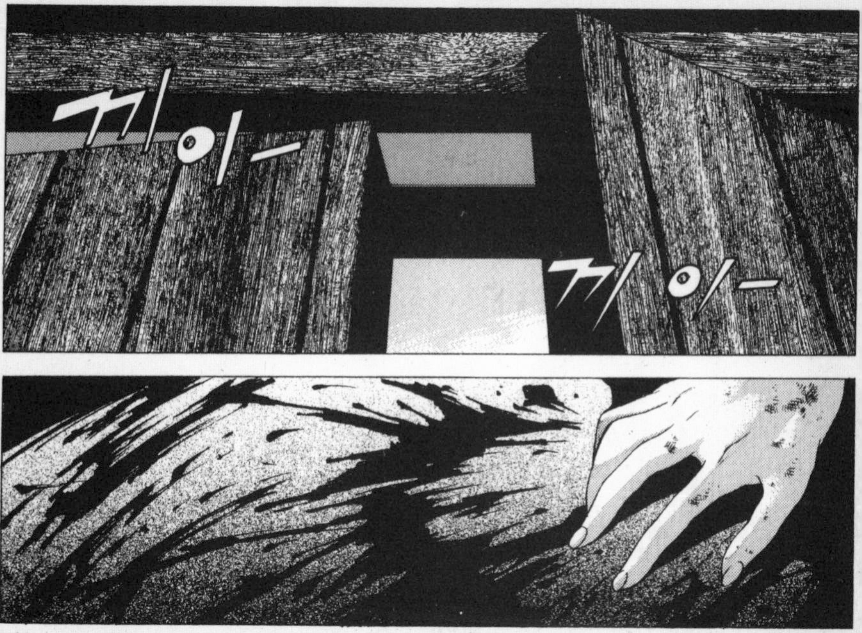
끼이-
끼이-

Chapter 19
Seed of Revenge

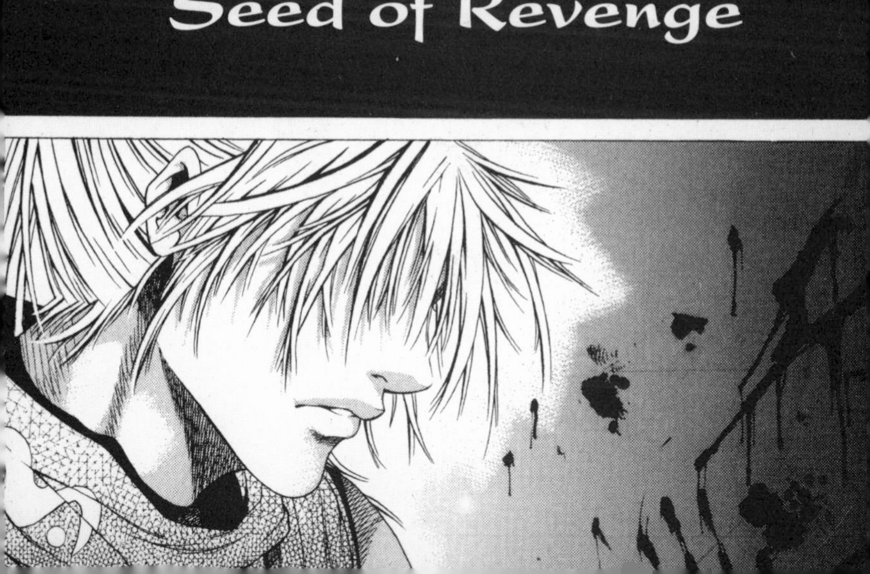

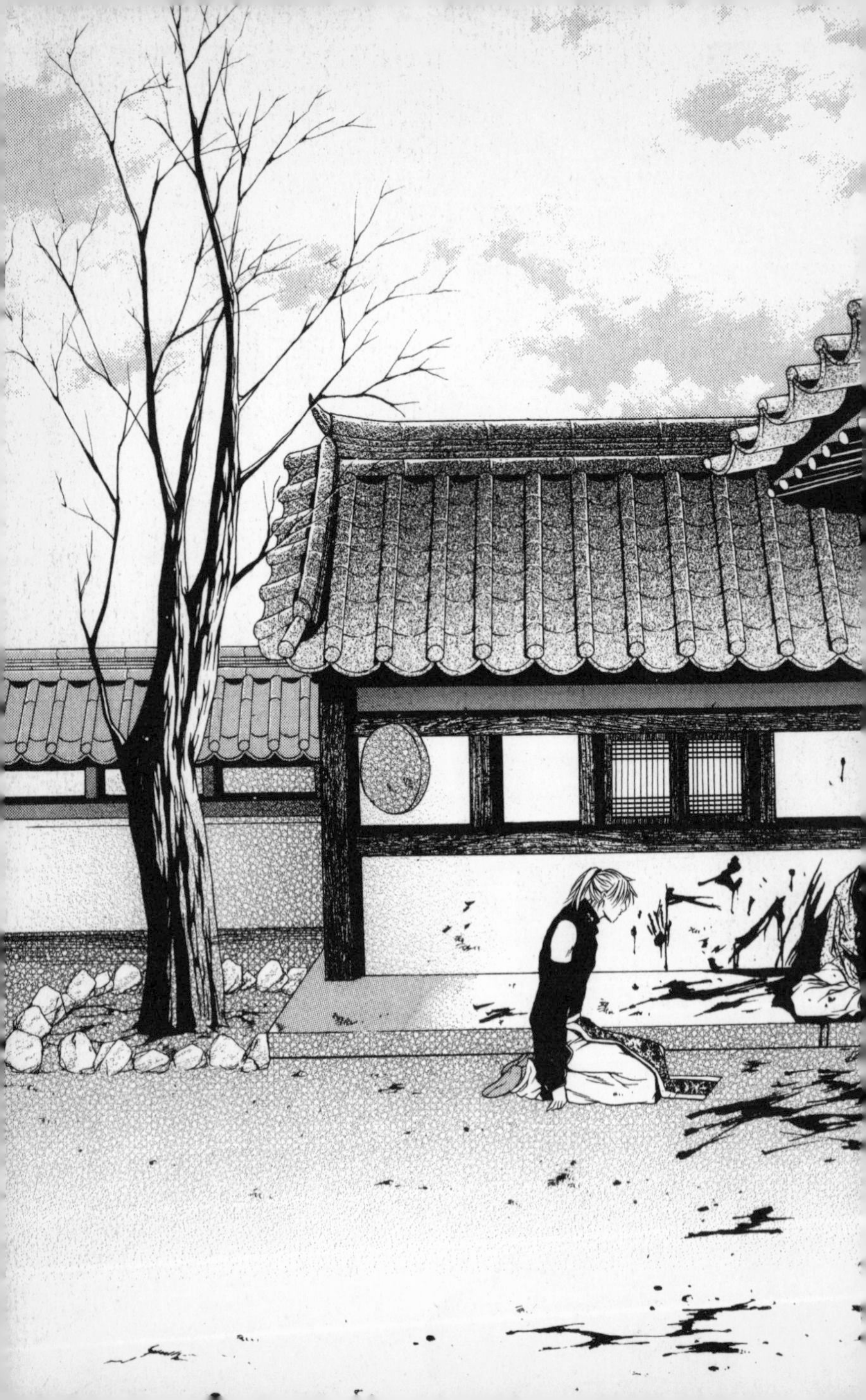

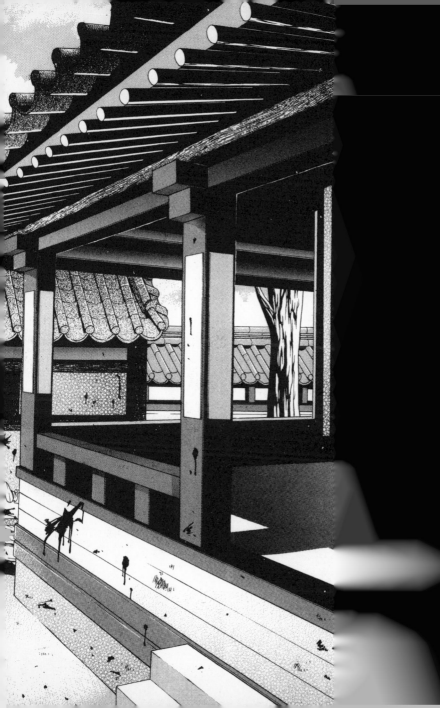

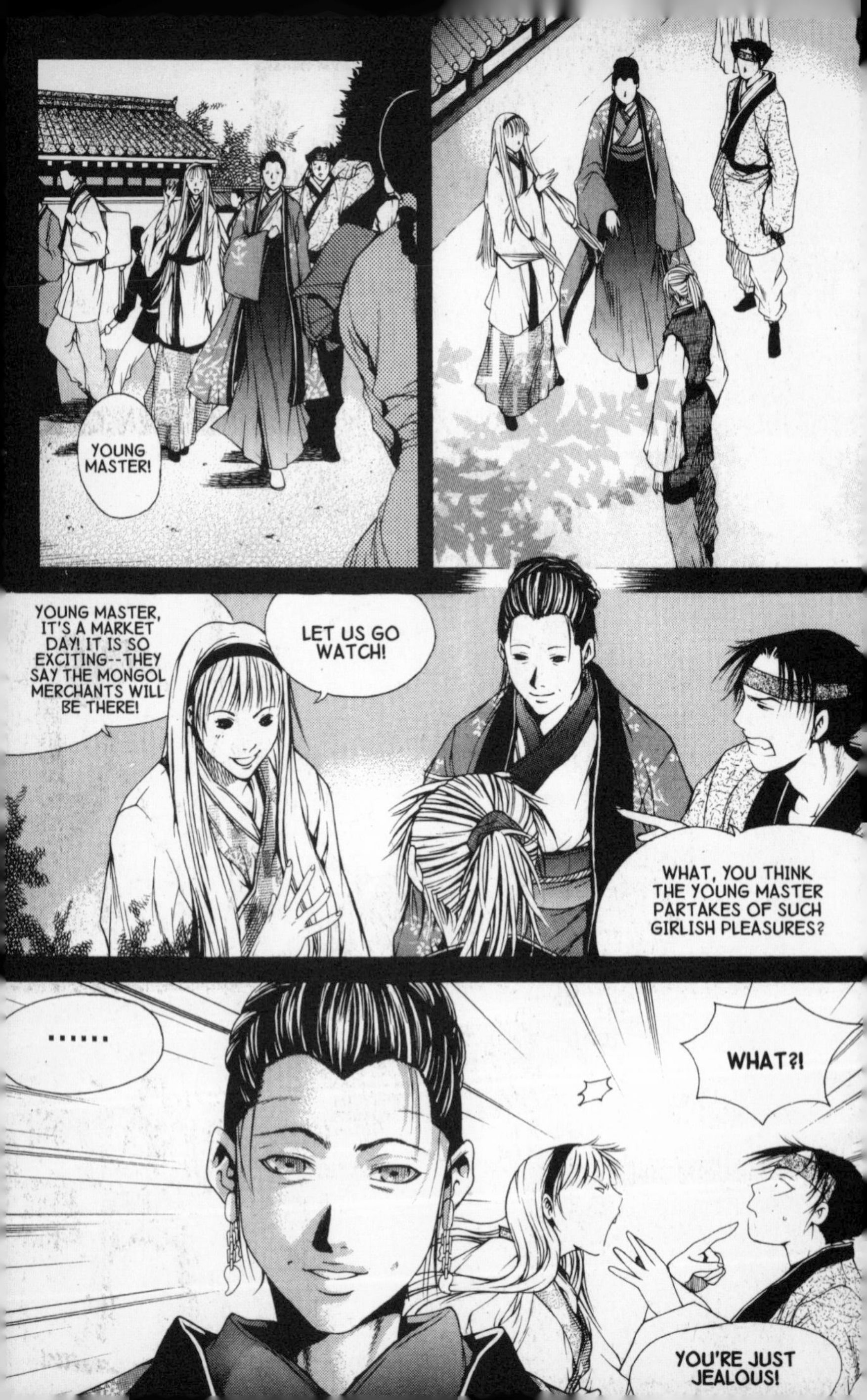
YOUNG MASTER!
YOUNG MASTER, IT'S A MARKET DAY! IT IS SO EXCITING--THEY SAY THE MONGOL MERCHANTS WILL BE THERE!
LET US GO WATCH!
WHAT, YOU THINK THE YOUNG MASTER PARTAKES OF SUCH GIRLISH PLEASURES?
......
WHAT?!
YOU'RE JUST JEALOUS!

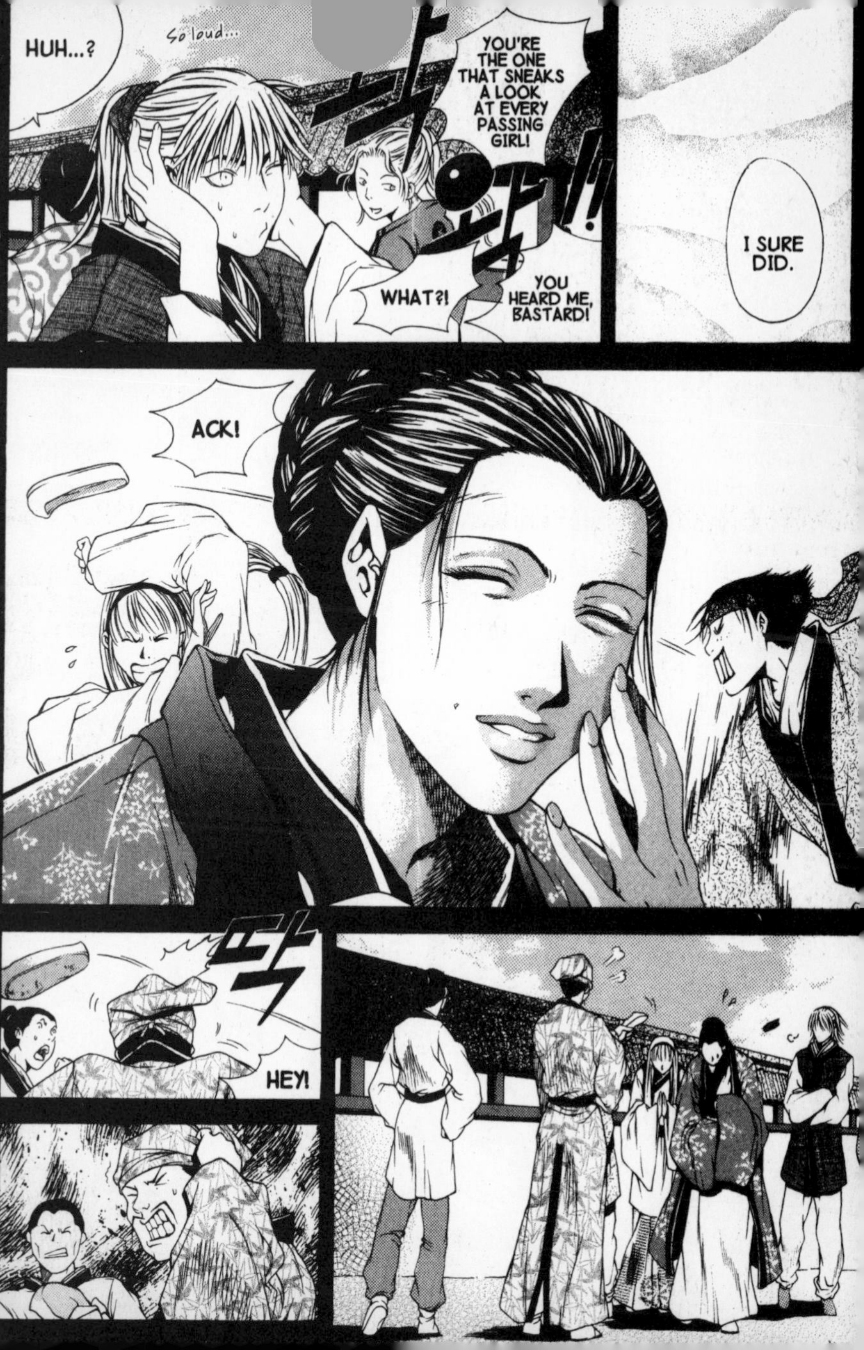
HUH...?
So loud...
YOU'RE THE ONE THAT SNEAKS A LOOK AT EVERY PASSING GIRL!
WHAT?!
YOU HEARD ME, BASTARD!
I SURE DID.
ACK!
HEY!

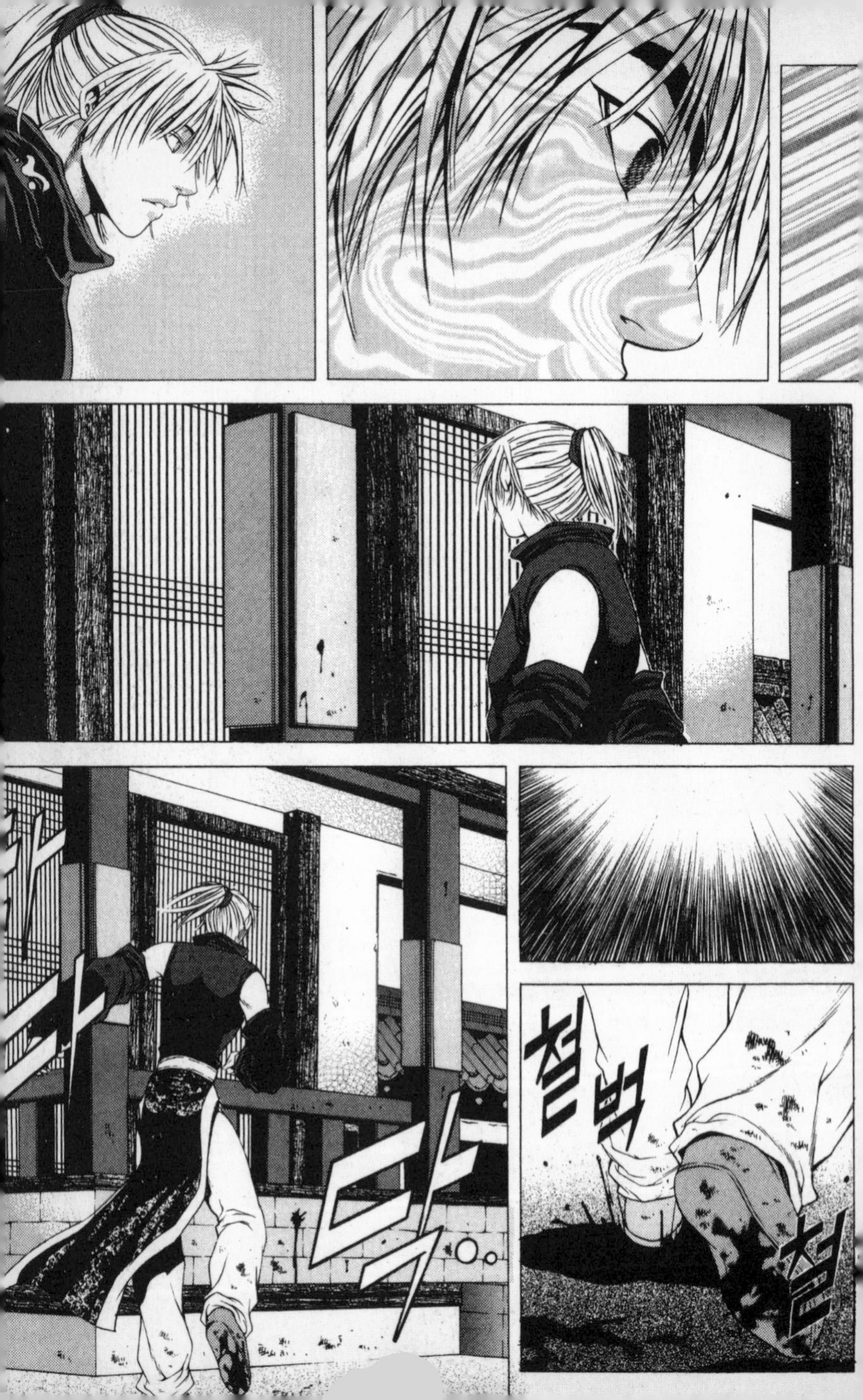
철벅
철

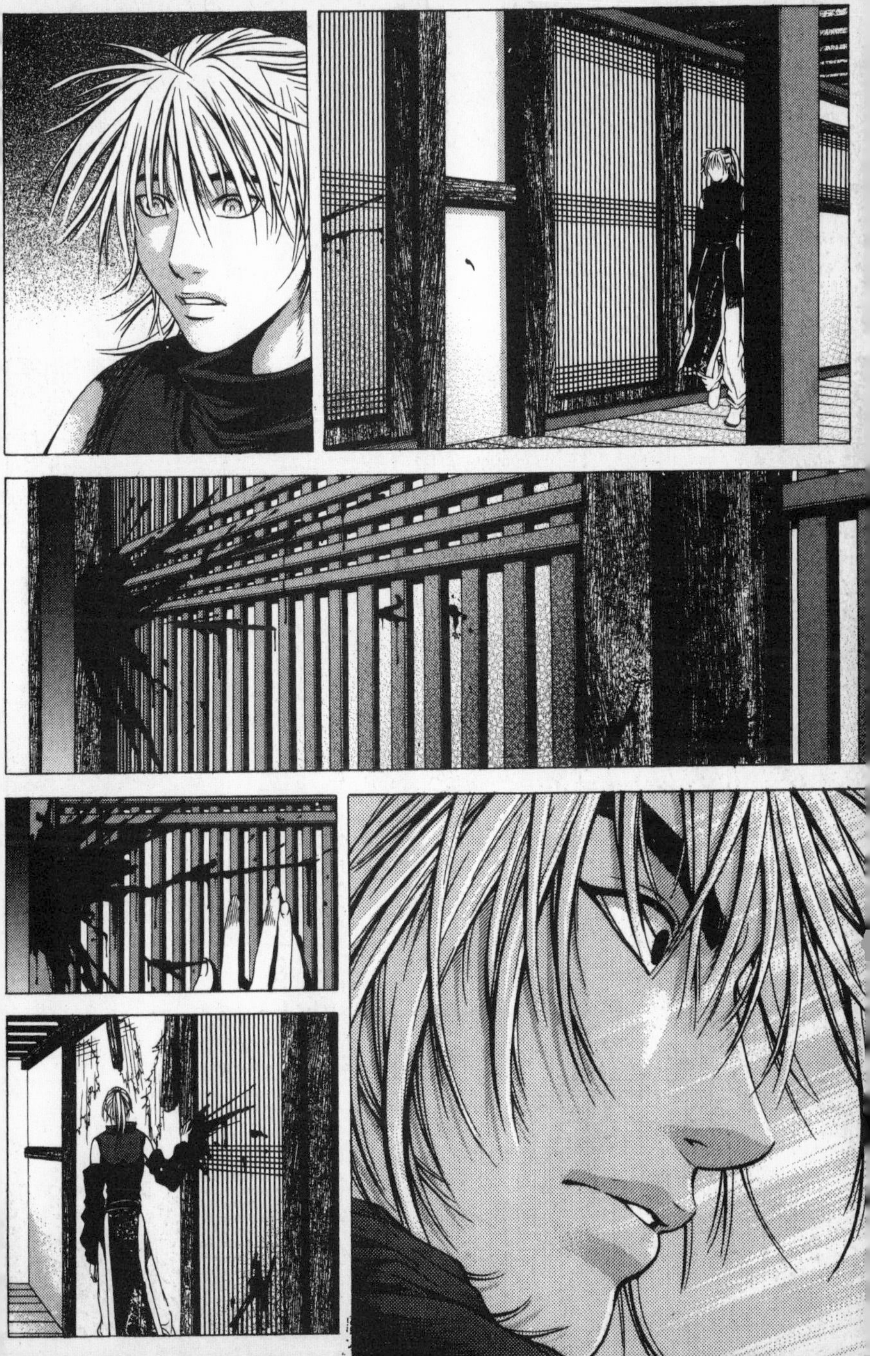

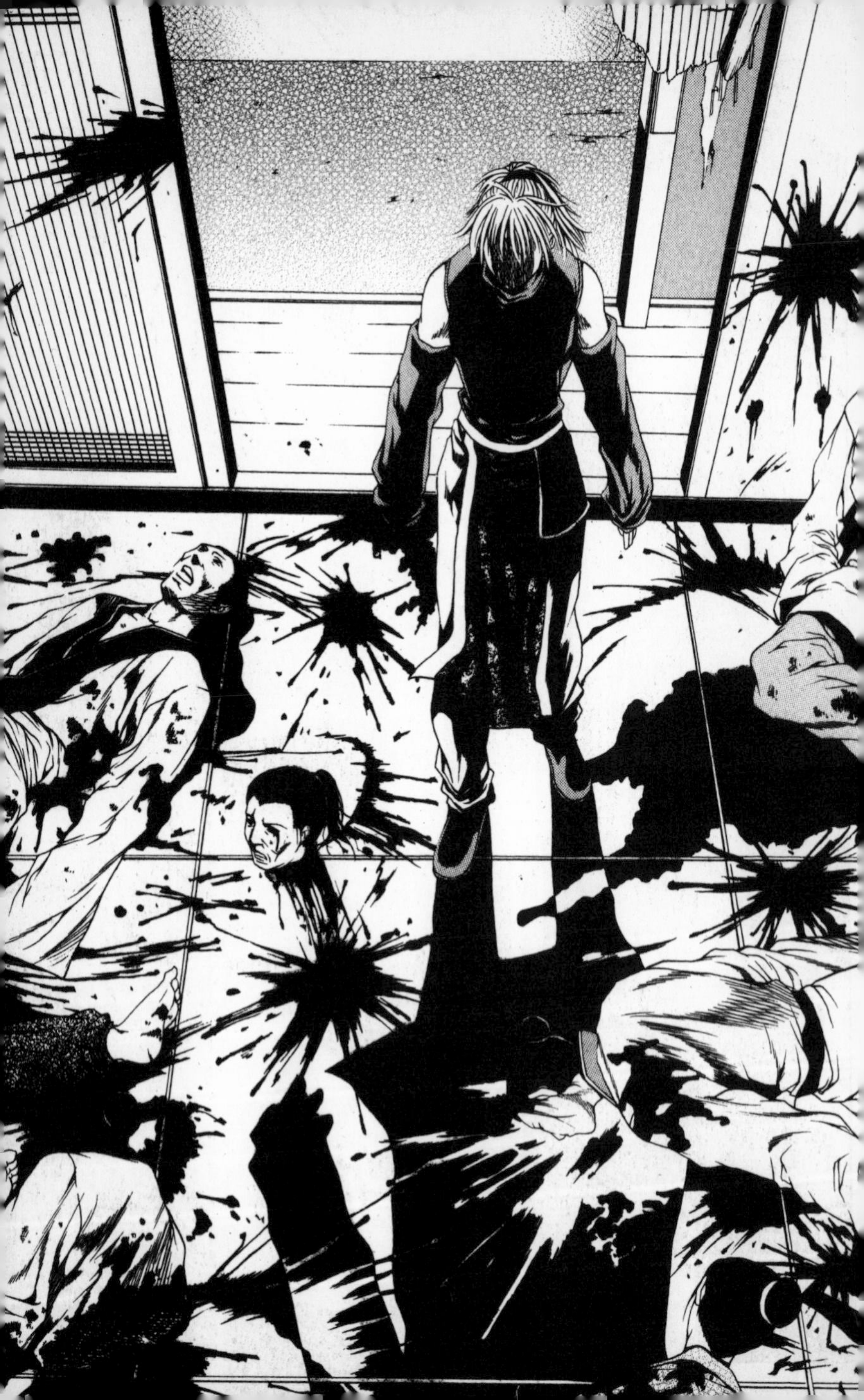

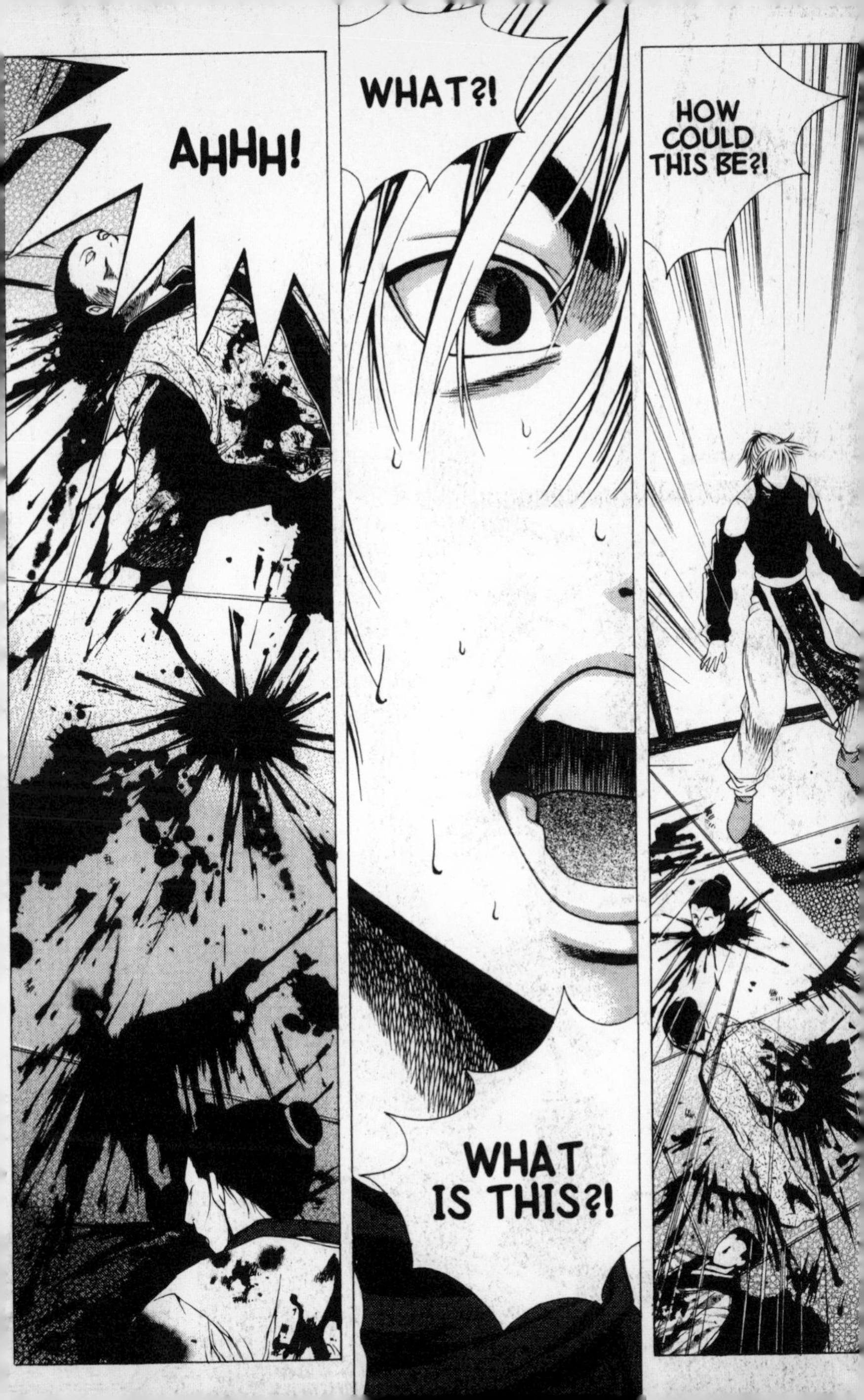
AHHH!
WHAT?!
WHAT IS THIS?!
HOW COULD THIS BE?!

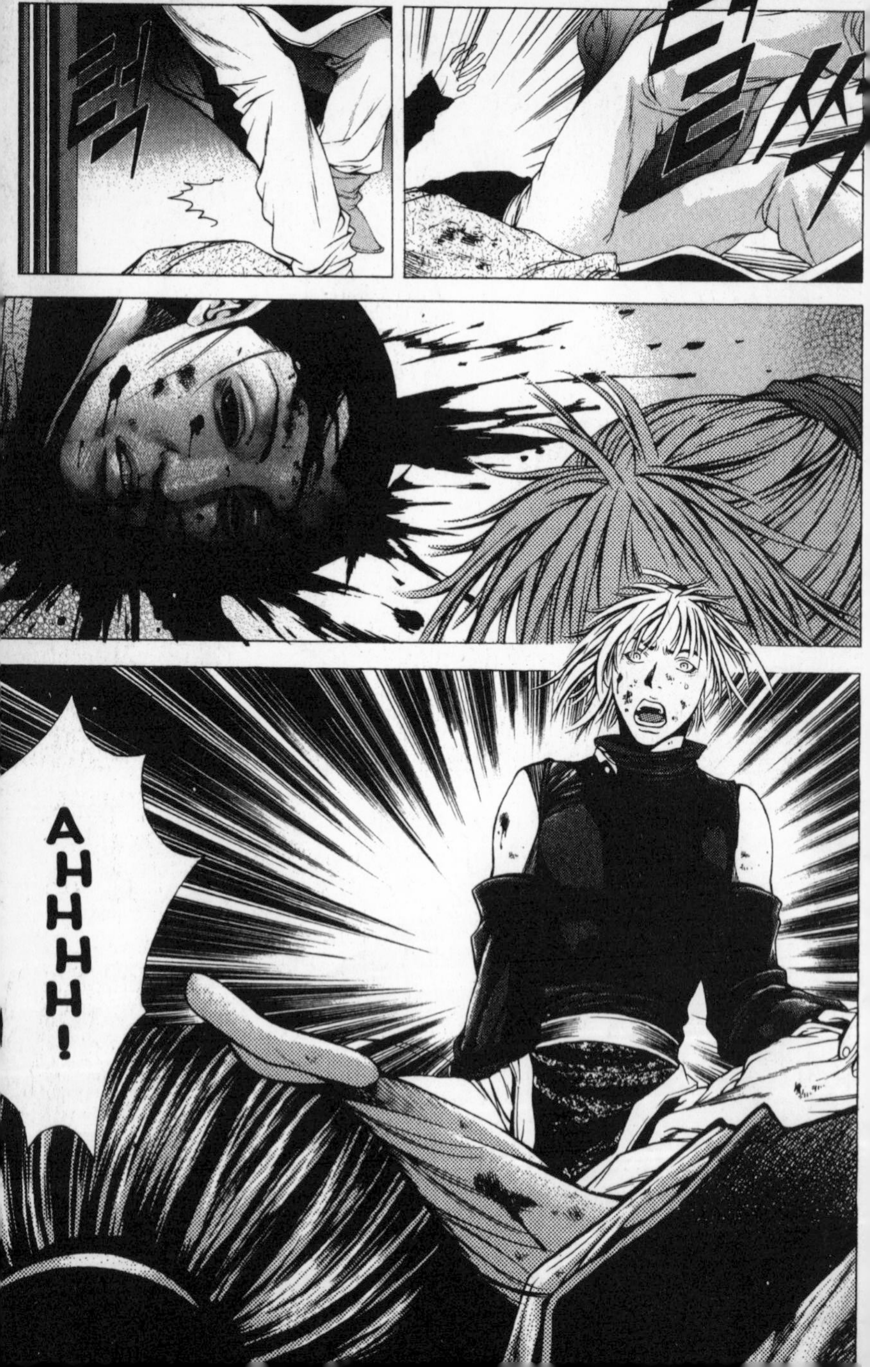
턱
털썩
AHHHH!

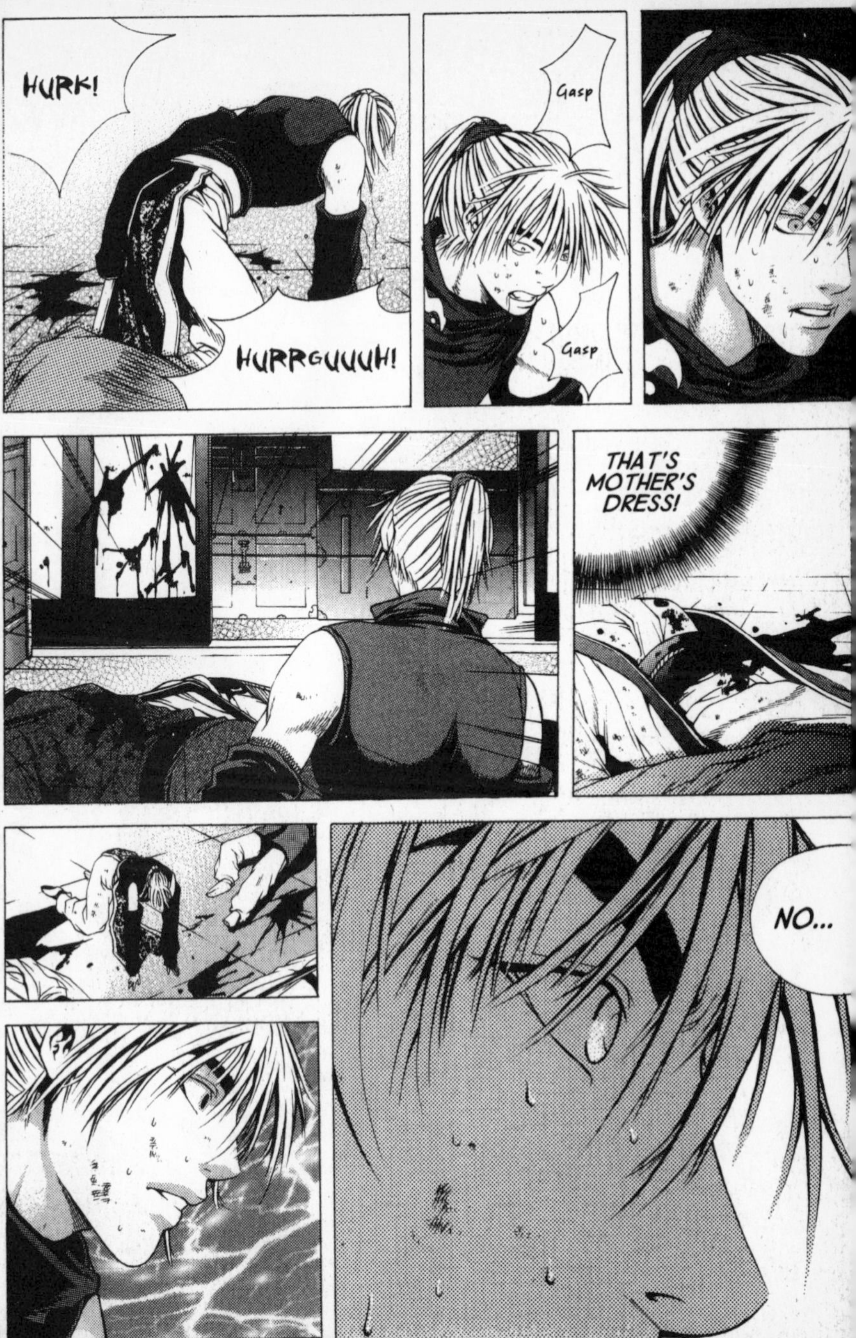
HURK!
HURRGUUUH!
Gasp
Gasp
THAT'S MOTHER'S DRESS!
NO...

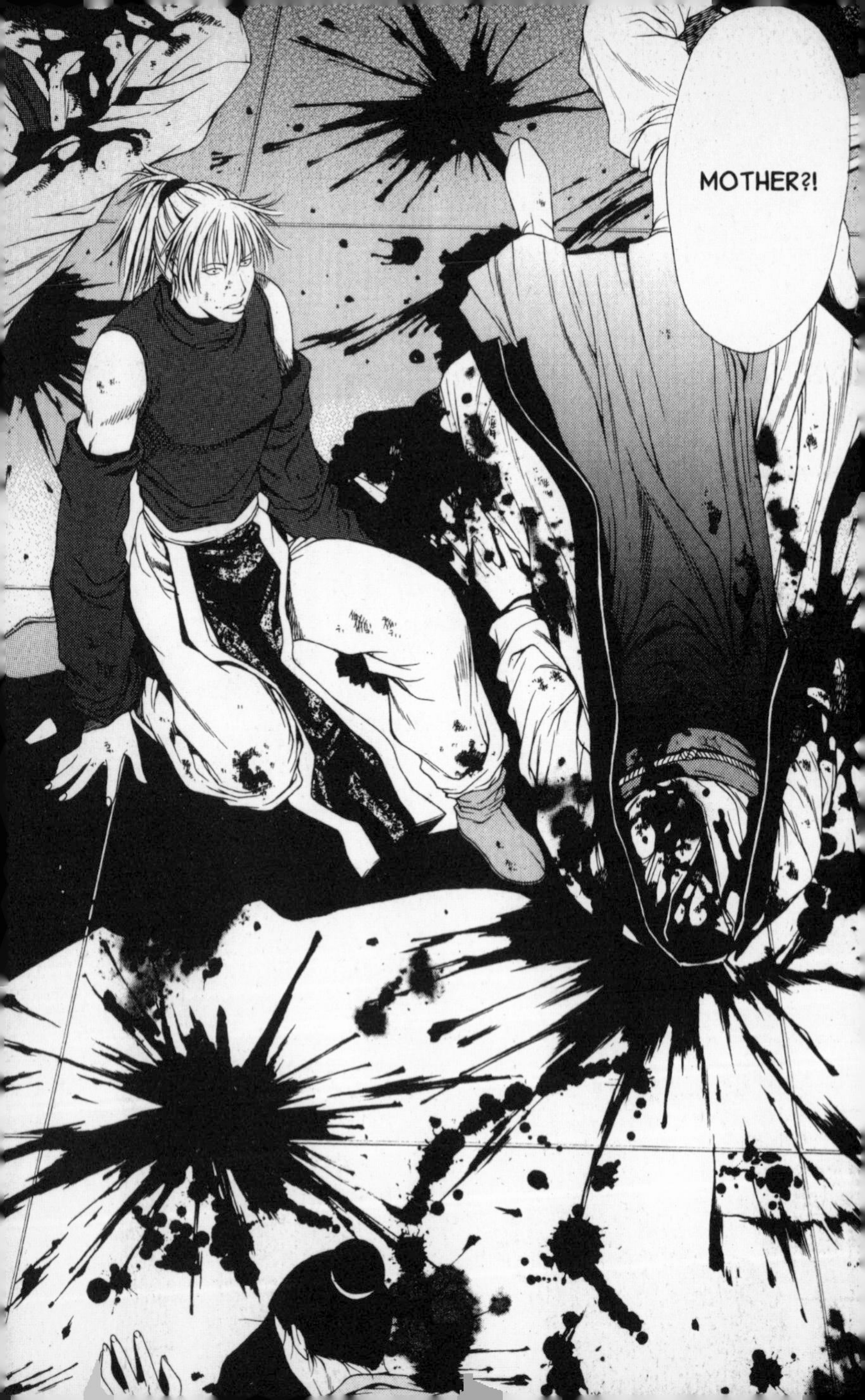
MOTHER?!

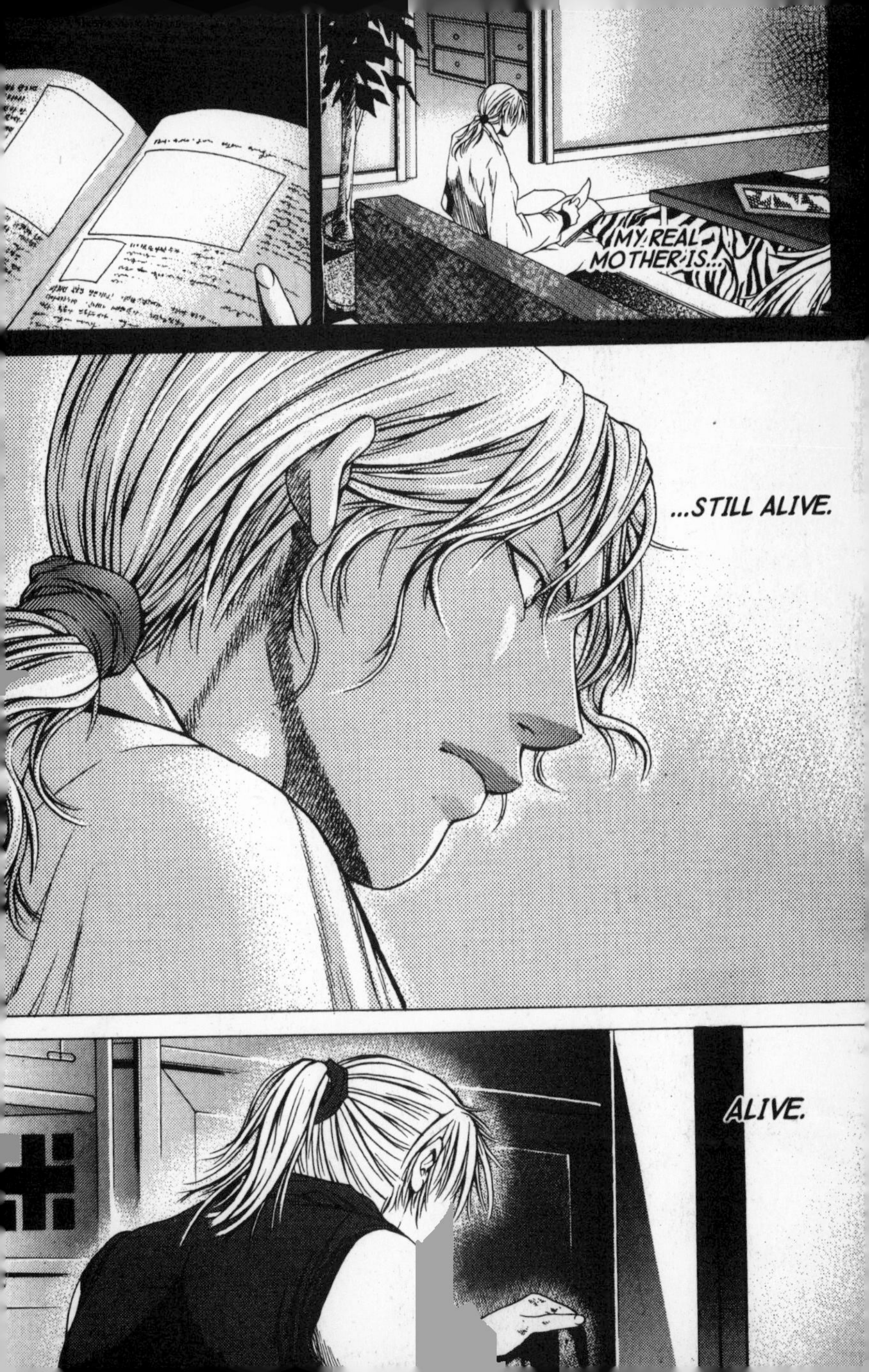
MY REAL MOTHER IS...
...STILL ALIVE.
ALIVE.

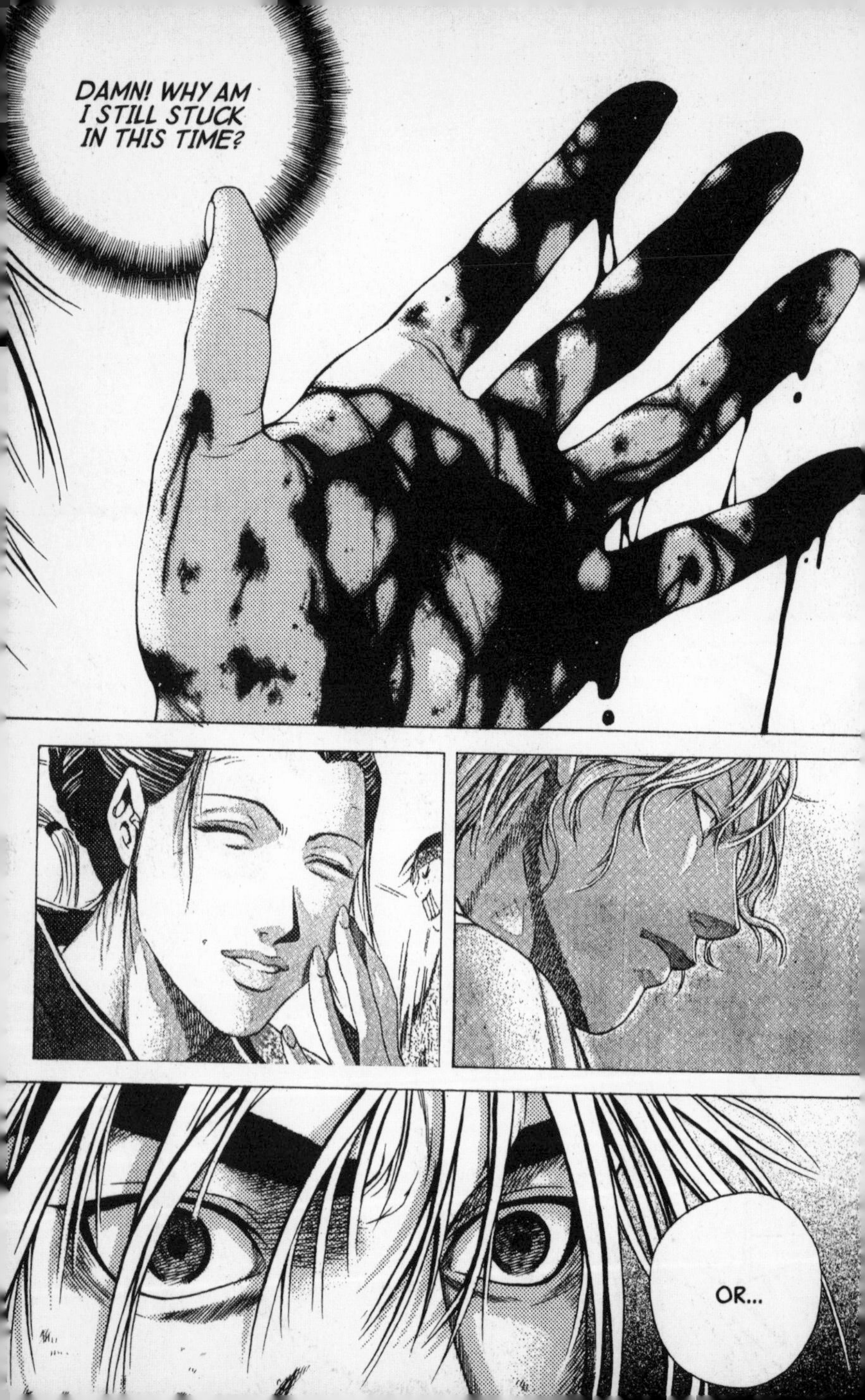
DAMN! WHY AM I STILL STUCK IN THIS TIME?
OR...

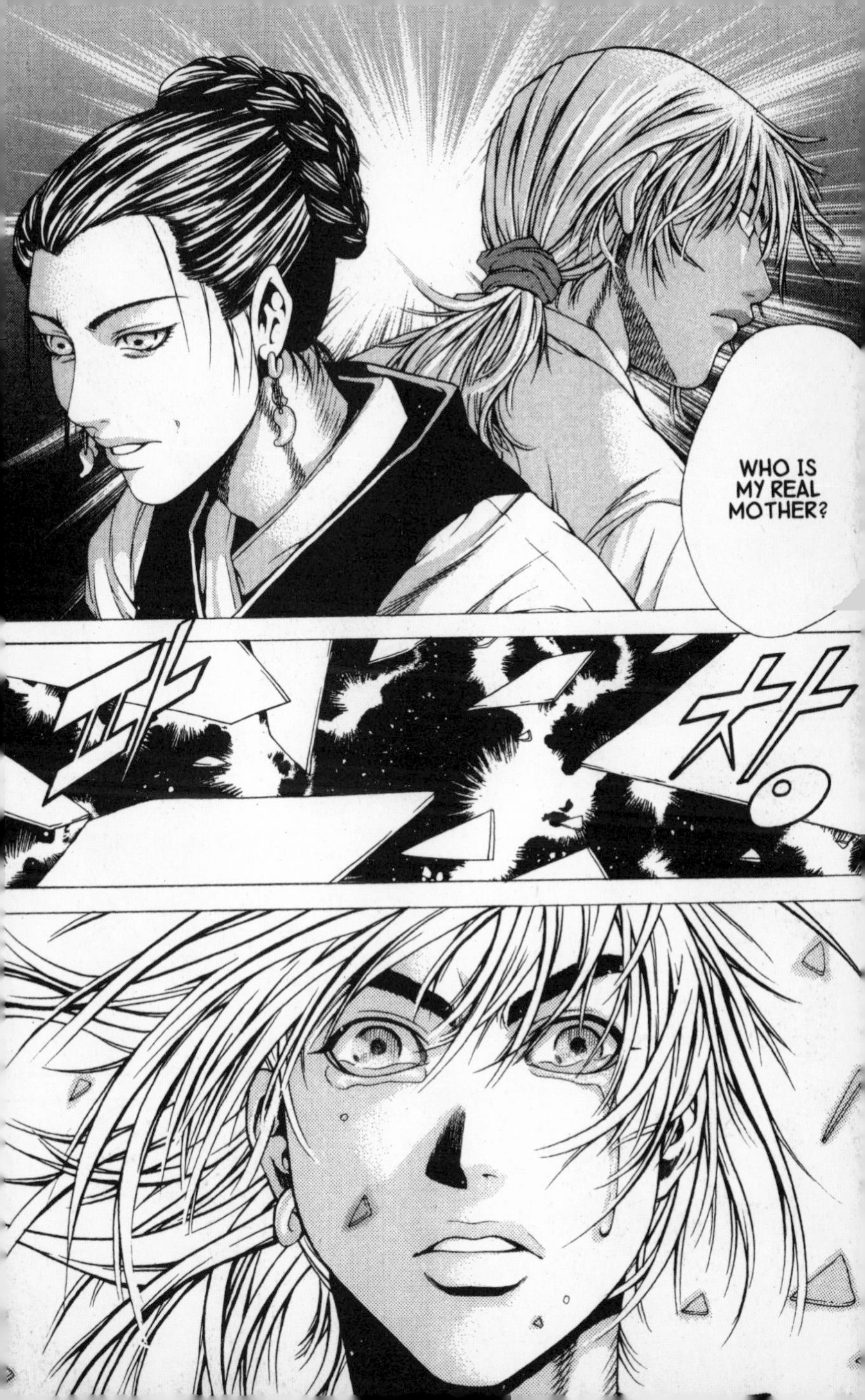
WHO IS MY REAL MOTHER?

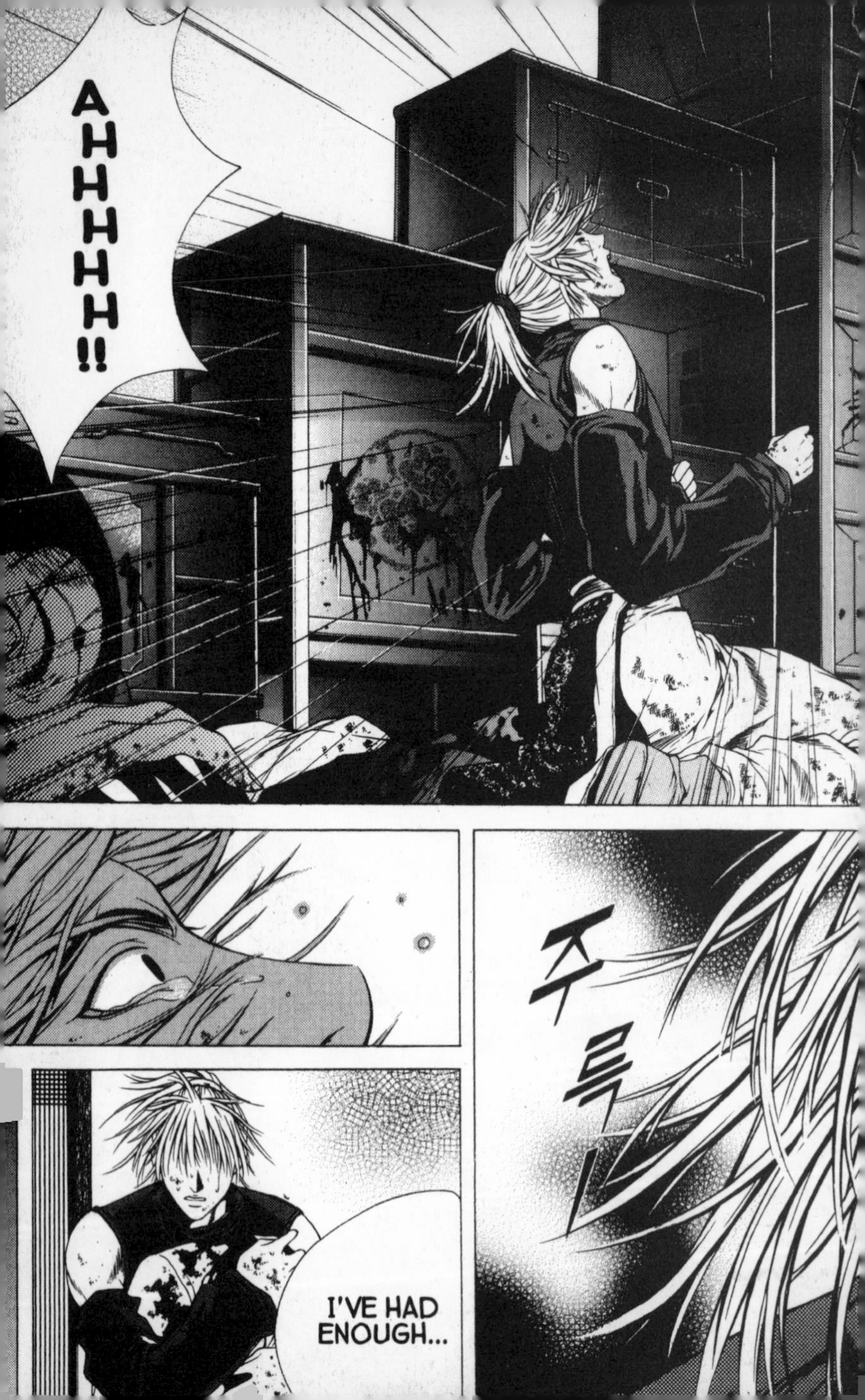
AHHHHH!!
주륵
I'VE HAD ENOUGH...

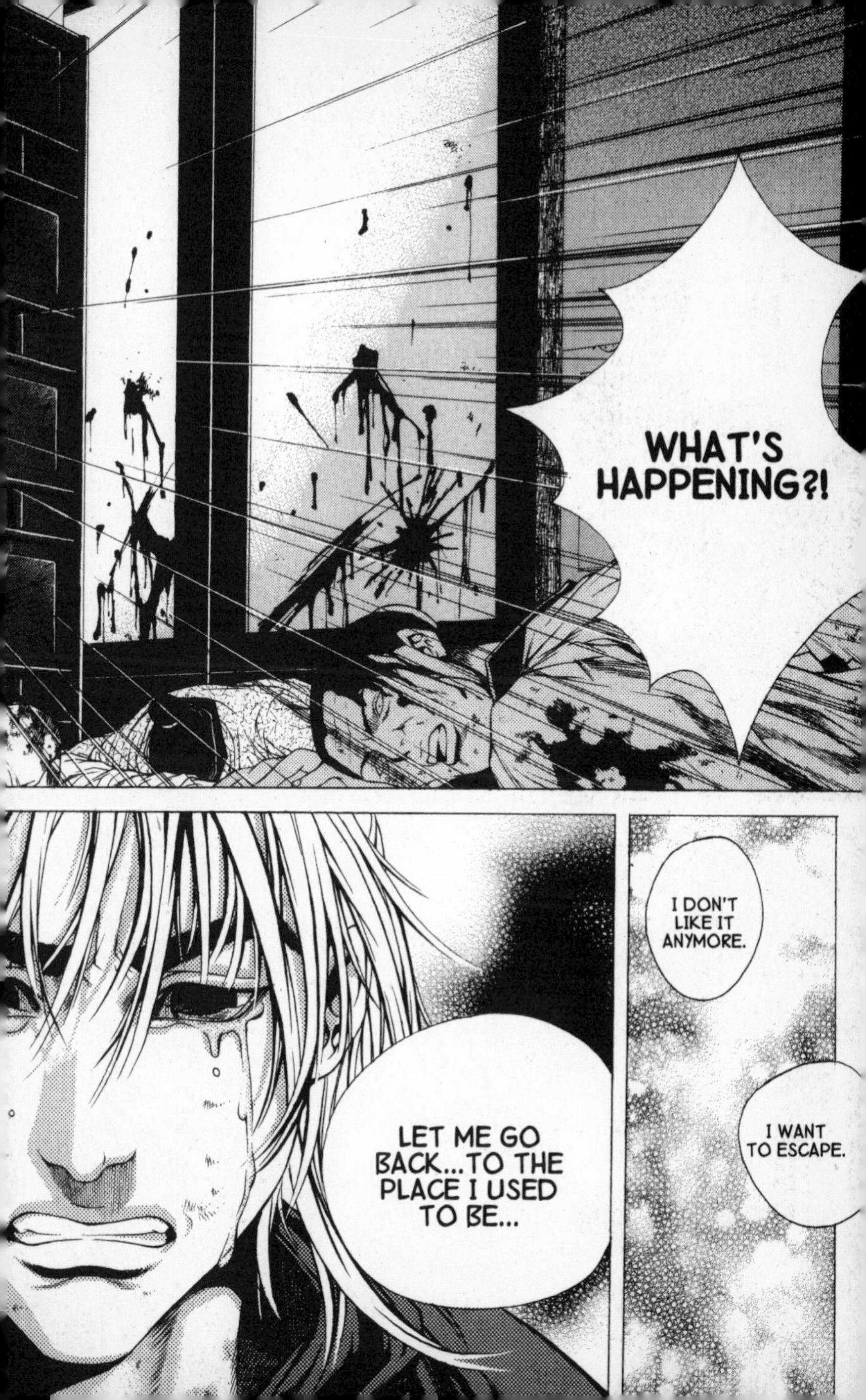
WHAT'S HAPPENING?!
LET ME GO BACK...TO THE PLACE I USED TO BE...
I DON'T LIKE IT ANYMORE.
I WANT TO ESCAPE.

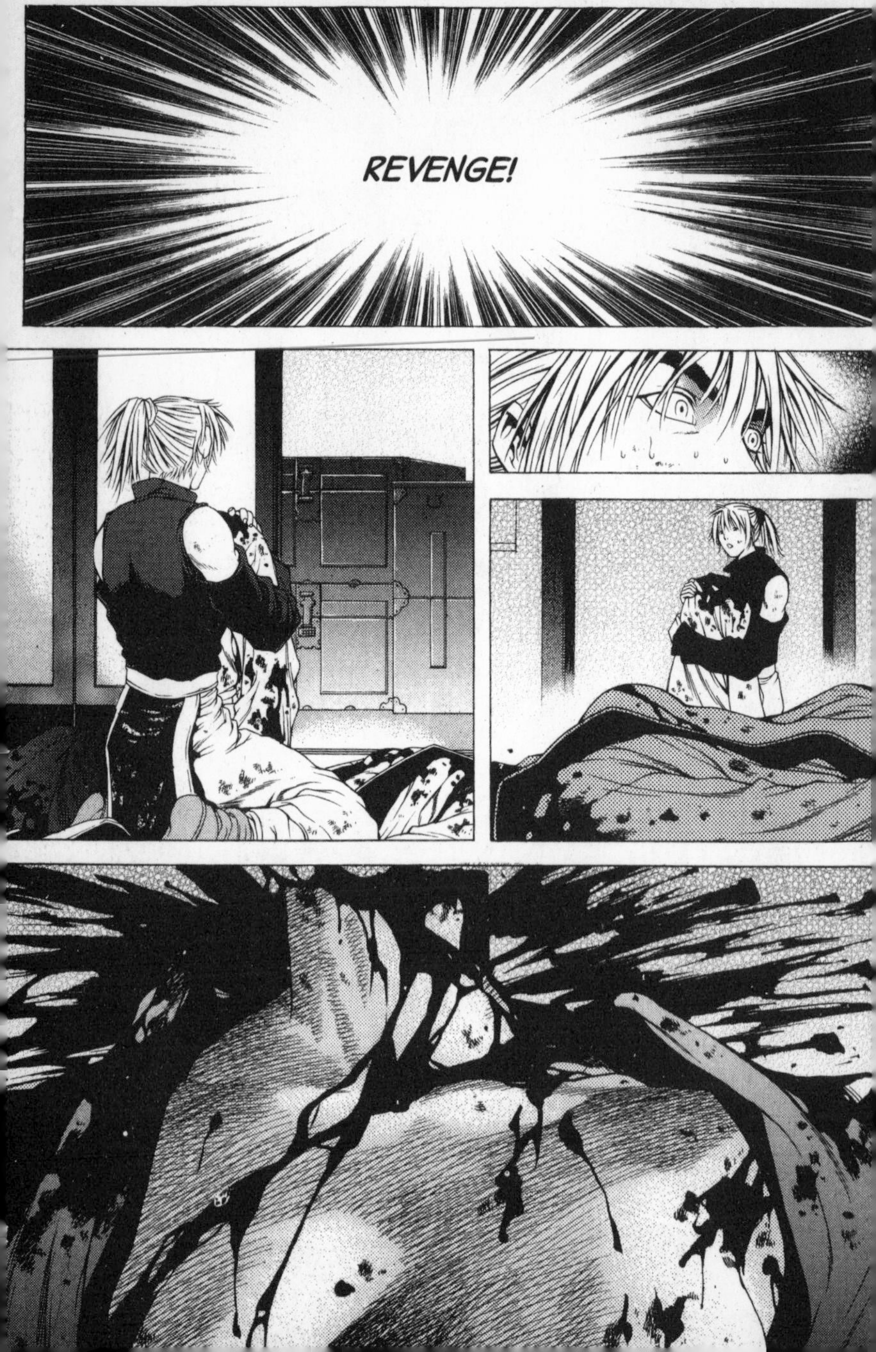
REVENGE!

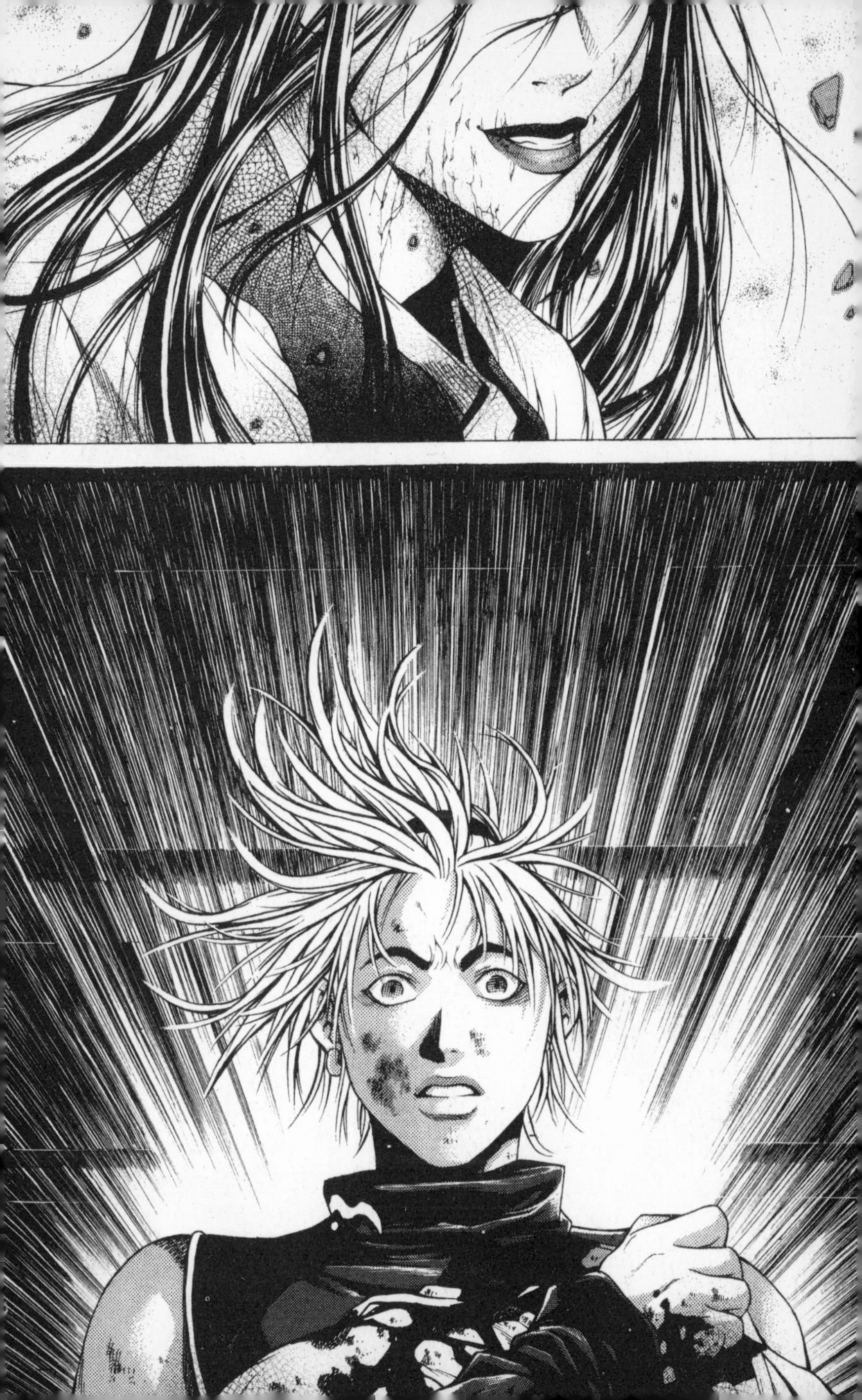

GENERAL SALI TAYI, YOU SUMMONED ME...?

...

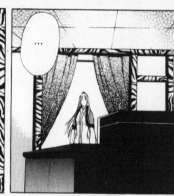

HE IS GONE?

IF HE ORDERS THE GRANDDAUGHTER OF THE GREAT KAHN TO APPEAR, HE SHOULD AT LEAST MAKE SURE TO RECEIVE ME.

THIS...

ISN'T IT SALT?!

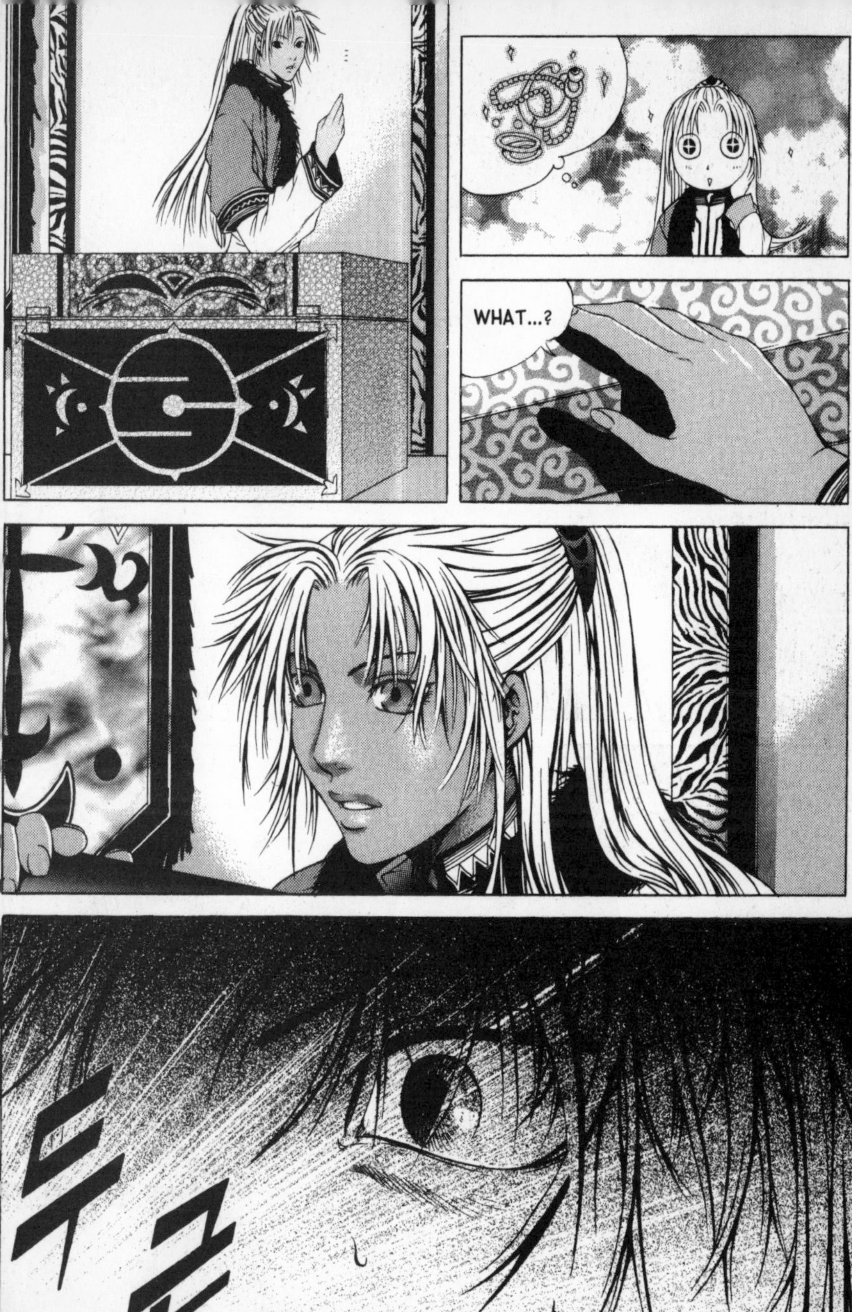
WHAT...?

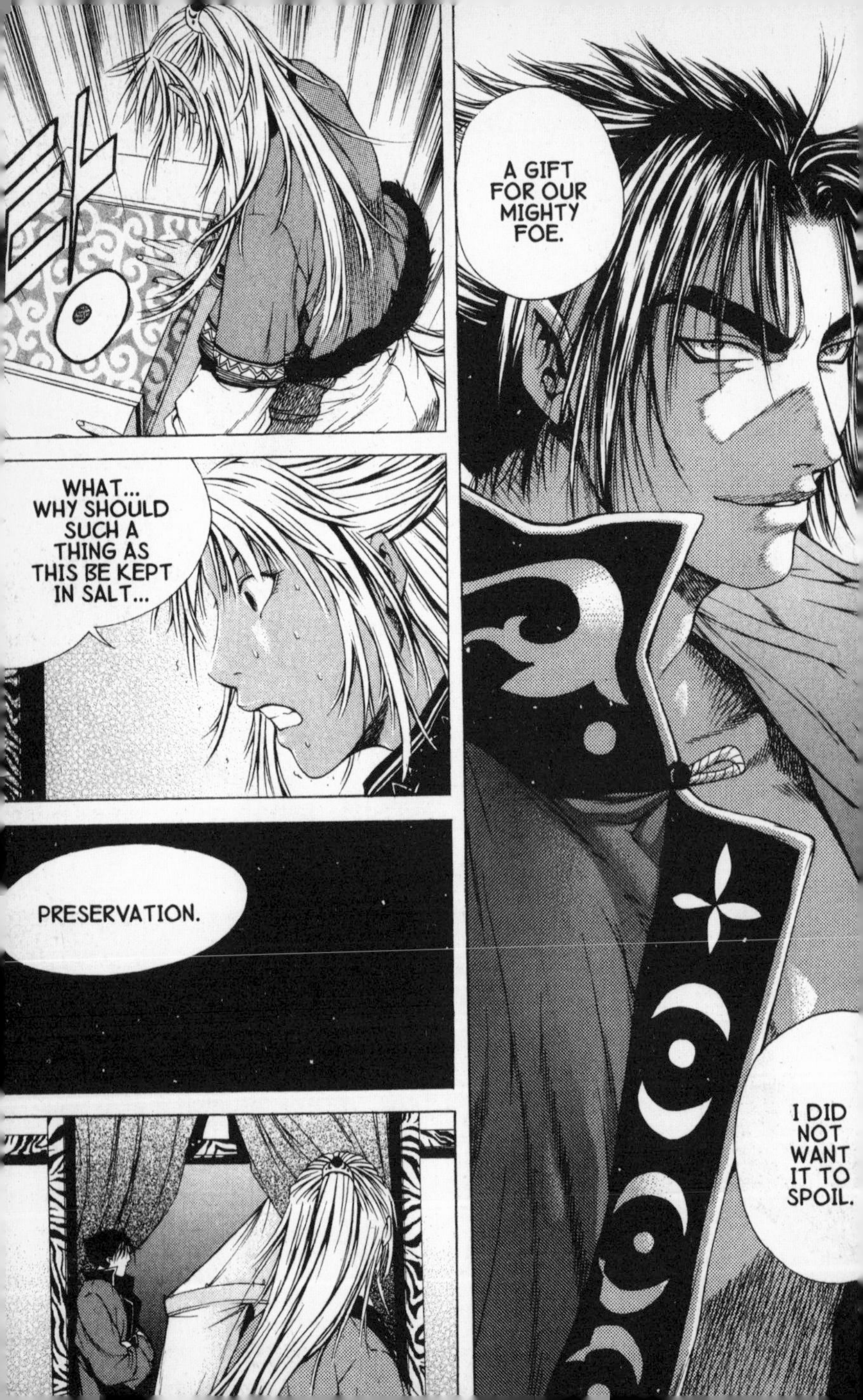
WHAT... WHY SHOULD SUCH A THING AS THIS BE KEPT IN SALT...
PRESERVATION.
A GIFT FOR OUR MIGHTY FOE.
I DID NOT WANT IT TO SPOIL.

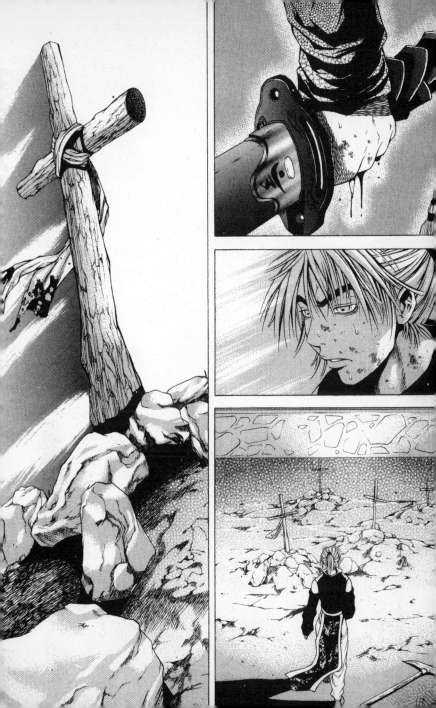

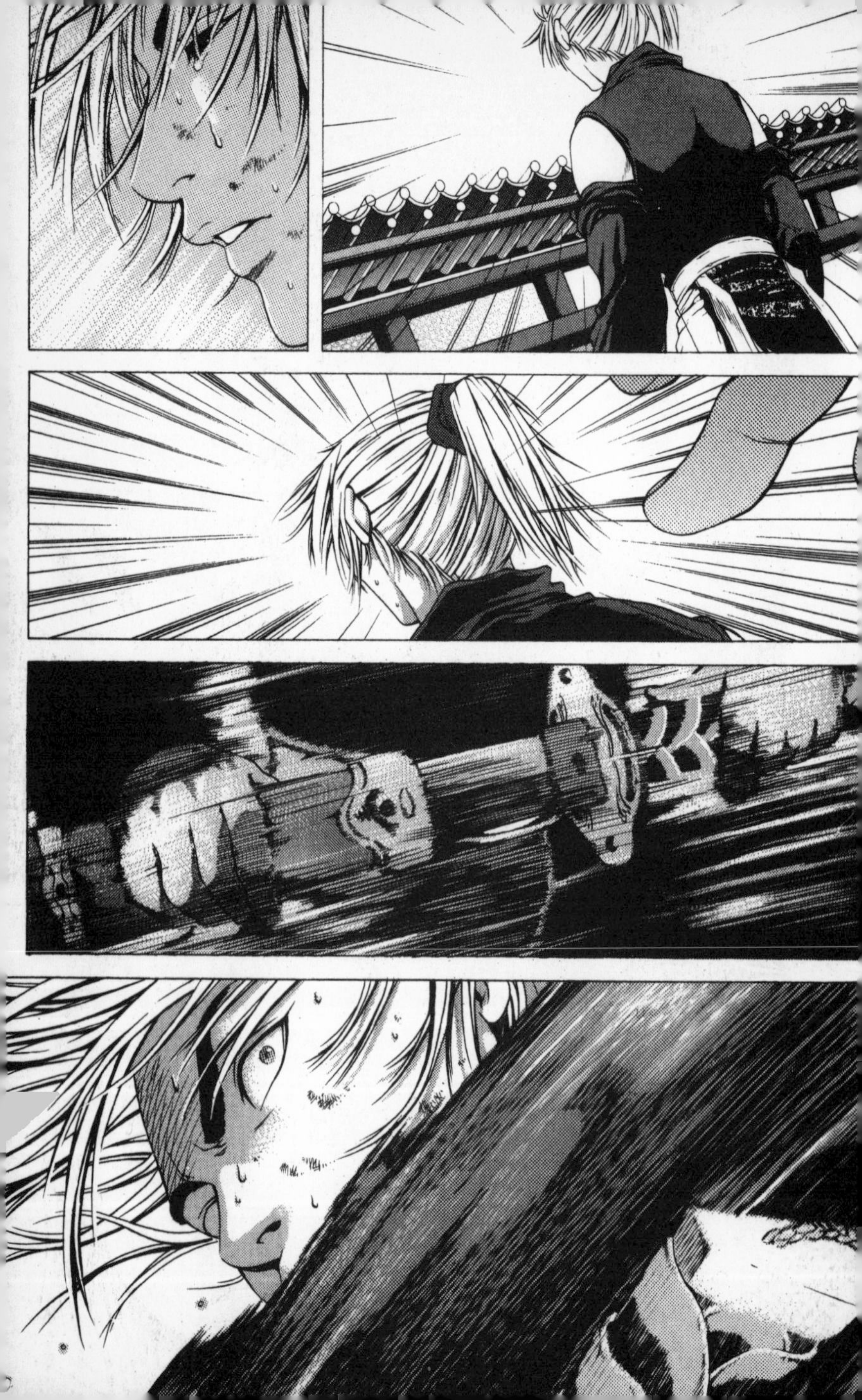

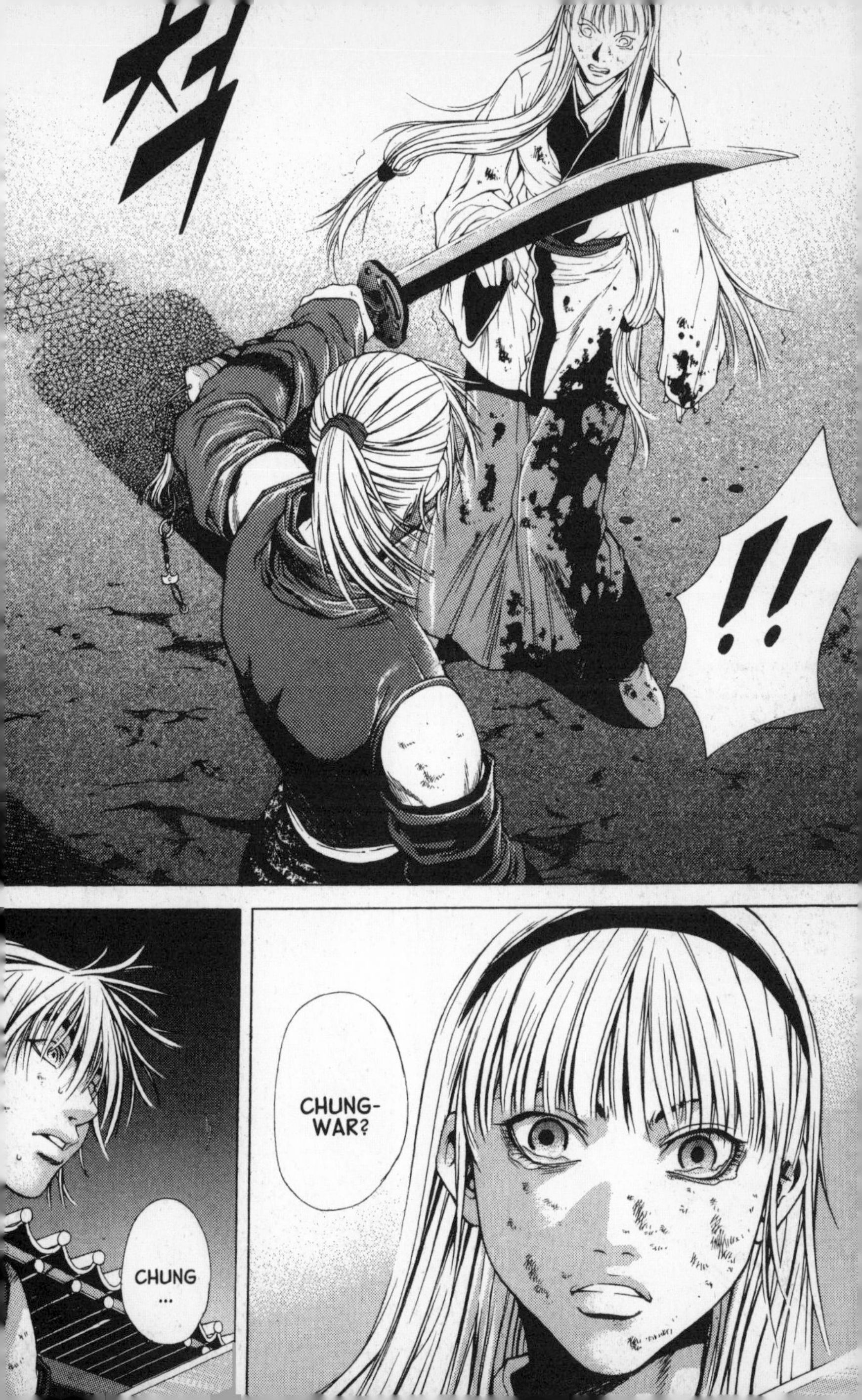
!!
CHUNG ...
CHUNG-WAR?

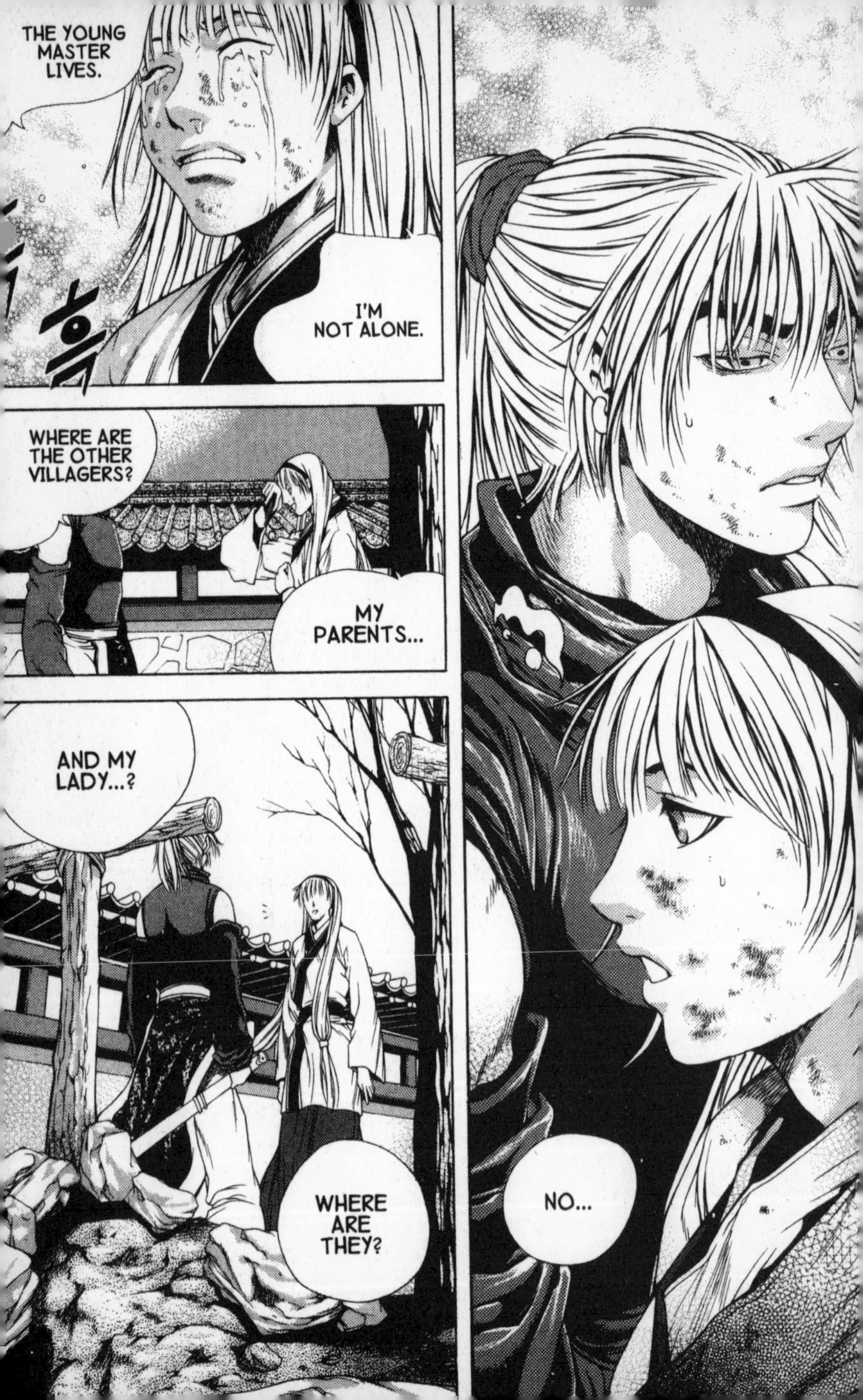
THE YOUNG MASTER LIVES.
I'M NOT ALONE.
WHERE ARE THE OTHER VILLAGERS?
MY PARENTS...
AND MY LADY...?
WHERE ARE THEY?
NO...

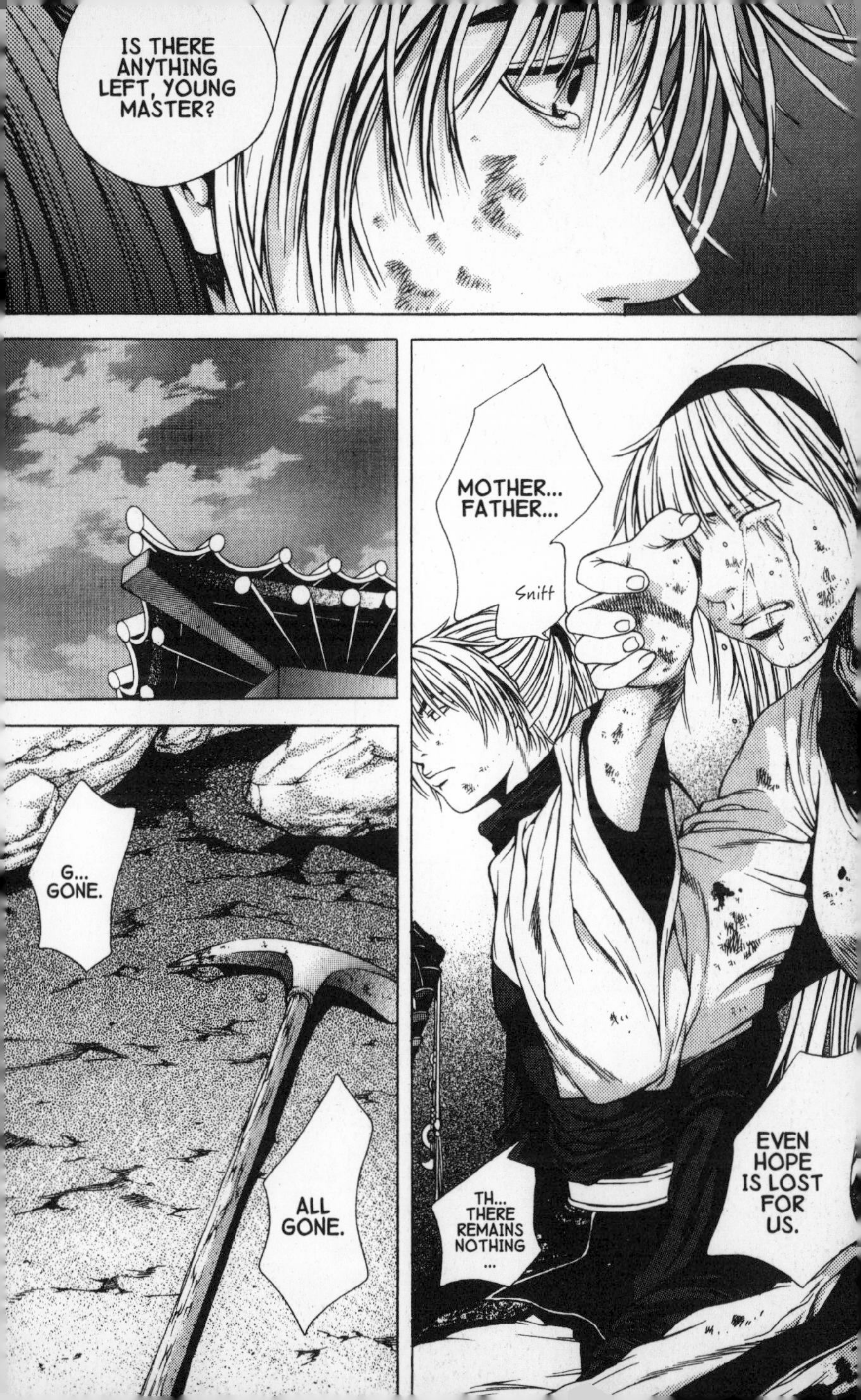
IS THERE ANYTHING LEFT, YOUNG MASTER?
G... GONE.
ALL GONE.
MOTHER... FATHER...
Sniff
TH... THERE REMAINS NOTHING ...
EVEN HOPE IS LOST FOR US.

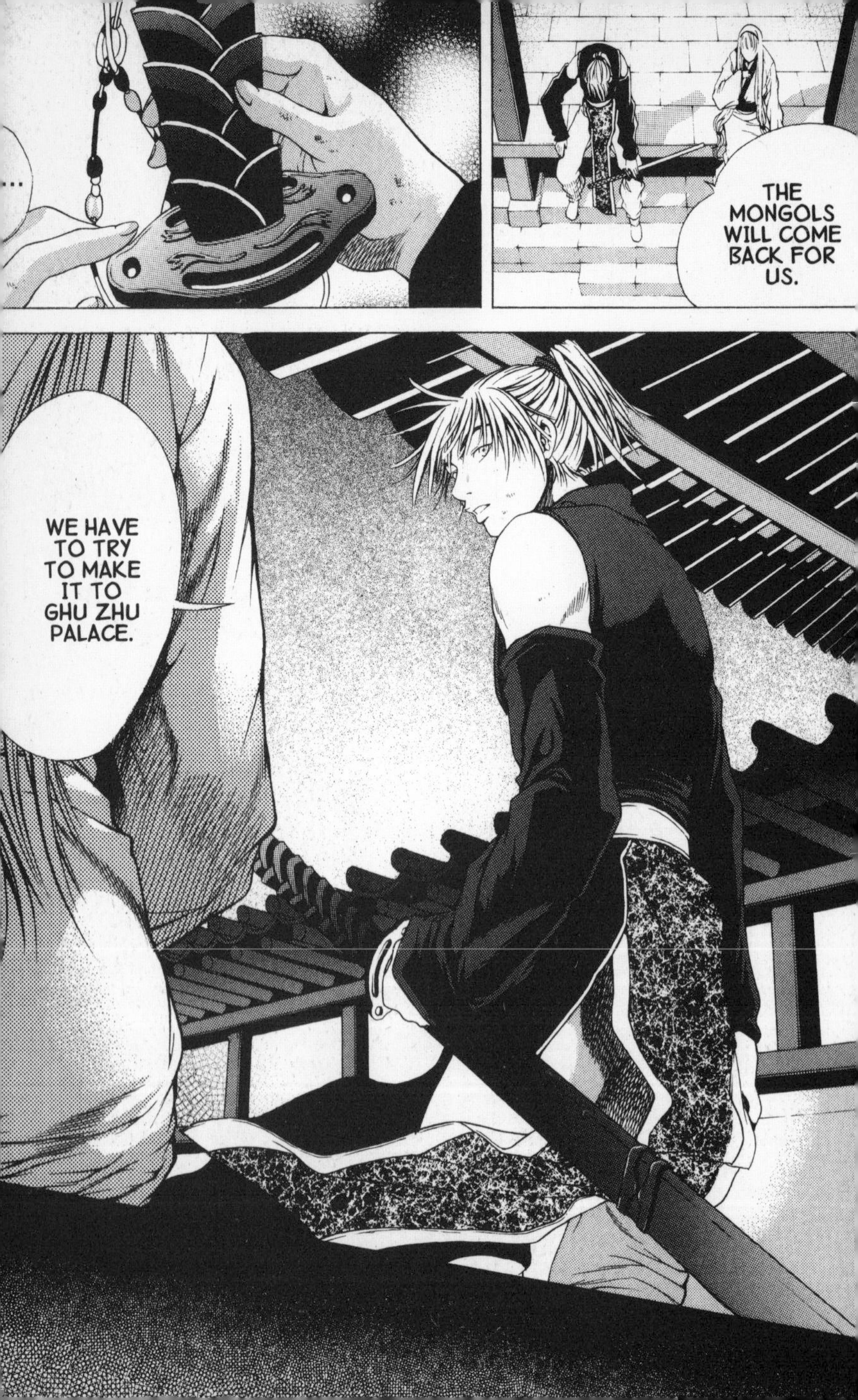
...
THE MONGOLS WILL COME BACK FOR US.
WE HAVE TO TRY TO MAKE IT TO GHU ZHU PALACE.

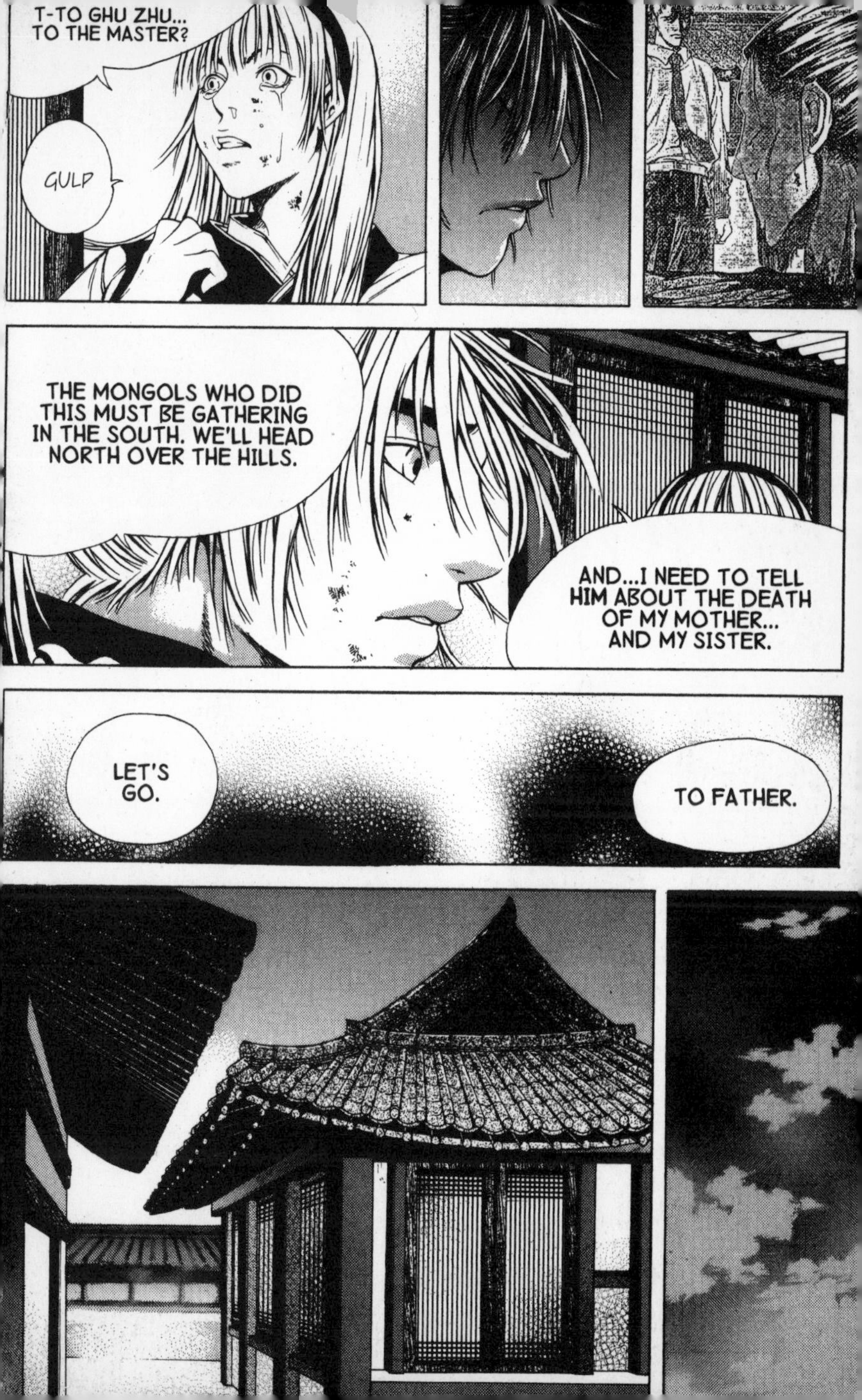
T-TO GHU ZHU...
TO THE MASTER?
GULP
THE MONGOLS WHO DID THIS MUST BE GATHERING IN THE SOUTH. WE'LL HEAD NORTH OVER THE HILLS.
AND...I NEED TO TELL HIM ABOUT THE DEATH OF MY MOTHER... AND MY SISTER.
LET'S GO.
TO FATHER.

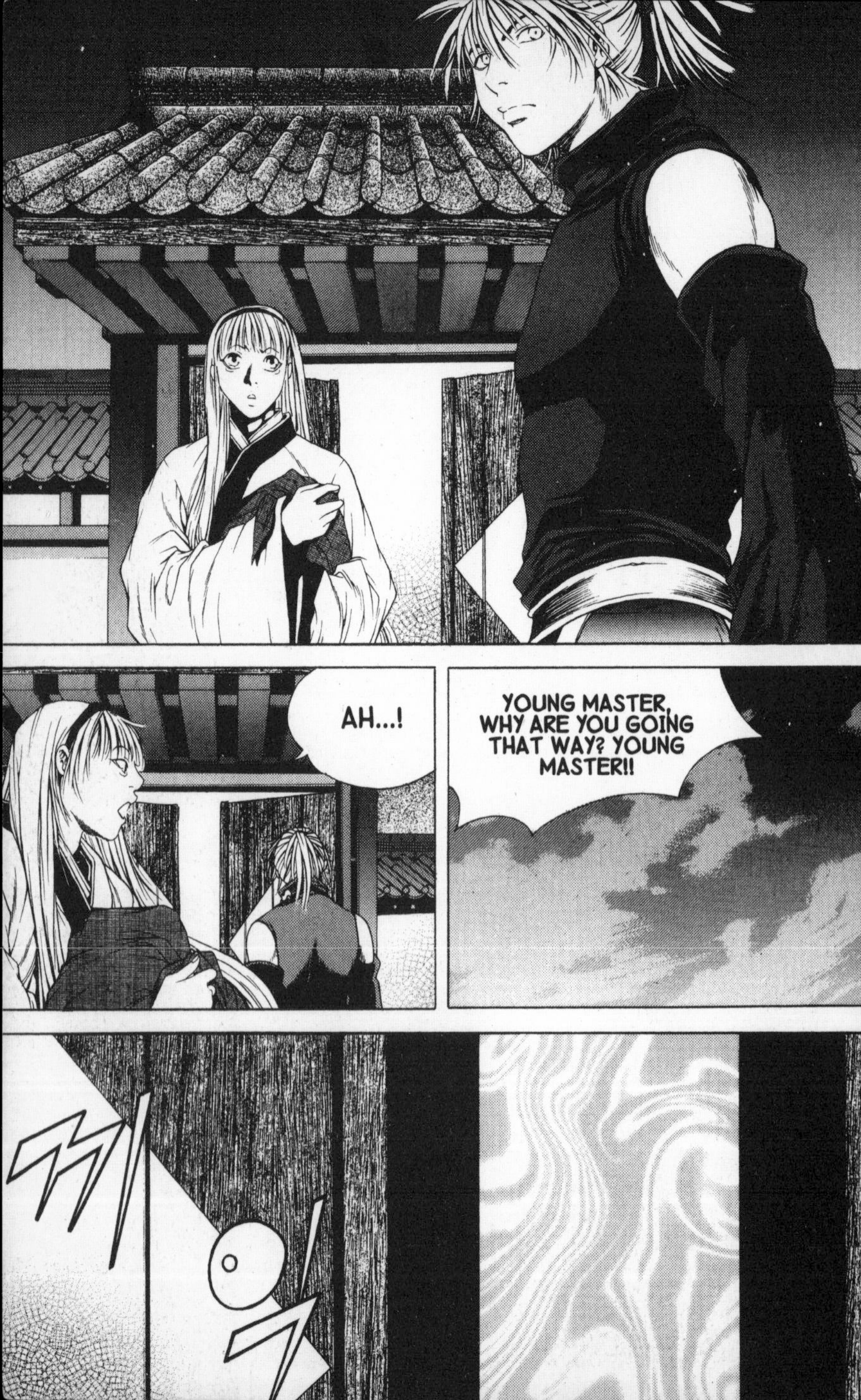
AH...!
YOUNG MASTER, WHY ARE YOU GOING THAT WAY? YOUNG MASTER!!

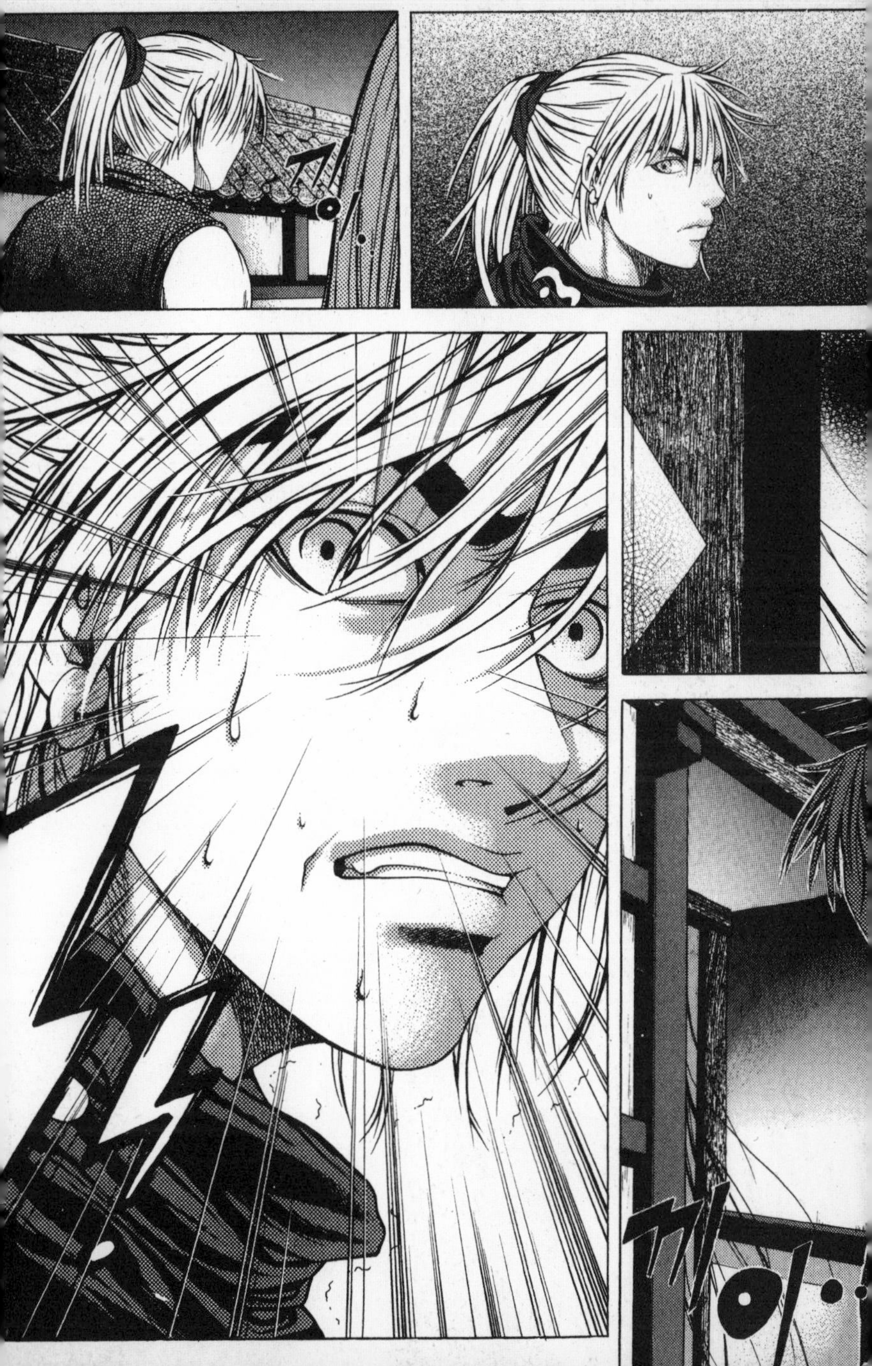

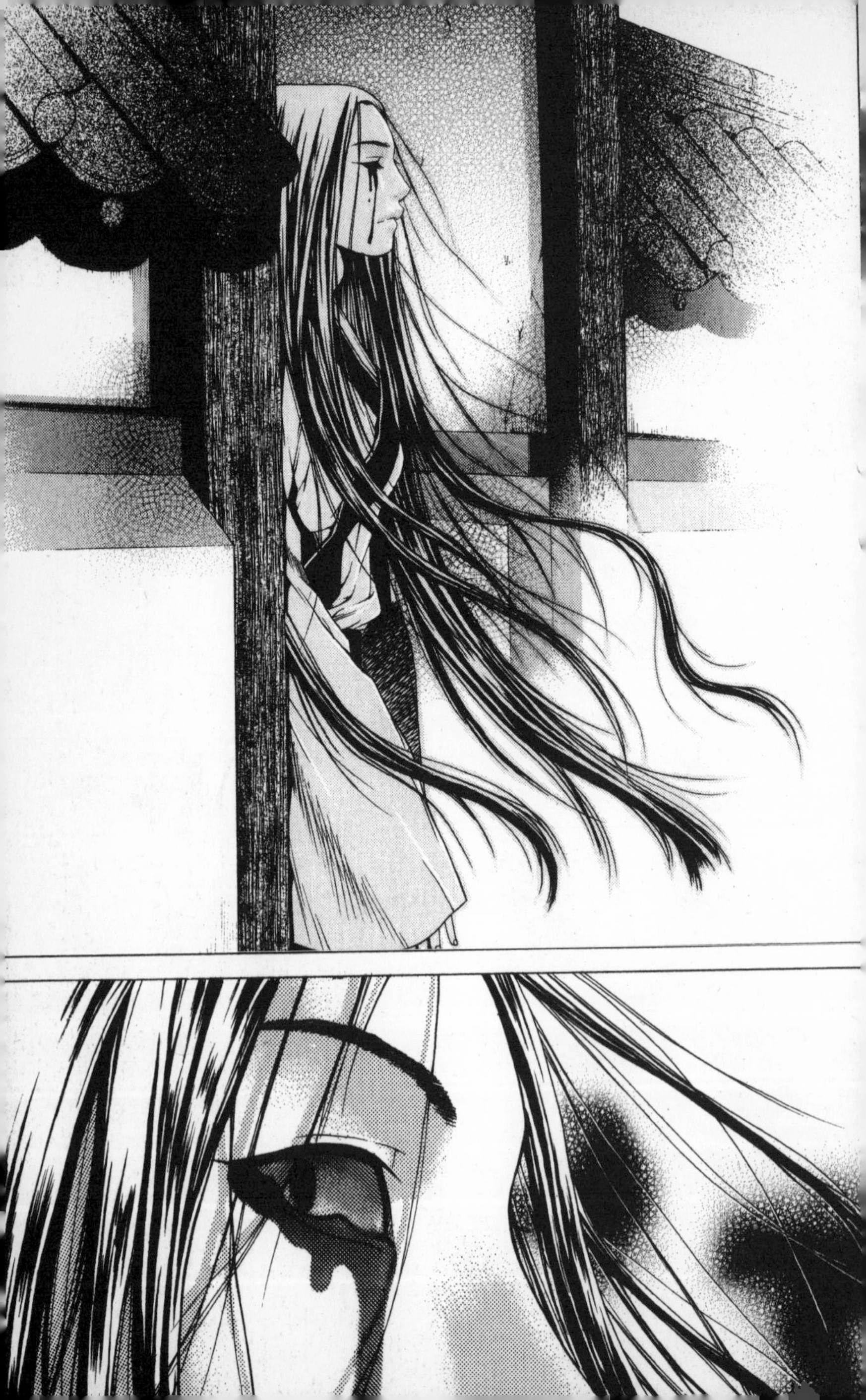

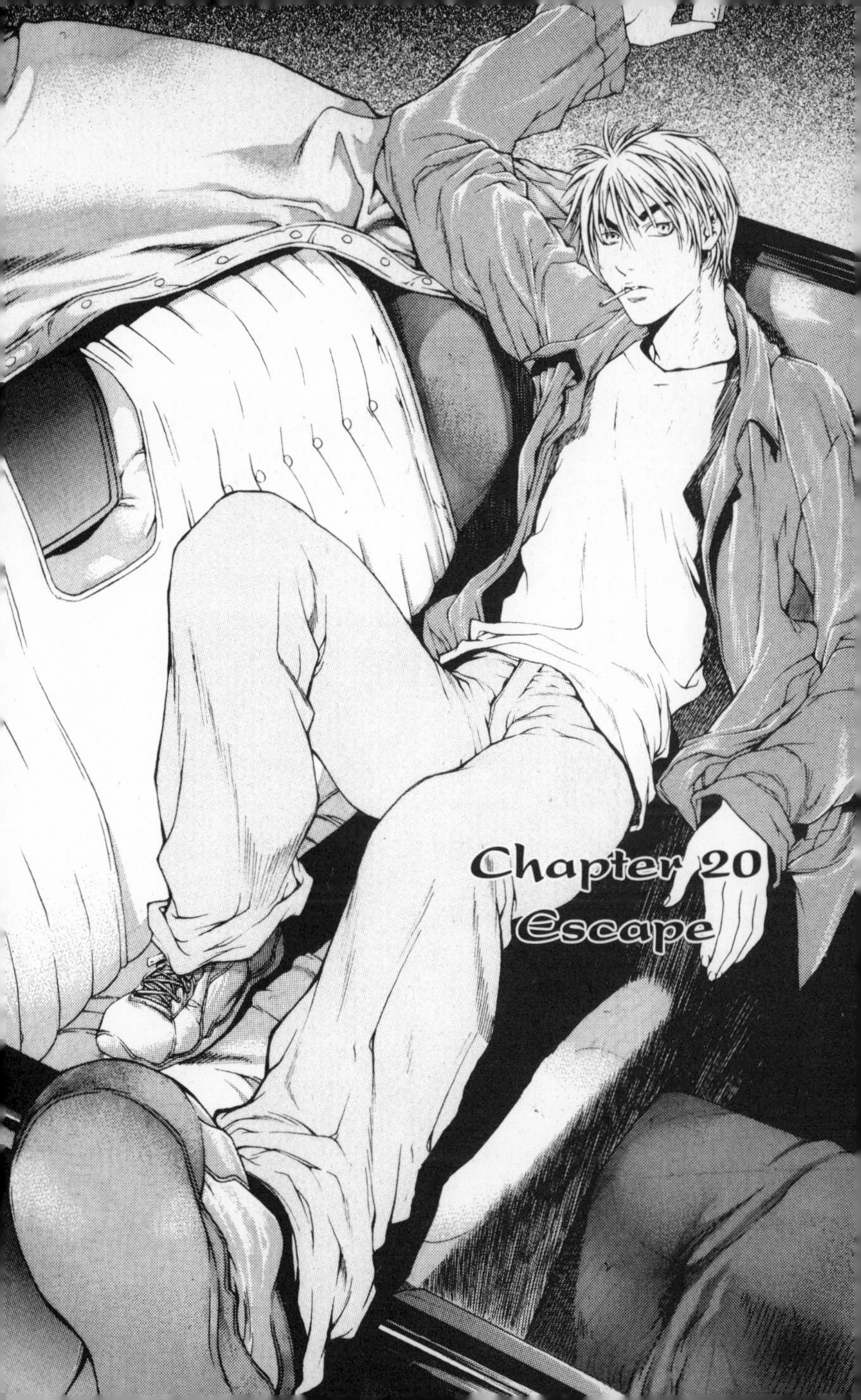
Chapter 20
Escape

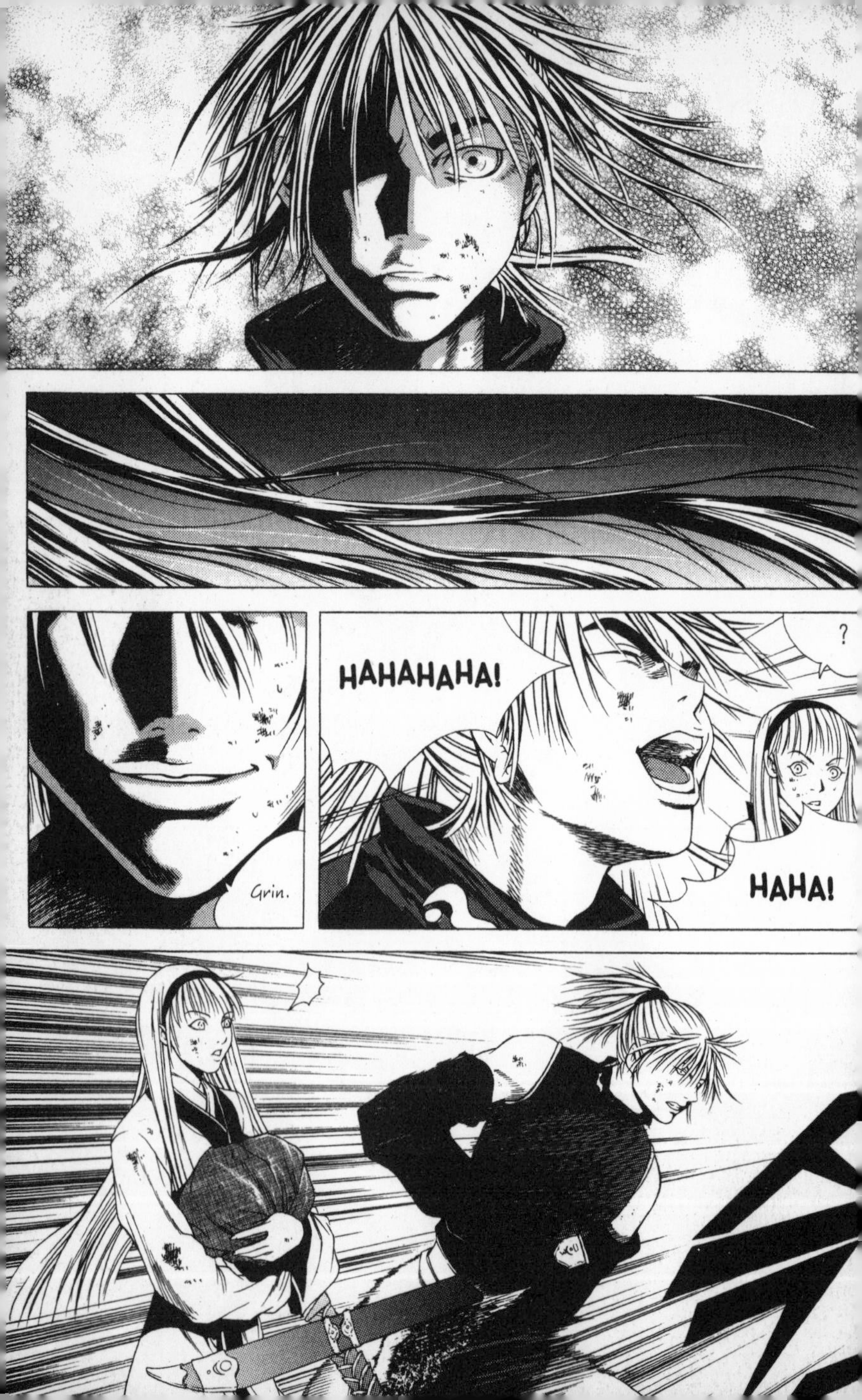
Grin.
HAHAHAHA!
?
HAHA!

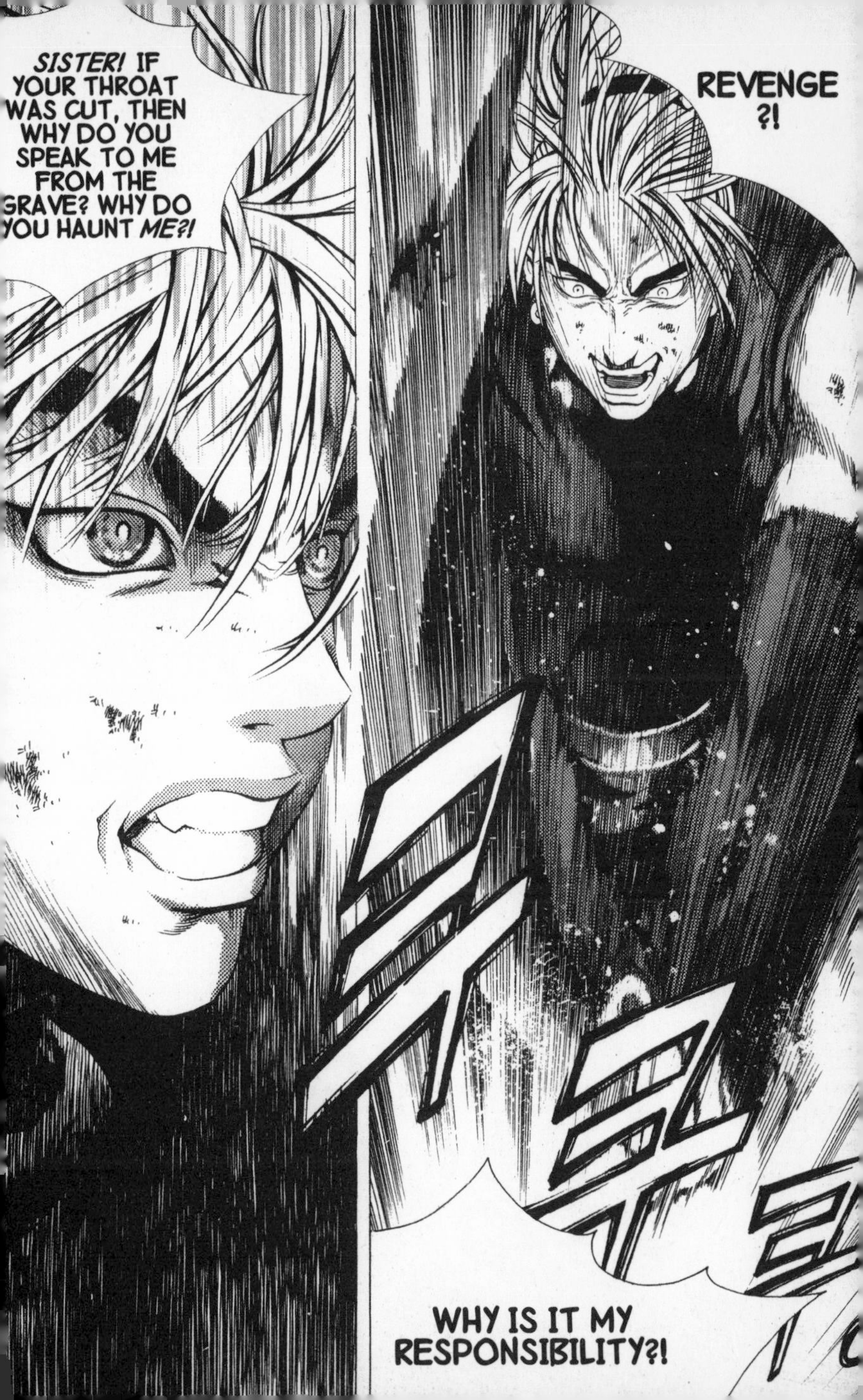
SISTER! IF YOUR THROAT WAS CUT, THEN WHY DO YOU SPEAK TO ME FROM THE GRAVE? WHY DO YOU HAUNT ME?!
REVENGE ?!
WHY IS IT MY RESPONSIBILITY?!

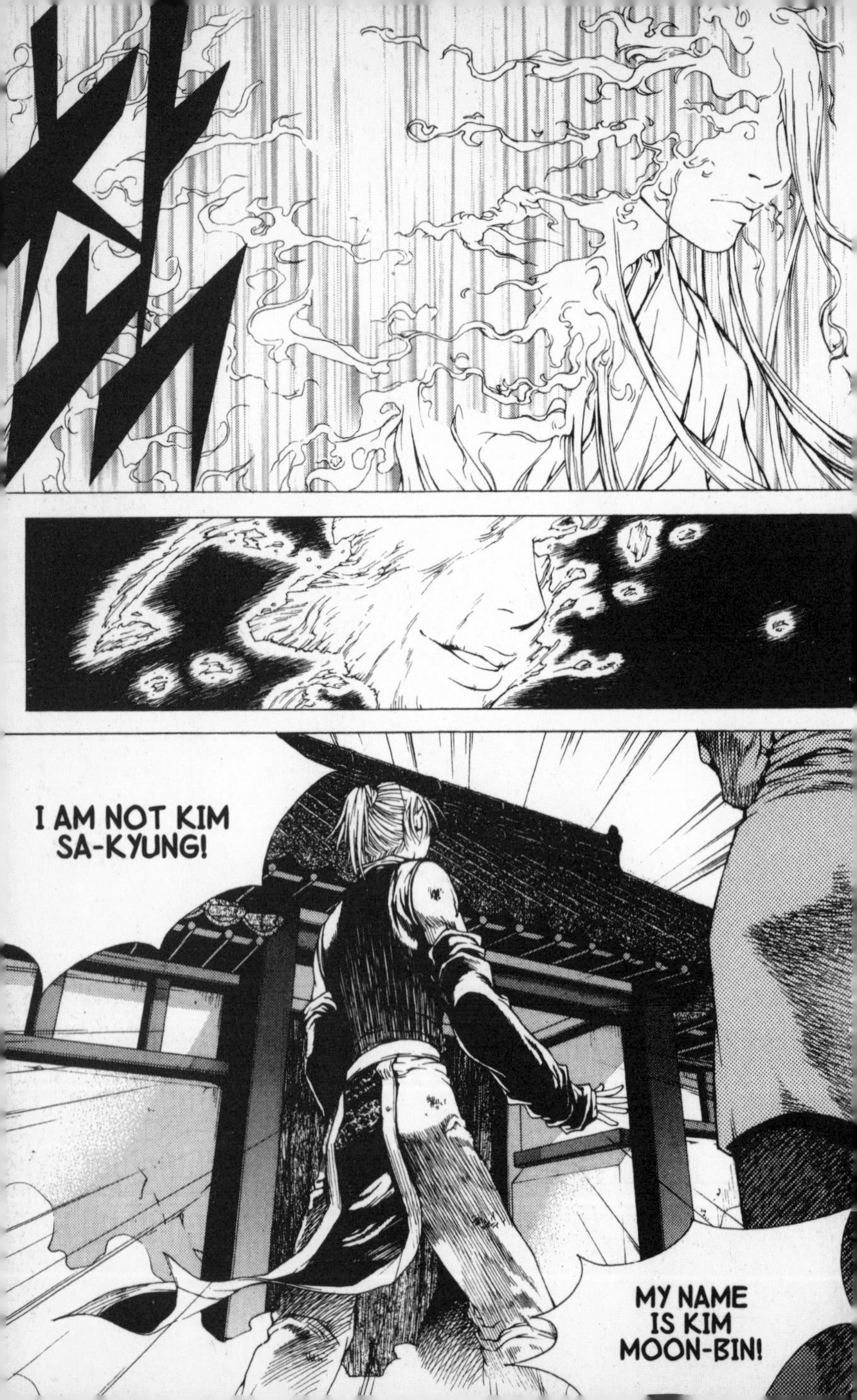

I AM NOT KIM SA-KYUNG!
MY NAME IS KIM MOON-BIN!

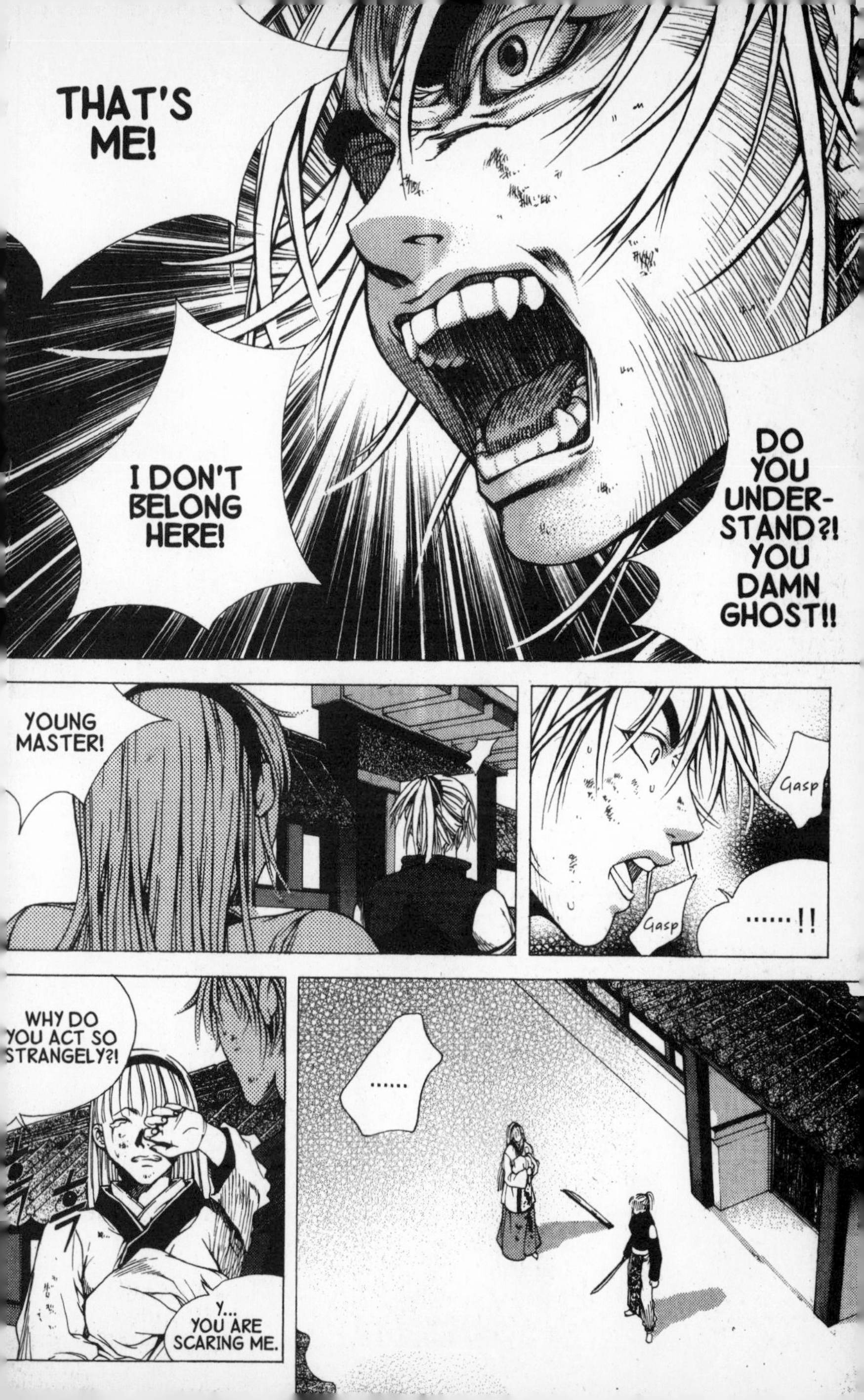
THAT'S ME!
I DON'T BELONG HERE!
DO YOU UNDER-STAND?! YOU DAMN GHOST!!
YOUNG MASTER!
Gasp
Gasp
......!!
WHY DO YOU ACT SO STRANGELY?!
Y... YOU ARE SCARING ME.
......

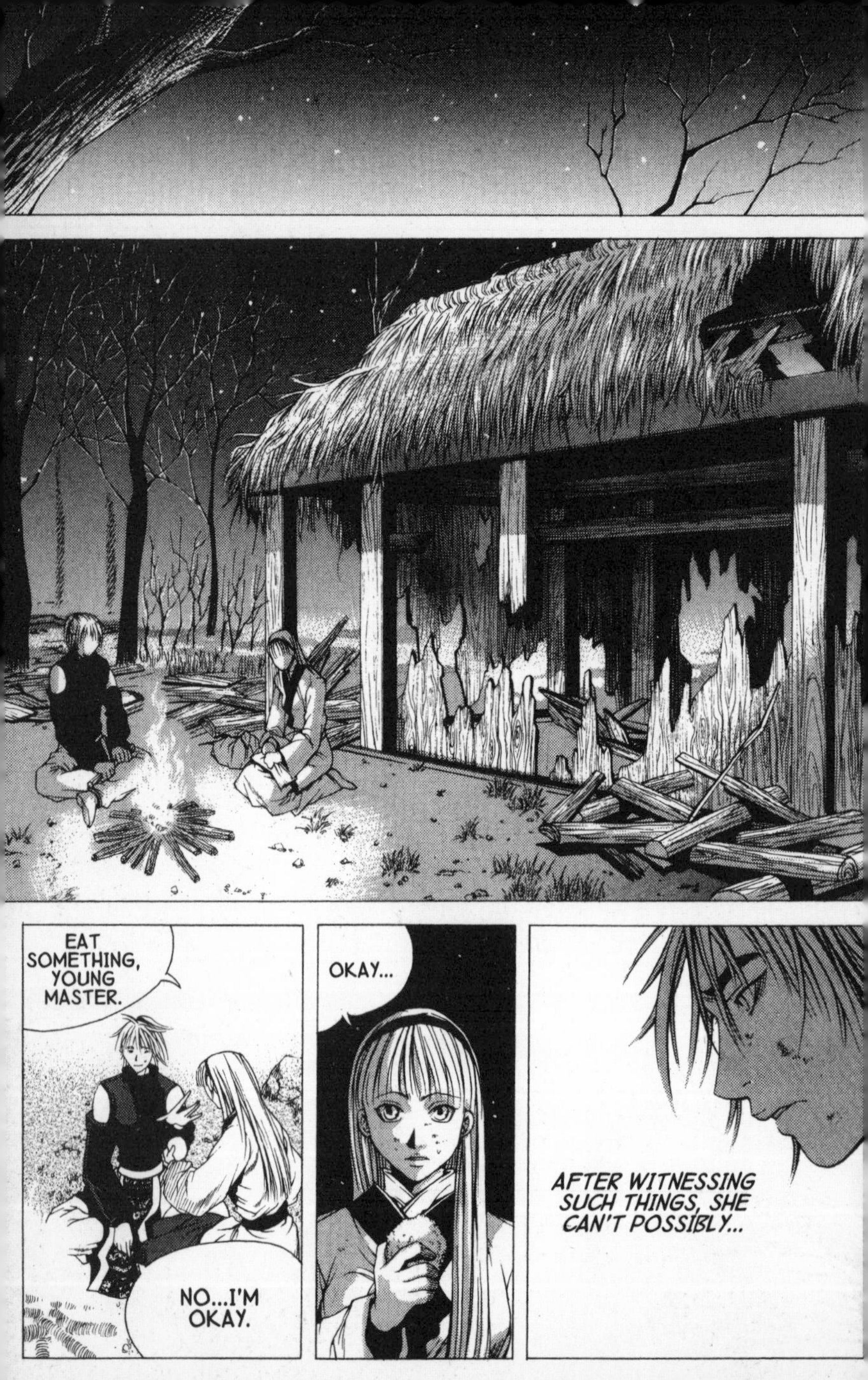
EAT SOMETHING, YOUNG MASTER.
NO...I'M OKAY.
OKAY...
AFTER WITNESSING SUCH THINGS, SHE CAN'T POSSIBLY...

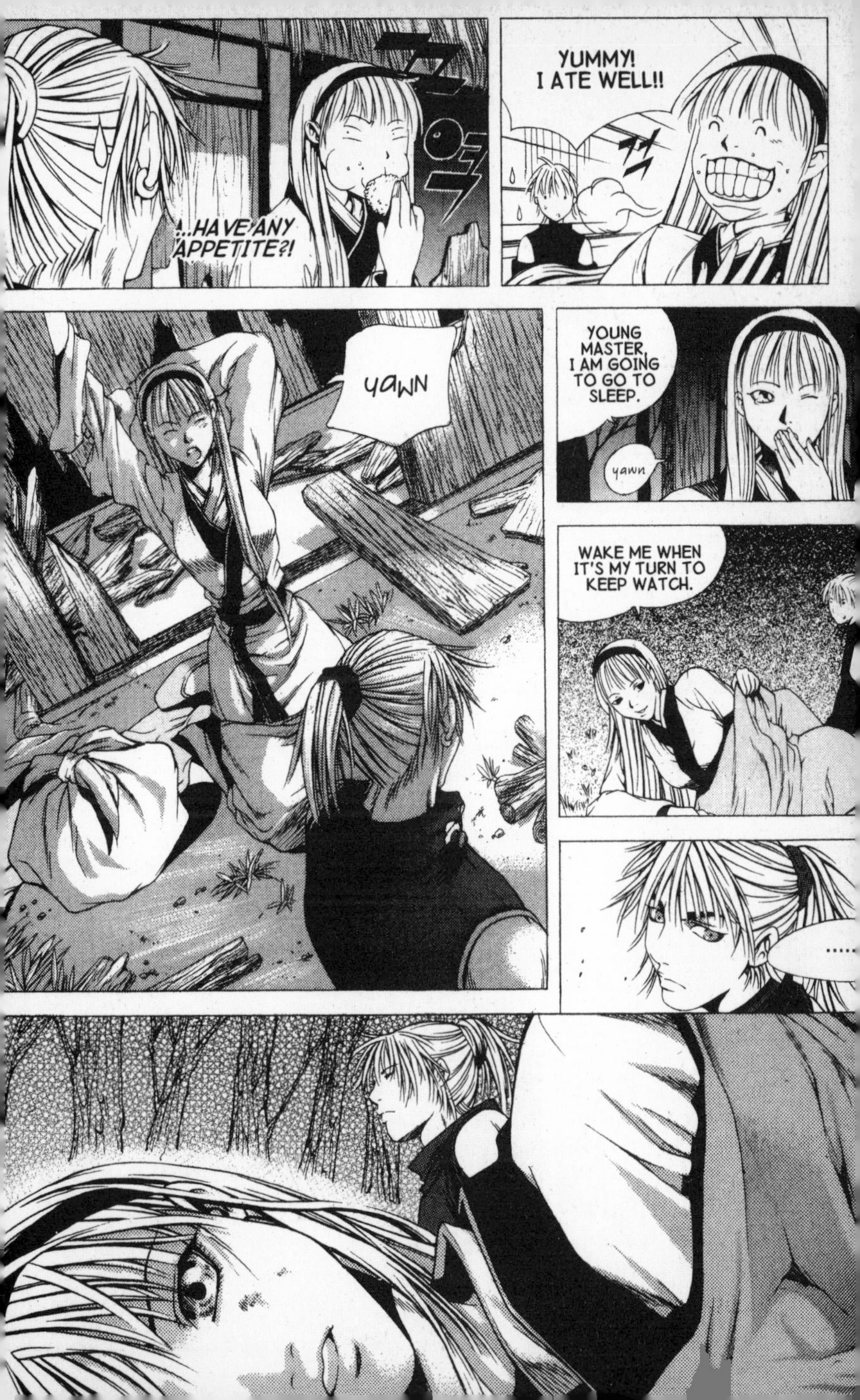
...HAVE ANY APPETITE?!
YUMMY! I ATE WELL!!
yawn
YOUNG MASTER, I AM GOING TO GO TO SLEEP.
yawn
WAKE ME WHEN IT'S MY TURN TO KEEP WATCH.
.....

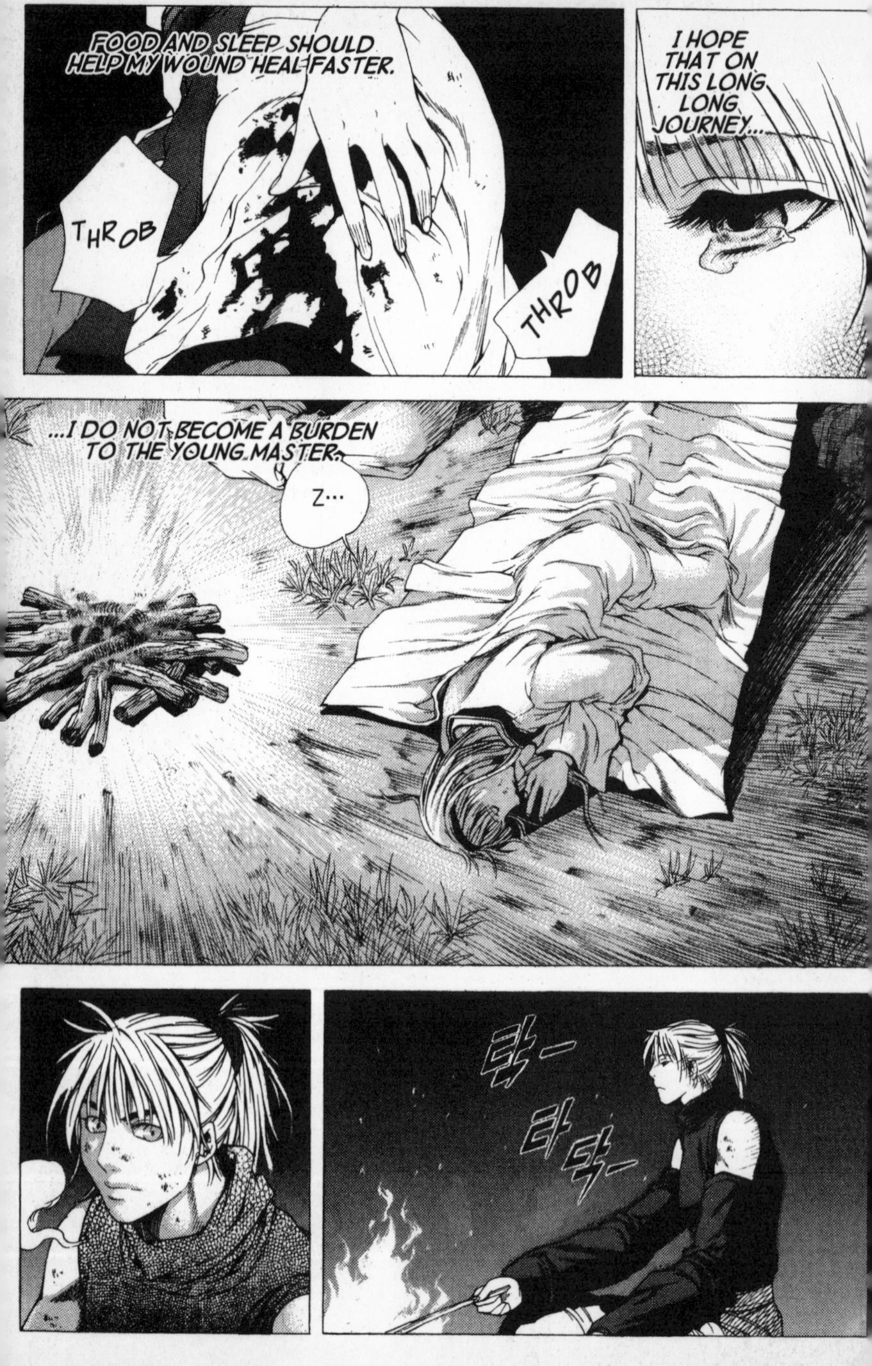
FOOD AND SLEEP SHOULD HELP MY WOUND HEAL FASTER.
THROB
THROB
I HOPE THAT ON THIS LONG LONG JOURNEY...
...I DO NOT BECOME A BURDEN TO THE YOUNG MASTER.
Z...
탁-
타
닥-

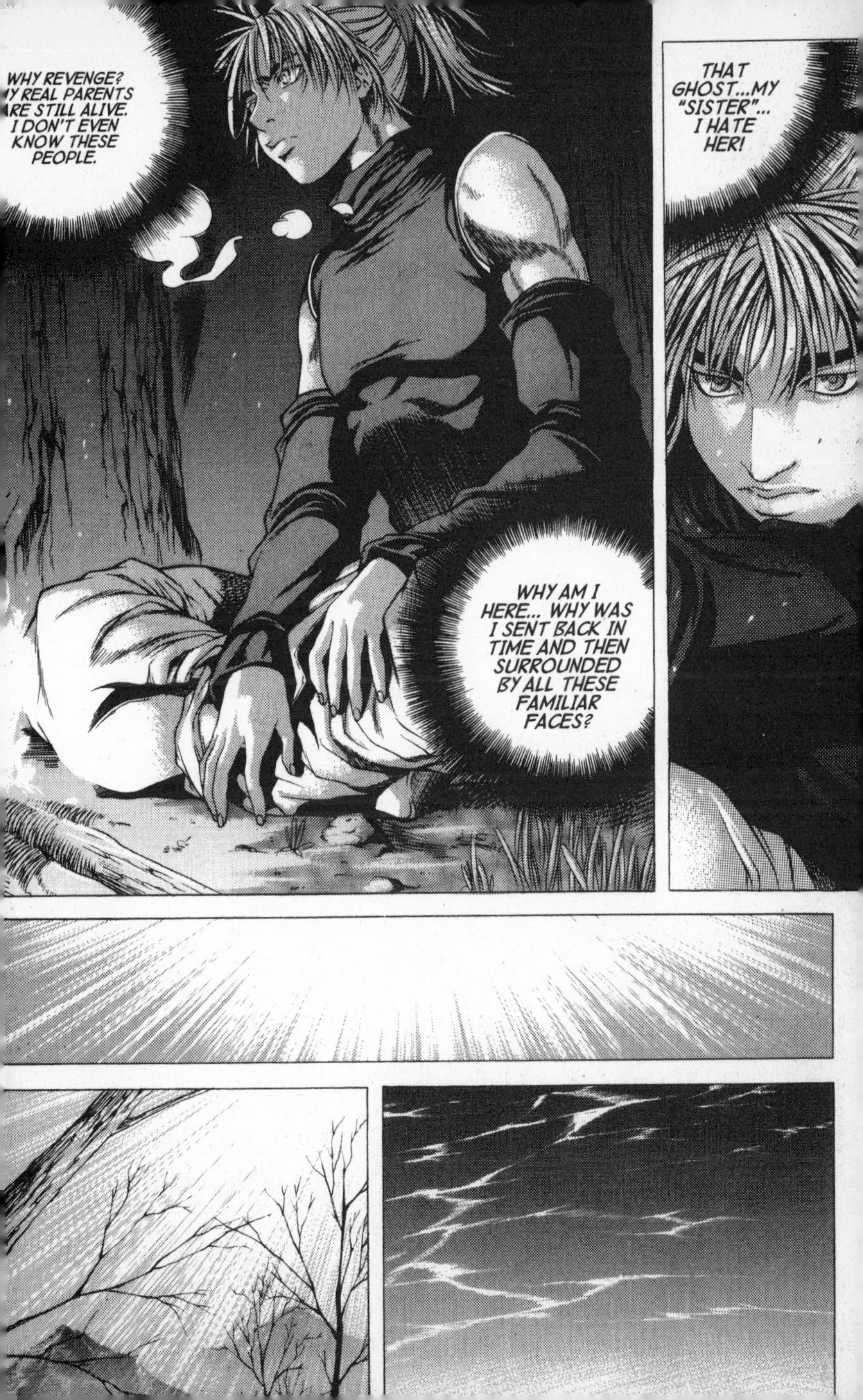
WHY REVENGE? MY REAL PARENTS ARE STILL ALIVE. I DON'T EVEN KNOW THESE PEOPLE.
WHY AM I HERE... WHY WAS I SENT BACK IN TIME AND THEN SURROUNDED BY ALL THESE FAMILIAR FACES?
THAT GHOST...MY "SISTER"... I HATE HER!

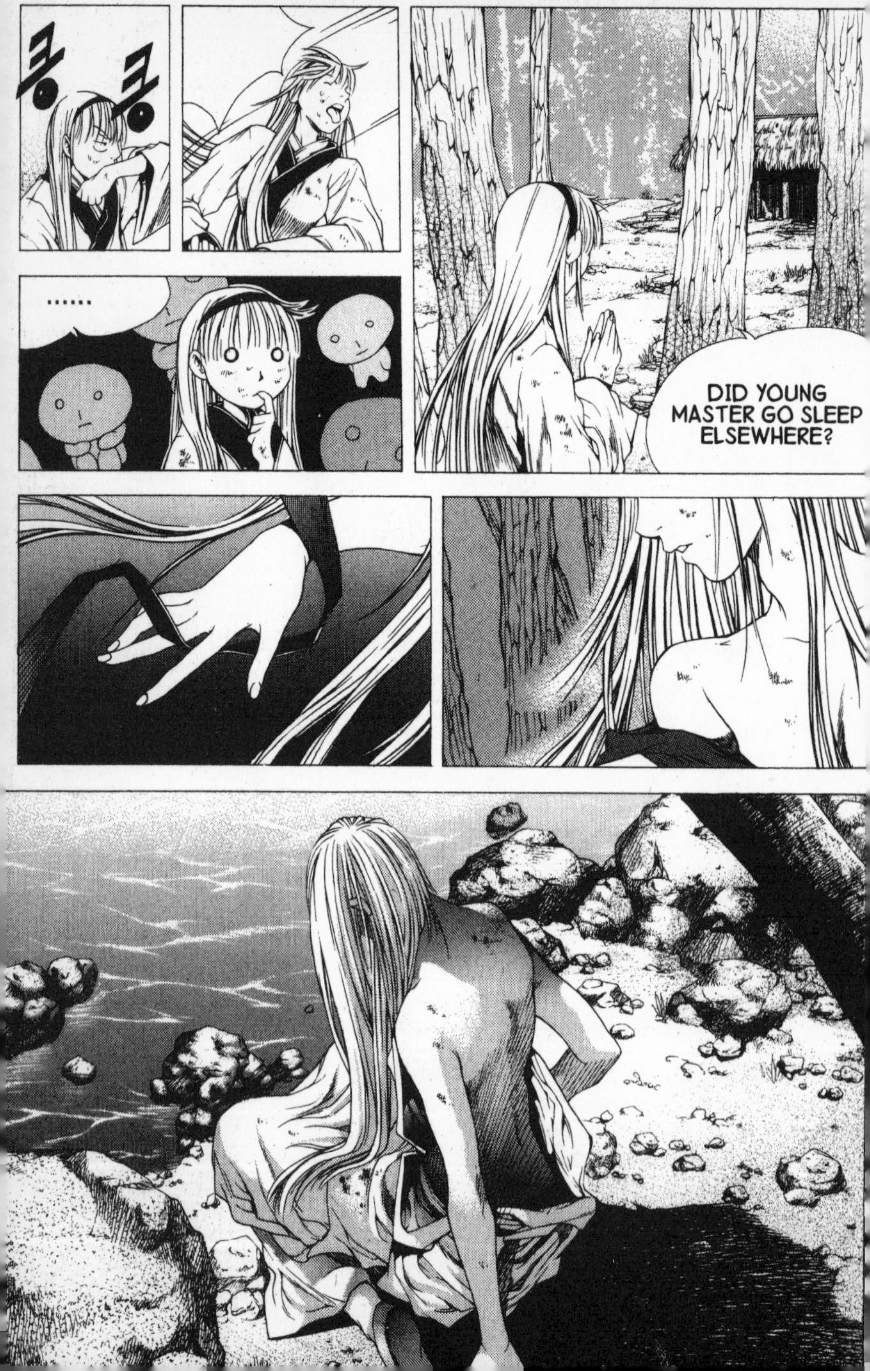
쿵
쿵
......
DID YOUNG MASTER GO SLEEP ELSEWHERE?

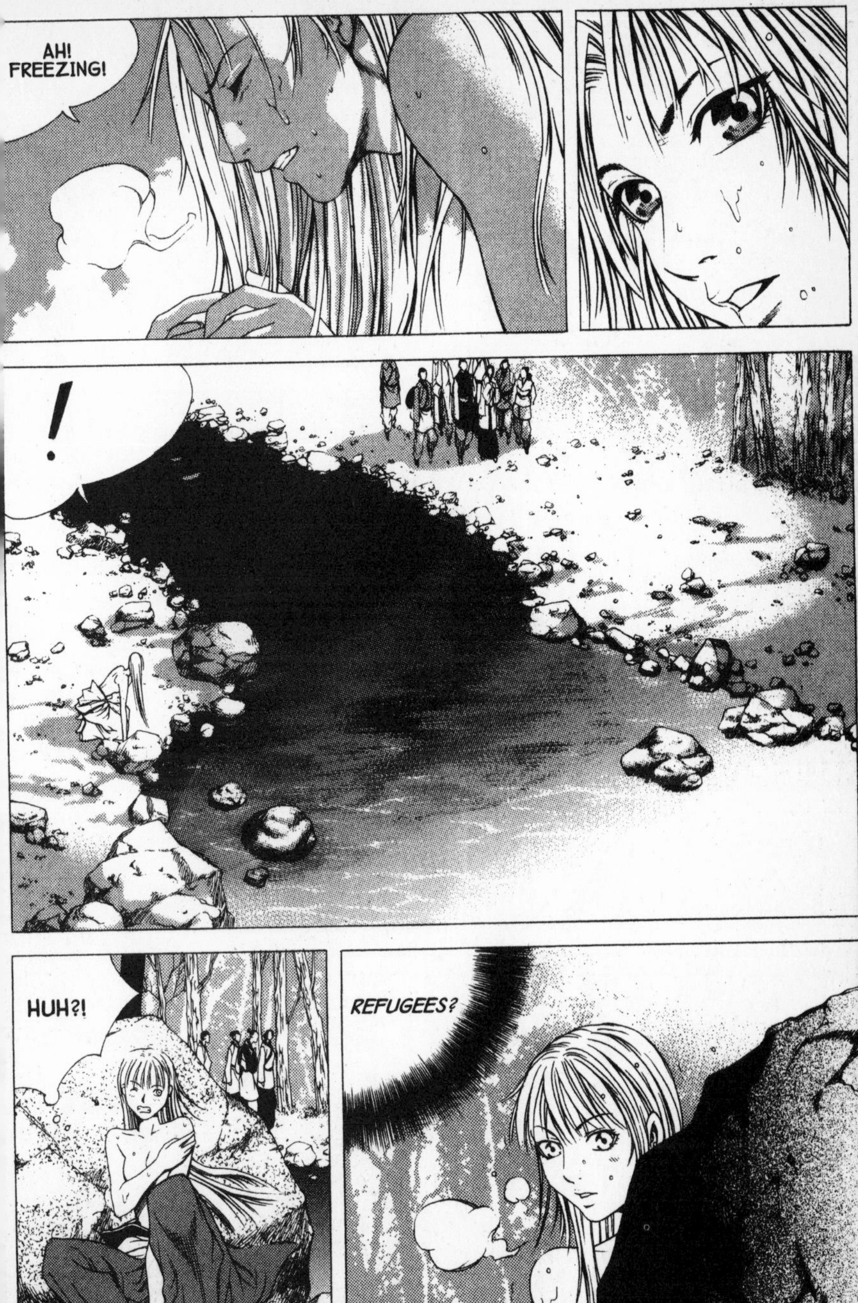
AH! FREEZING!
!
HUH?!
REFUGEES?

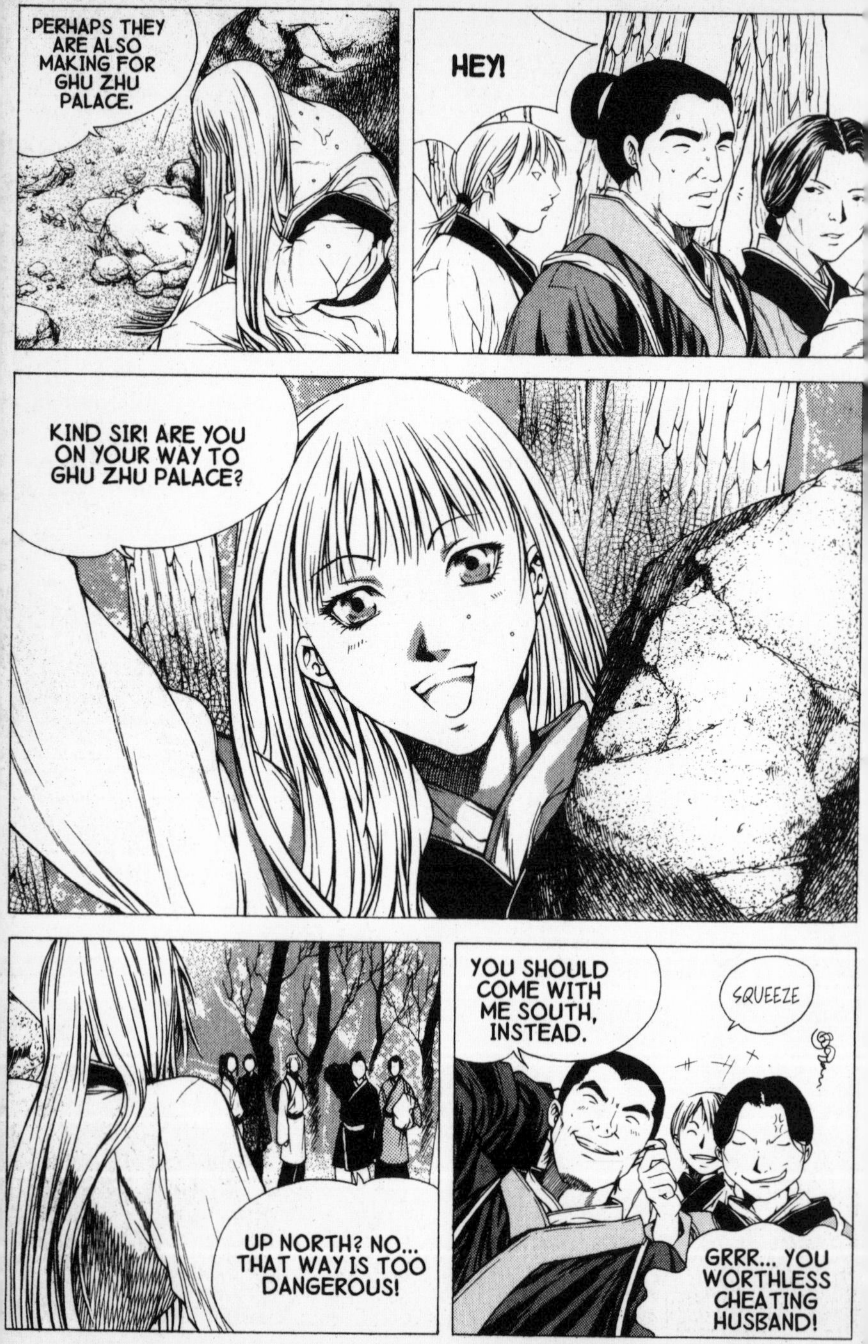
PERHAPS THEY ARE ALSO MAKING FOR GHU ZHU PALACE.
HEY!
KIND SIR! ARE YOU ON YOUR WAY TO GHU ZHU PALACE?
UP NORTH? NO... THAT WAY IS TOO DANGEROUS!
YOU SHOULD COME WITH ME SOUTH, INSTEAD.
SQUEEZE
GRRR... YOU WORTHLESS CHEATING HUSBAND!

GAHH!

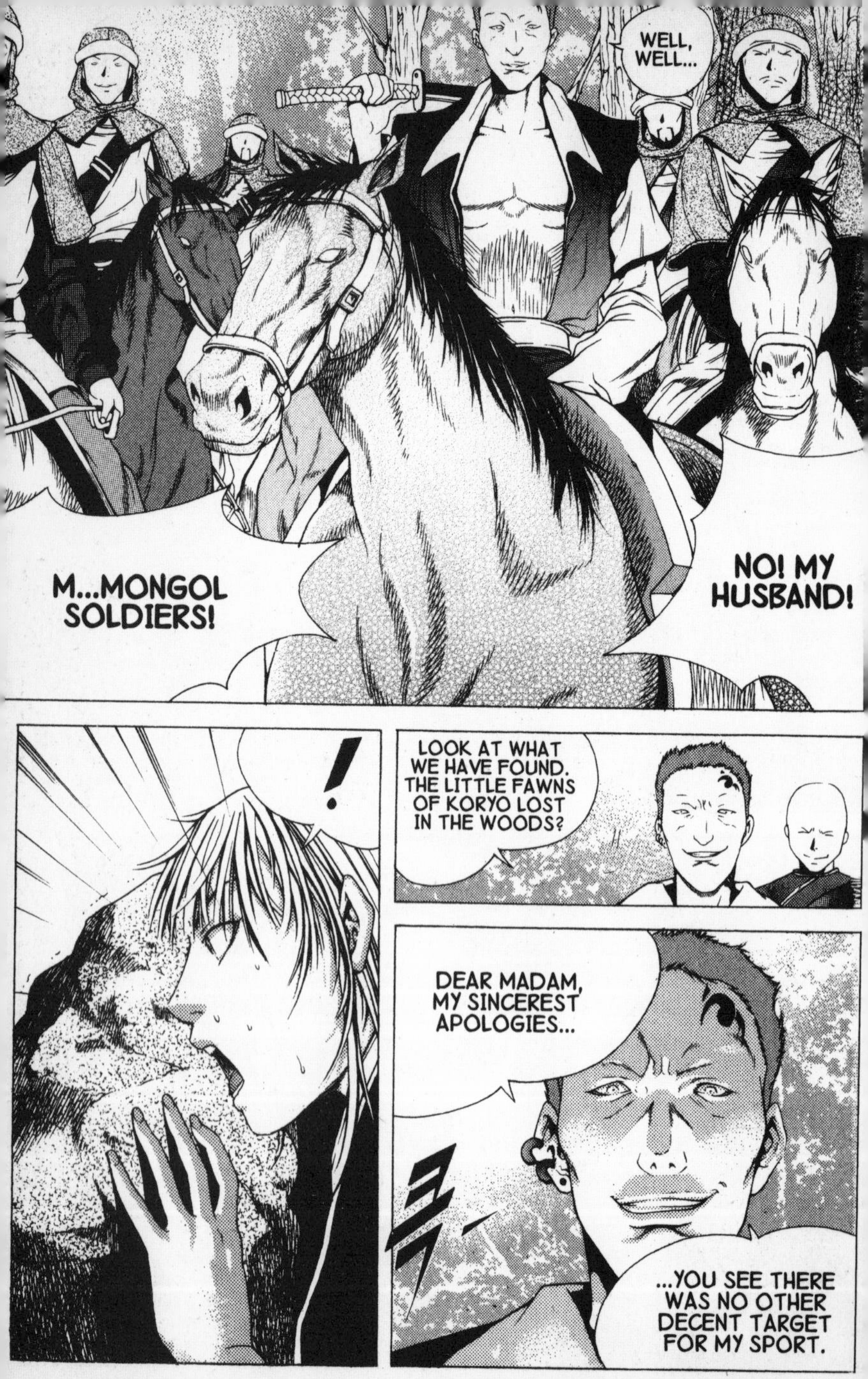
WELL, WELL...
M...MONGOL SOLDIERS!
NO! MY HUSBAND!
!
LOOK AT WHAT WE HAVE FOUND. THE LITTLE FAWNS OF KORYO LOST IN THE WOODS?
DEAR MADAM, MY SINCEREST APOLOGIES...
...YOU SEE THERE WAS NO OTHER DECENT TARGET FOR MY SPORT.

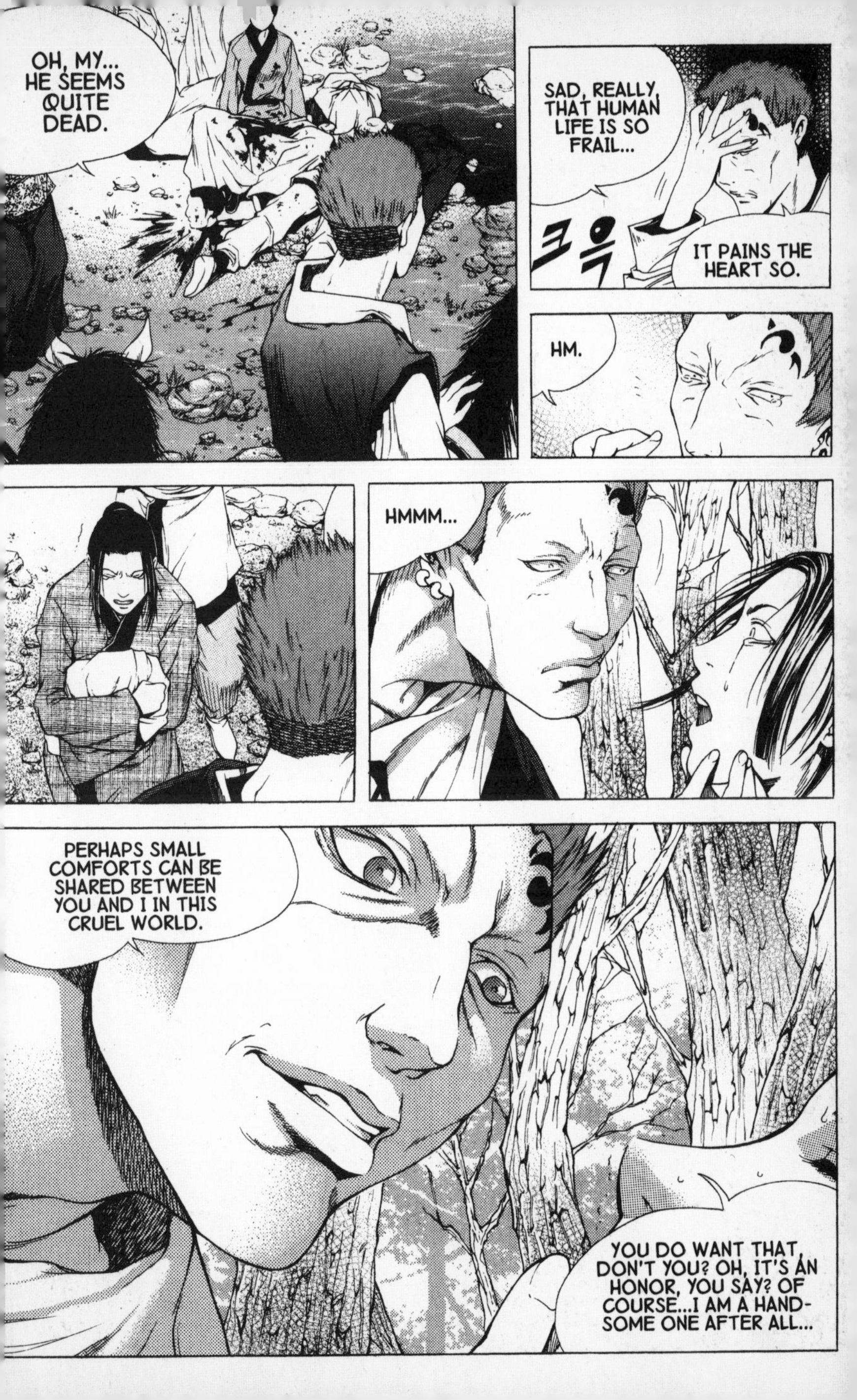
OH, MY... HE SEEMS QUITE DEAD.
SAD, REALLY, THAT HUMAN LIFE IS SO FRAIL...
크윽
IT PAINS THE HEART SO.
HM.
HMMM...
PERHAPS SMALL COMFORTS CAN BE SHARED BETWEEN YOU AND I IN THIS CRUEL WORLD.
YOU DO WANT THAT, DON'T YOU? OH, IT'S AN HONOR, YOU SAY? OF COURSE...I AM A HAND-SOME ONE AFTER ALL...

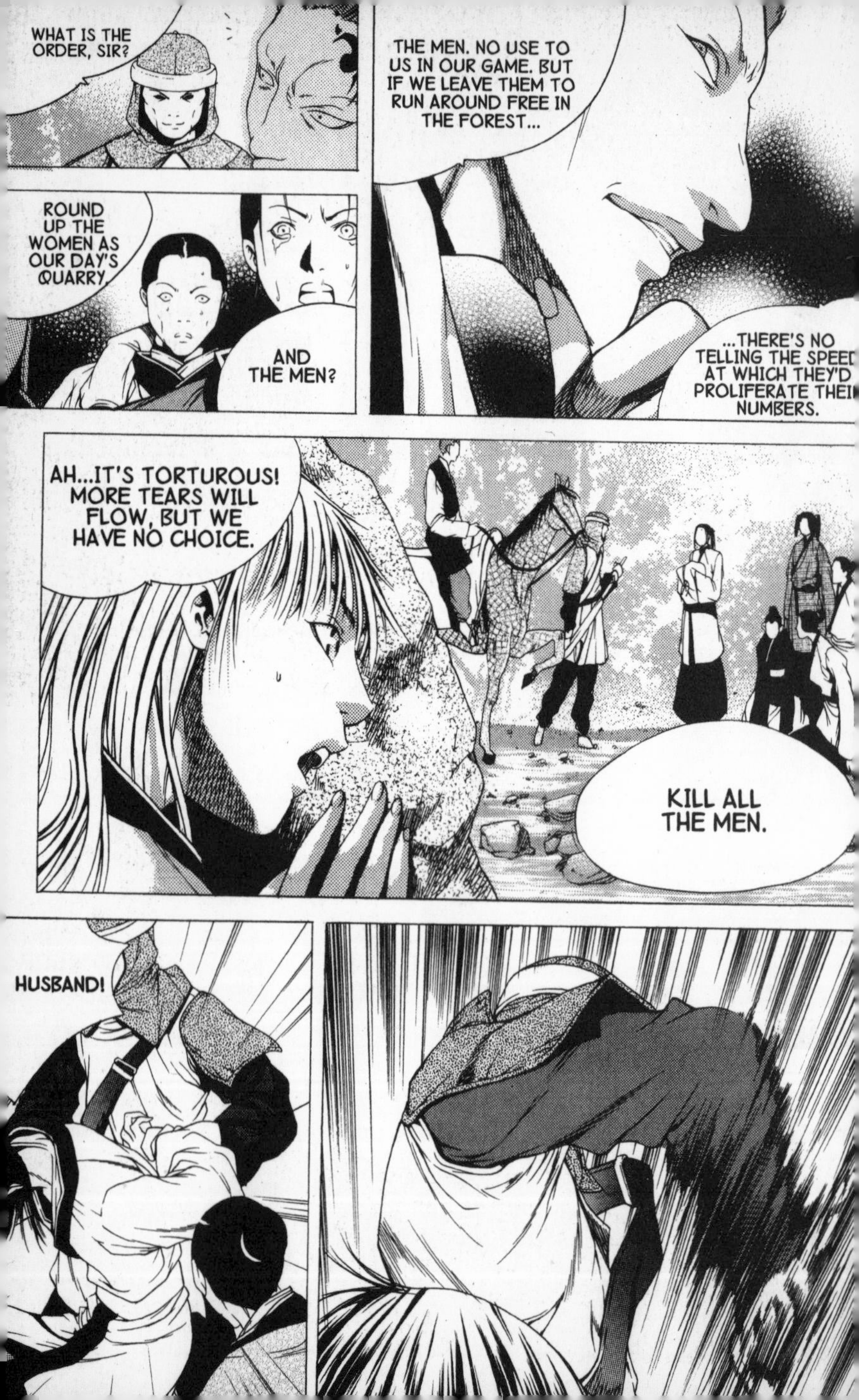
WHAT IS THE ORDER, SIR?
ROUND UP THE WOMEN AS OUR DAY'S QUARRY.
AND THE MEN?
THE MEN. NO USE TO US IN OUR GAME. BUT IF WE LEAVE THEM TO RUN AROUND FREE IN THE FOREST...
...THERE'S NO TELLING THE SPEED AT WHICH THEY'D PROLIFERATE THEIR NUMBERS.
AH...IT'S TORTUROUS! MORE TEARS WILL FLOW, BUT WE HAVE NO CHOICE.
KILL ALL THE MEN.
HUSBAND!

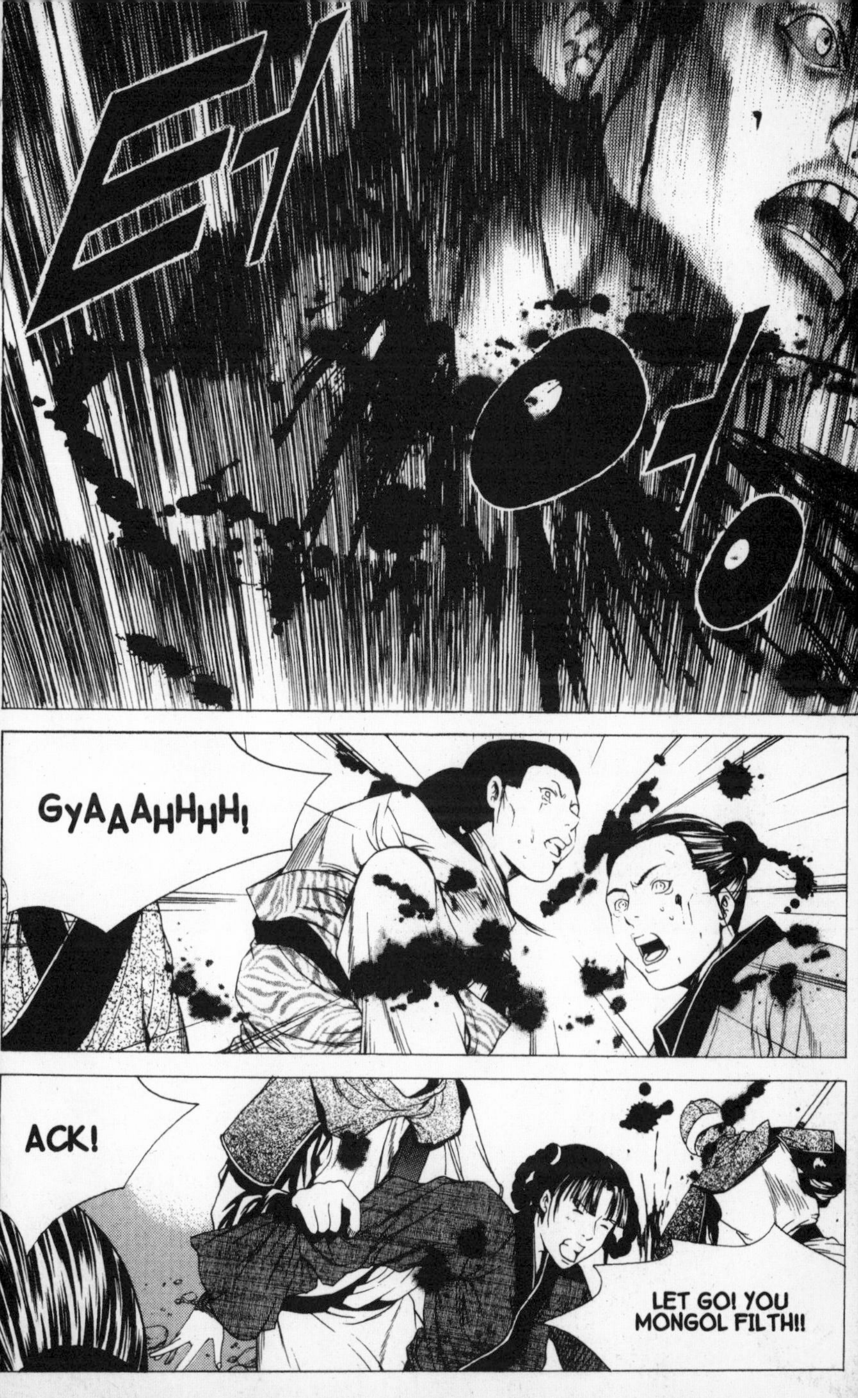
GYAAAHHHH!
ACK!
LET GO! YOU MONGOL FILTH!!

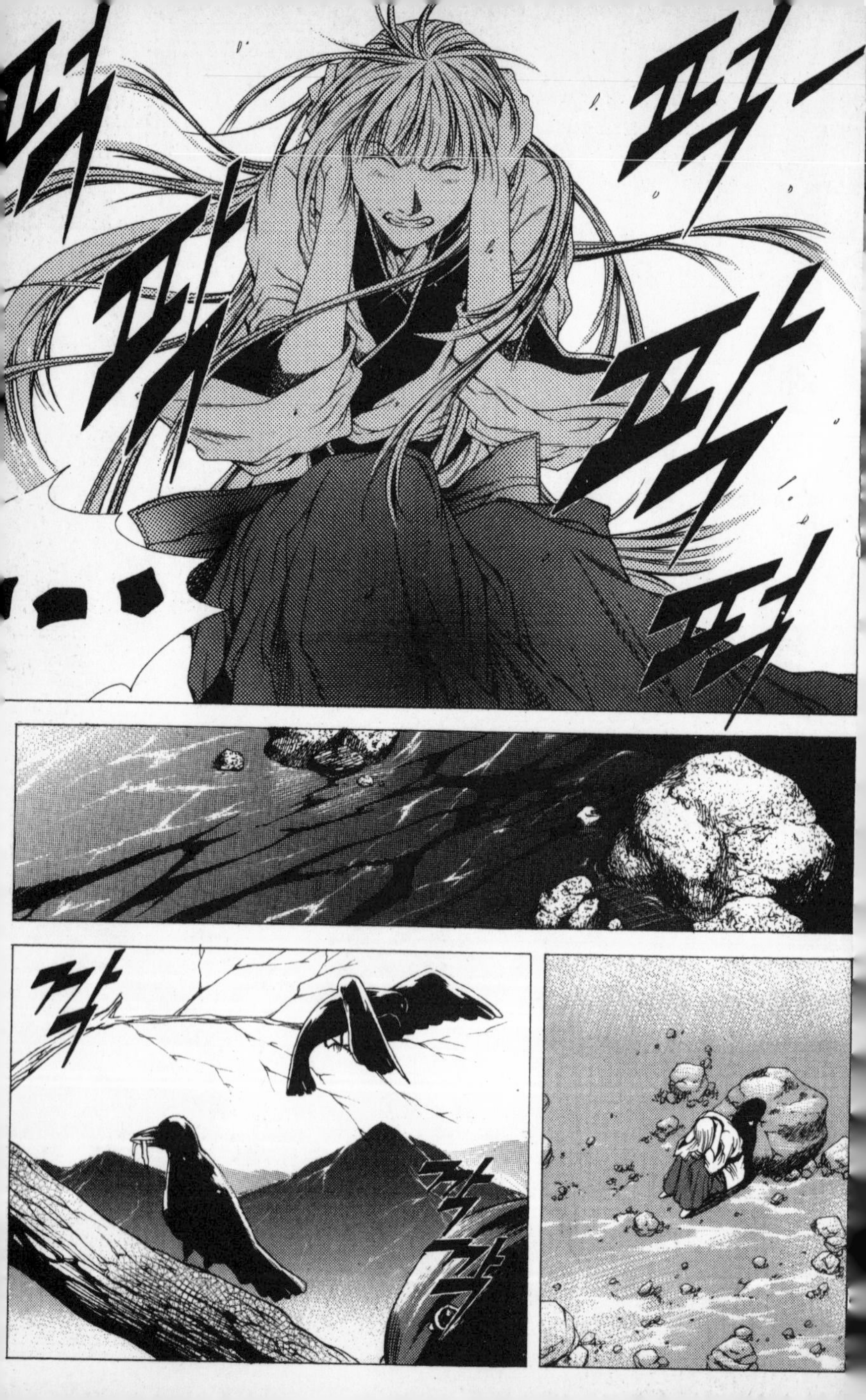
....

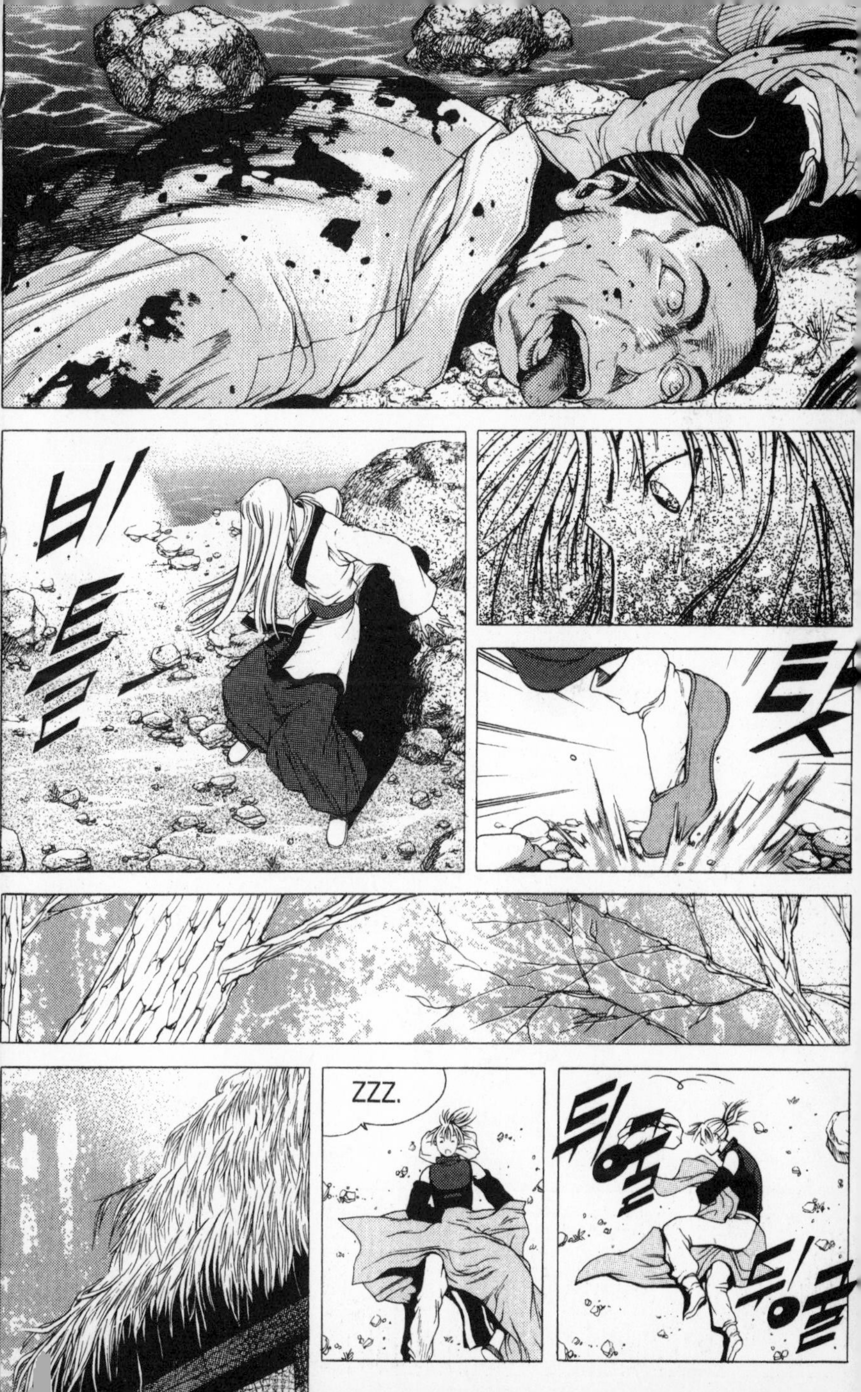
비틀
탓
ZZZ.
뒹굴
뒹굴

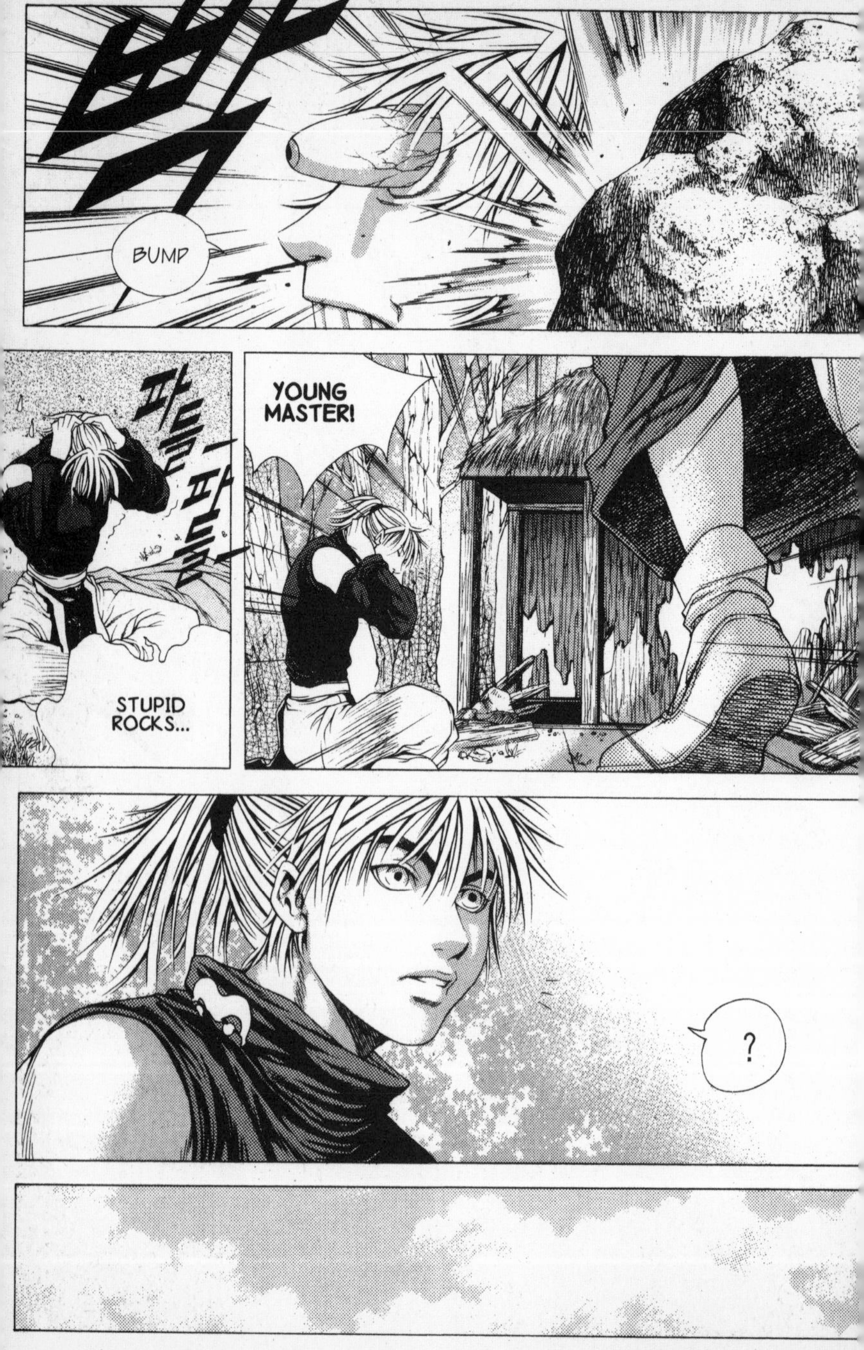
빡
BUMP
파들- 파들-
STUPID ROCKS...
YOUNG MASTER!
?

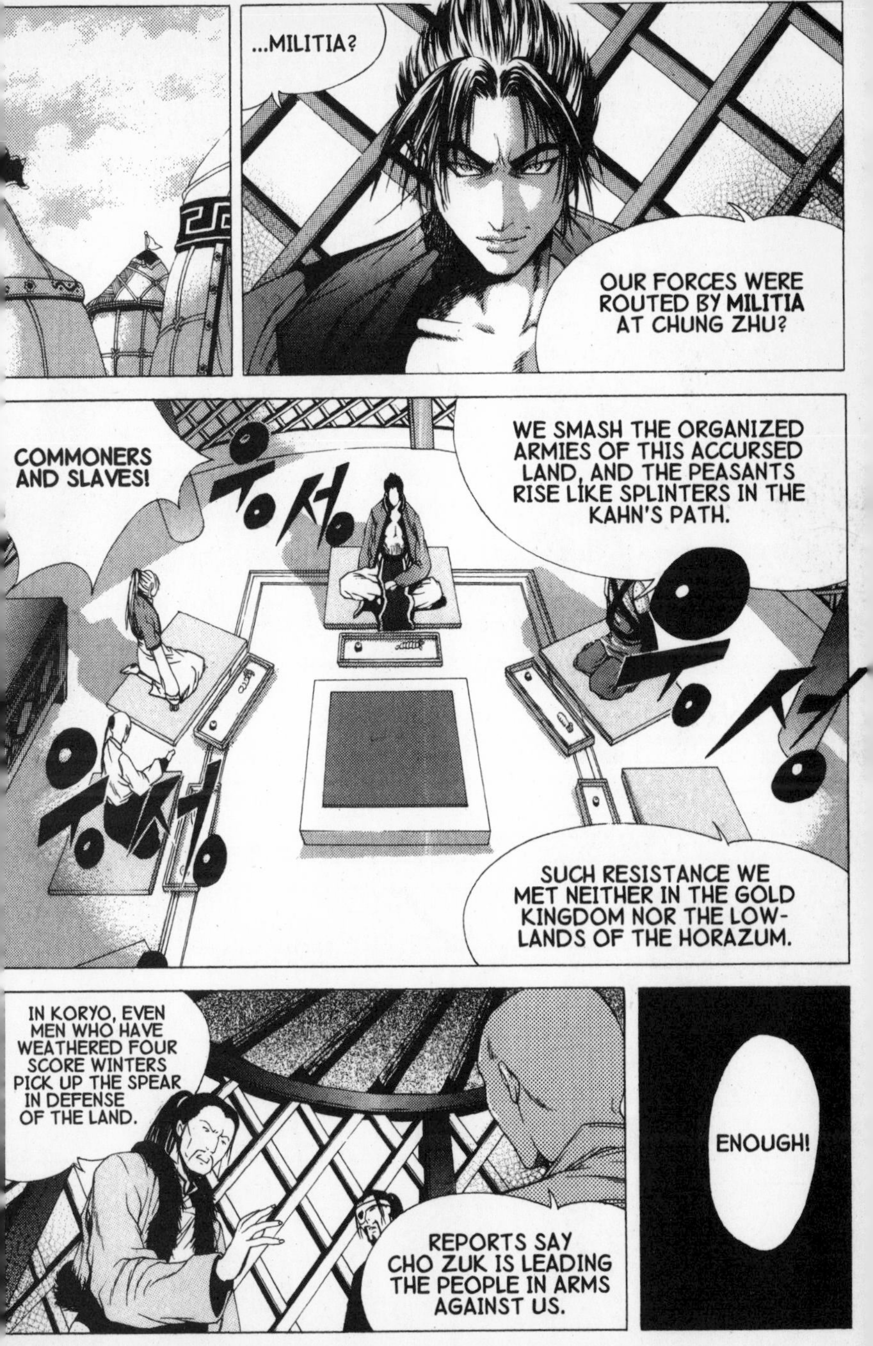

...MILITIA?
OUR FORCES WERE ROUTED BY MILITIA AT CHUNG ZHU?
COMMONERS AND SLAVES!
WE SMASH THE ORGANIZED ARMIES OF THIS ACCURSED LAND, AND THE PEASANTS RISE LIKE SPLINTERS IN THE KAHN'S PATH.
SUCH RESISTANCE WE MET NEITHER IN THE GOLD KINGDOM NOR THE LOW-LANDS OF THE HORAZUM.
IN KORYO, EVEN MEN WHO HAVE WEATHERED FOUR SCORE WINTERS PICK UP THE SPEAR IN DEFENSE OF THE LAND.
REPORTS SAY CHO ZUK IS LEADING THE PEOPLE IN ARMS AGAINST US.
ENOUGH!

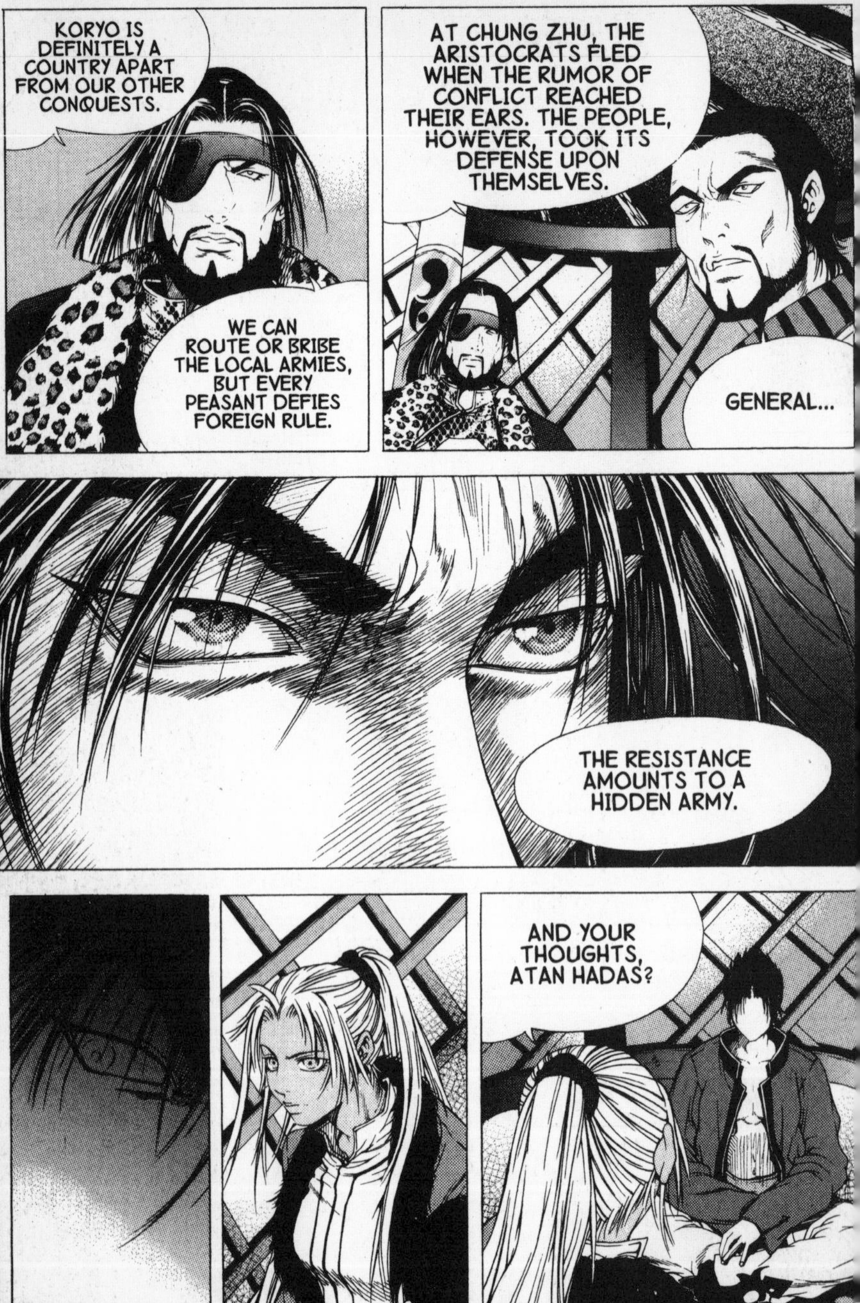
KORYO IS DEFINITELY A COUNTRY APART FROM OUR OTHER CONQUESTS.
WE CAN ROUTE OR BRIBE THE LOCAL ARMIES, BUT EVERY PEASANT DEFIES FOREIGN RULE.
AT CHUNG ZHU, THE ARISTOCRATS FLED WHEN THE RUMOR OF CONFLICT REACHED THEIR EARS. THE PEOPLE, HOWEVER, TOOK ITS DEFENSE UPON THEMSELVES.
GENERAL...
THE RESISTANCE AMOUNTS TO A HIDDEN ARMY.
AND YOUR THOUGHTS, ATAN HADAS?

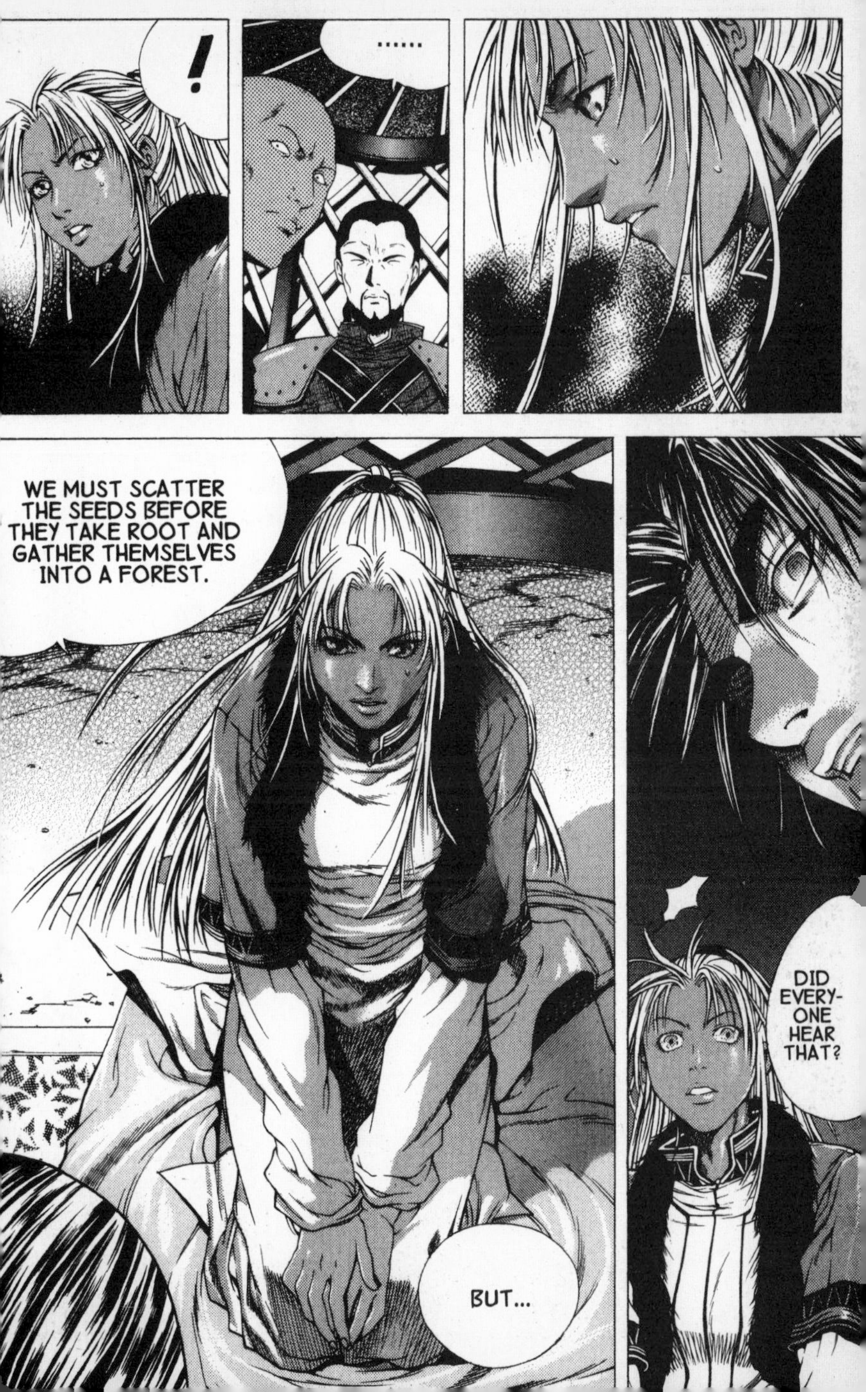
!
......
WE MUST SCATTER THE SEEDS BEFORE THEY TAKE ROOT AND GATHER THEMSELVES INTO A FOREST.
BUT...
DID EVERY-ONE HEAR THAT?

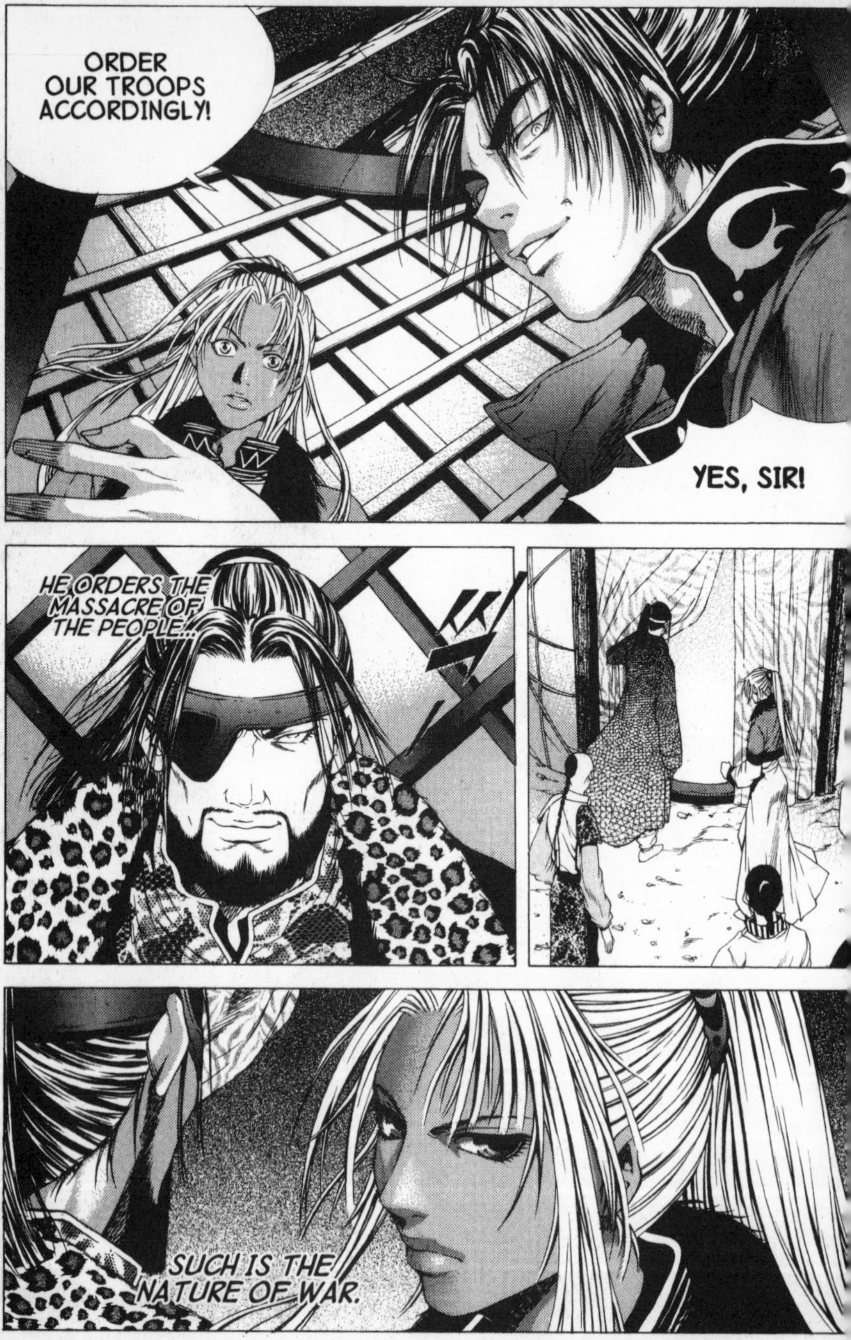
ORDER OUR TROOPS ACCORDINGLY!
YES, SIR!
HE ORDERS THE MASSACRE OF THE PEOPLE...
SUCH IS THE NATURE OF WAR.

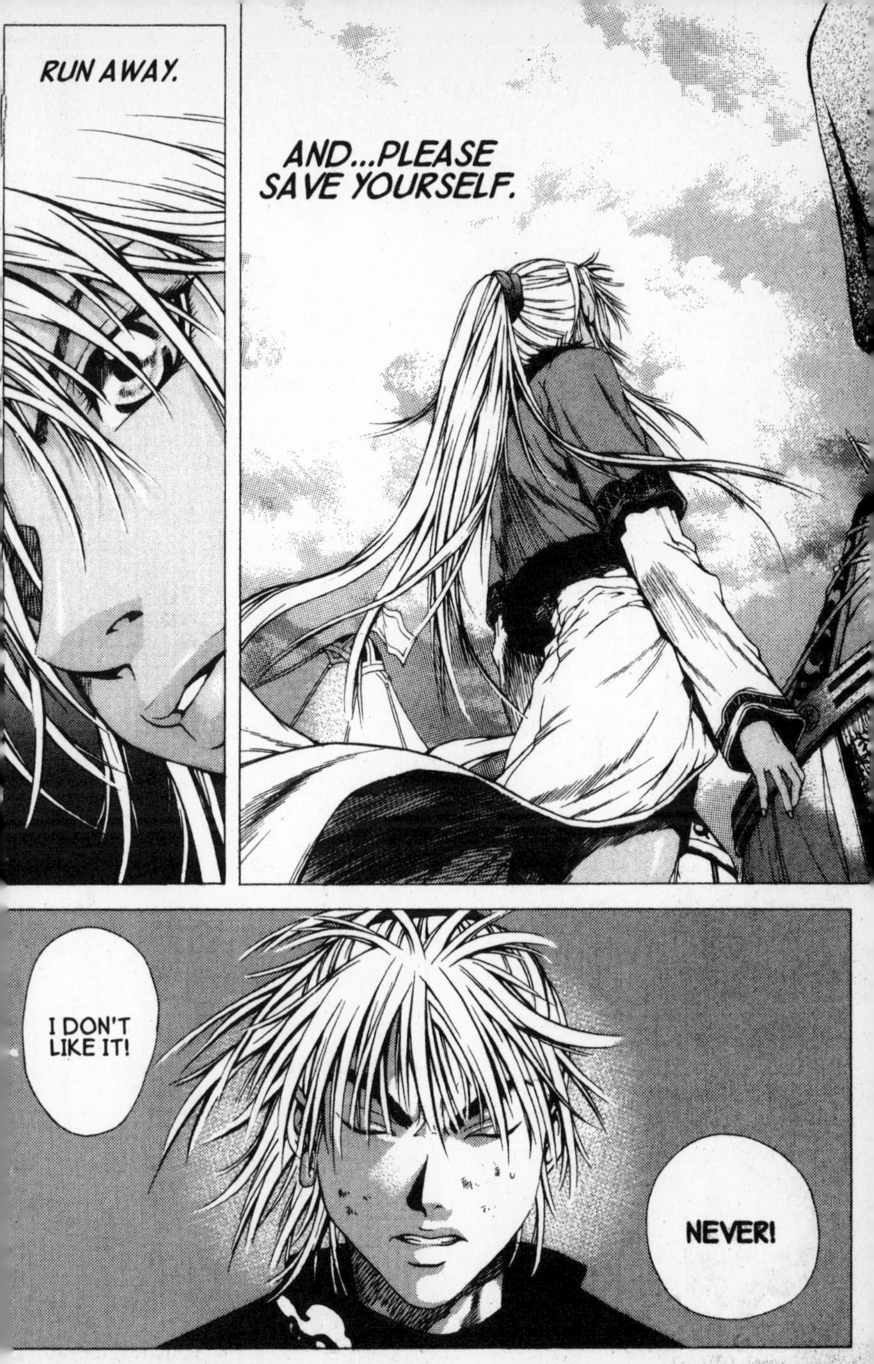
RUN AWAY.
AND...PLEASE SAVE YOURSELF.
I DON'T LIKE IT!
NEVER!

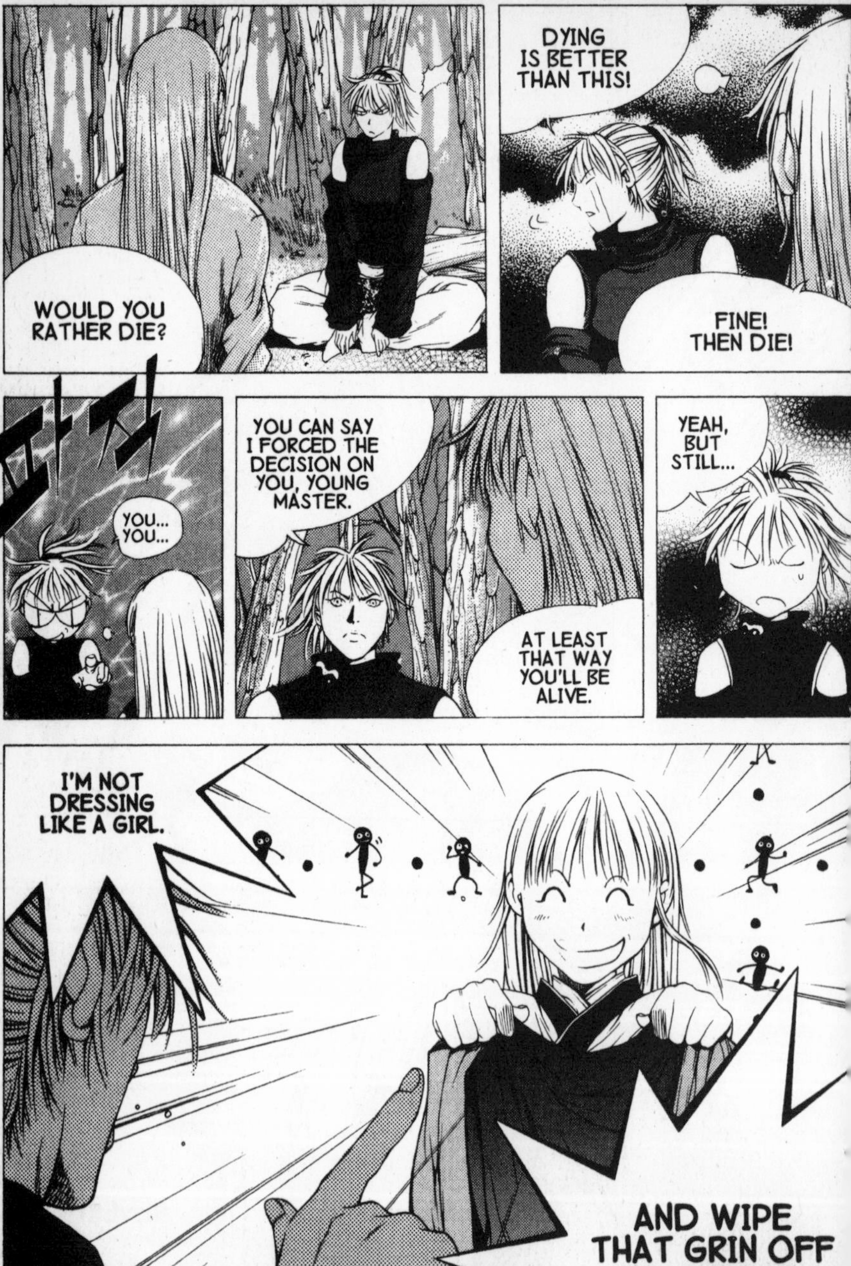
WOULD YOU RATHER DIE?
DYING IS BETTER THAN THIS!
FINE! THEN DIE!
YOU... YOU...
YOU CAN SAY I FORCED THE DECISION ON YOU, YOUNG MASTER.
AT LEAST THAT WAY YOU'LL BE ALIVE.
YEAH, BUT STILL...
I'M NOT DRESSING LIKE A GIRL.
AND WIPE THAT GRIN OFF YOUR FACE.

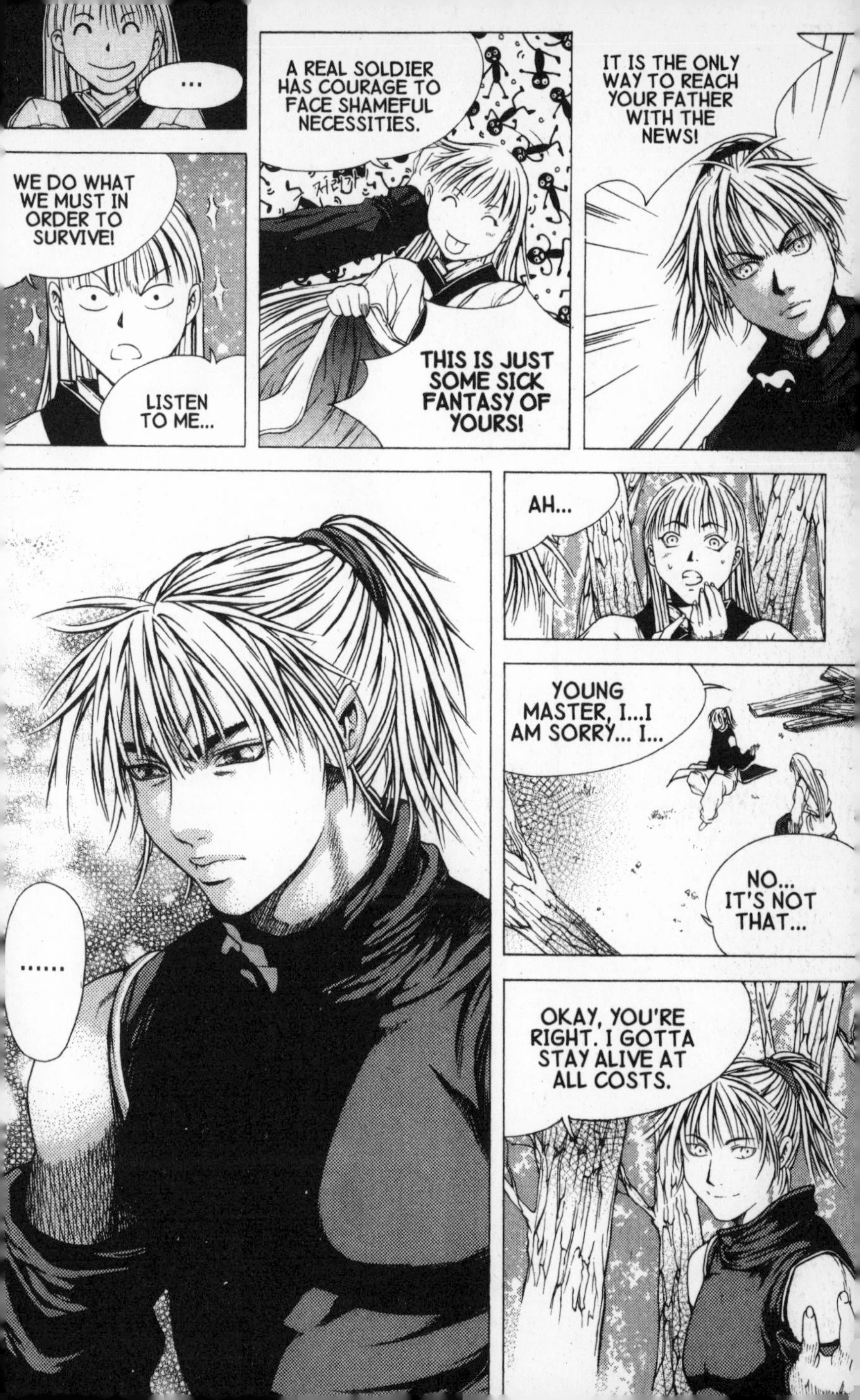
...
WE DO WHAT WE MUST IN ORDER TO SURVIVE!
LISTEN TO ME...
A REAL SOLDIER HAS COURAGE TO FACE SHAMEFUL NECESSITIES.
저리가
THIS IS JUST SOME SICK FANTASY OF YOURS!
IT IS THE ONLY WAY TO REACH YOUR FATHER WITH THE NEWS!
......
AH...
YOUNG MASTER, I...I AM SORRY... I...
NO... IT'S NOT THAT...
OKAY, YOU'RE RIGHT. I GOTTA STAY ALIVE AT ALL COSTS.

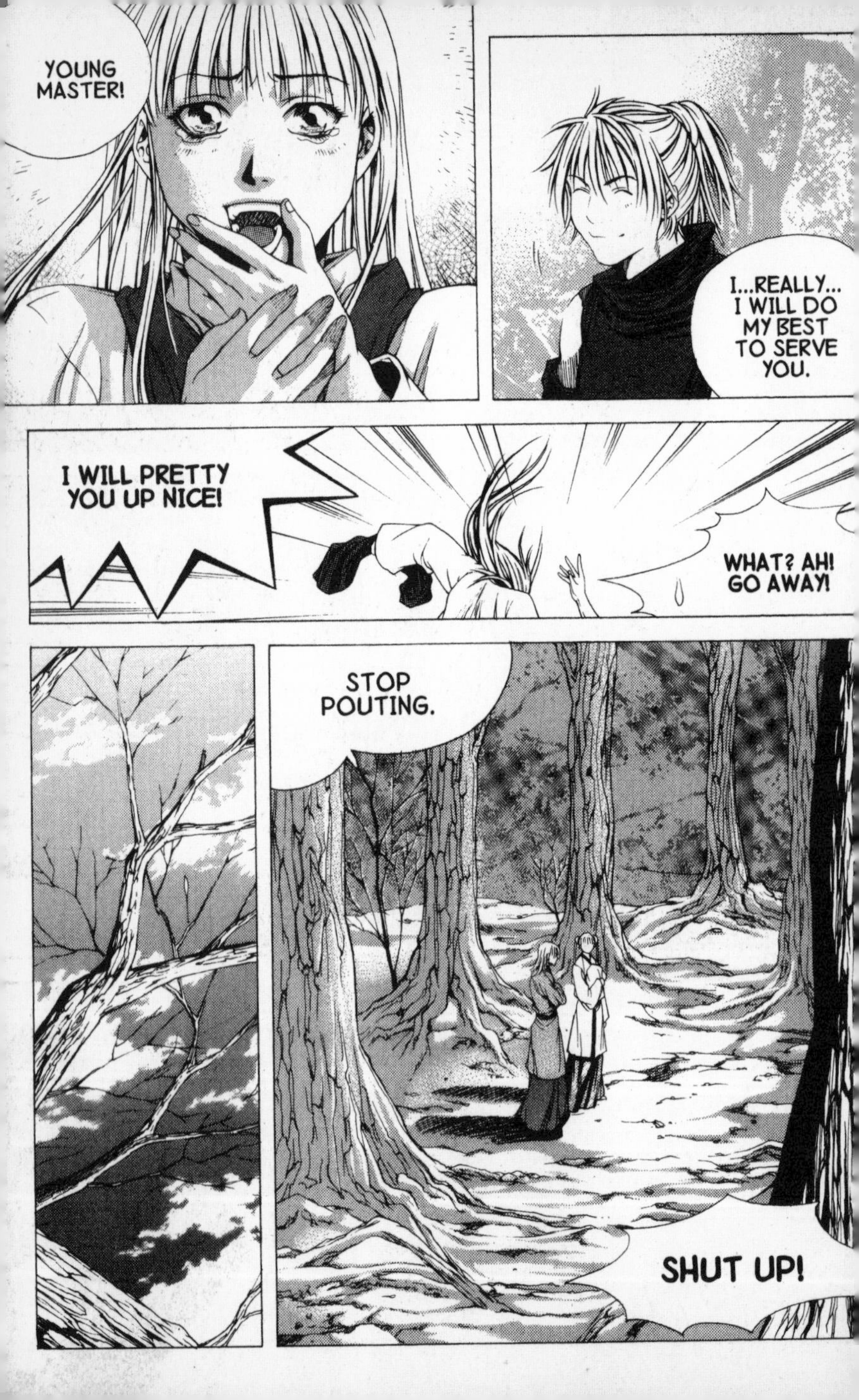
YOUNG MASTER!
I...REALLY... I WILL DO MY BEST TO SERVE YOU.
I WILL PRETTY YOU UP NICE!
WHAT? AH! GO AWAY!
STOP POUTING.
SHUT UP!

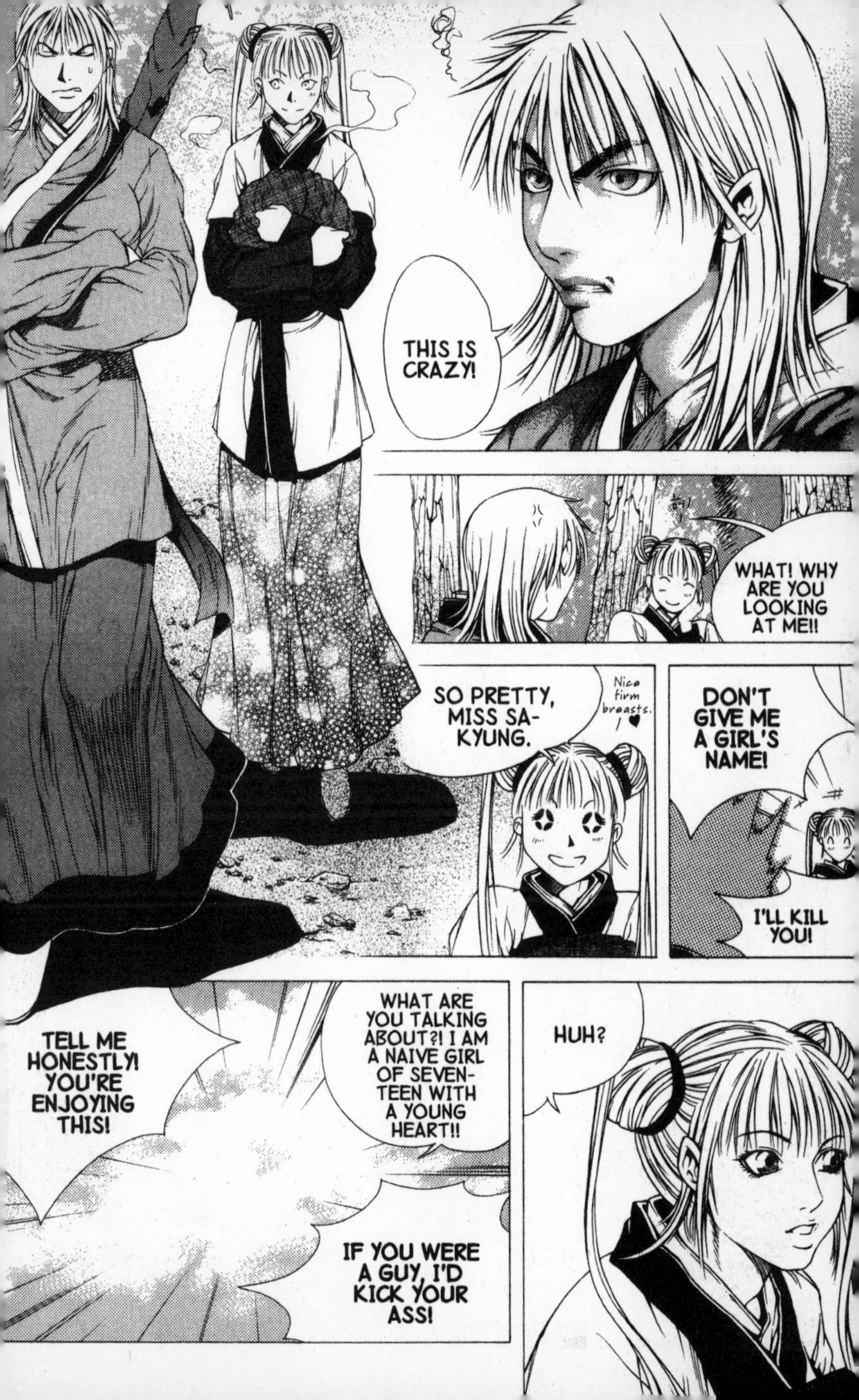
THIS IS CRAZY!
WHAT! WHY ARE YOU LOOKING AT ME!!
SO PRETTY, MISS SA-KYUNG.
Nice firm breasts. ♥
DON'T GIVE ME A GIRL'S NAME!
I'LL KILL YOU!
TELL ME HONESTLY! YOU'RE ENJOYING THIS!
WHAT ARE YOU TALKING ABOUT?! I AM A NAIVE GIRL OF SEVEN-TEEN WITH A YOUNG HEART!!
IF YOU WERE A GUY, I'D KICK YOUR ASS!
HUH?

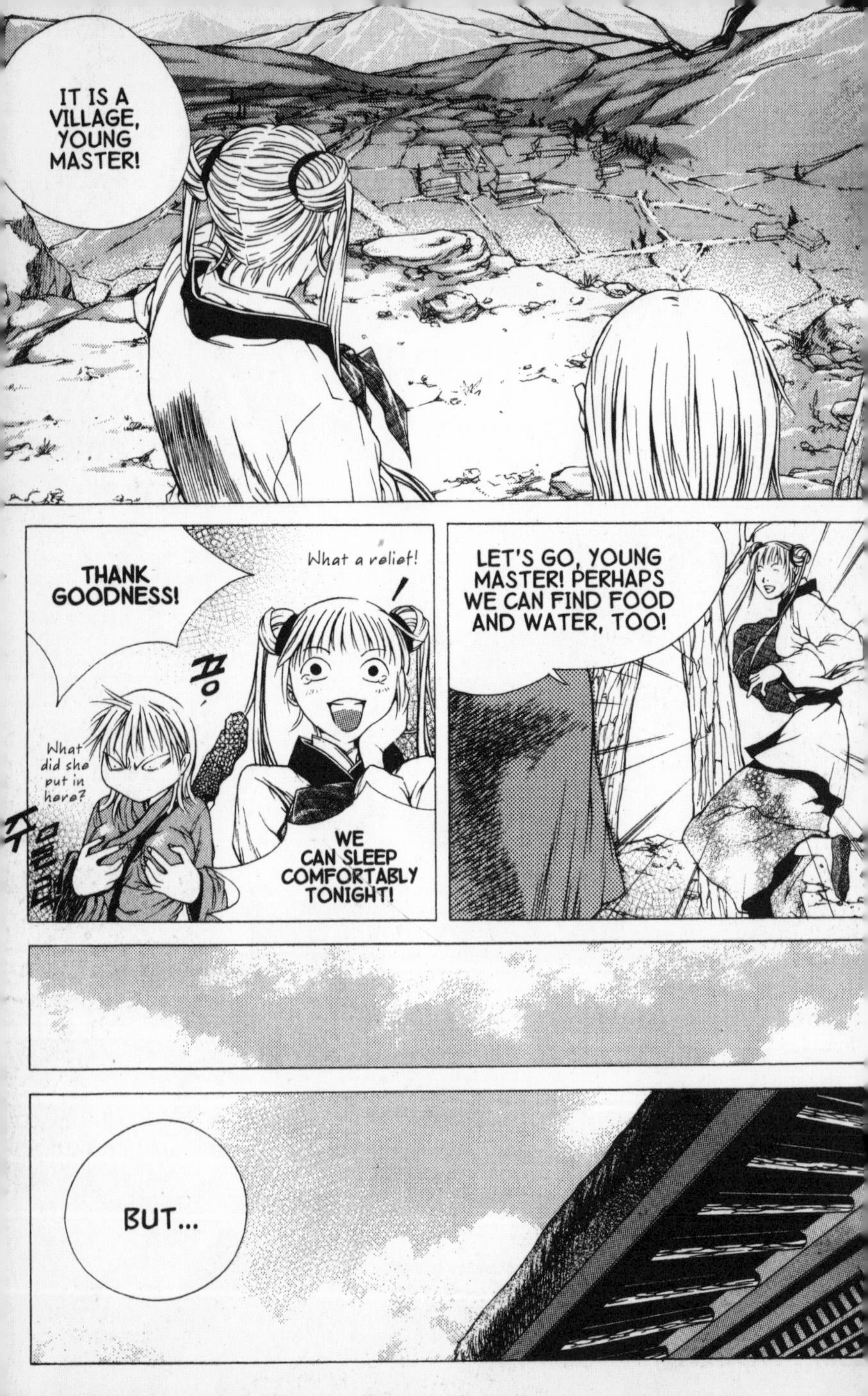
IT IS A VILLAGE, YOUNG MASTER!
THANK GOODNESS!
What a relief!
!
What did she put in here?
WE CAN SLEEP COMFORTABLY TONIGHT!
LET'S GO, YOUNG MASTER! PERHAPS WE CAN FIND FOOD AND WATER, TOO!
BUT...

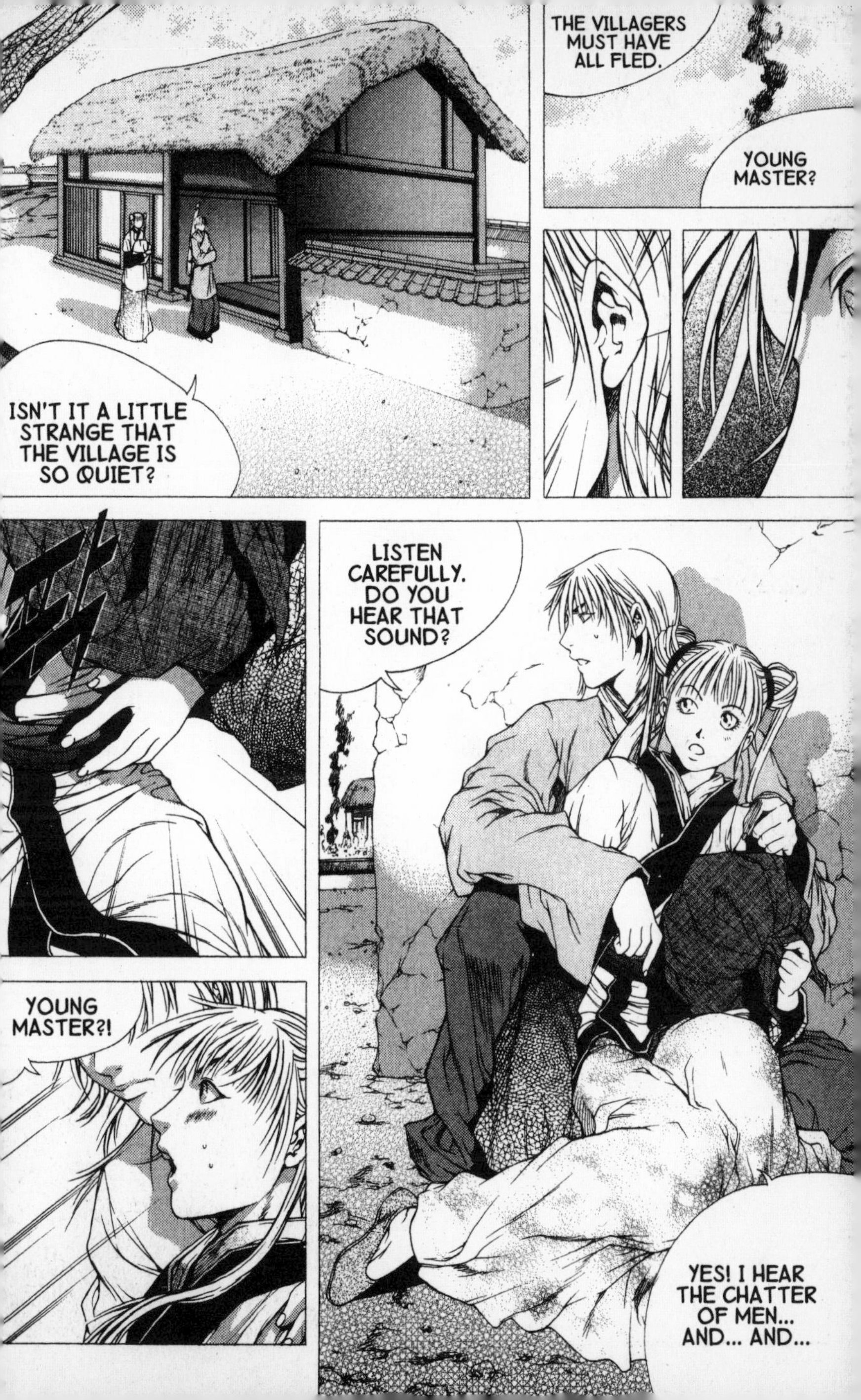
ISN'T IT A LITTLE STRANGE THAT THE VILLAGE IS SO QUIET?
THE VILLAGERS MUST HAVE ALL FLED.
YOUNG MASTER?
YOUNG MASTER?!
LISTEN CAREFULLY. DO YOU HEAR THAT SOUND?
YES! I HEAR THE CHATTER OF MEN... AND... AND...

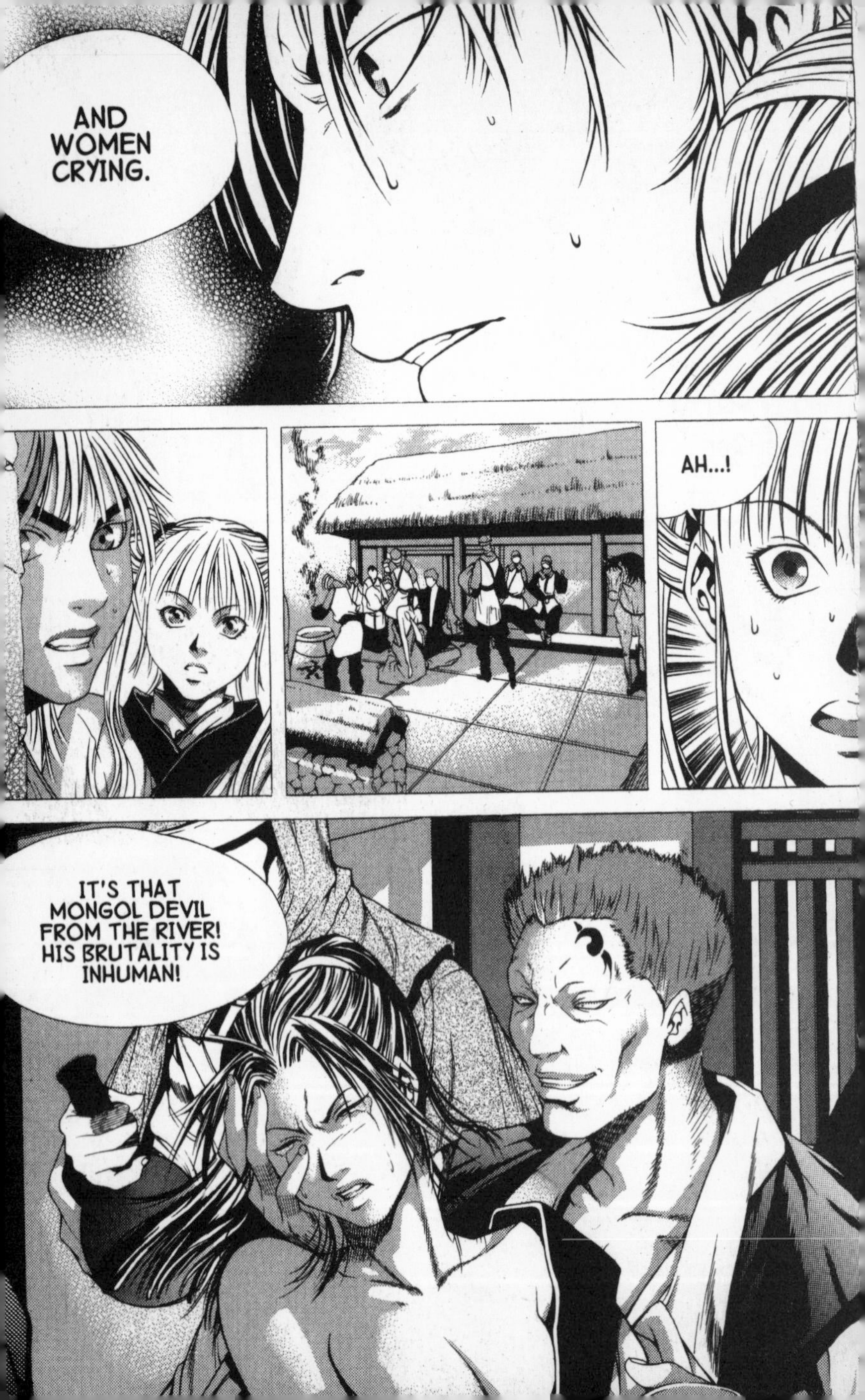
AND WOMEN CRYING.
AH...!
IT'S THAT MONGOL DEVIL FROM THE RIVER! HIS BRUTALITY IS INHUMAN!

HE'S CAPTURED A GIRL!

WE HAVE TO GO BACK.

THERE'S NOTHING WE CAN DO...

벅석

!

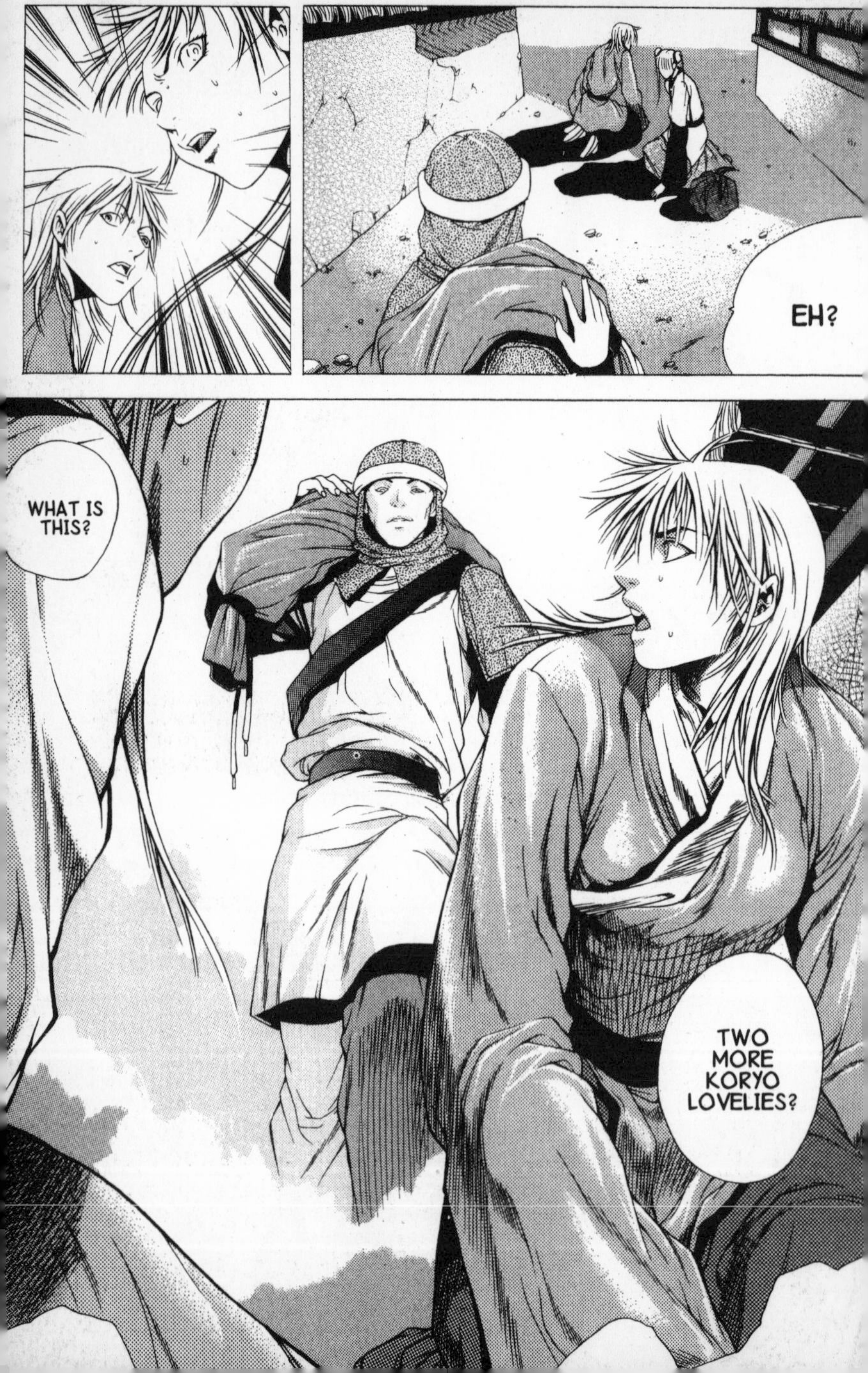
EH?
WHAT IS THIS?
TWO MORE KORYO LOVELIES?

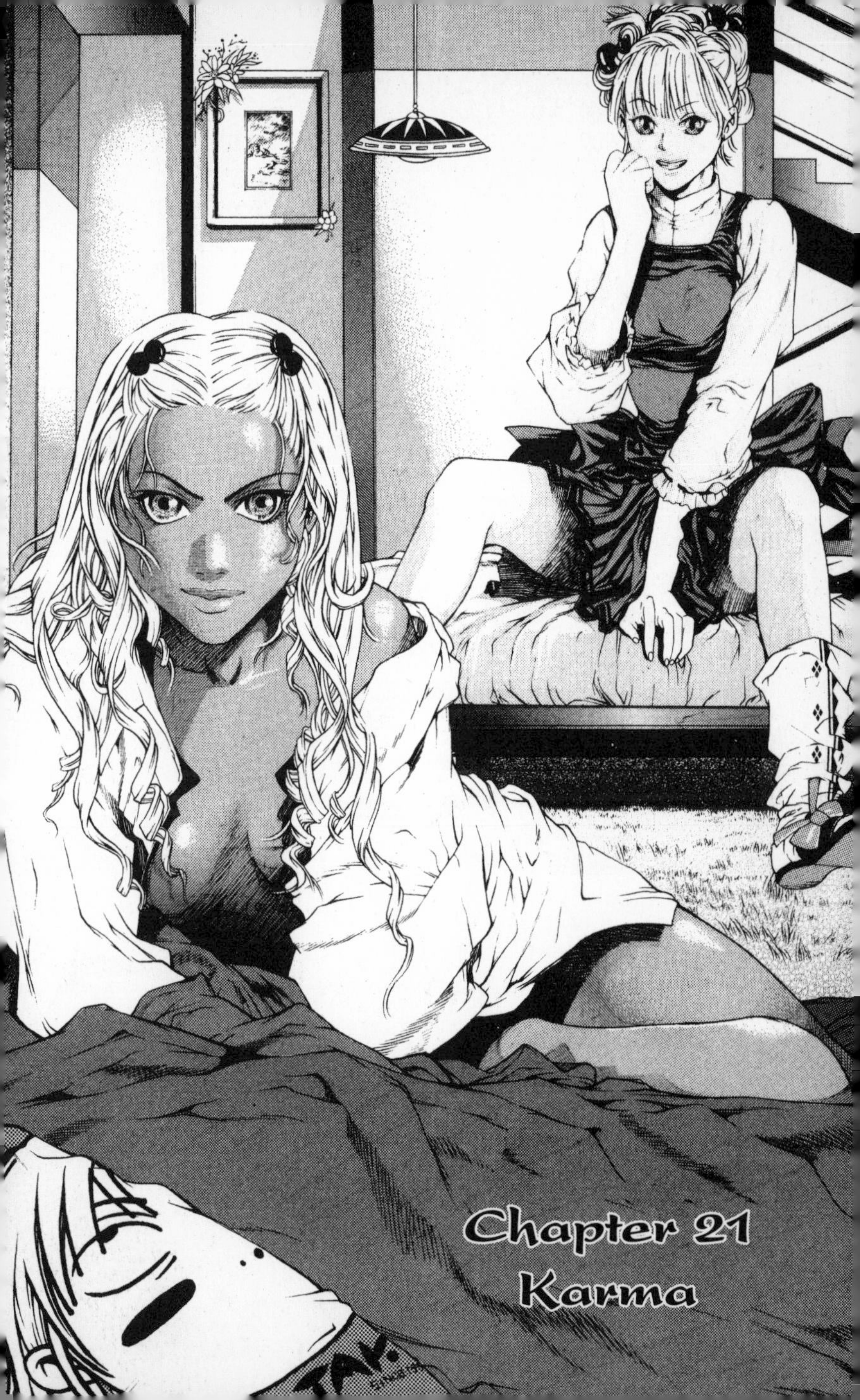
Chapter 21
Karma

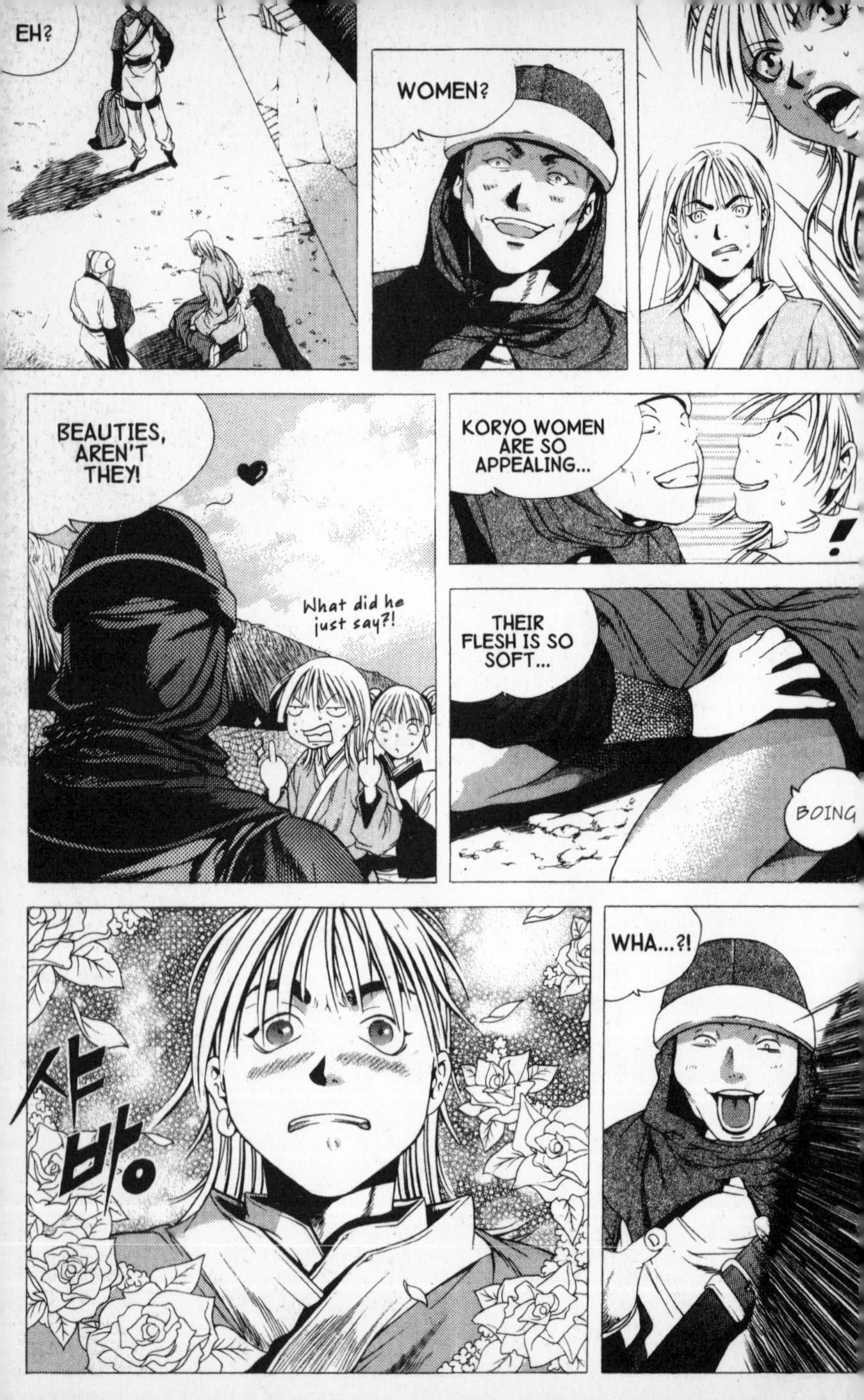
EH?
WOMEN?
BEAUTIES, AREN'T THEY!
What did he just say?!
KORYO WOMEN ARE SO APPEALING...
!
THEIR FLESH IS SO SOFT...
BOING
샤방
WHA...?!

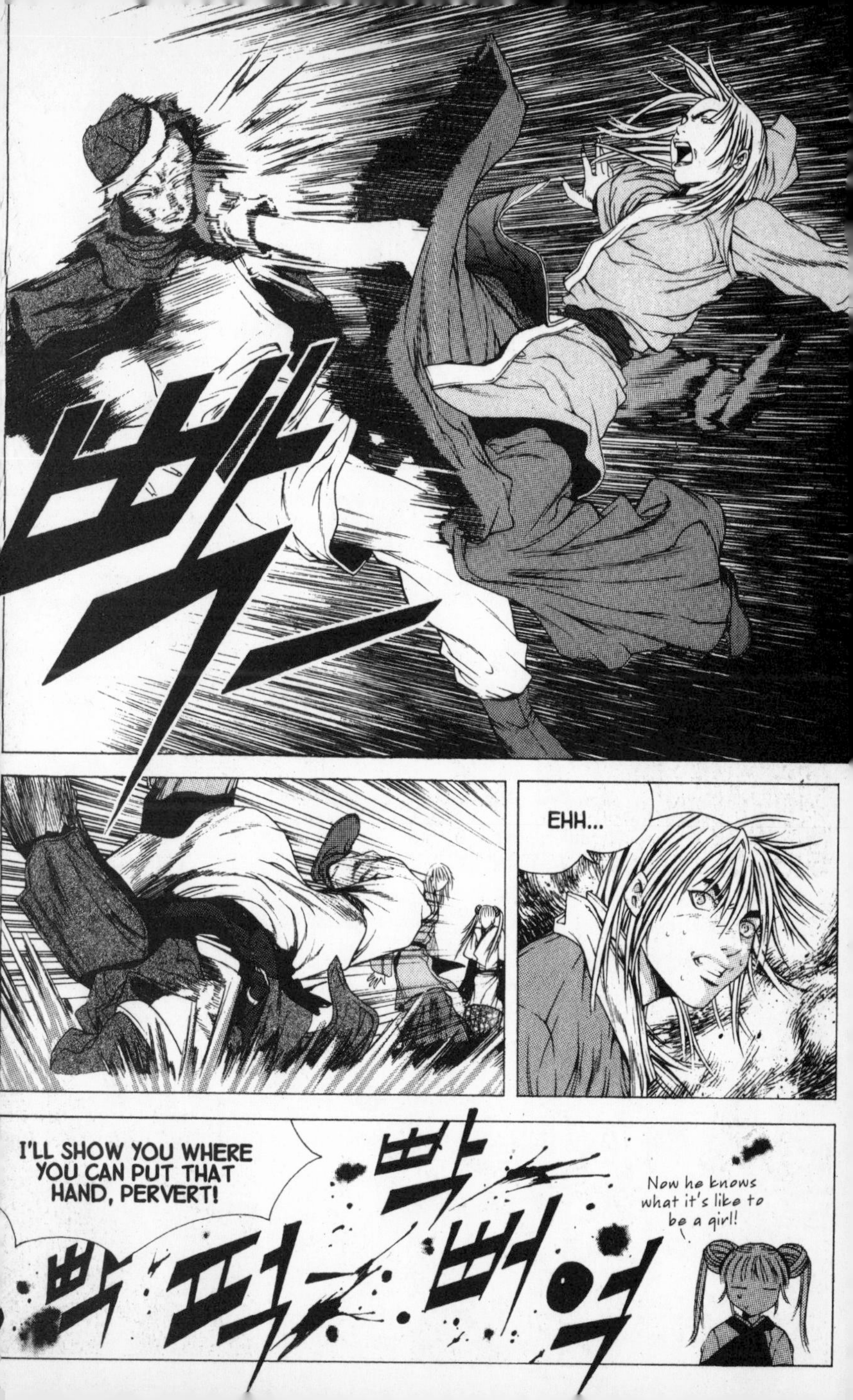
EHH...
I'LL SHOW YOU WHERE YOU CAN PUT THAT HAND, PERVERT!
빡
퍽
빡
뻐억
Now he knows what it's like to be a girl!

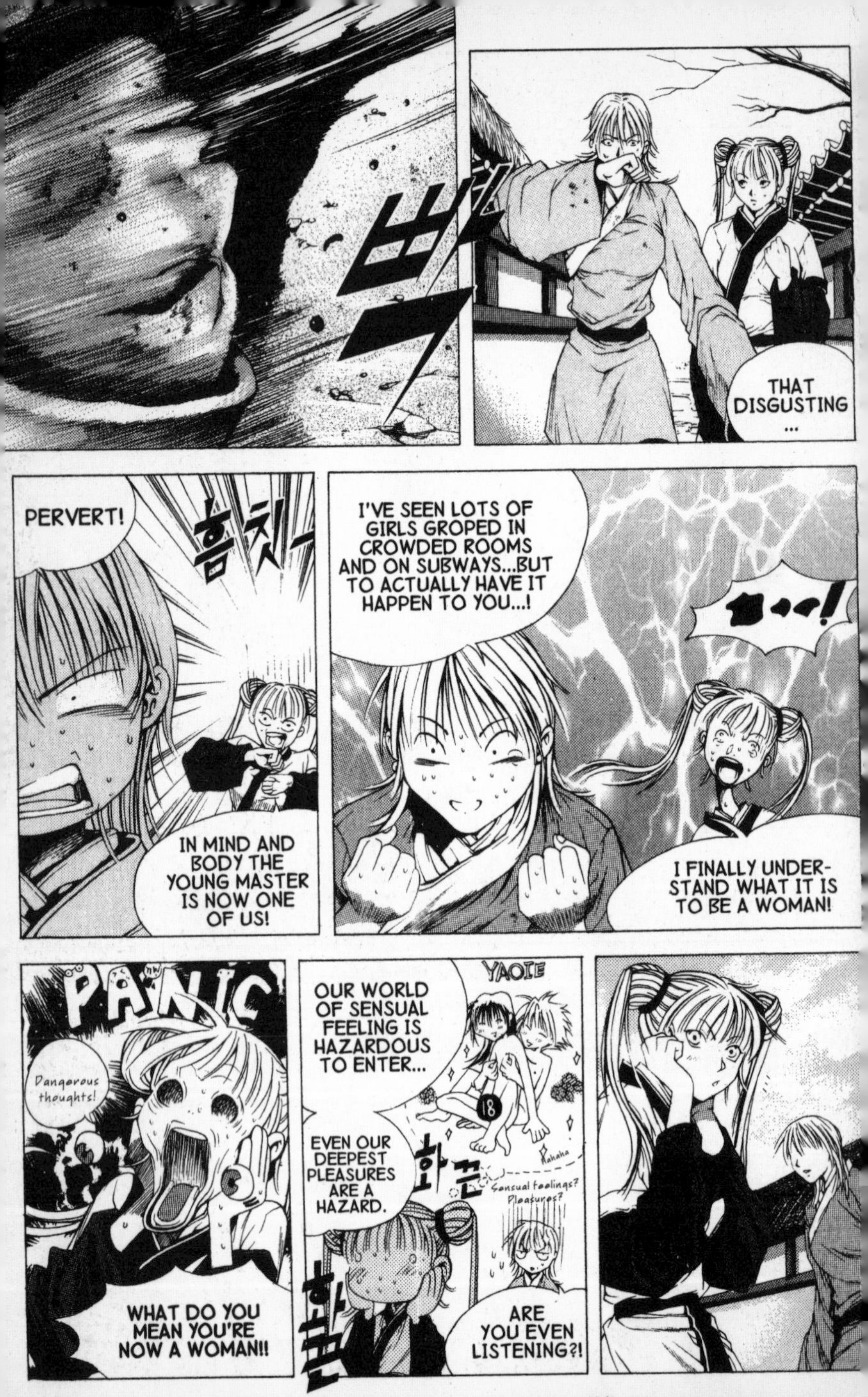
THAT DISGUSTING ...
PERVERT!
흠칫
IN MIND AND BODY THE YOUNG MASTER IS NOW ONE OF US!
I'VE SEEN LOTS OF GIRLS GROPED IN CROWDED ROOMS AND ON SUBWAYS...BUT TO ACTUALLY HAVE IT HAPPEN TO YOU...!
I FINALLY UNDER-STAND WHAT IT IS TO BE A WOMAN!
PANIC
Dangerous thoughts!
WHAT DO YOU MEAN YOU'RE NOW A WOMAN!!
OUR WORLD OF SENSUAL FEELING IS HAZARDOUS TO ENTER...
YAOI
18
EVEN OUR DEEPEST PLEASURES ARE A HAZARD.
화끈
Hahaha
Sensual feelings? Pleasures?
ARE YOU EVEN LISTENING?!

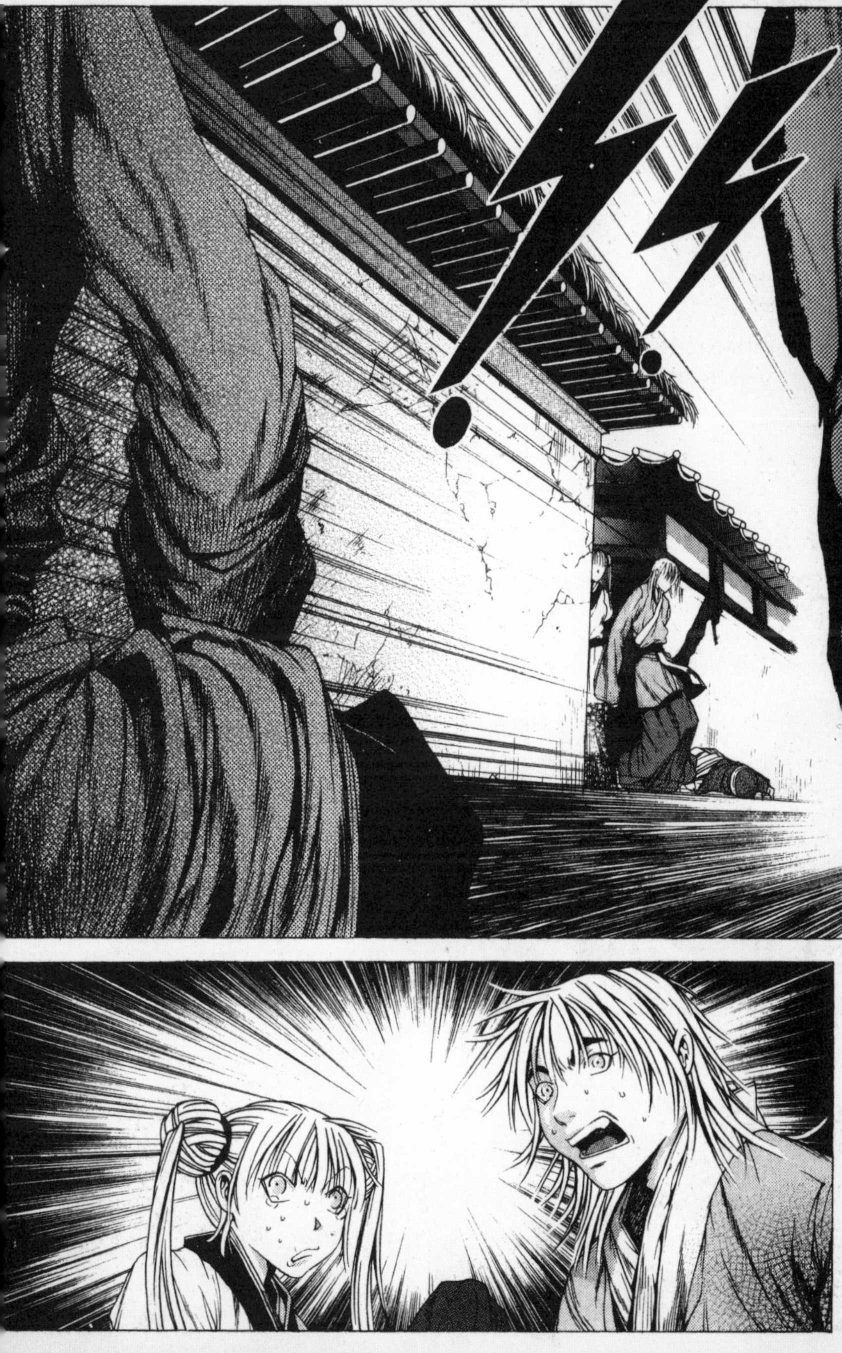

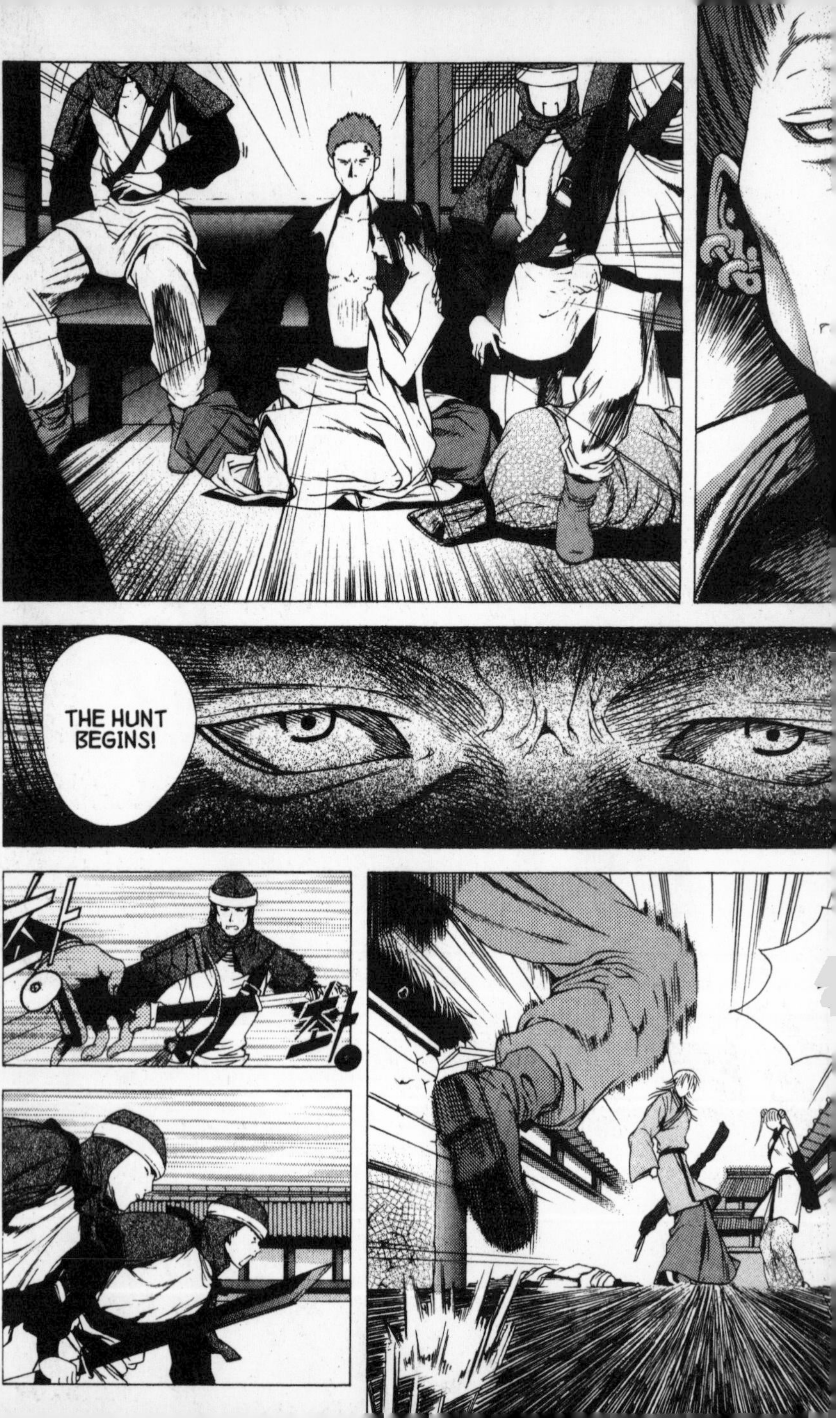
THE HUNT BEGINS!

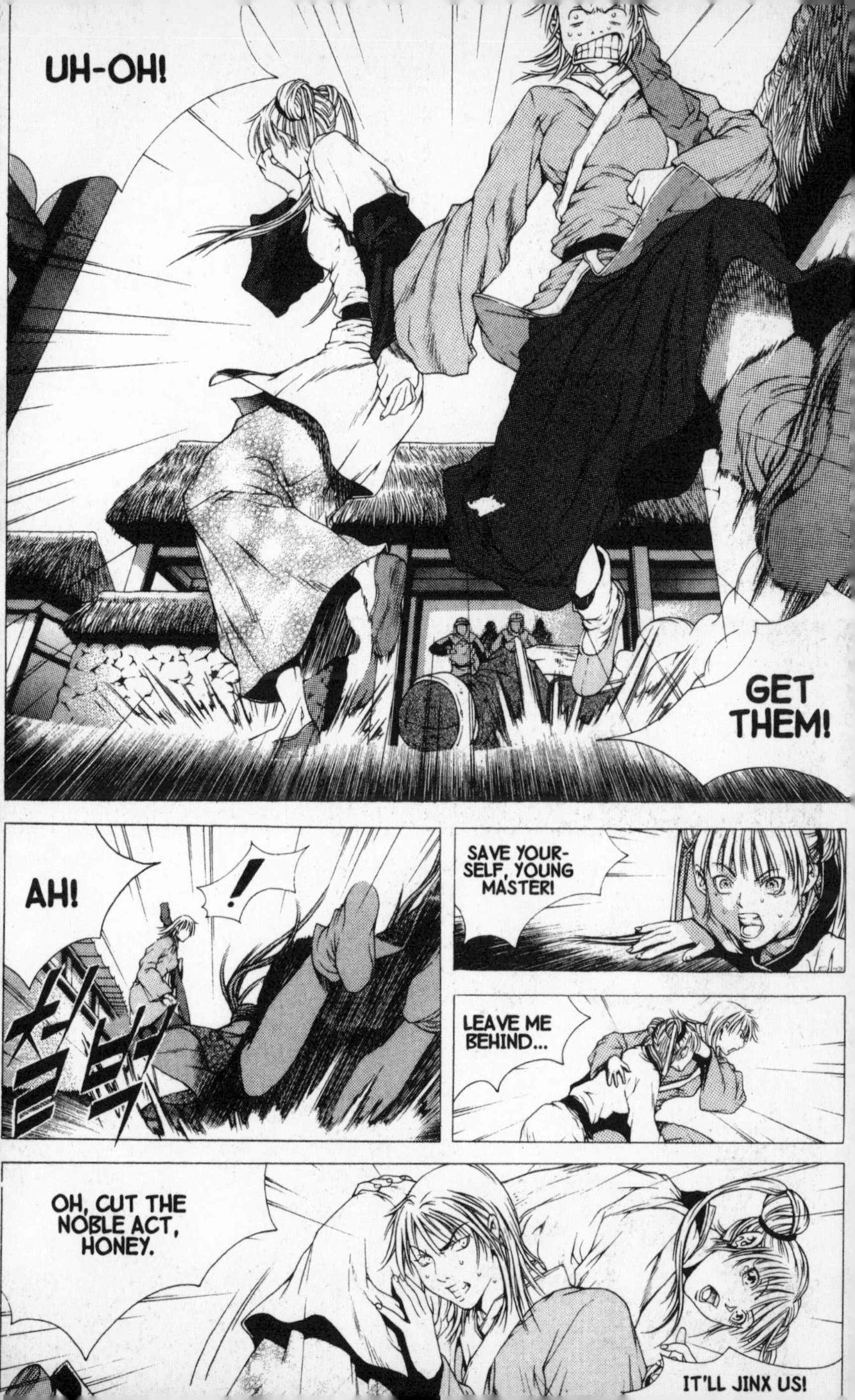
UH-OH!
GET THEM!
AH!
!
SAVE YOUR-SELF, YOUNG MASTER!
LEAVE ME BEHIND...
OH, CUT THE NOBLE ACT, HONEY.
IT'LL JINX US!

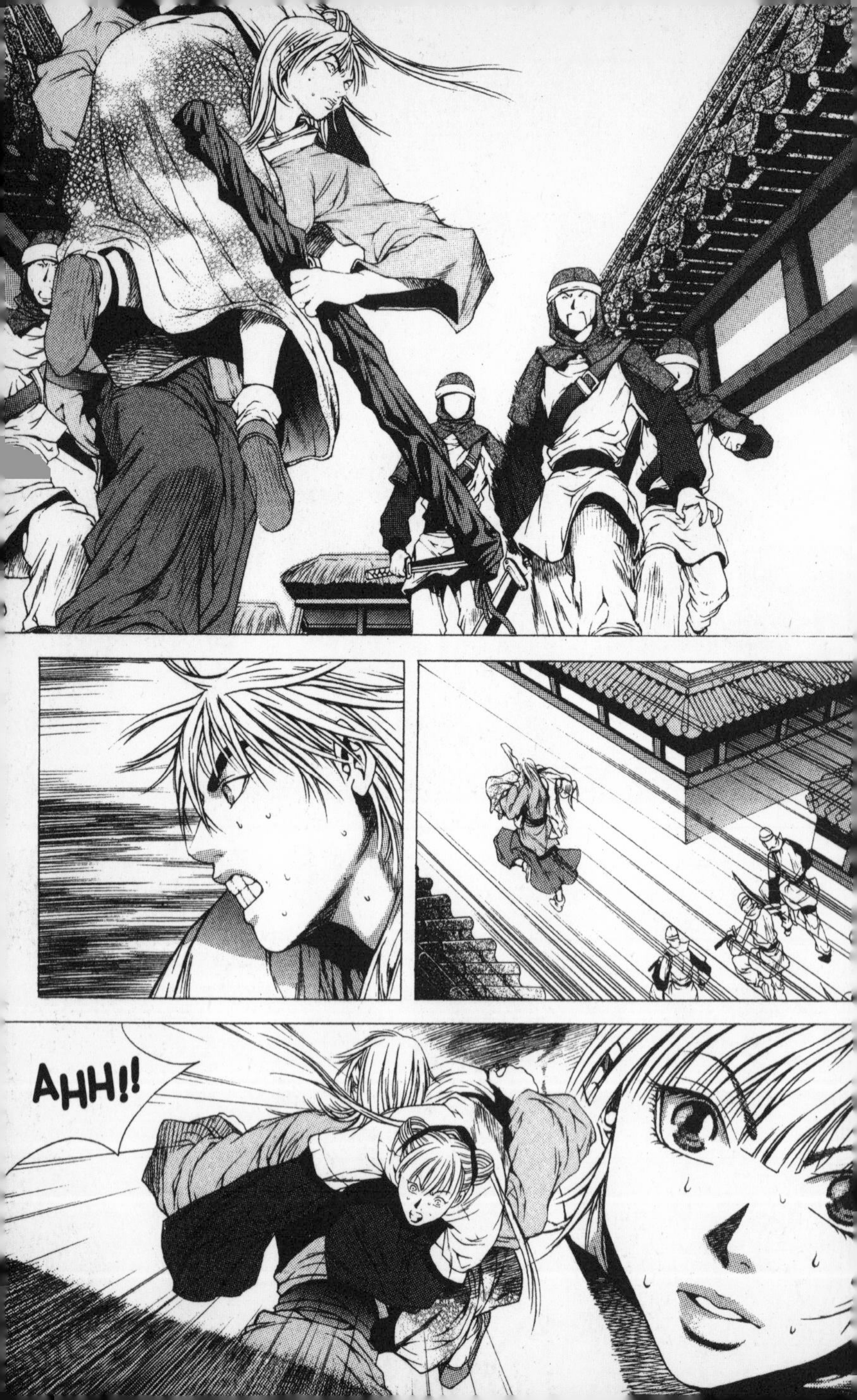
AHH!!

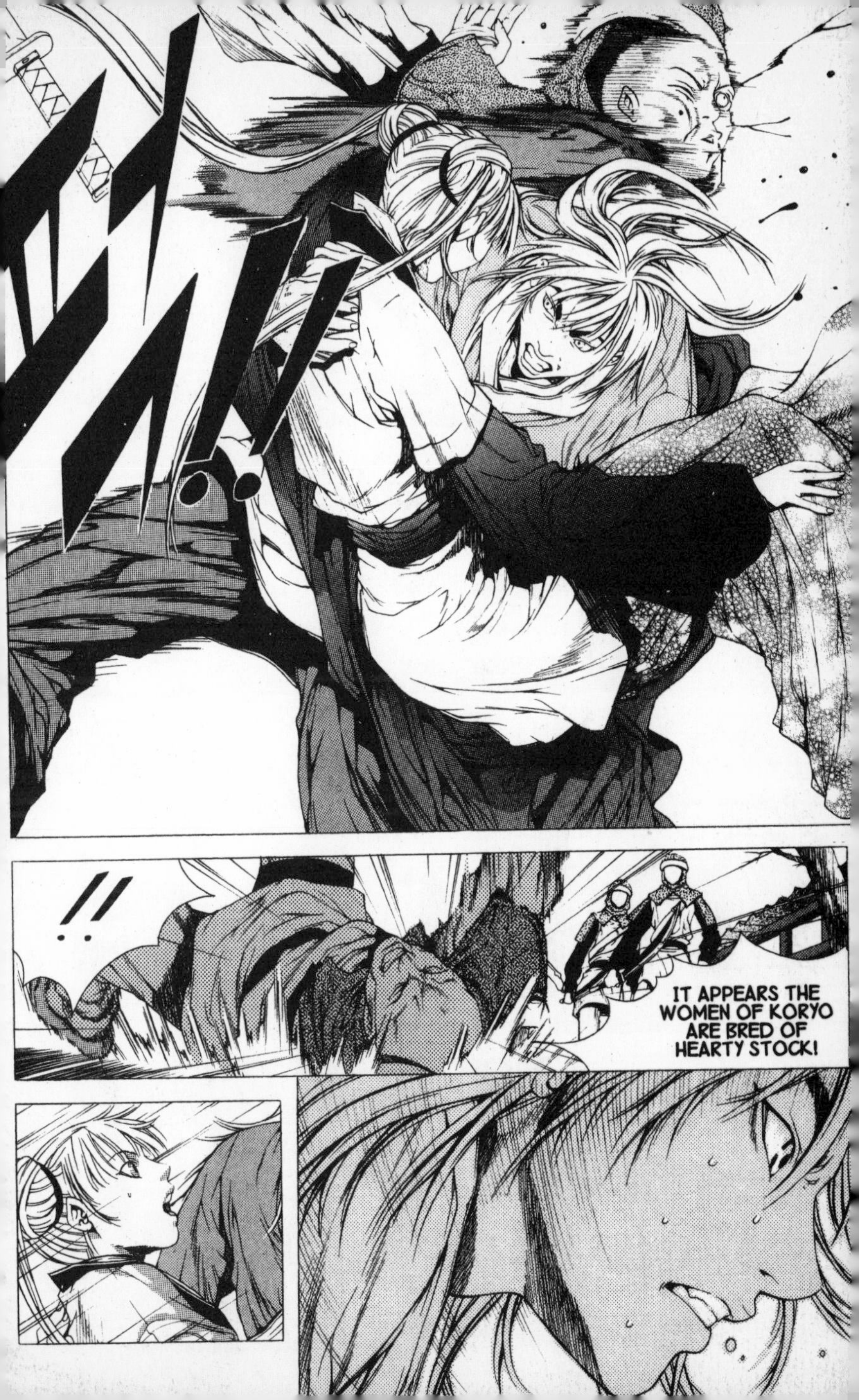
!!
!!
IT APPEARS THE WOMEN OF KORYO ARE BRED OF HEARTY STOCK!

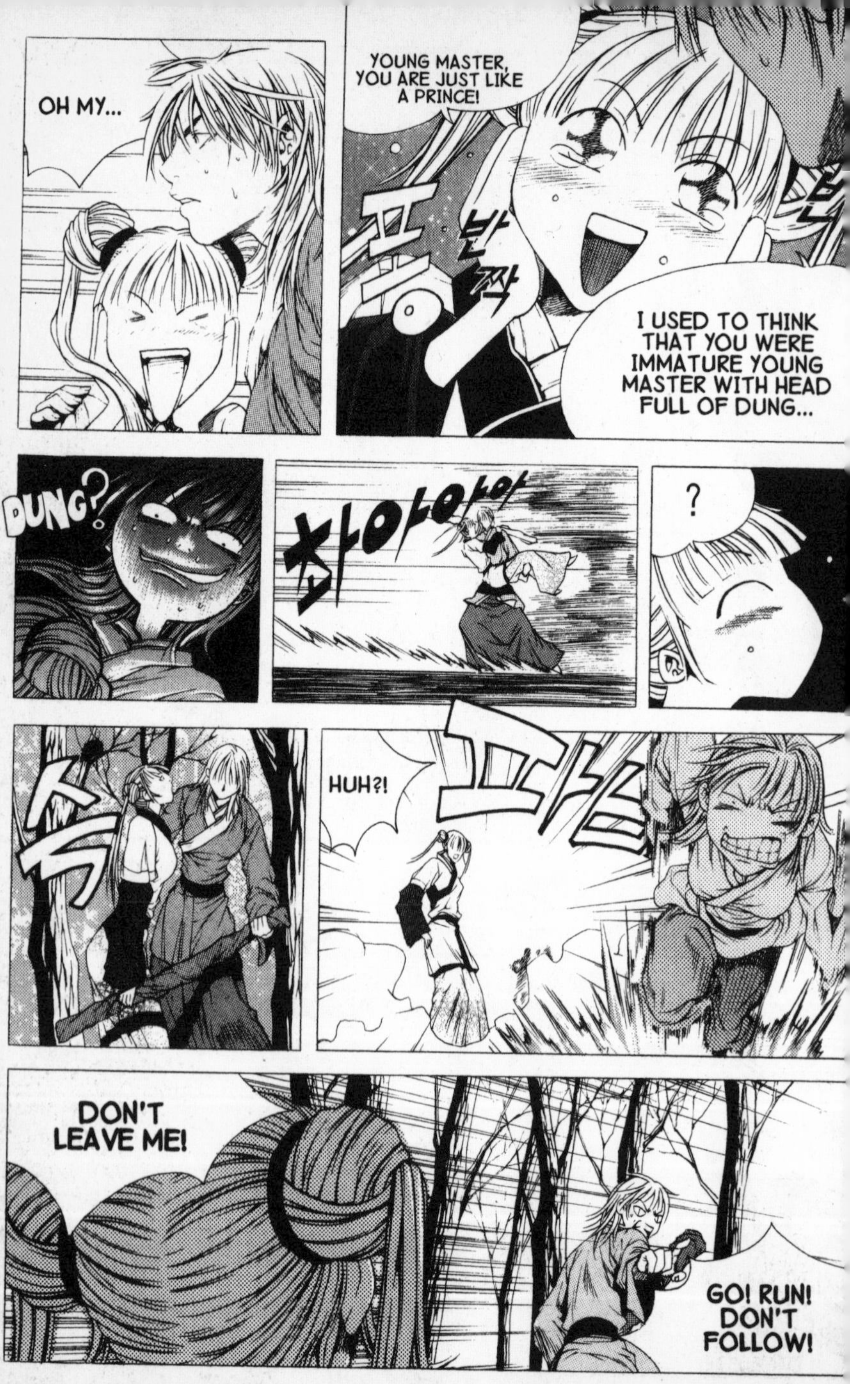
OH MY...
YOUNG MASTER, YOU ARE JUST LIKE A PRINCE!
반짝
I USED TO THINK THAT YOU WERE IMMATURE YOUNG MASTER WITH HEAD FULL OF DUNG...
DUNG?
?
HUH?!
DON'T LEAVE ME!
GO! RUN! DON'T FOLLOW!

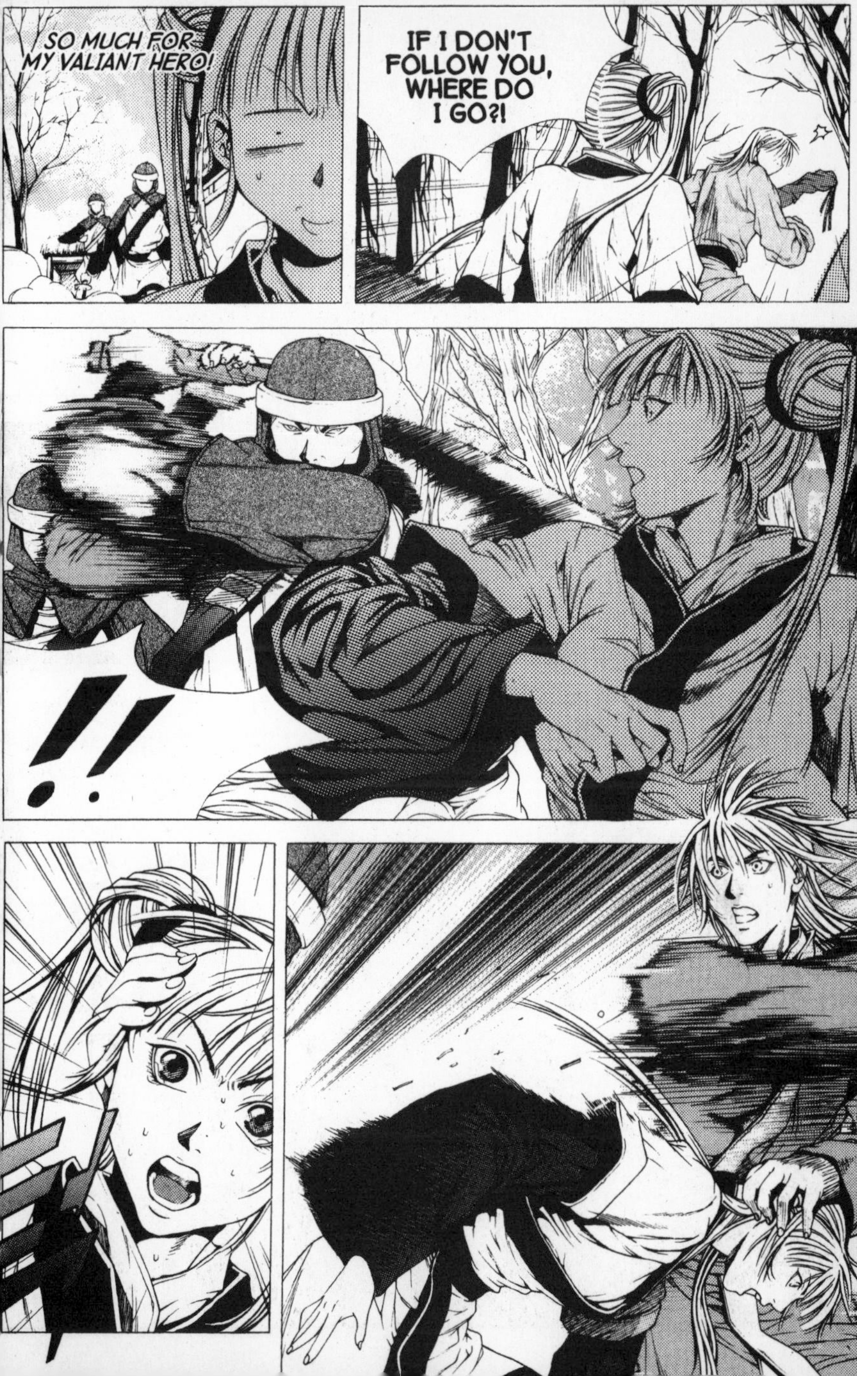

SO MUCH FOR MY VALIANT HERO!
IF I DON'T FOLLOW YOU, WHERE DO I GO?!
!!

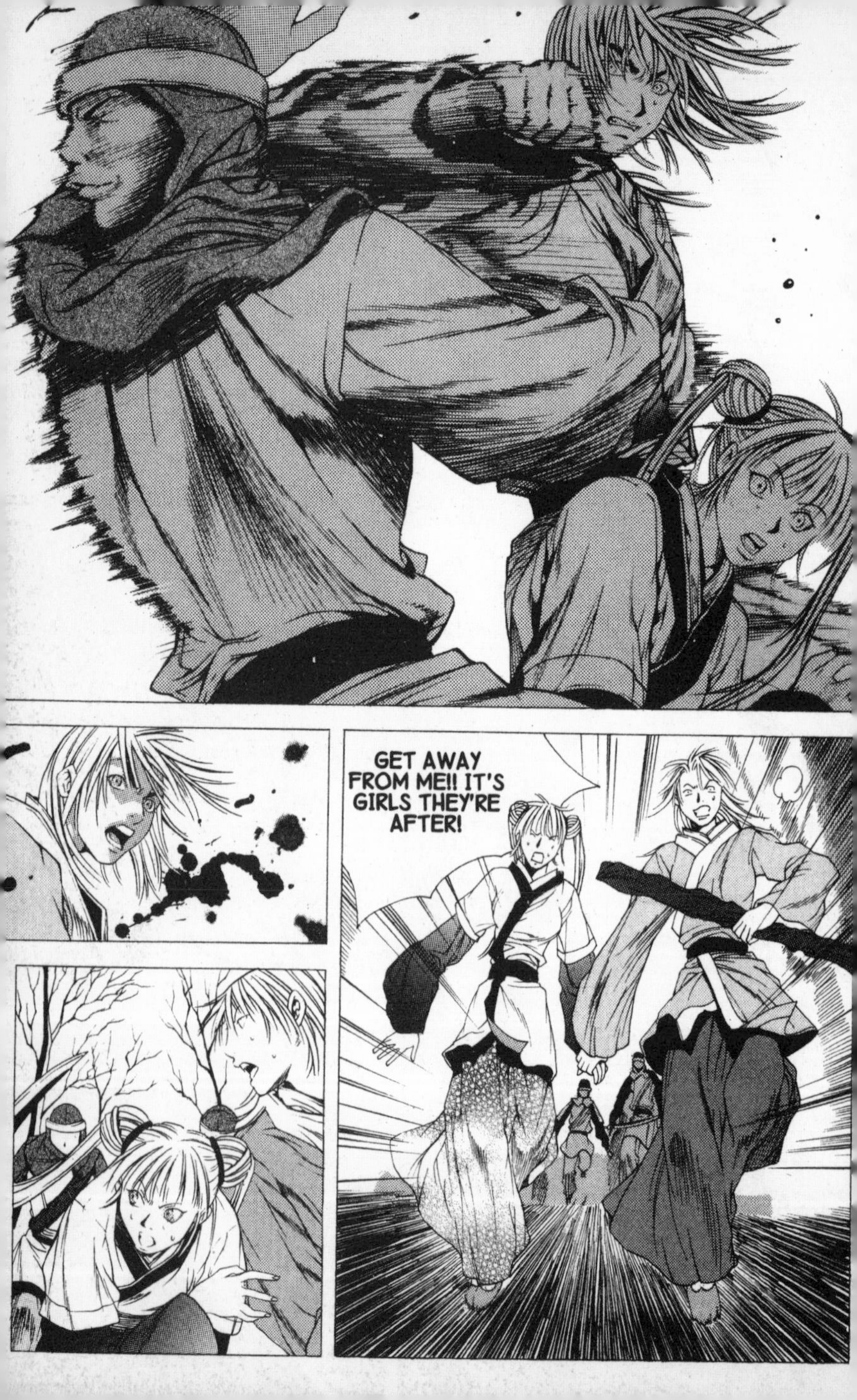
GET AWAY FROM ME!! IT'S GIRLS THEY'RE AFTER!

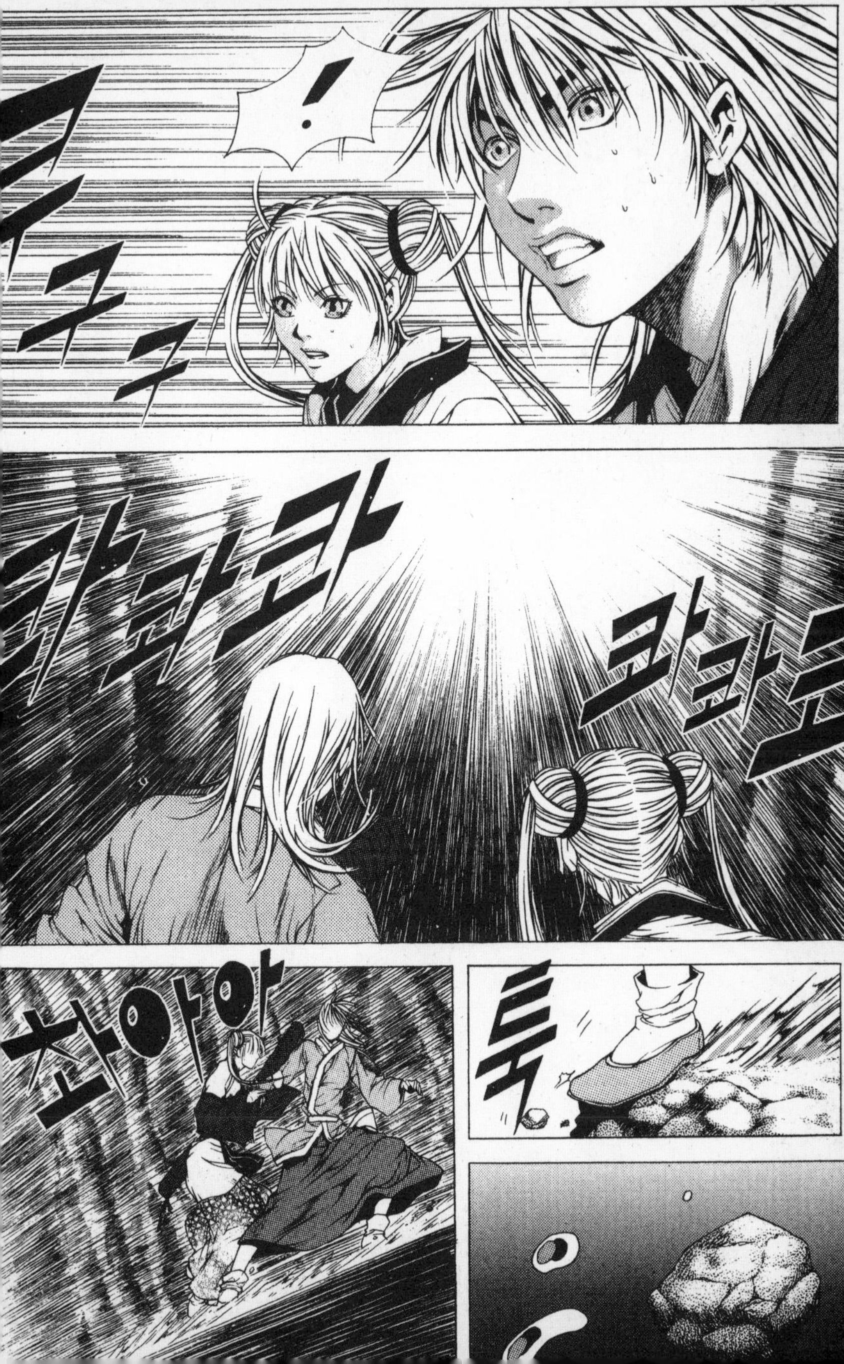
!
촤아아
툭.

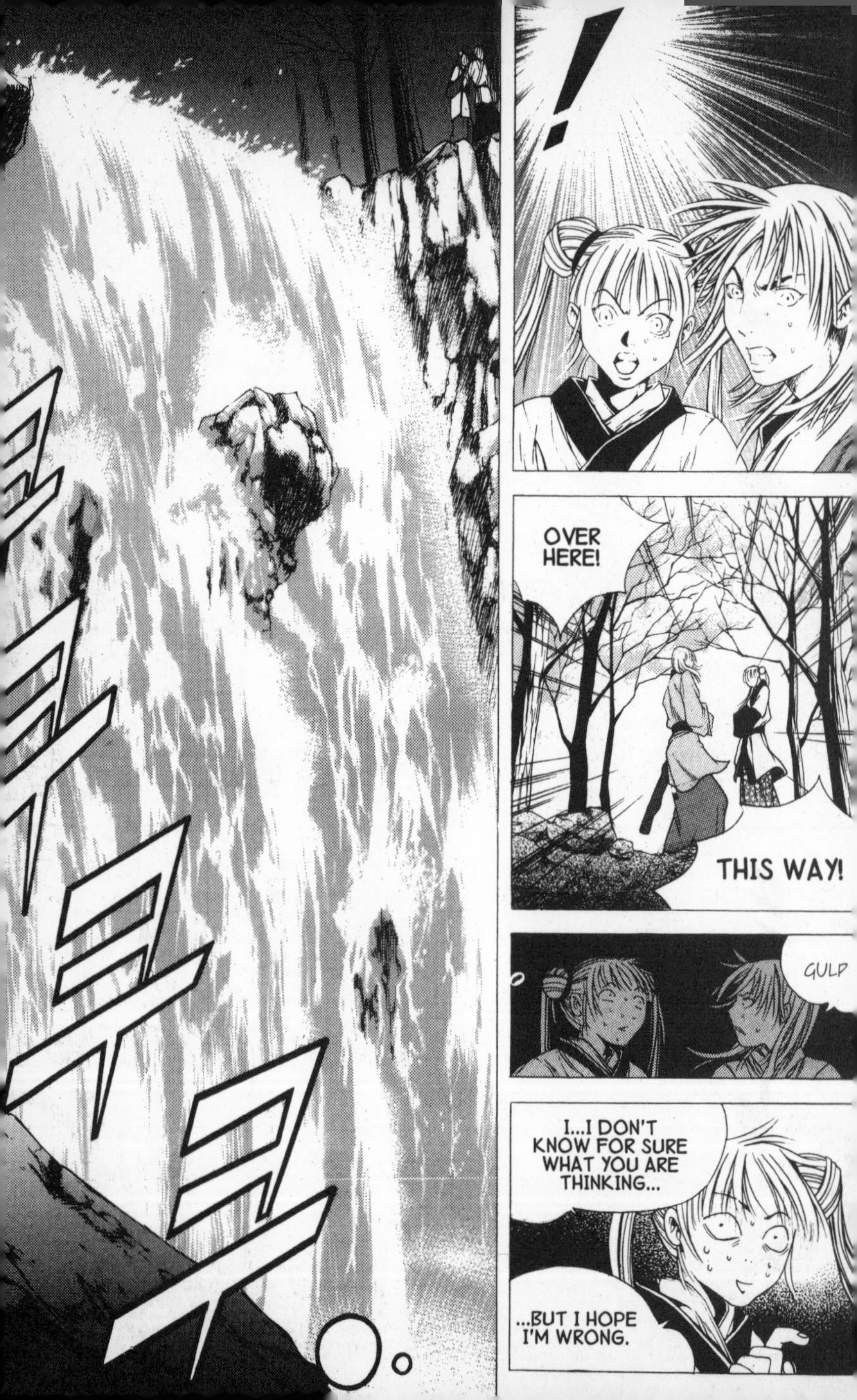
!
OVER HERE!
THIS WAY!
GULP
I...I DON'T KNOW FOR SURE WHAT YOU ARE THINKING...
...BUT I HOPE I'M WRONG.

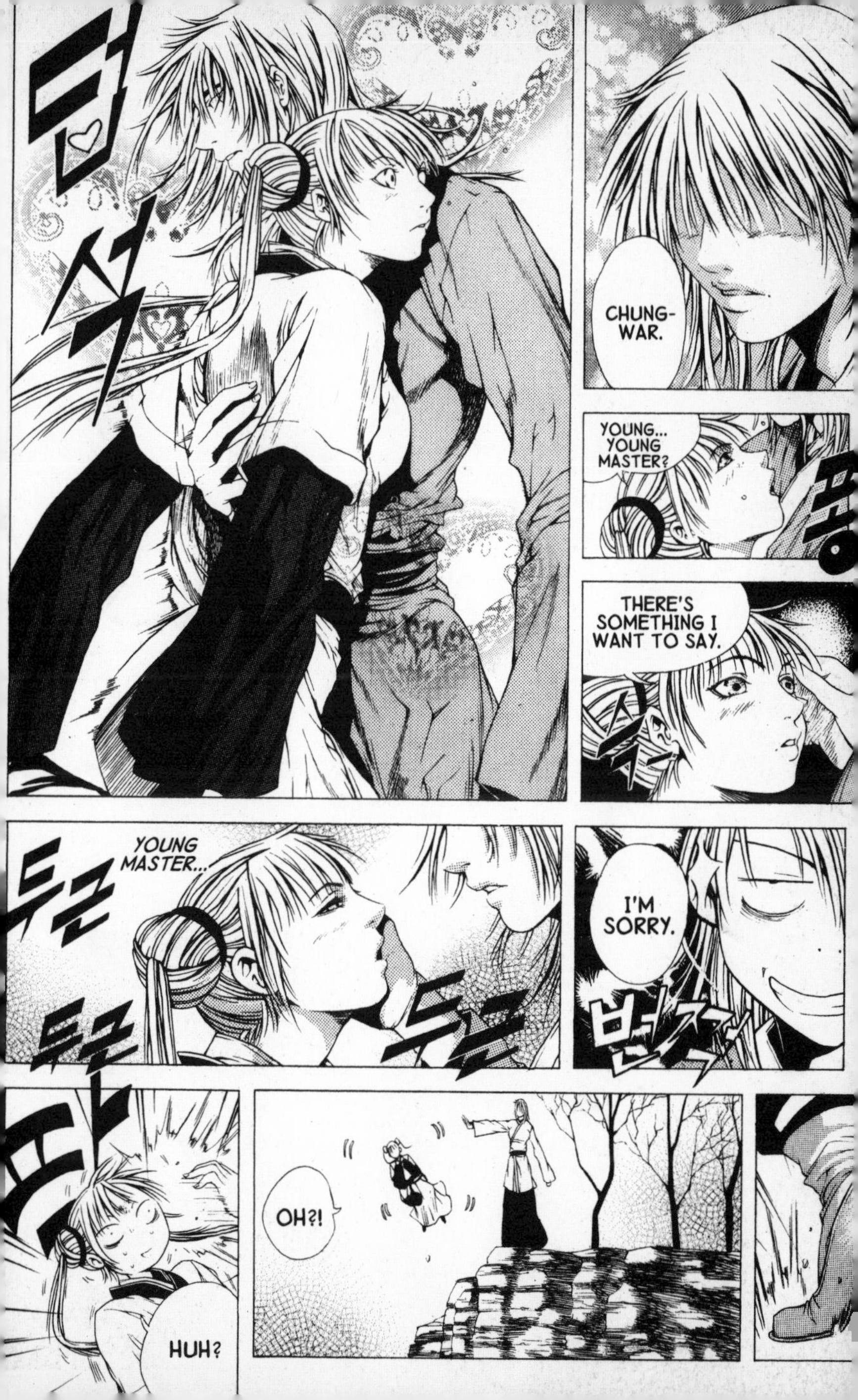
CHUNG-WAR.
YOUNG... YOUNG MASTER?
THERE'S SOMETHING I WANT TO SAY.
YOUNG MASTER...
I'M SORRY.
HUH?
OH?!

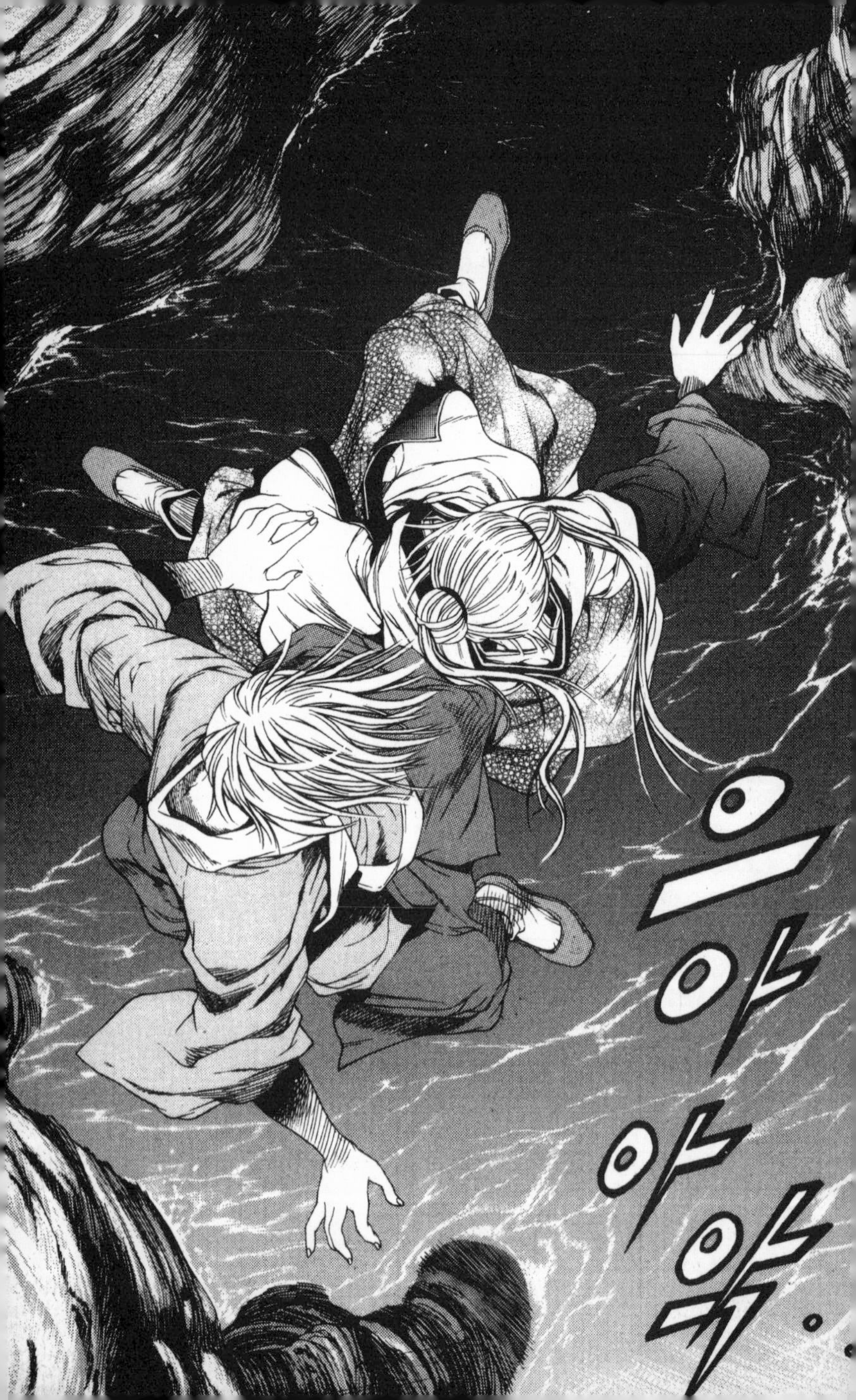
으아아악..

THIS IS MADNESS!
AHHHHH!

SOMEONE SAVE ME!

HANG ON!

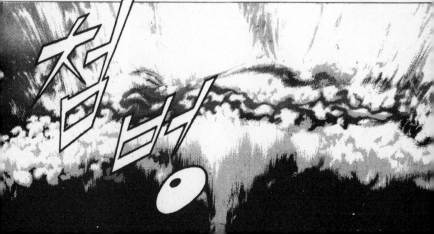

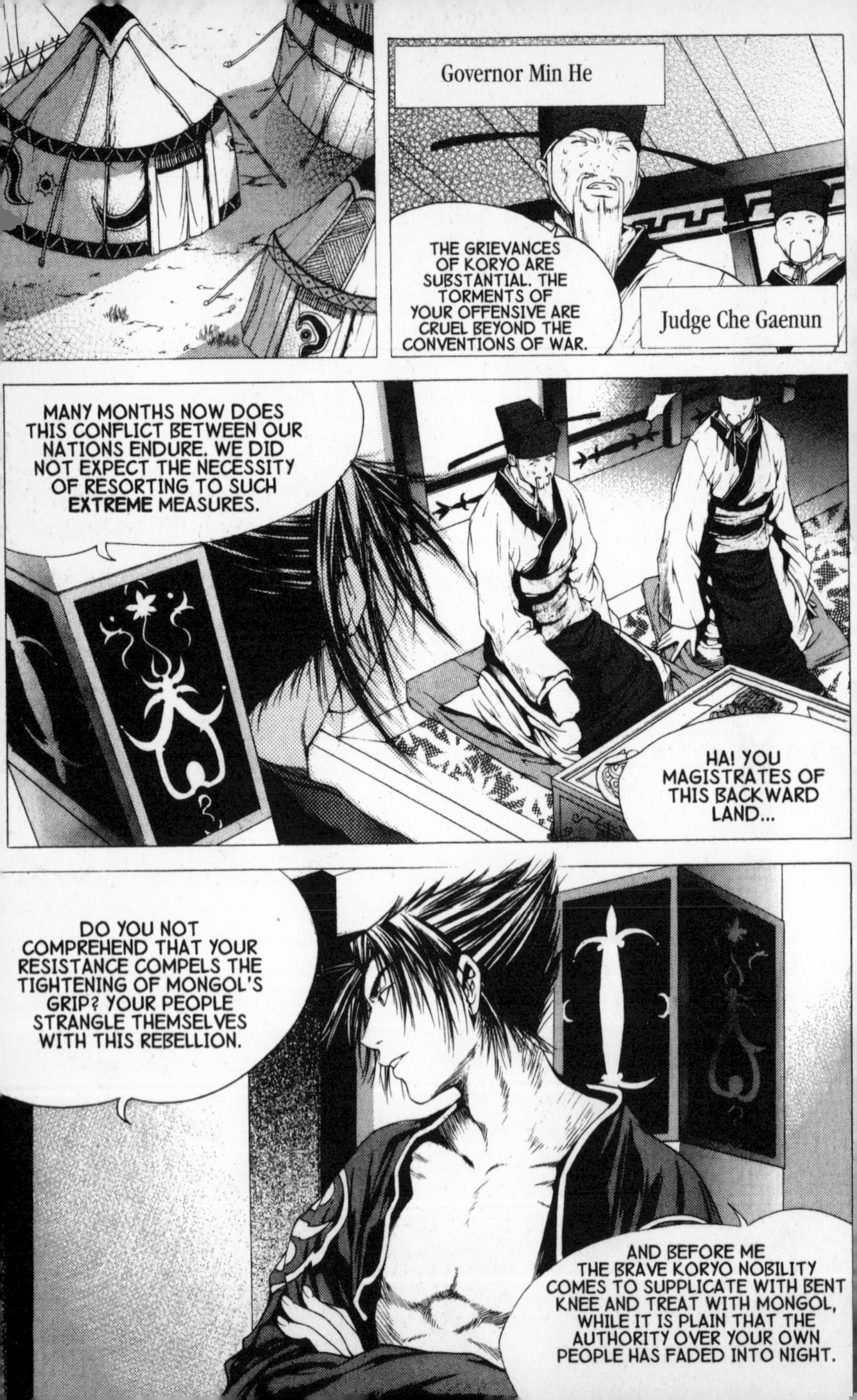
Governor Min He
THE GRIEVANCES OF KORYO ARE SUBSTANTIAL. THE TORMENTS OF YOUR OFFENSIVE ARE CRUEL BEYOND THE CONVENTIONS OF WAR.
Judge Che Gaenun
MANY MONTHS NOW DOES THIS CONFLICT BETWEEN OUR NATIONS ENDURE. WE DID NOT EXPECT THE NECESSITY OF RESORTING TO SUCH EXTREME MEASURES.
HA! YOU MAGISTRATES OF THIS BACKWARD LAND...
DO YOU NOT COMPREHEND THAT YOUR RESISTANCE COMPELS THE TIGHTENING OF MONGOL'S GRIP? YOUR PEOPLE STRANGLE THEMSELVES WITH THIS REBELLION.
AND BEFORE ME THE BRAVE KORYO NOBILITY COMES TO SUPPLICATE WITH BENT KNEE AND TREAT WITH MONGOL, WHILE IT IS PLAIN THAT THE AUTHORITY OVER YOUR OWN PEOPLE HAS FADED INTO NIGHT.

THESE TRUTHS TELL ME THAT KING CHE OO LORDS OVER NOTHING SAVE EXPIRED MEMORIES!

SALI TAYI! YOU ARE TOO BOLD WITH YOUR INSULTS!!

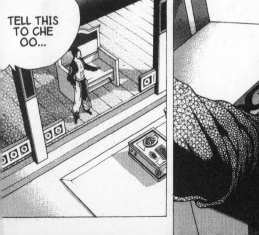

TELL THIS TO CHE OO...

HE MAY YIELD TO THE SERVANTS OF OGODEI THE GREAT KAHN...

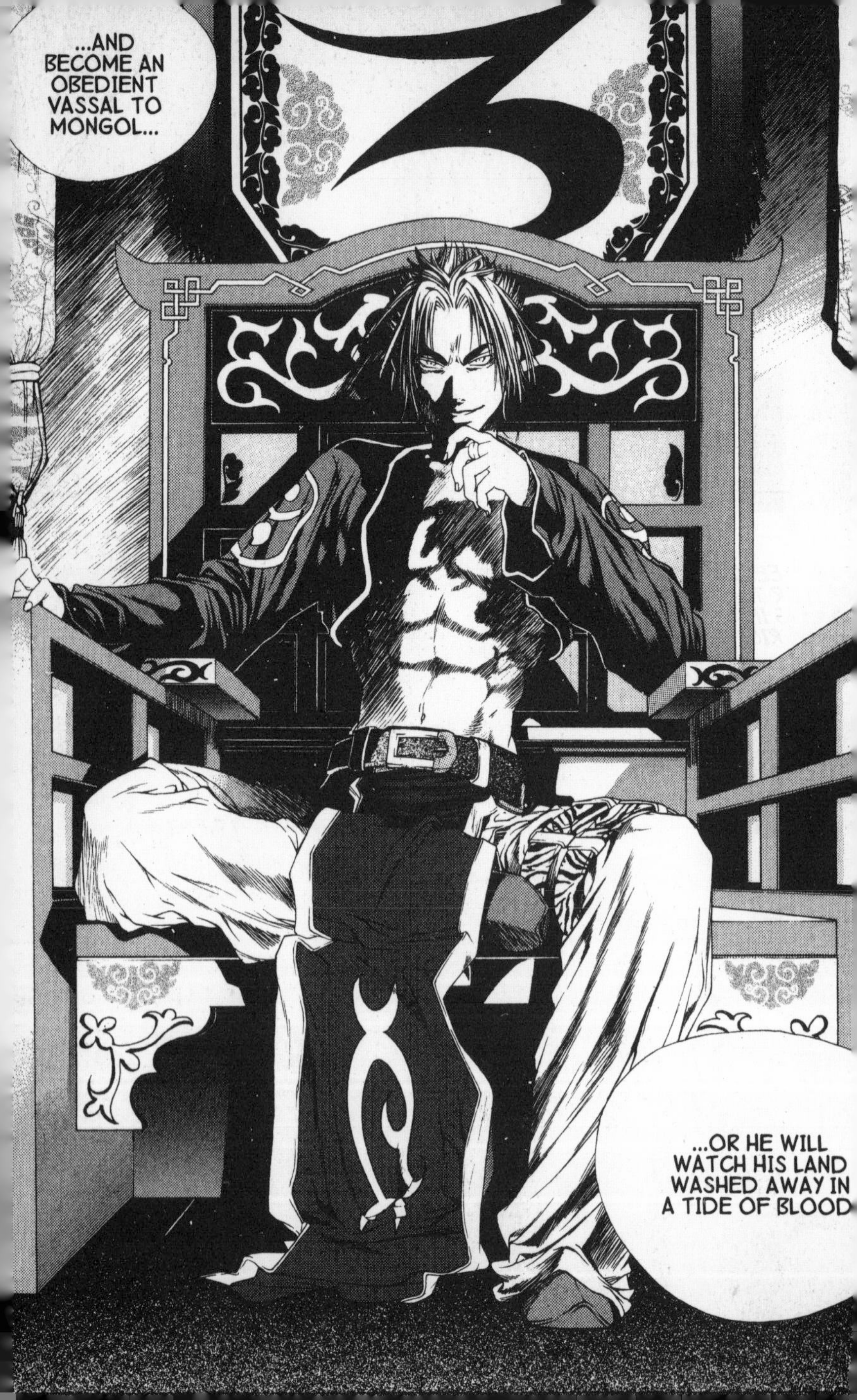
...AND BECOME AN OBEDIENT VASSAL TO MONGOL...
...OR HE WILL WATCH HIS LAND WASHED AWAY IN A TIDE OF BLOOD

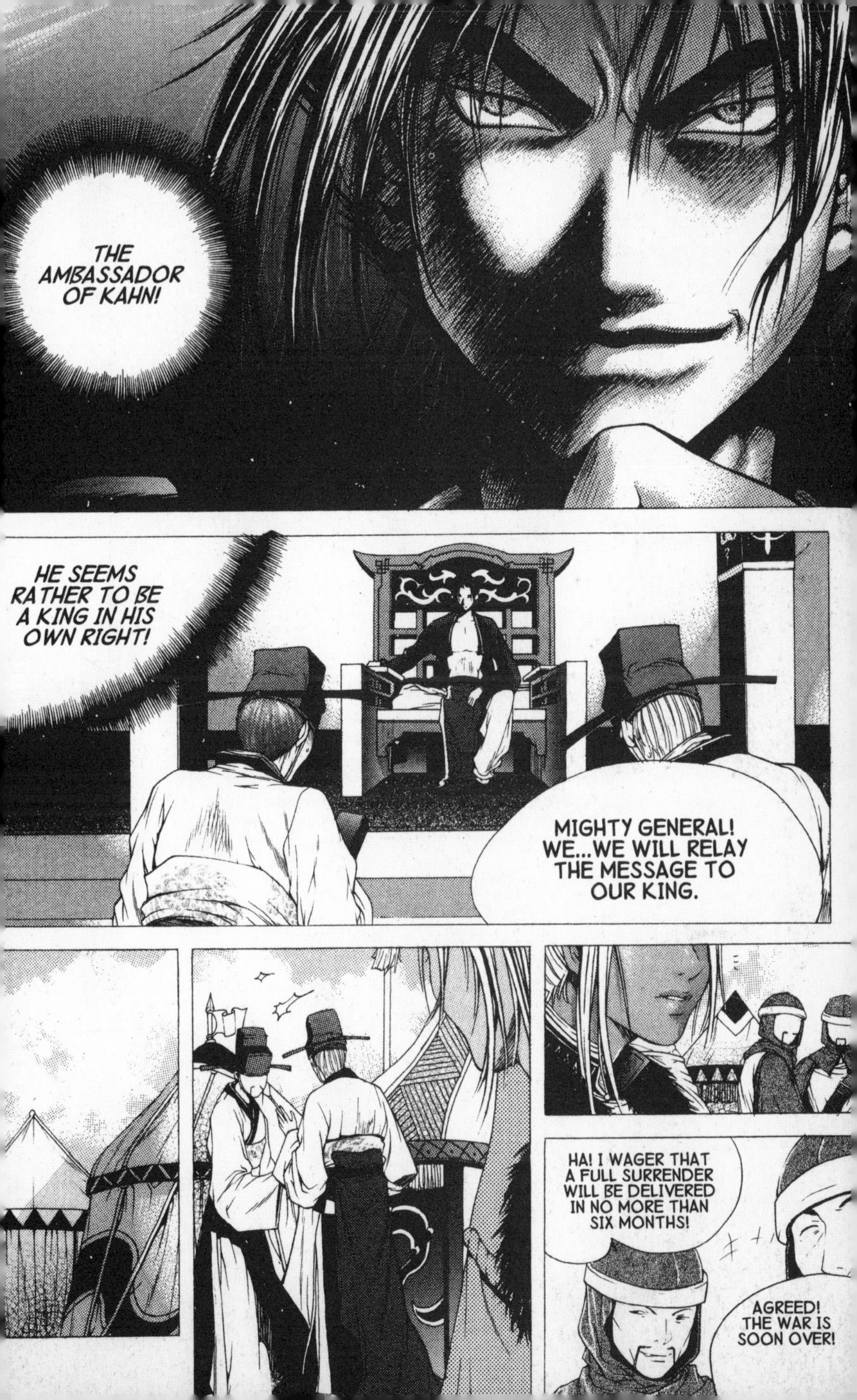
THE AMBASSADOR OF KAHN!
HE SEEMS RATHER TO BE A KING IN HIS OWN RIGHT!
MIGHTY GENERAL! WE...WE WILL RELAY THE MESSAGE TO OUR KING.
HA! I WAGER THAT A FULL SURRENDER WILL BE DELIVERED IN NO MORE THAN SIX MONTHS!
AGREED! THE WAR IS SOON OVER!

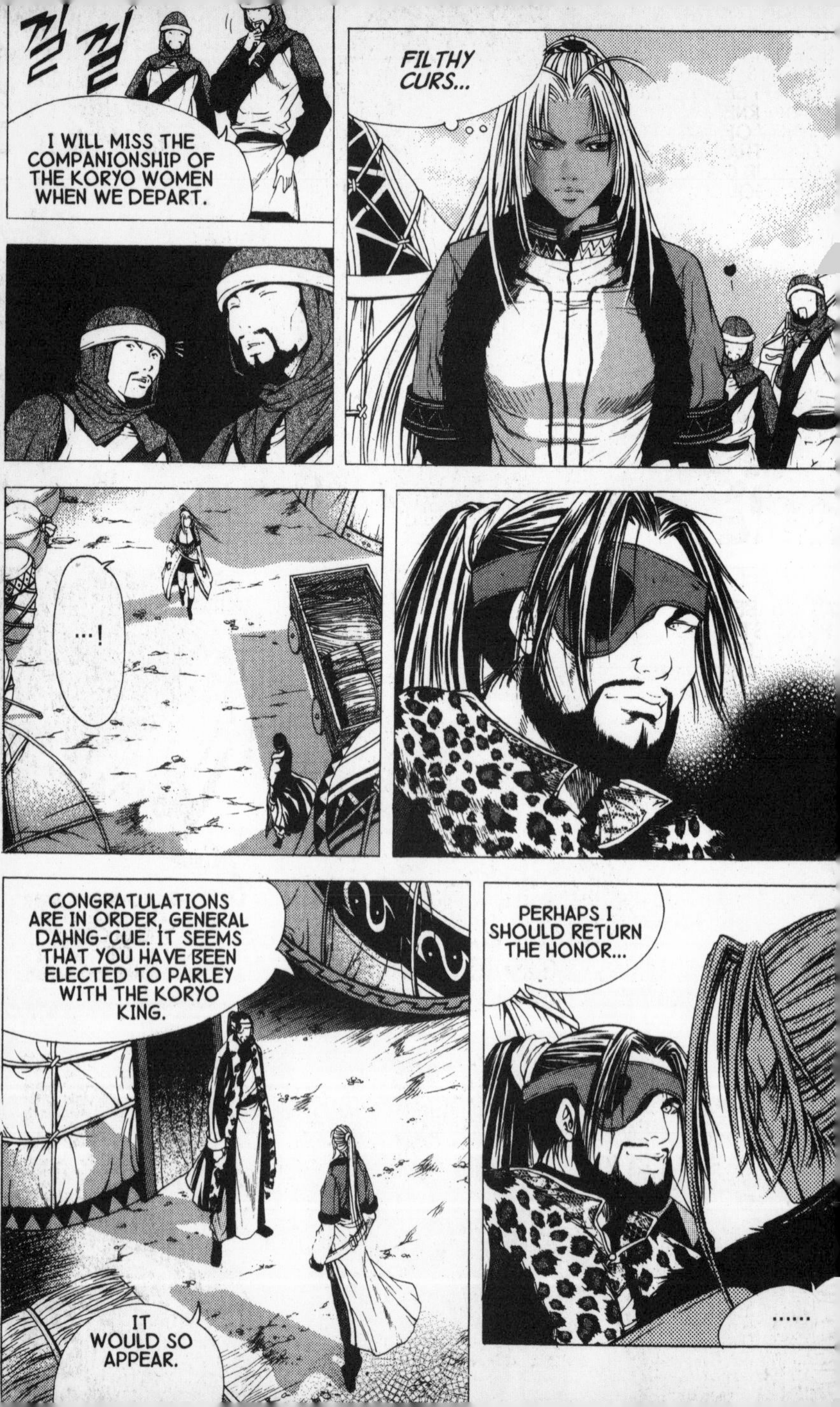

낄낄
I WILL MISS THE COMPANIONSHIP OF THE KORYO WOMEN WHEN WE DEPART.
FILTHY CURS...
...!
CONGRATULATIONS ARE IN ORDER, GENERAL DAHNG-CUE. IT SEEMS THAT YOU HAVE BEEN ELECTED TO PARLEY WITH THE KORYO KING.
IT WOULD SO APPEAR.
PERHAPS I SHOULD RETURN THE HONOR...
......

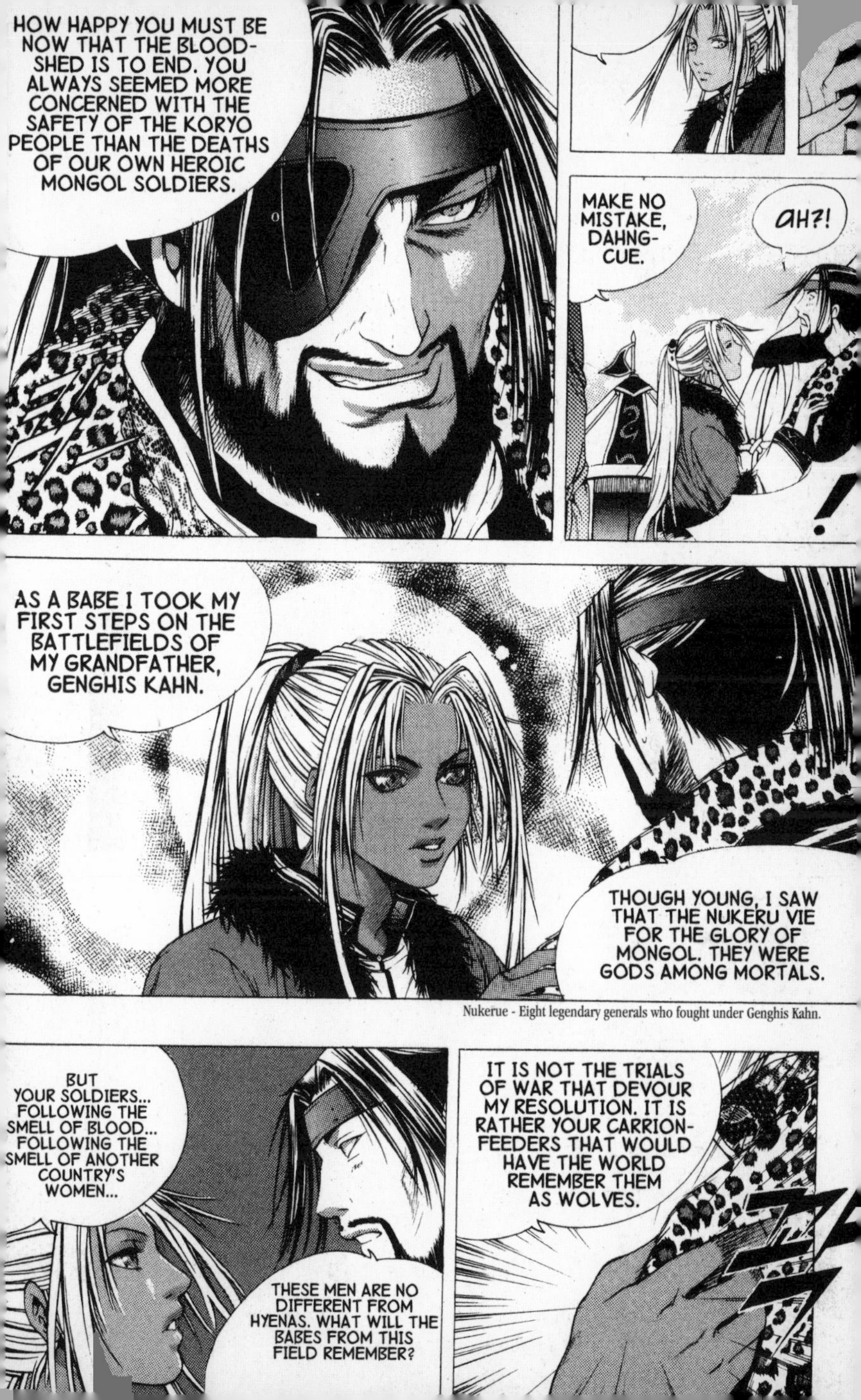
HOW HAPPY YOU MUST BE NOW THAT THE BLOOD-SHED IS TO END. YOU ALWAYS SEEMED MORE CONCERNED WITH THE SAFETY OF THE KORYO PEOPLE THAN THE DEATHS OF OUR OWN HEROIC MONGOL SOLDIERS.
MAKE NO MISTAKE, DAHNG-CUE.
ah?!
!
AS A BABE I TOOK MY FIRST STEPS ON THE BATTLEFIELDS OF MY GRANDFATHER, GENGHIS KAHN.
THOUGH YOUNG, I SAW THAT THE NUKERU VIE FOR THE GLORY OF MONGOL. THEY WERE GODS AMONG MORTALS.
BUT YOUR SOLDIERS... FOLLOWING THE SMELL OF BLOOD... FOLLOWING THE SMELL OF ANOTHER COUNTRY'S WOMEN...
THESE MEN ARE NO DIFFERENT FROM HYENAS. WHAT WILL THE BABES FROM THIS FIELD REMEMBER?
IT IS NOT THE TRIALS OF WAR THAT DEVOUR MY RESOLUTION. IT IS RATHER YOUR CARRION-FEEDERS THAT WOULD HAVE THE WORLD REMEMBER THEM AS WOLVES.
Nukerue - Eight legendary generals who fought under Genghis Kahn.

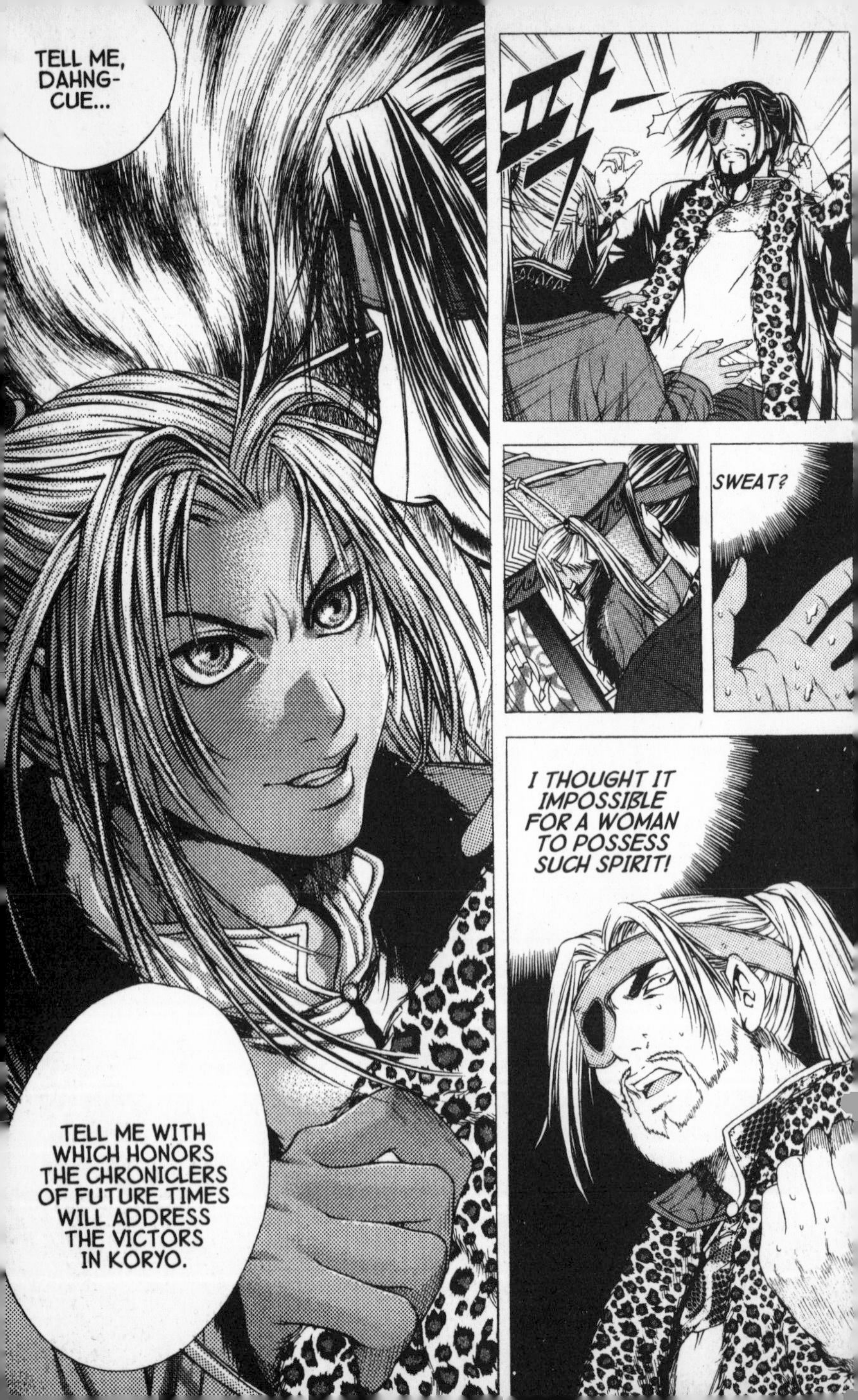
TELL ME, DAHNG-CUE...
TELL ME WITH WHICH HONORS THE CHRONICLERS OF FUTURE TIMES WILL ADDRESS THE VICTORS IN KORYO.
SWEAT?
I THOUGHT IT IMPOSSIBLE FOR A WOMAN TO POSSESS SUCH SPIRIT!

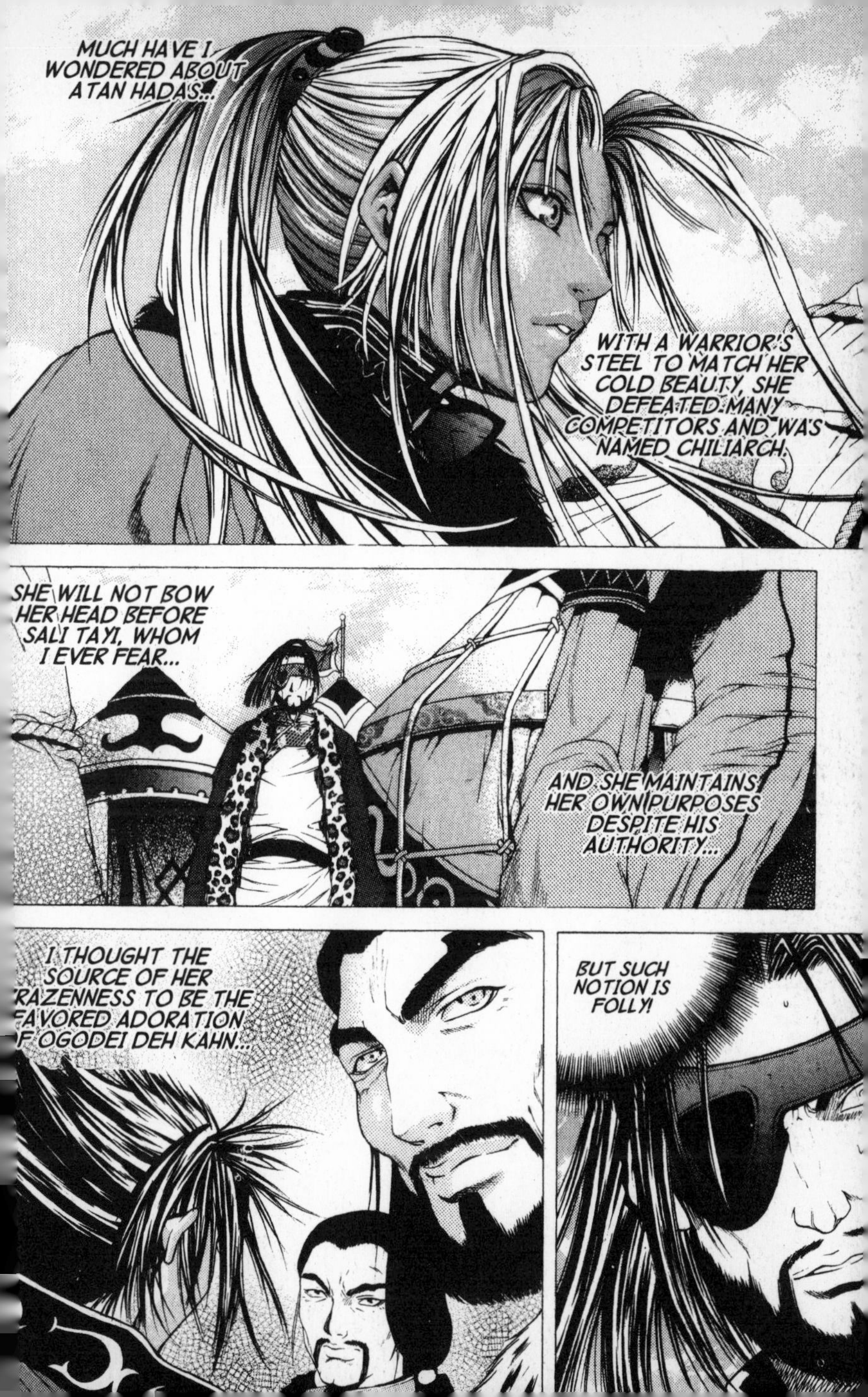
MUCH HAVE I WONDERED ABOUT ATAN HADAS...
WITH A WARRIOR'S STEEL TO MATCH HER COLD BEAUTY, SHE DEFEATED MANY COMPETITORS AND WAS NAMED CHILIARCH.
SHE WILL NOT BOW HER HEAD BEFORE SALI TAYI, WHOM I EVER FEAR...
AND SHE MAINTAINS HER OWN PURPOSES DESPITE HIS AUTHORITY...
I THOUGHT THE SOURCE OF HER RAZENNESS TO BE THE FAVORED ADORATION OF OGODEI DEH KAHN...
BUT SUCH NOTION IS FOLLY!

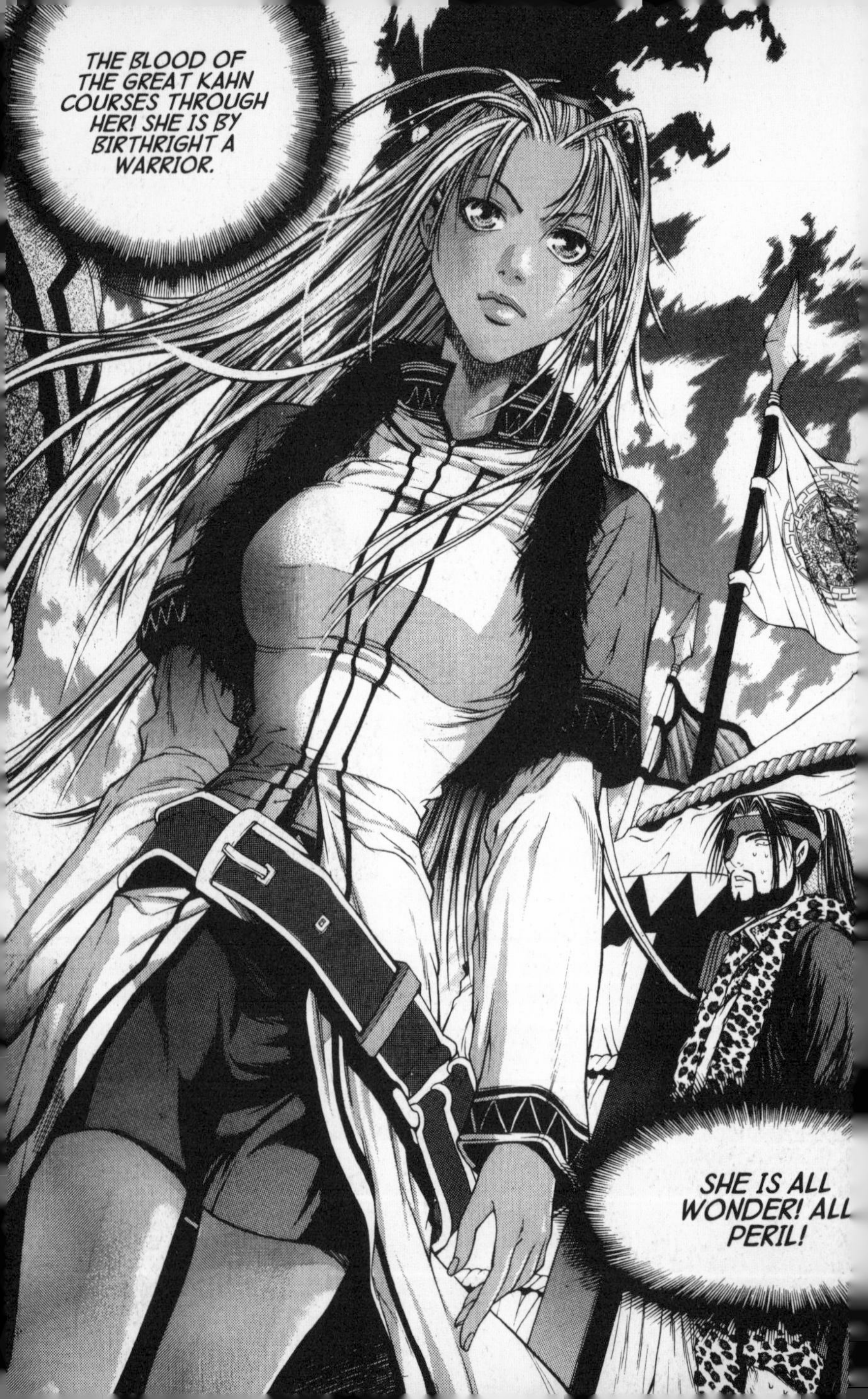
THE BLOOD OF THE GREAT KAHN COURSES THROUGH HER! SHE IS BY BIRTHRIGHT A WARRIOR.
SHE IS ALL WONDER! ALL PERIL!

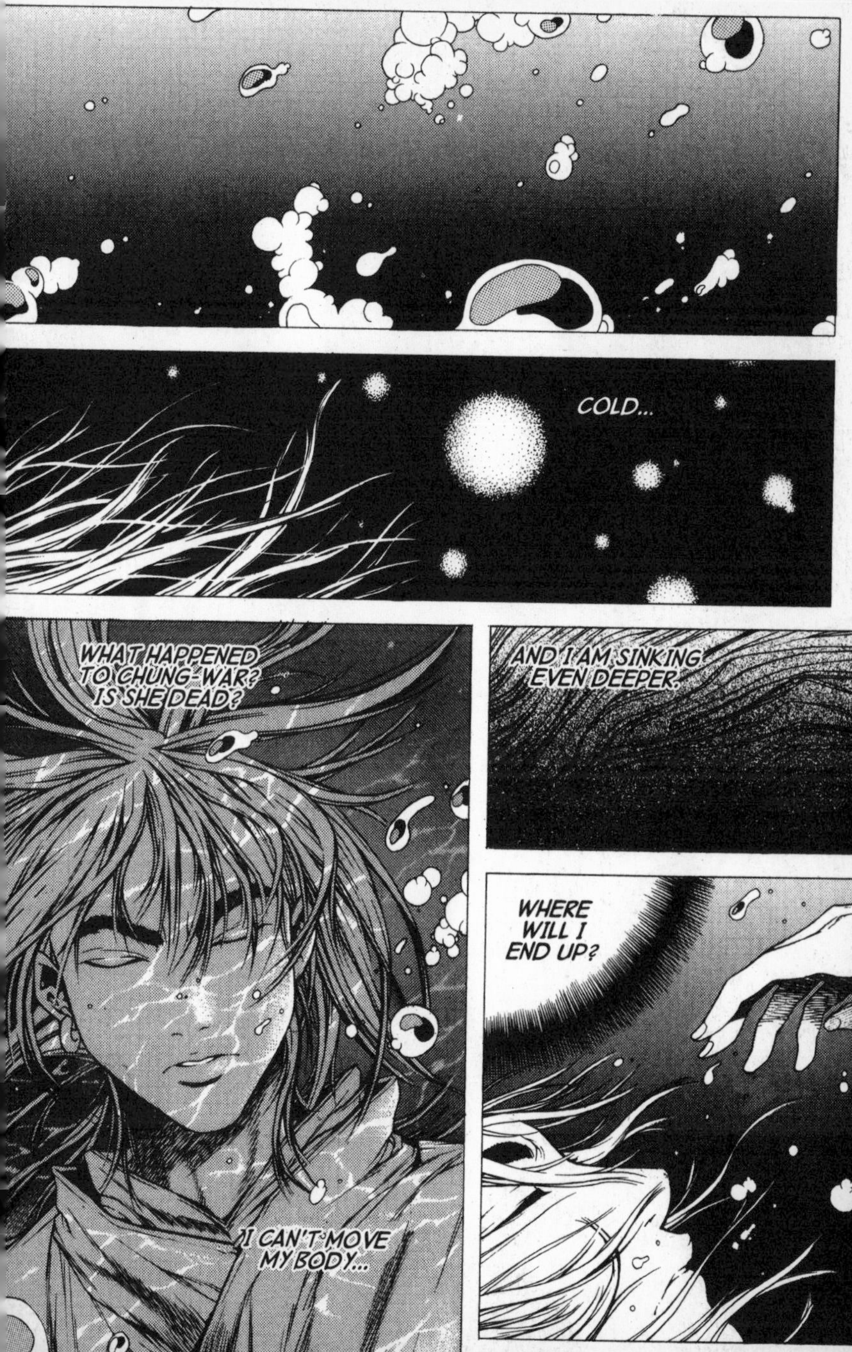
COLD...
WHAT HAPPENED TO CHUNG-WAR? IS SHE DEAD?
I CAN'T MOVE MY BODY...
AND I AM SINKING EVEN DEEPER.
WHERE WILL I END UP?

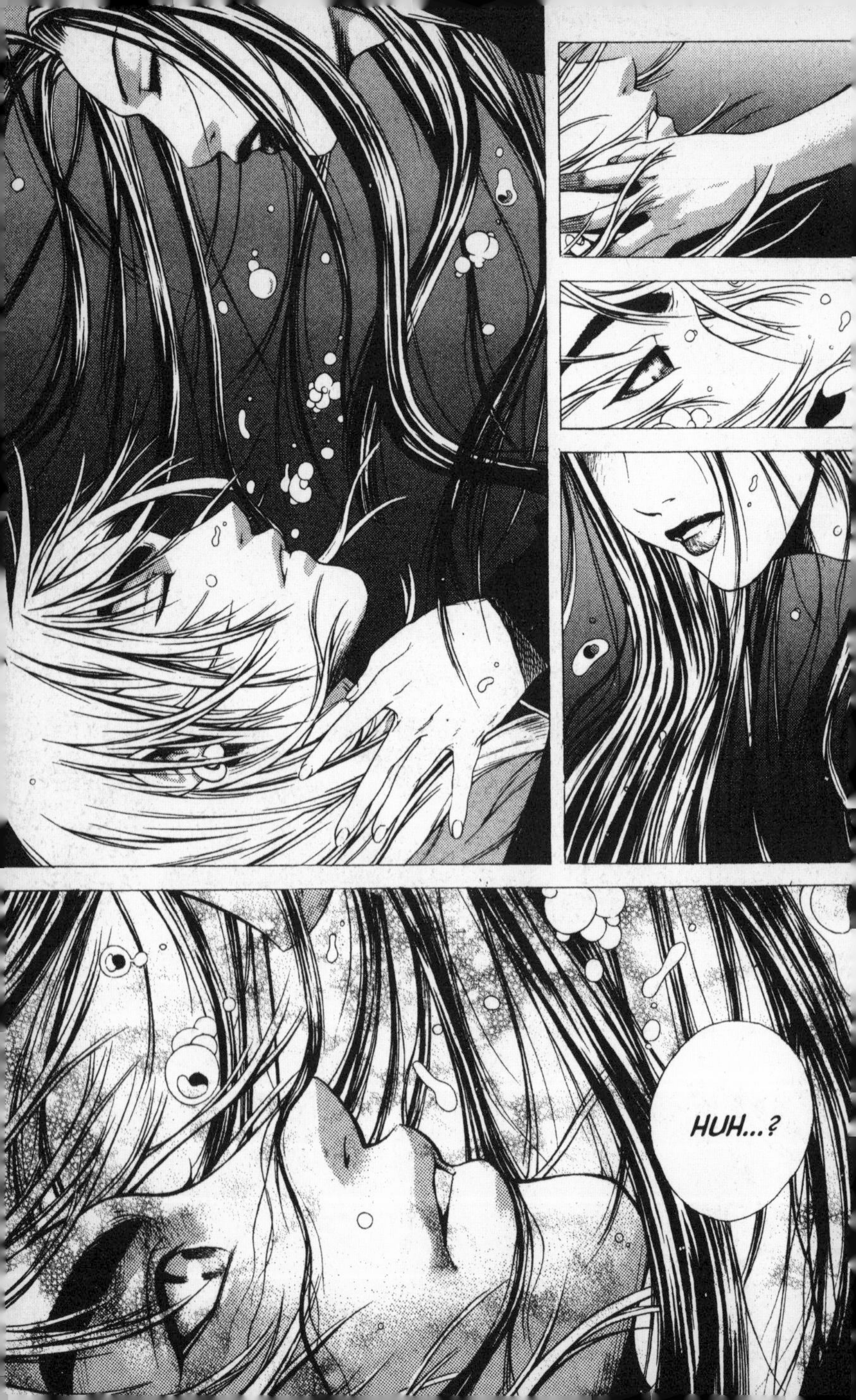
HUH...?

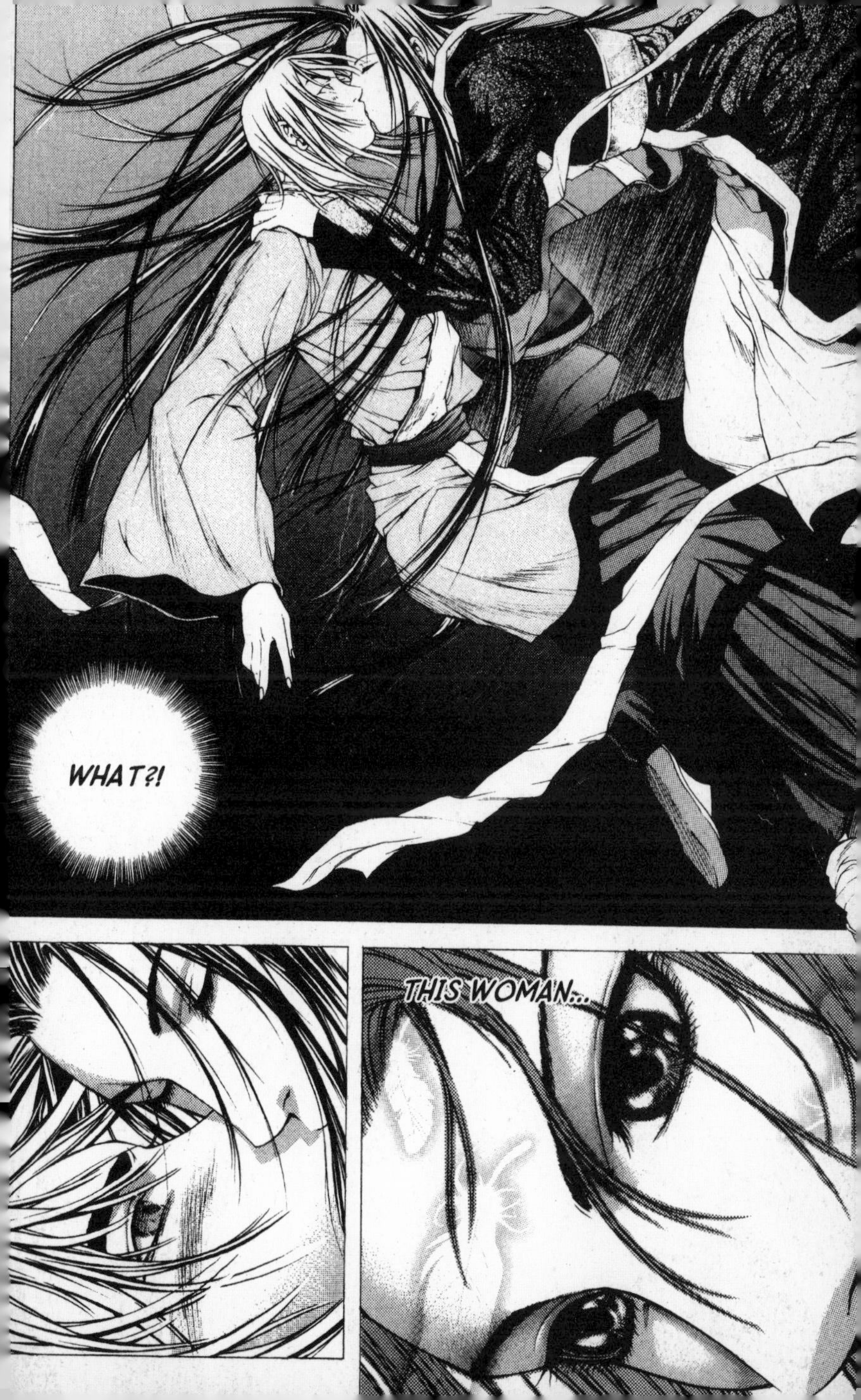
WHAT?!
THIS WOMAN...

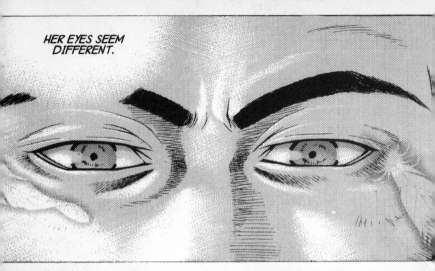

*HER EYES SEEM
DIFFERENT.*

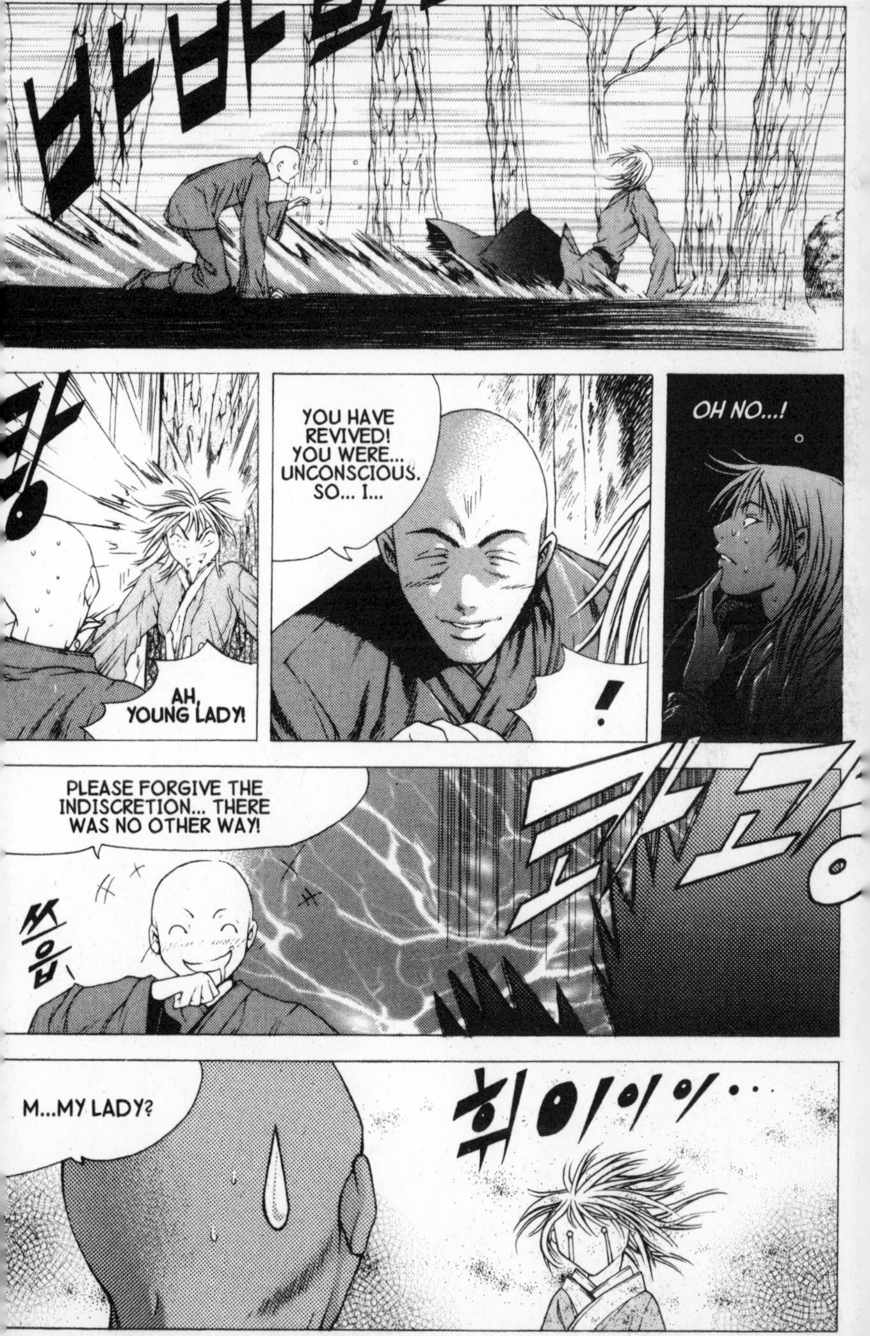
바바박
AH, YOUNG LADY!
YOU HAVE REVIVED! YOU WERE... UNCONSCIOUS. SO... I...
!
OH NO...!
PLEASE FORGIVE THE INDISCRETION... THERE WAS NO OTHER WAY!
쓰읍
M...MY LADY?
휘이이이..

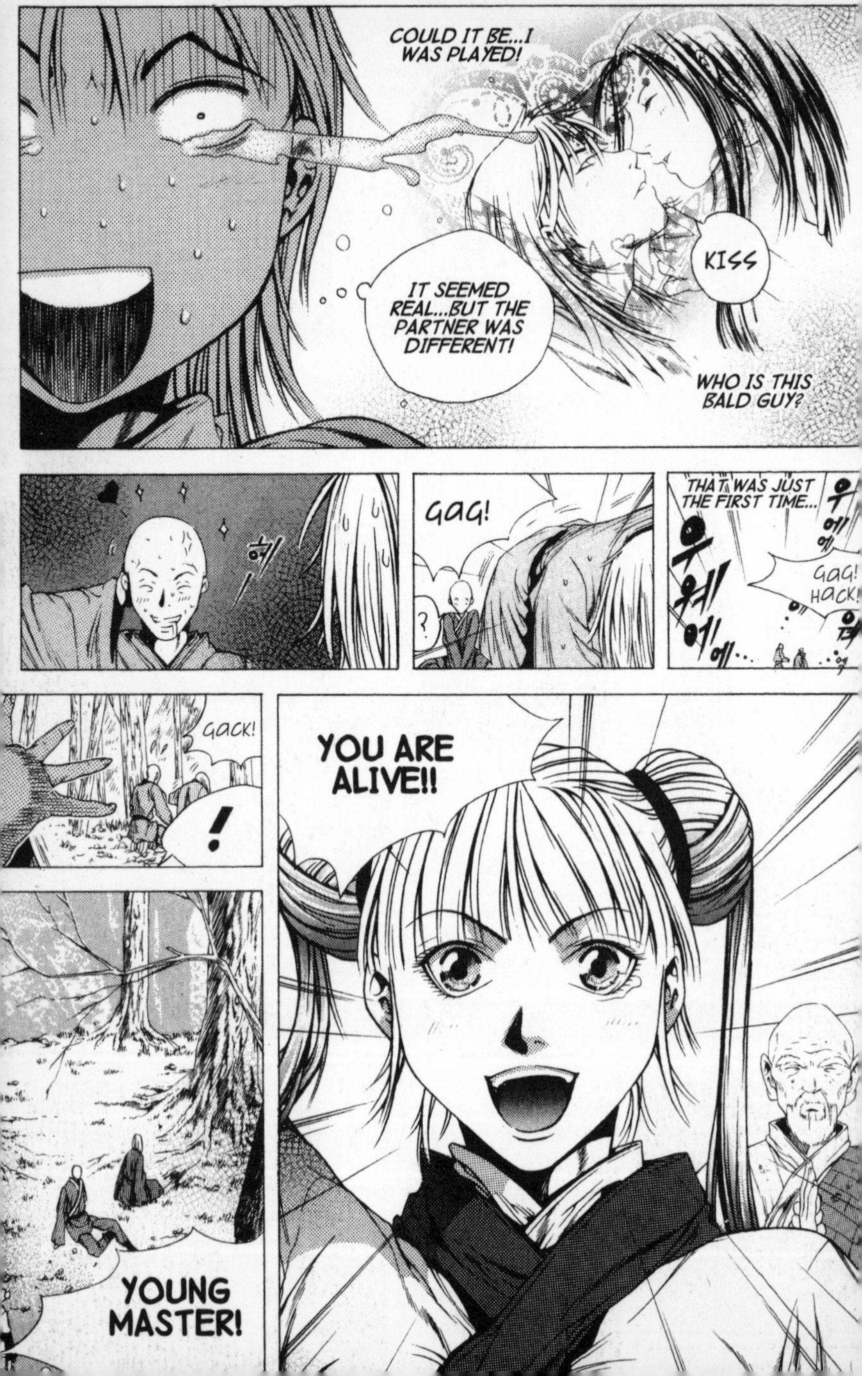
COULD IT BE...I WAS PLAYED!
IT SEEMED REAL...BUT THE PARTNER WAS DIFFERENT!
KISS
WHO IS THIS BALD GUY?
GAG!
?
THAT WAS JUST THE FIRST TIME...
우웨에에...
GAG! HACK!
GACK!
!
YOUNG MASTER!
YOU ARE ALIVE!!

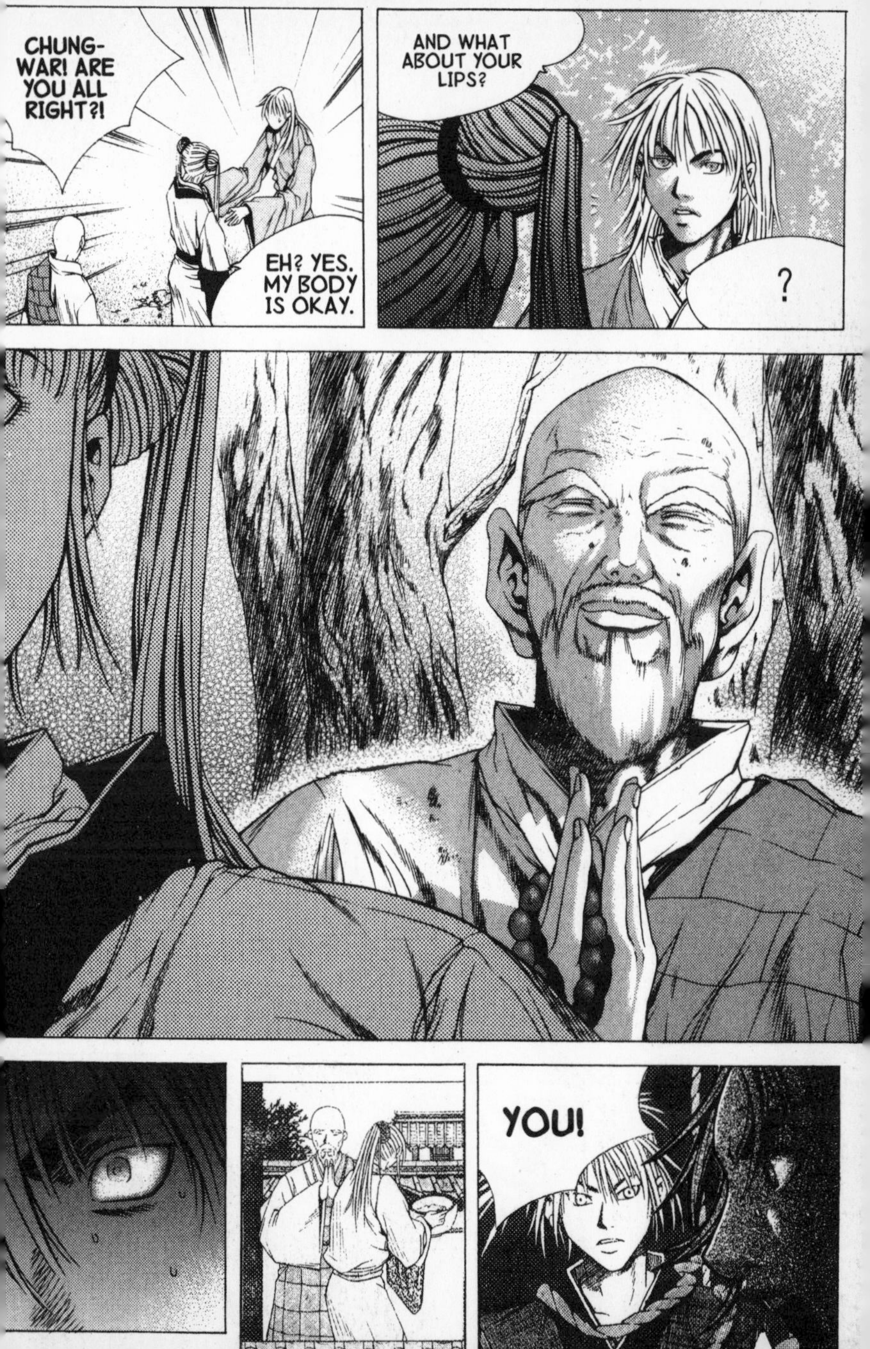
CHUNG-WAR! ARE YOU ALL RIGHT?!
EH? YES. MY BODY IS OKAY.
AND WHAT ABOUT YOUR LIPS?
?
YOU!

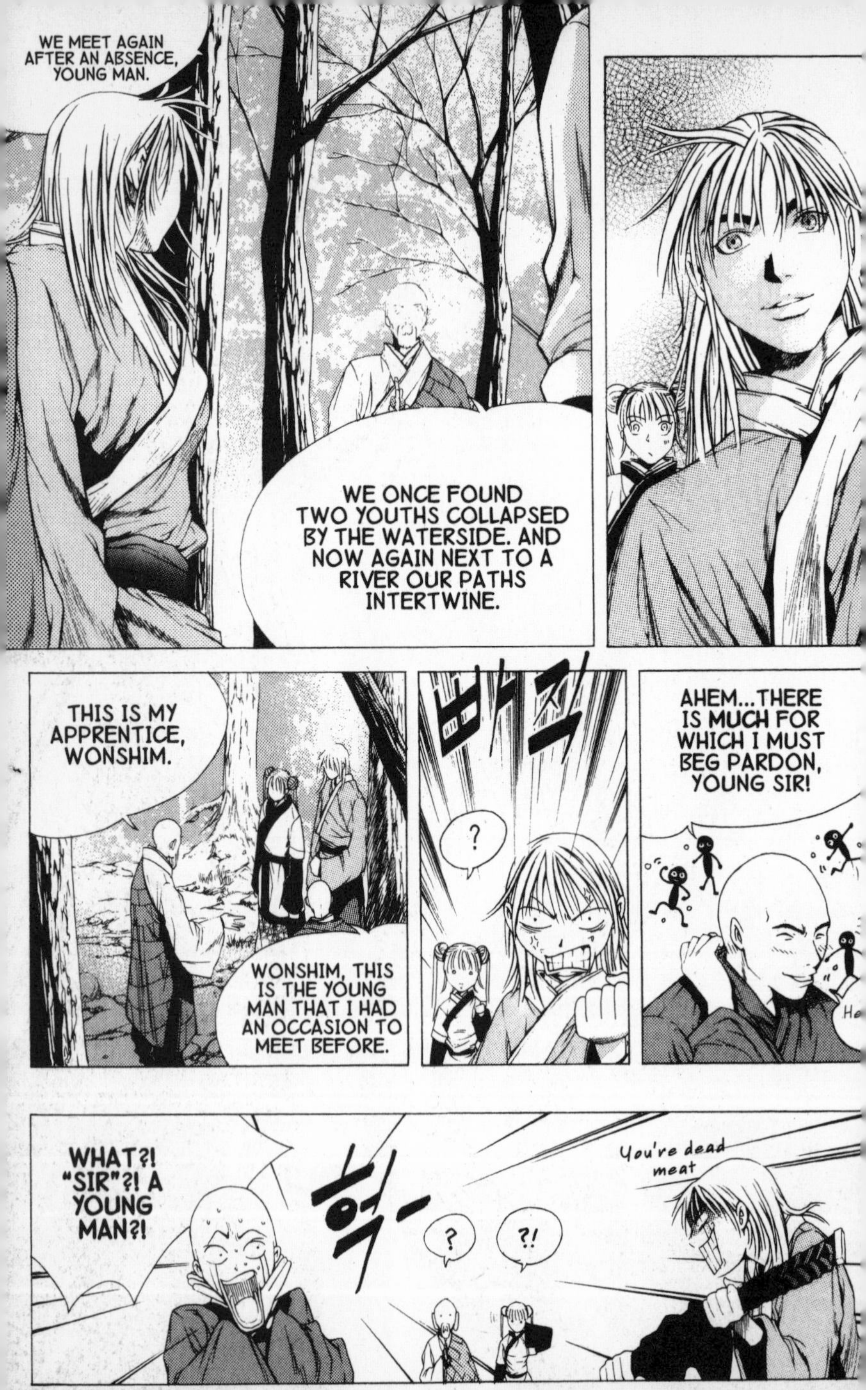
WE MEET AGAIN AFTER AN ABSENCE, YOUNG MAN.
WE ONCE FOUND TWO YOUTHS COLLAPSED BY THE WATERSIDE. AND NOW AGAIN NEXT TO A RIVER OUR PATHS INTERTWINE.
THIS IS MY APPRENTICE, WONSHIM.
WONSHIM, THIS IS THE YOUNG MAN THAT I HAD AN OCCASION TO MEET BEFORE.
빠직
?
AHEM...THERE IS MUCH FOR WHICH I MUST BEG PARDON, YOUNG SIR!
He
WHAT?! "SIR"?! A YOUNG MAN?!
헉-
?
?!
You're dead meat

Chapter 22
Uprising

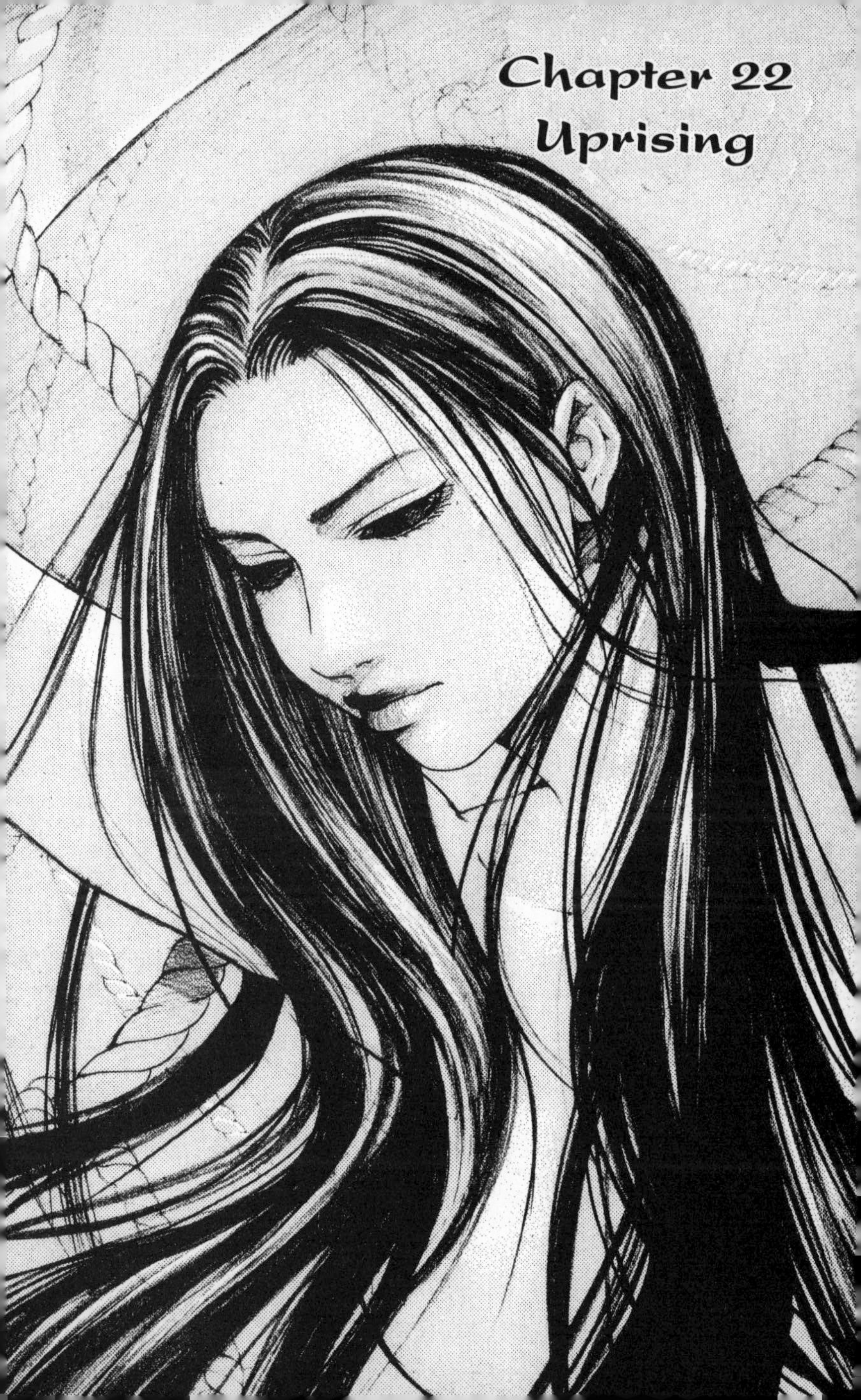

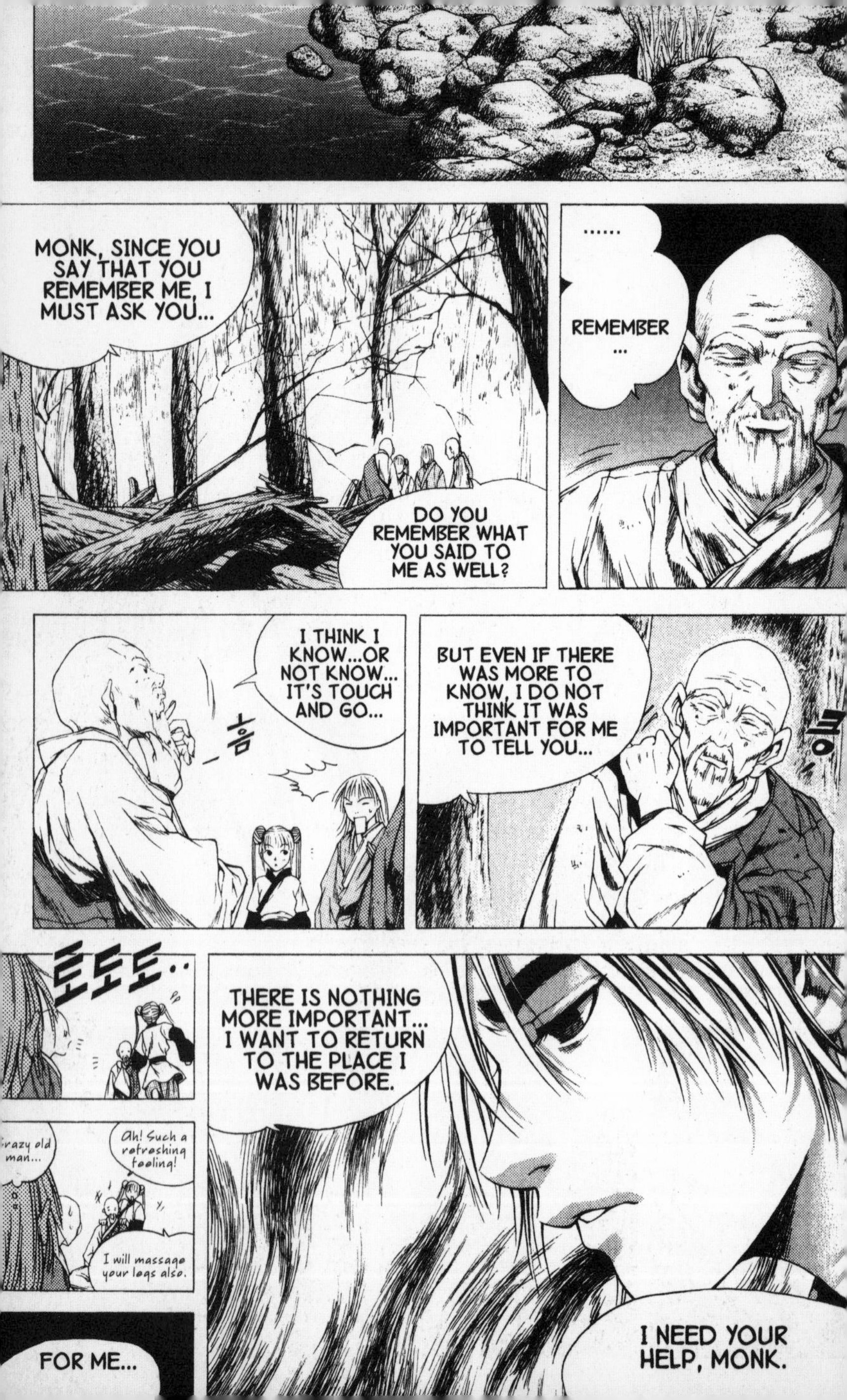

MONK, SINCE YOU SAY THAT YOU REMEMBER ME, I MUST ASK YOU...
DO YOU REMEMBER WHAT YOU SAID TO ME AS WELL?
......
REMEMBER ...
I THINK I KNOW...OR NOT KNOW... IT'S TOUCH AND GO...
흠
BUT EVEN IF THERE WAS MORE TO KNOW, I DO NOT THINK IT WAS IMPORTANT FOR ME TO TELL YOU...
토도도..
Crazy old man...
Ah! Such a refreshing feeling!
I will massage your legs also.
FOR ME...
THERE IS NOTHING MORE IMPORTANT... I WANT TO RETURN TO THE PLACE I WAS BEFORE.
I NEED YOUR HELP, MONK.

PLEASE TELL ME ALL THAT YOU KNOW ABOUT MY SITUATION.

I DON'T HAVE THE STRENGTH TO DO THIS ON MY OWN. I... I WAS JUST A HIGH SCHOOL KID.

PLEASE...

HELP ME.

......

I AM SORRY...

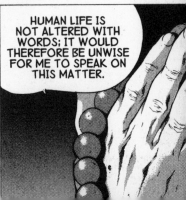

HUMAN LIFE IS NOT ALTERED WITH WORDS; IT WOULD THEREFORE BE UNWISE FOR ME TO SPEAK ON THIS MATTER.

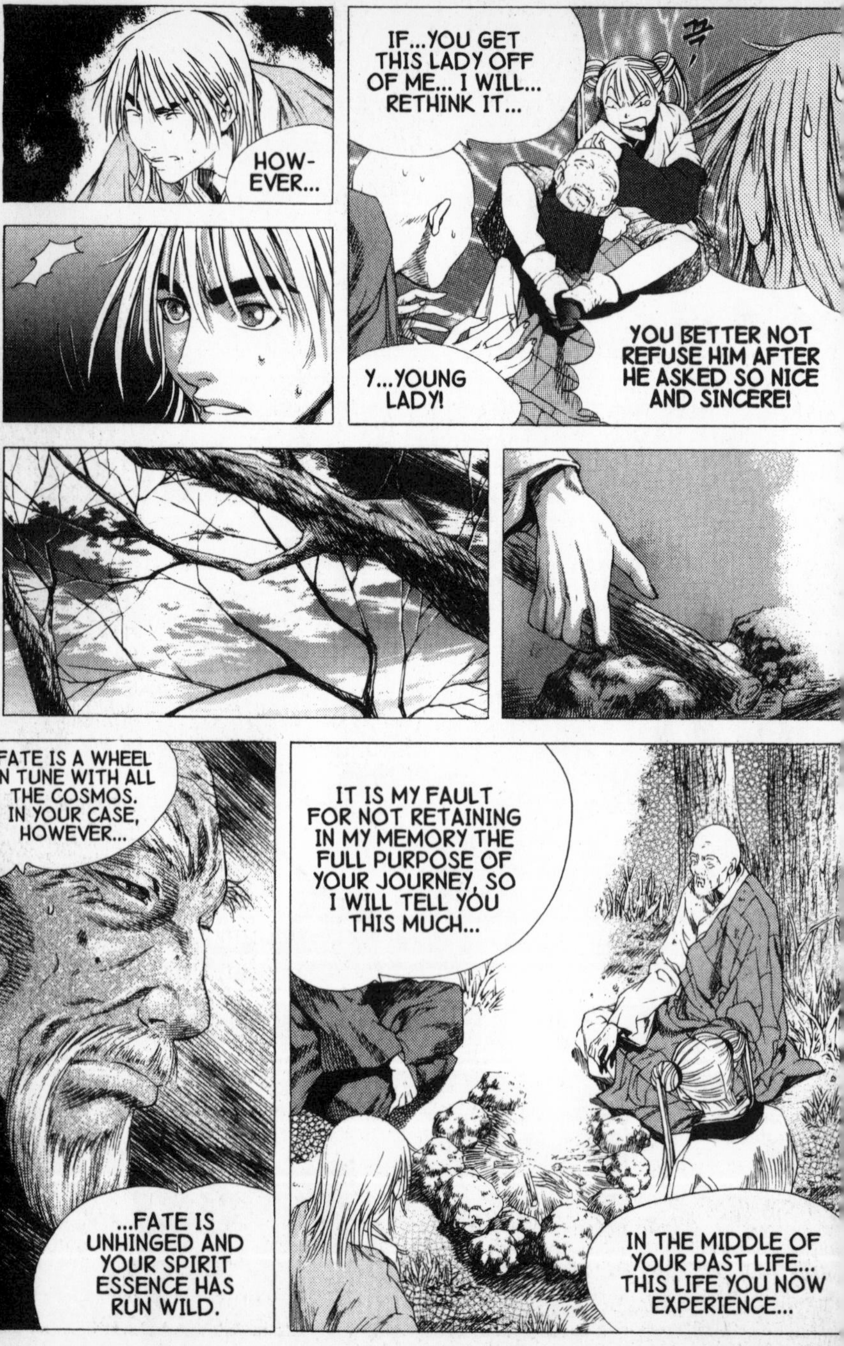
HOW-EVER...
IF...YOU GET THIS LADY OFF OF ME... I WILL... RETHINK IT...
Y...YOUNG LADY!
YOU BETTER NOT REFUSE HIM AFTER HE ASKED SO NICE AND SINCERE!
FATE IS A WHEEL IN TUNE WITH ALL THE COSMOS. IN YOUR CASE, HOWEVER...
...FATE IS UNHINGED AND YOUR SPIRIT ESSENCE HAS RUN WILD.
IT IS MY FAULT FOR NOT RETAINING IN MY MEMORY THE FULL PURPOSE OF YOUR JOURNEY, SO I WILL TELL YOU THIS MUCH...
IN THE MIDDLE OF YOUR PAST LIFE... THIS LIFE YOU NOW EXPERIENCE...

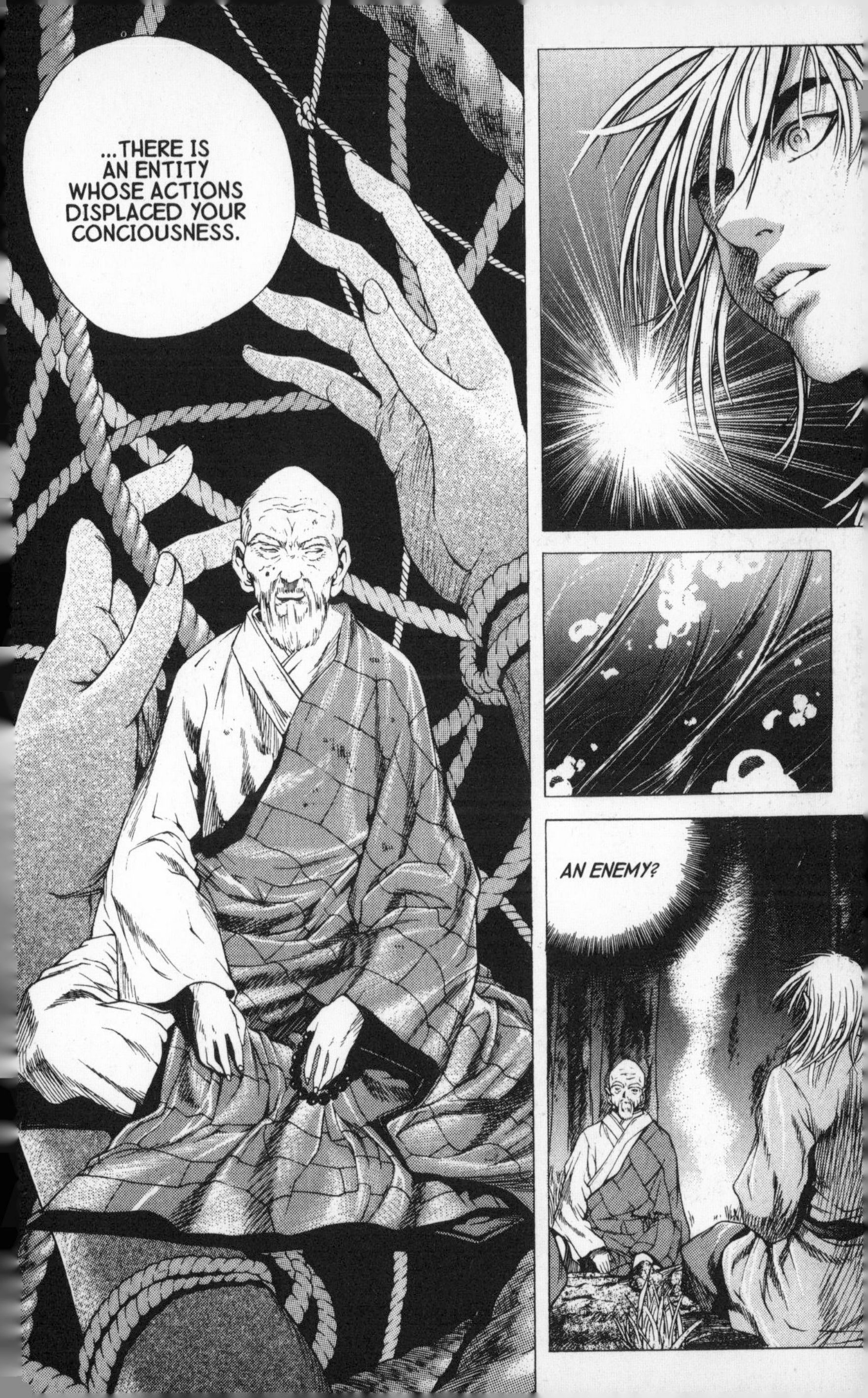
...THERE IS AN ENTITY WHOSE ACTIONS DISPLACED YOUR CONCIOUSNESS.
AN ENEMY?

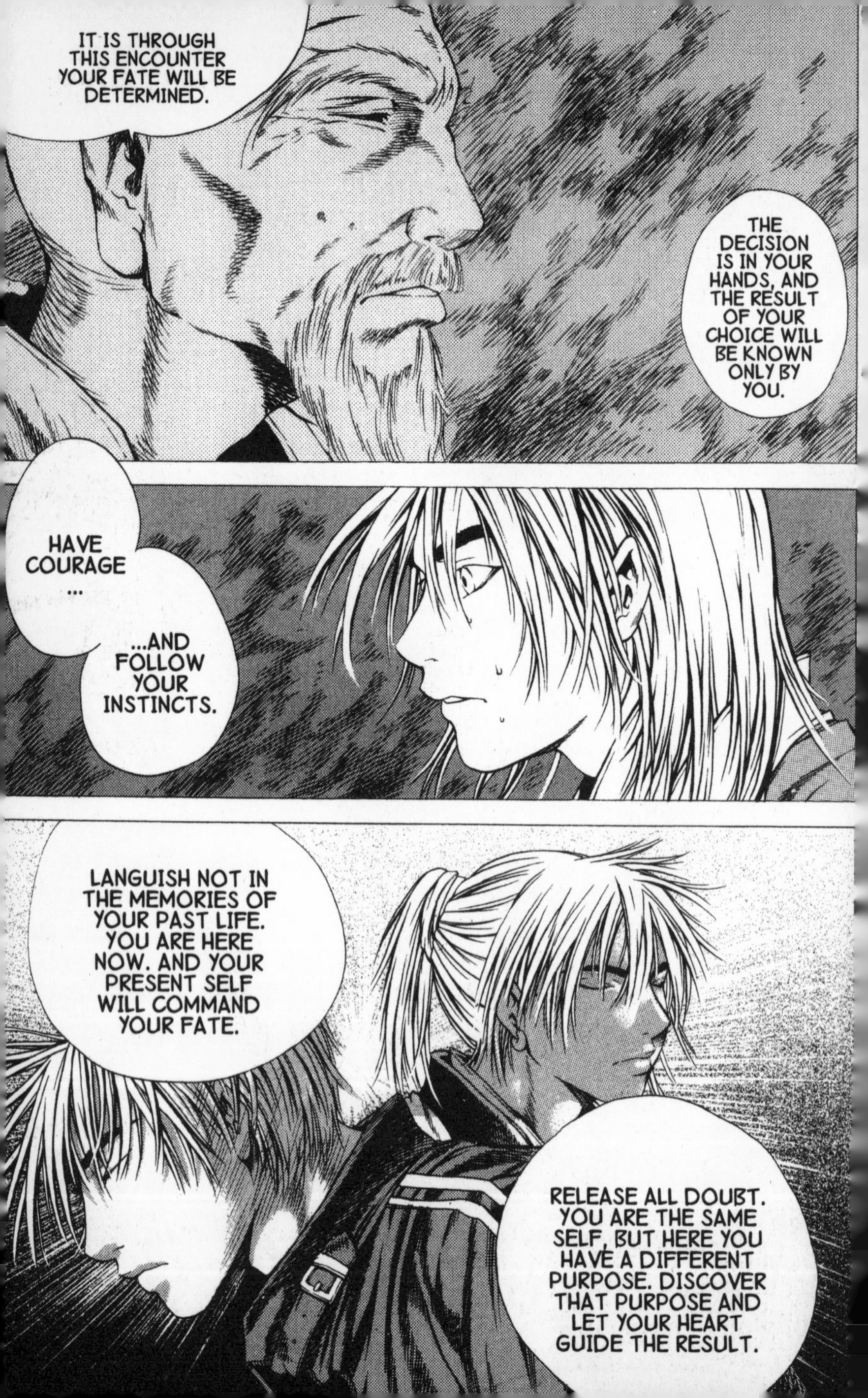
IT IS THROUGH THIS ENCOUNTER YOUR FATE WILL BE DETERMINED.
THE DECISION IS IN YOUR HANDS, AND THE RESULT OF YOUR CHOICE WILL BE KNOWN ONLY BY YOU.
HAVE COURAGE ...
...AND FOLLOW YOUR INSTINCTS.
LANGUISH NOT IN THE MEMORIES OF YOUR PAST LIFE. YOU ARE HERE NOW. AND YOUR PRESENT SELF WILL COMMAND YOUR FATE.
RELEASE ALL DOUBT. YOU ARE THE SAME SELF, BUT HERE YOU HAVE A DIFFERENT PURPOSE. DISCOVER THAT PURPOSE AND LET YOUR HEART GUIDE THE RESULT.

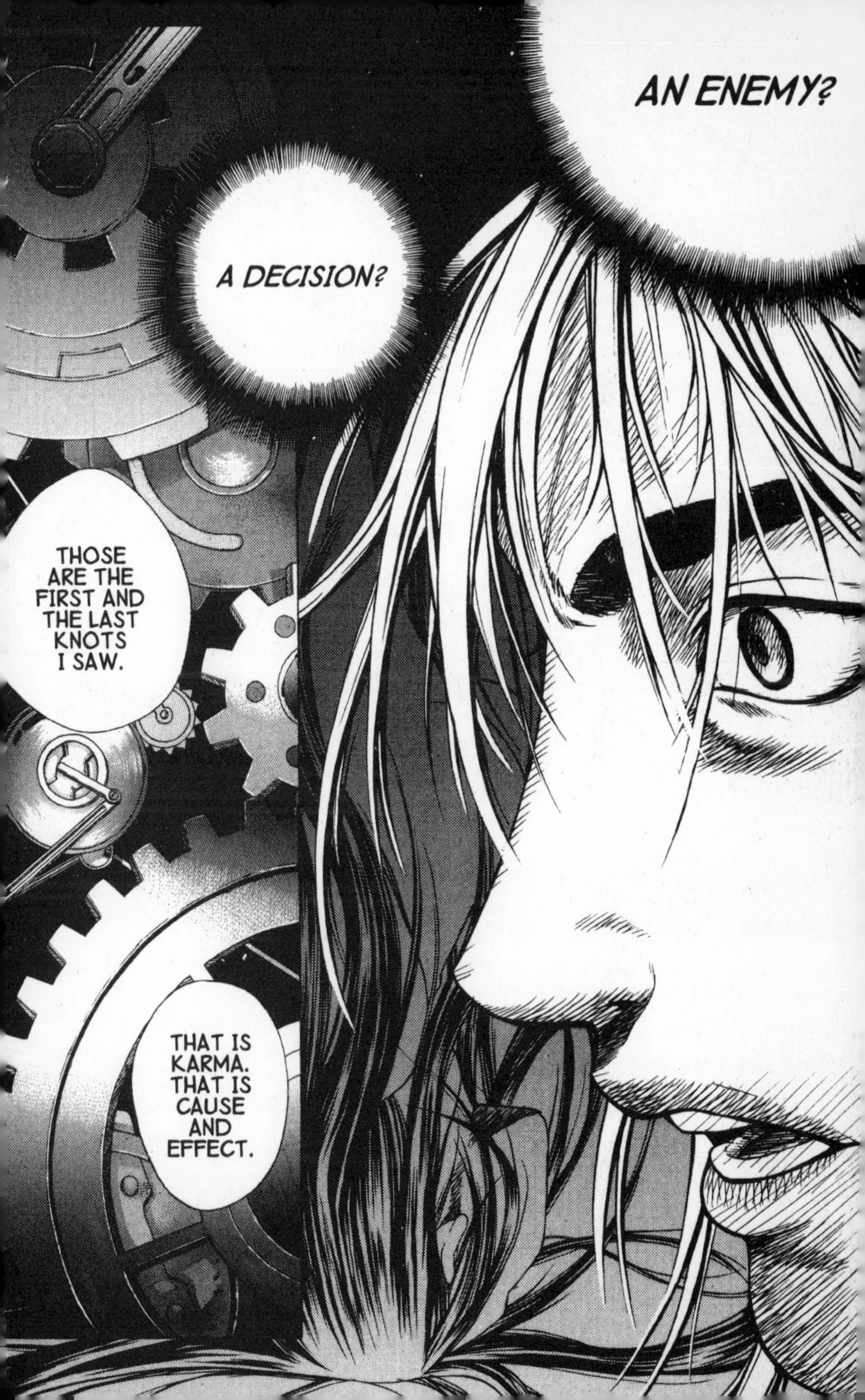
AN ENEMY?
A DECISION?
THOSE ARE THE FIRST AND THE LAST KNOTS I SAW.
THAT IS KARMA. THAT IS CAUSE AND EFFECT.

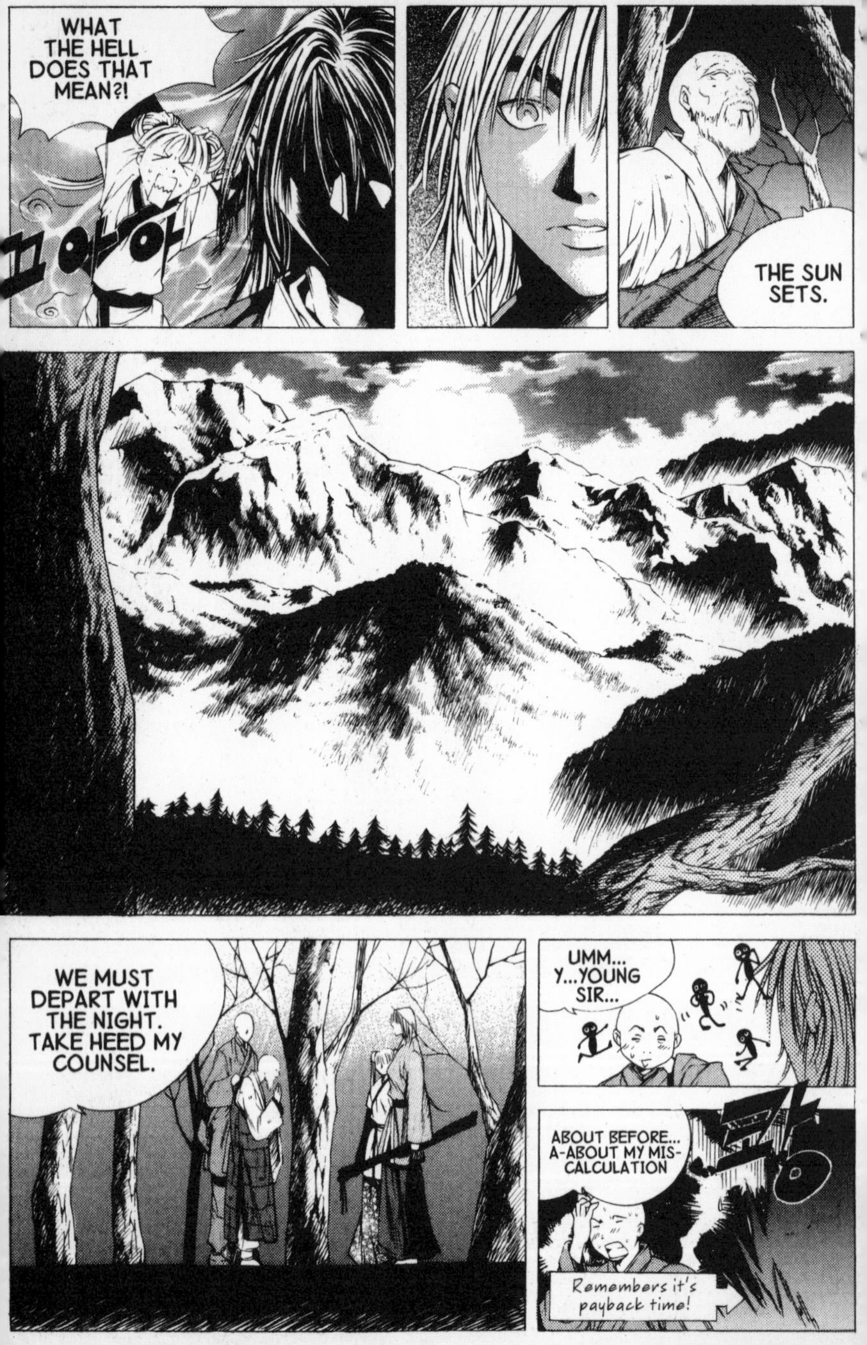
WHAT THE HELL DOES THAT MEAN?!
THE SUN SETS.
WE MUST DEPART WITH THE NIGHT. TAKE HEED MY COUNSEL.
UMM... Y...YOUNG SIR...
ABOUT BEFORE... A-ABOUT MY MIS-CALCULATION
Remembers it's payback time!

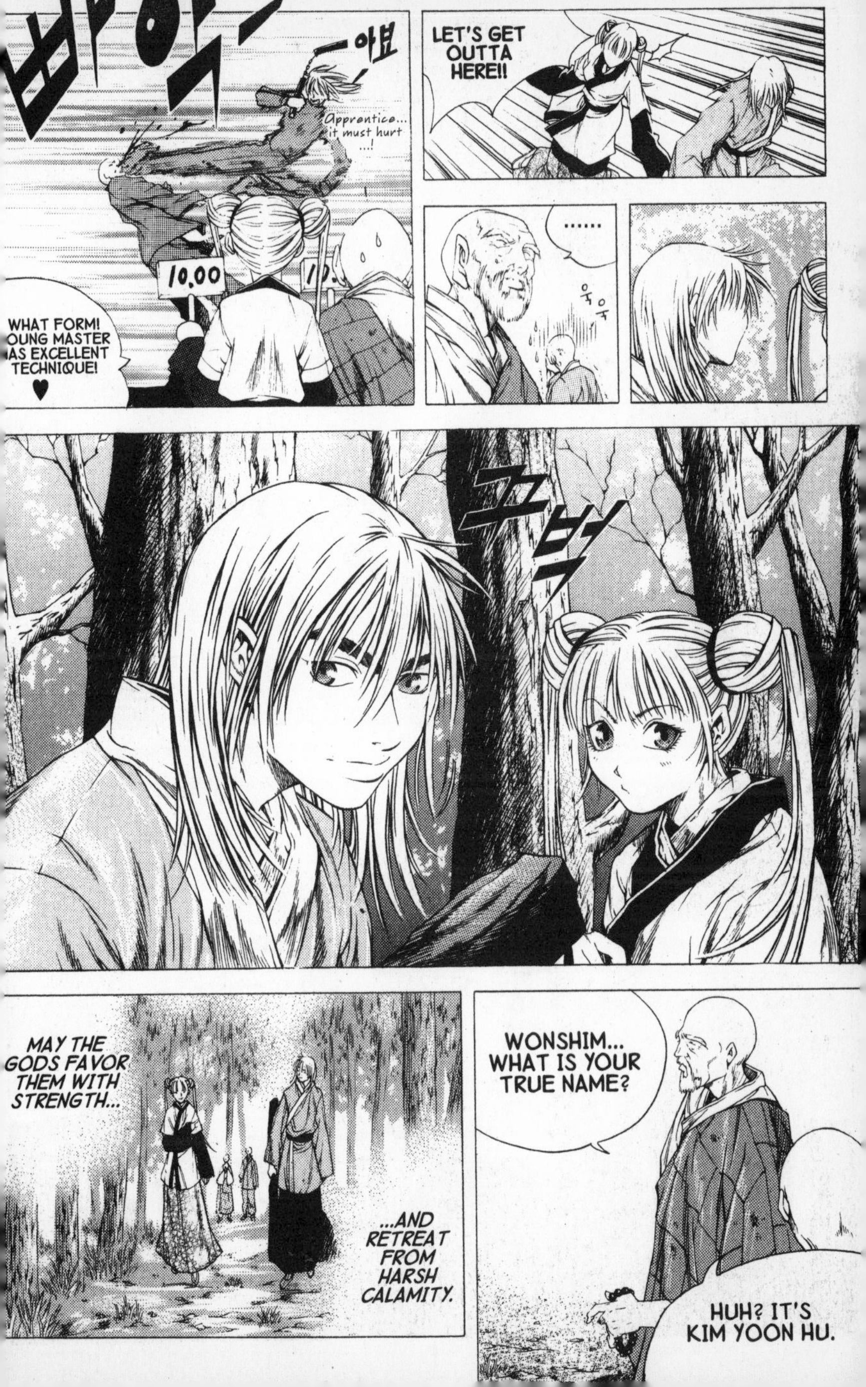
빠악-
-아뵤
Apprentice... it must hurt ...!
10.00
WHAT FORM! YOUNG MASTER HAS EXCELLENT TECHNIQUE! ♥
LET'S GET OUTTA HERE!!
......
MAY THE GODS FAVOR THEM WITH STRENGTH...
...AND RETREAT FROM HARSH CALAMITY.
WONSHIM... WHAT IS YOUR TRUE NAME?
HUH? IT'S KIM YOON HU.

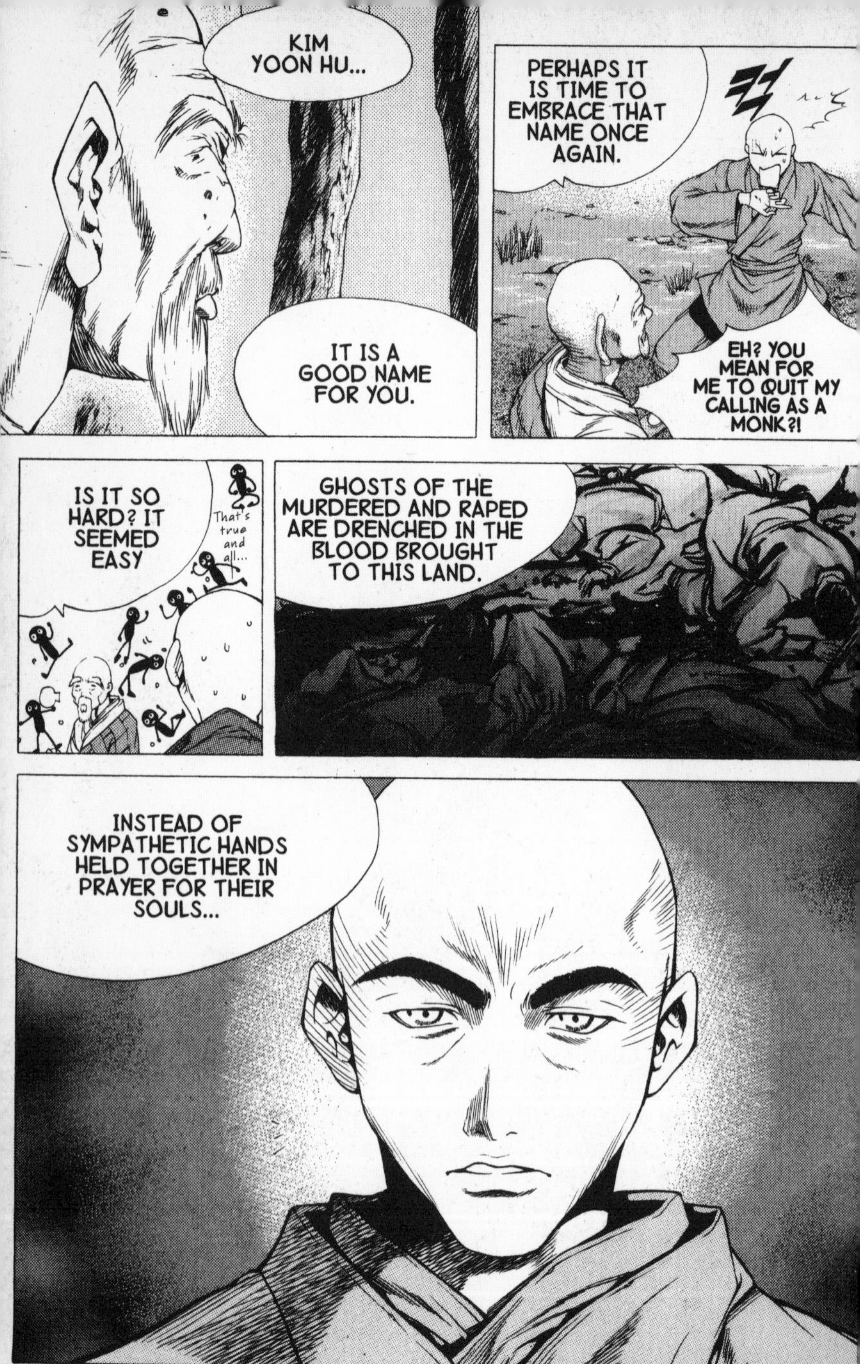
KIM YOON HU...
IT IS A GOOD NAME FOR YOU.
PERHAPS IT IS TIME TO EMBRACE THAT NAME ONCE AGAIN.
EH? YOU MEAN FOR ME TO QUIT MY CALLING AS A MONK?!
IS IT SO HARD? IT SEEMED EASY
That's true and all...
GHOSTS OF THE MURDERED AND RAPED ARE DRENCHED IN THE BLOOD BROUGHT TO THIS LAND.
INSTEAD OF SYMPATHETIC HANDS HELD TOGETHER IN PRAYER FOR THEIR SOULS...

Note - Buddhist monks are given a new name when entering the order...when you give up that new name, you are giving up the monk's life

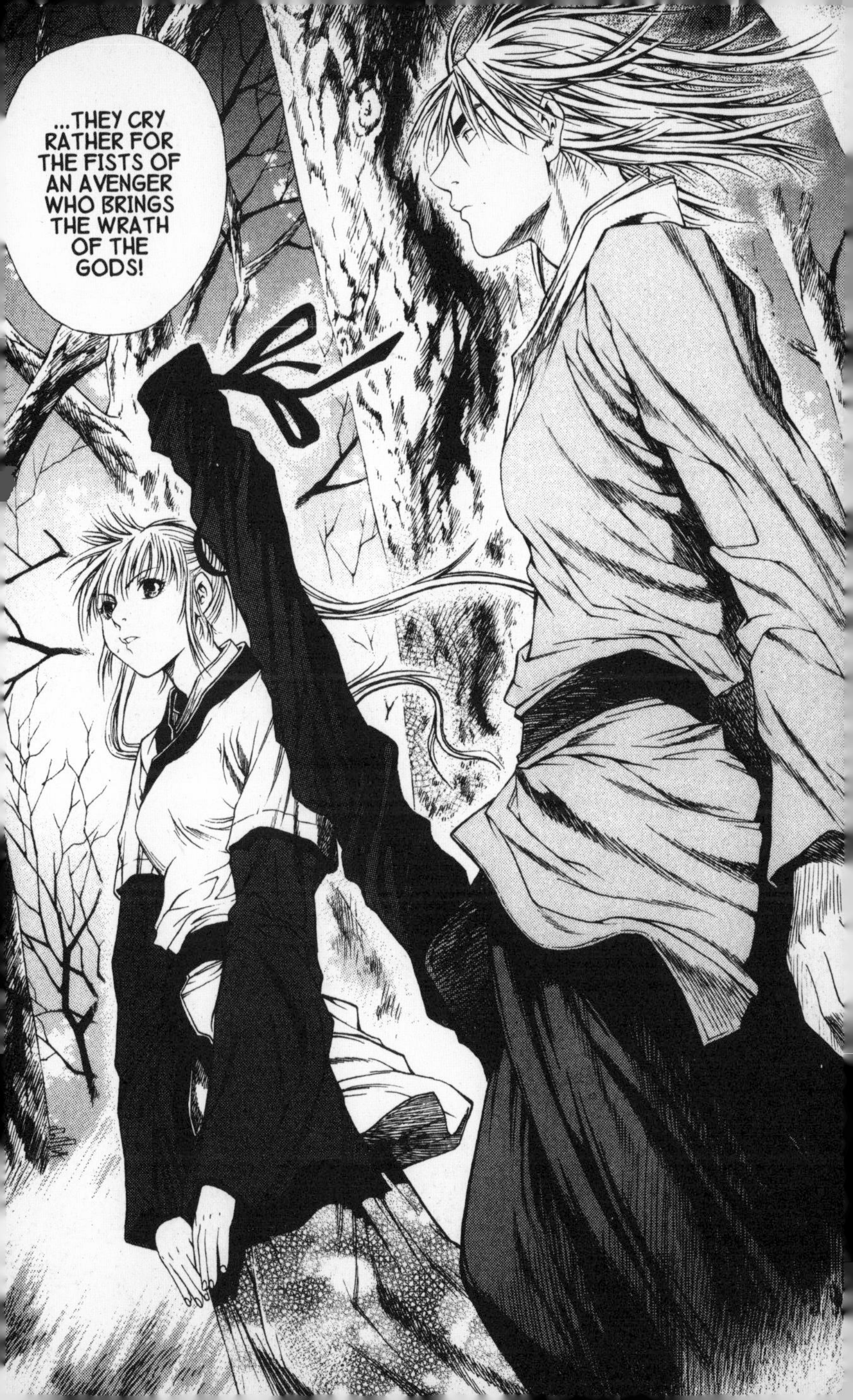
...THEY CRY RATHER FOR THE FISTS OF AN AVENGER WHO BRINGS THE WRATH OF THE GODS!

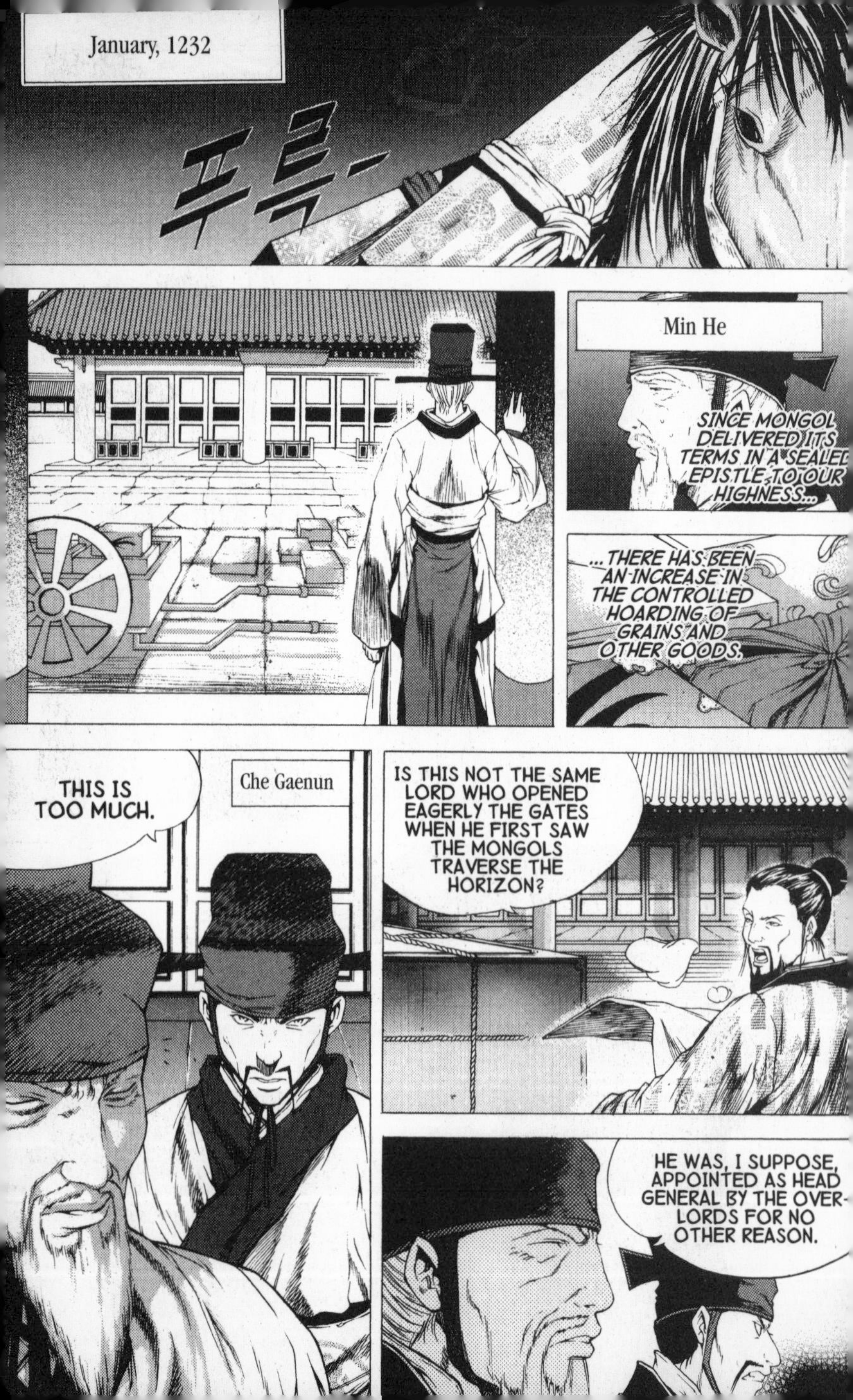
January, 1232
푸륵-
Min He
SINCE MONGOL DELIVERED ITS TERMS IN A SEALED EPISTLE TO OUR HIGHNESS...
...THERE HAS BEEN AN INCREASE IN THE CONTROLLED HOARDING OF GRAINS AND OTHER GOODS.
THIS IS TOO MUCH.
Che Gaenun
IS THIS NOT THE SAME LORD WHO OPENED EAGERLY THE GATES WHEN HE FIRST SAW THE MONGOLS TRAVERSE THE HORIZON?
HE WAS, I SUPPOSE, APPOINTED AS HEAD GENERAL BY THE OVER-LORDS FOR NO OTHER REASON.

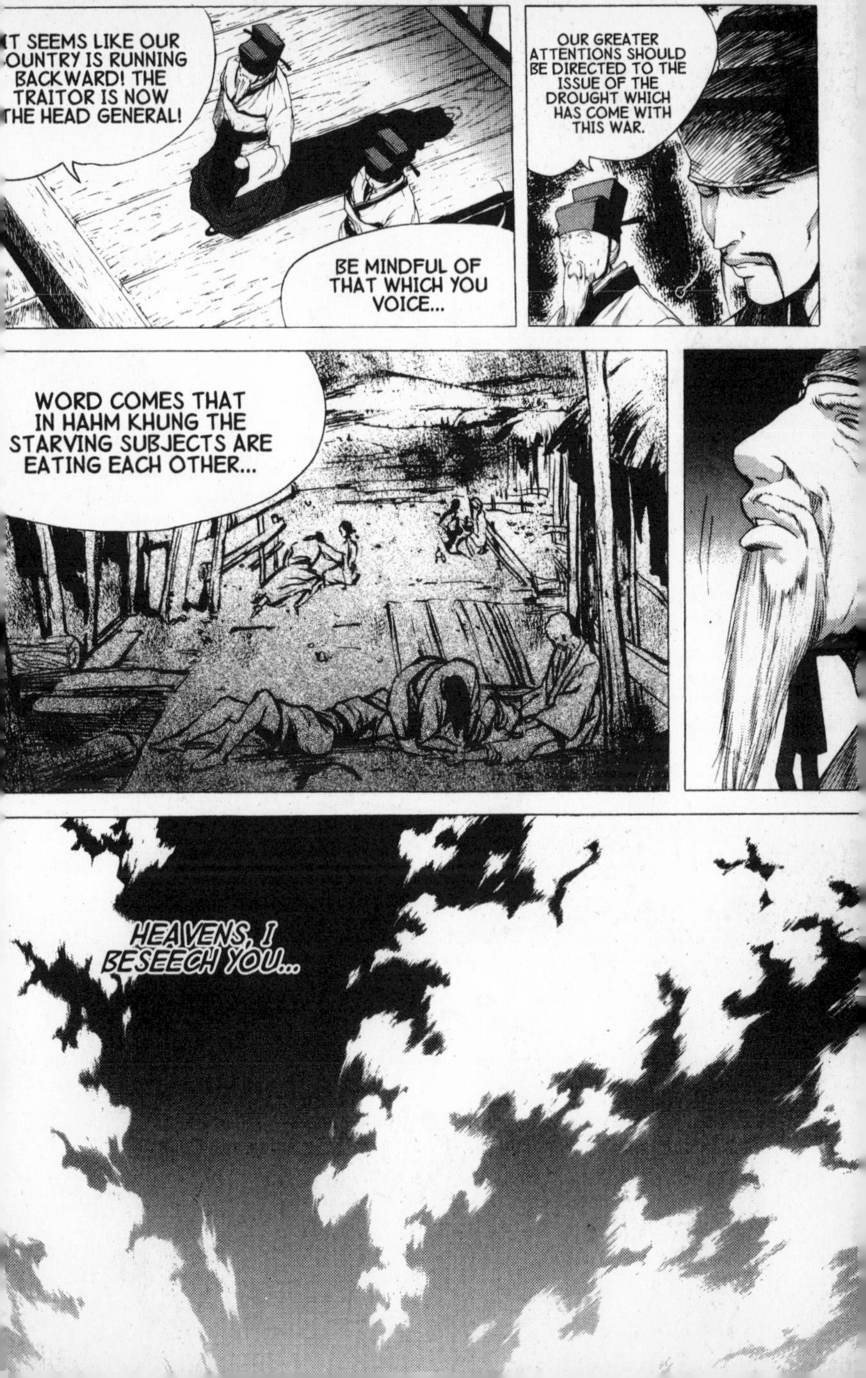
IT SEEMS LIKE OUR COUNTRY IS RUNNING BACKWARD! THE TRAITOR IS NOW THE HEAD GENERAL!
BE MINDFUL OF THAT WHICH YOU VOICE...
OUR GREATER ATTENTIONS SHOULD BE DIRECTED TO THE ISSUE OF THE DROUGHT WHICH HAS COME WITH THIS WAR.
WORD COMES THAT IN HAHM KHUNG THE STARVING SUBJECTS ARE EATING EACH OTHER...
HEAVENS, I BESEECH YOU...

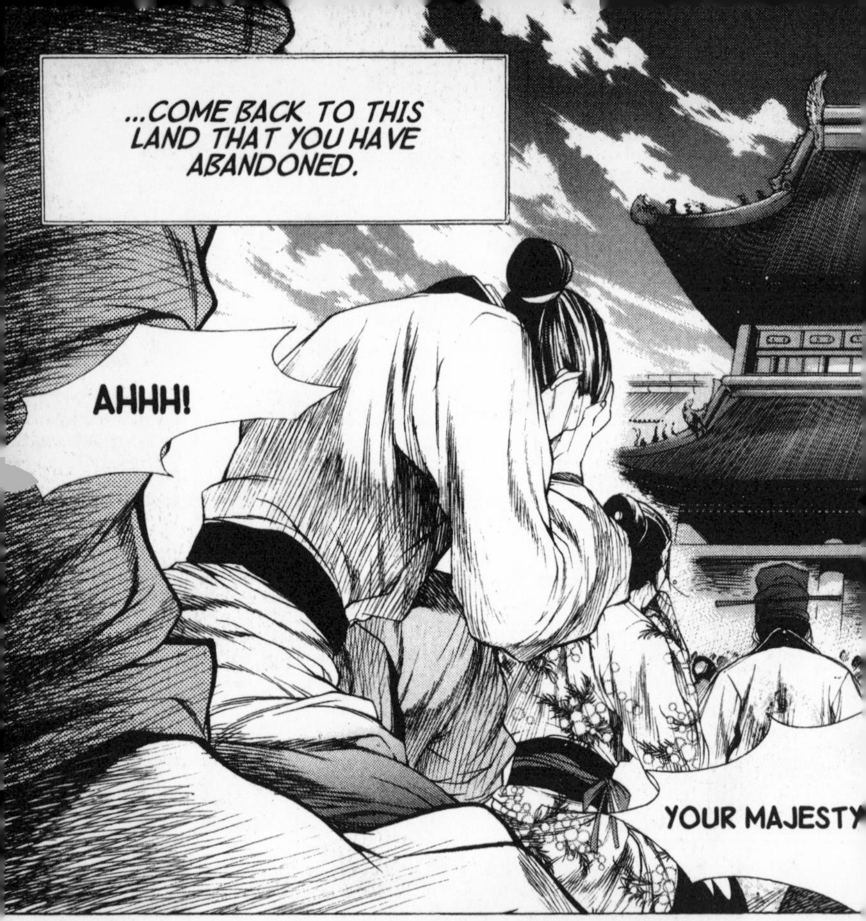
...COME BACK TO THIS LAND THAT YOU HAVE ABANDONED.
AHHH!
YOUR MAJESTY
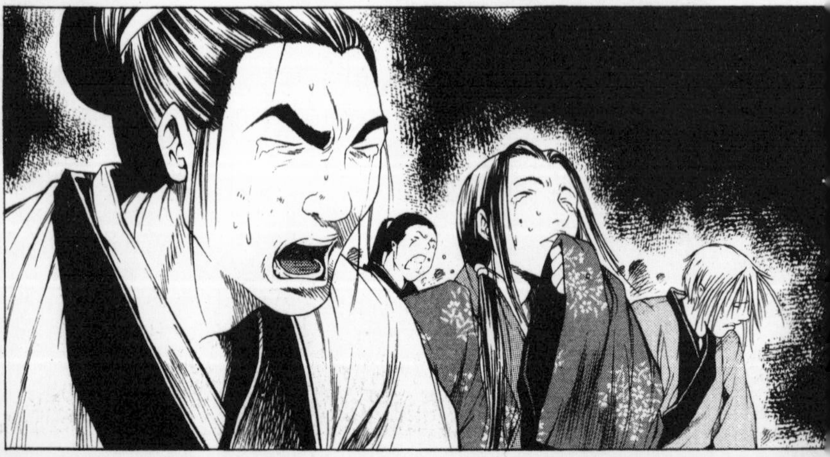

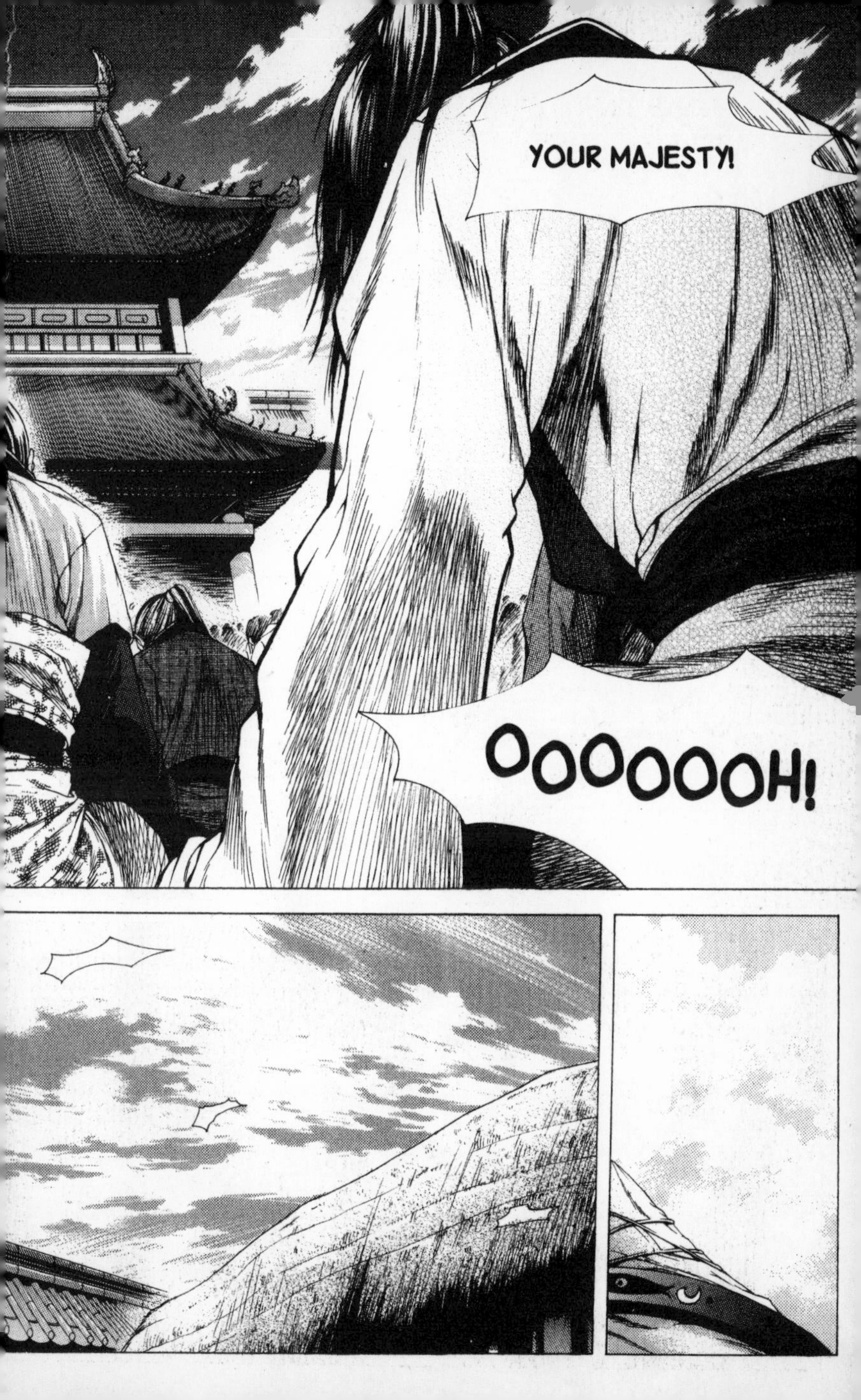
YOUR MAJESTY!
OOOOOOH!

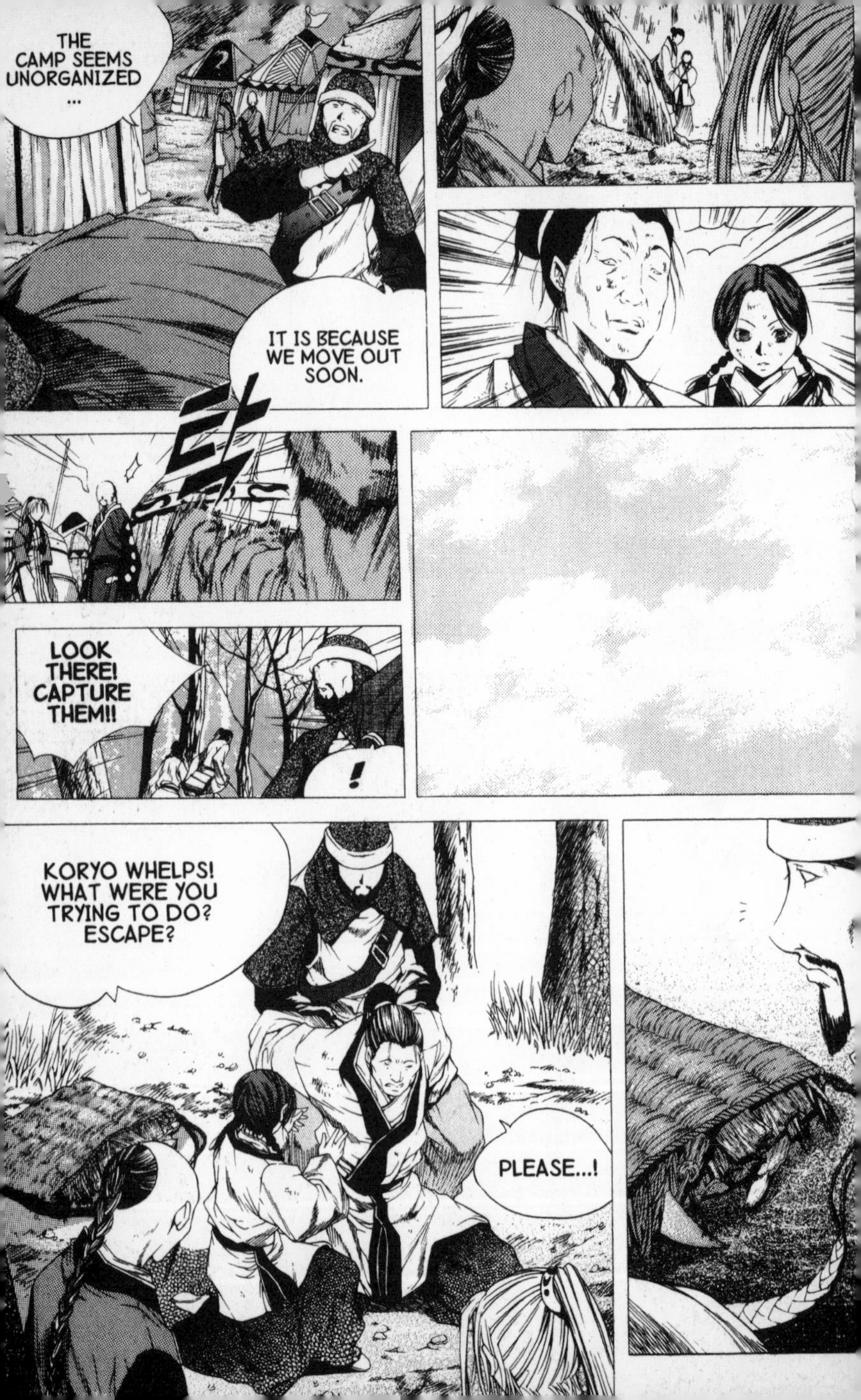
THE CAMP SEEMS UNORGANIZED ...
IT IS BECAUSE WE MOVE OUT SOON.
LOOK THERE! CAPTURE THEM!!
!
KORYO WHELPS! WHAT WERE YOU TRYING TO DO? ESCAPE?
PLEASE...!

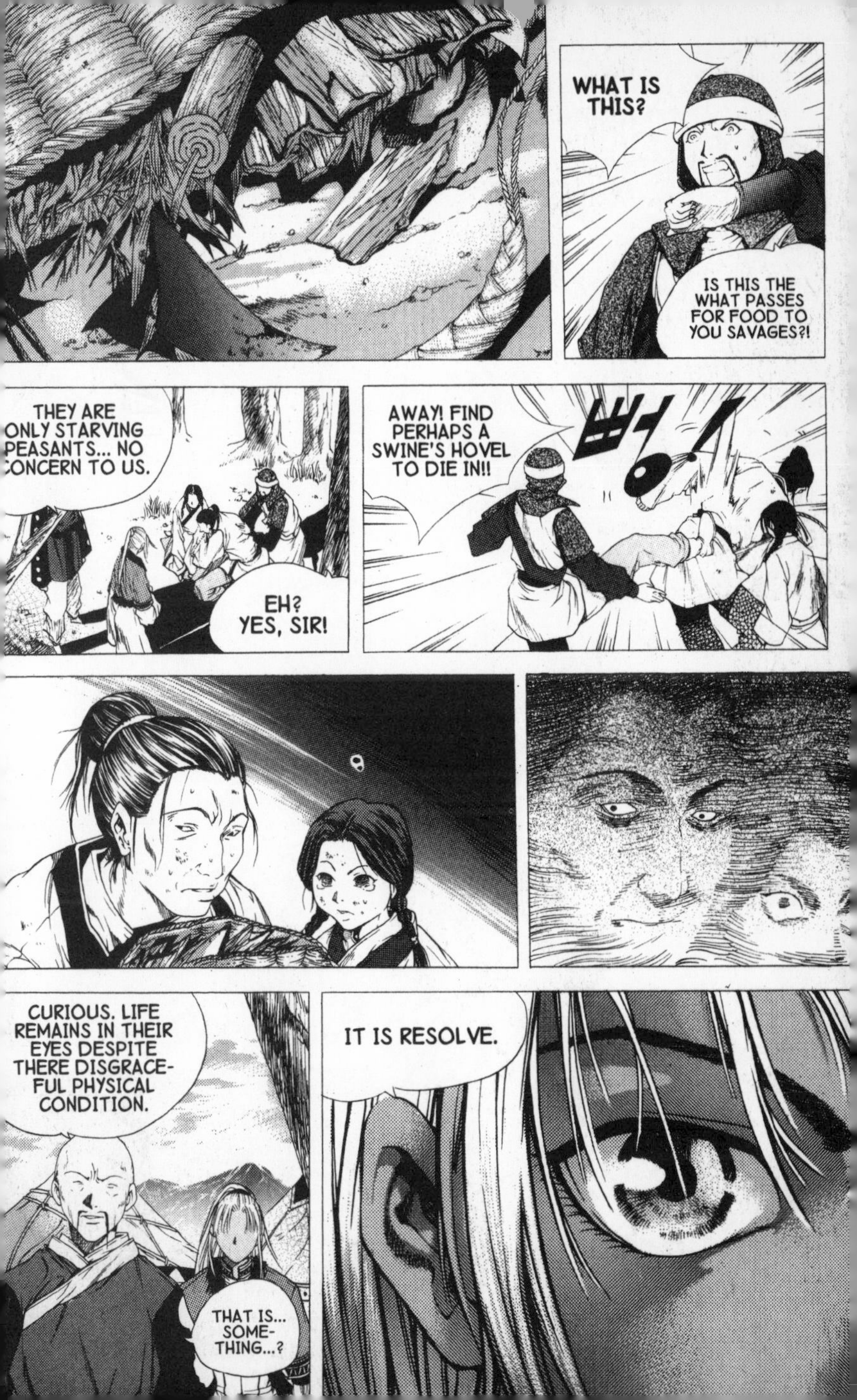
WHAT IS THIS?
IS THIS THE WHAT PASSES FOR FOOD TO YOU SAVAGES?!
THEY ARE ONLY STARVING PEASANTS... NO CONCERN TO US.
EH? YES, SIR!
AWAY! FIND PERHAPS A SWINE'S HOVEL TO DIE IN!!
CURIOUS. LIFE REMAINS IN THEIR EYES DESPITE THERE DISGRACE-FUL PHYSICAL CONDITION.
THAT IS... SOME-THING...?
IT IS RESOLVE.

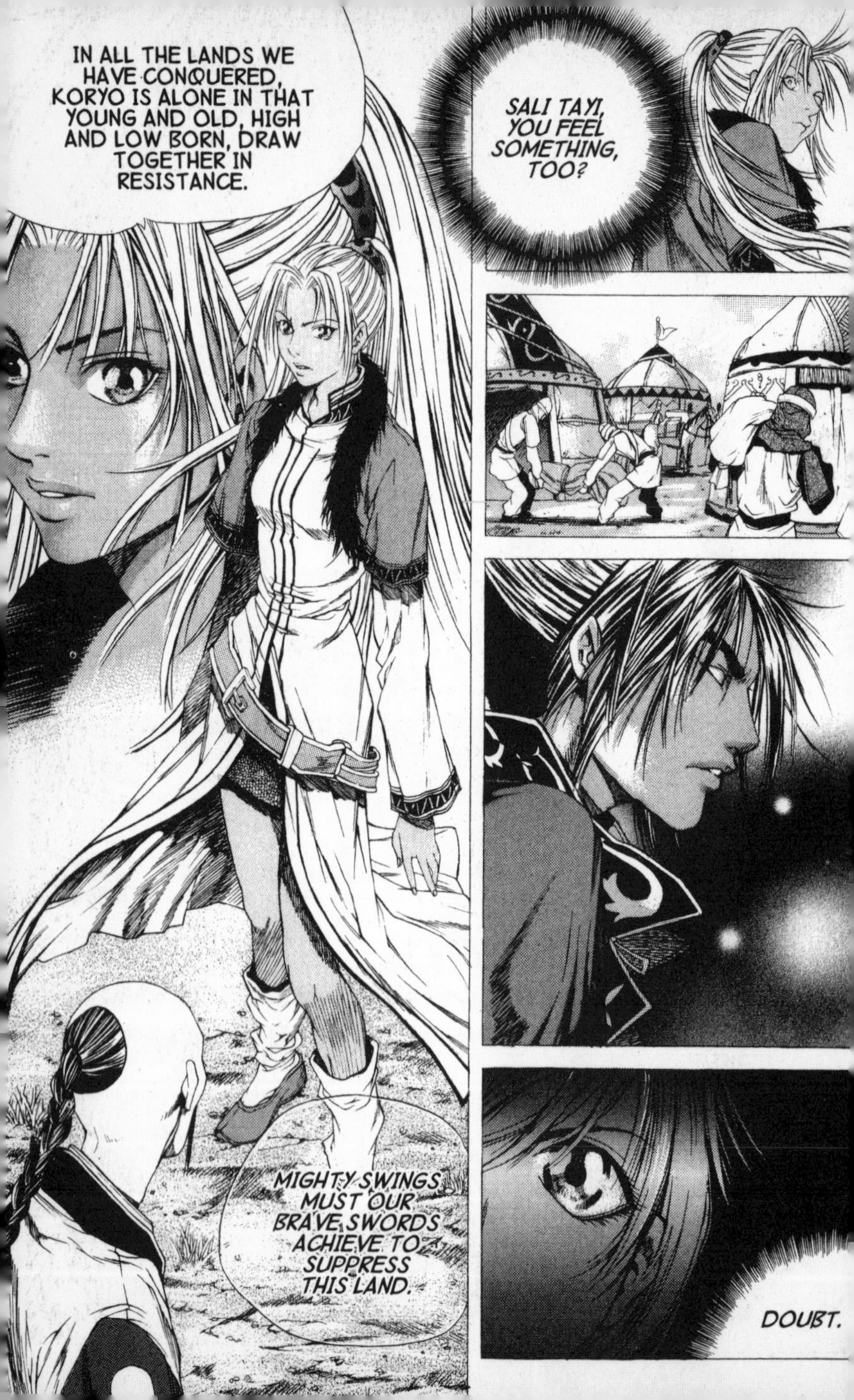
IN ALL THE LANDS WE HAVE CONQUERED, KORYO IS ALONE IN THAT YOUNG AND OLD, HIGH AND LOW BORN, DRAW TOGETHER IN RESISTANCE.
MIGHTY SWINGS MUST OUR BRAVE SWORDS ACHIEVE TO SUPPRESS THIS LAND.
SALI TAYI, YOU FEEL SOMETHING, TOO?
DOUBT.

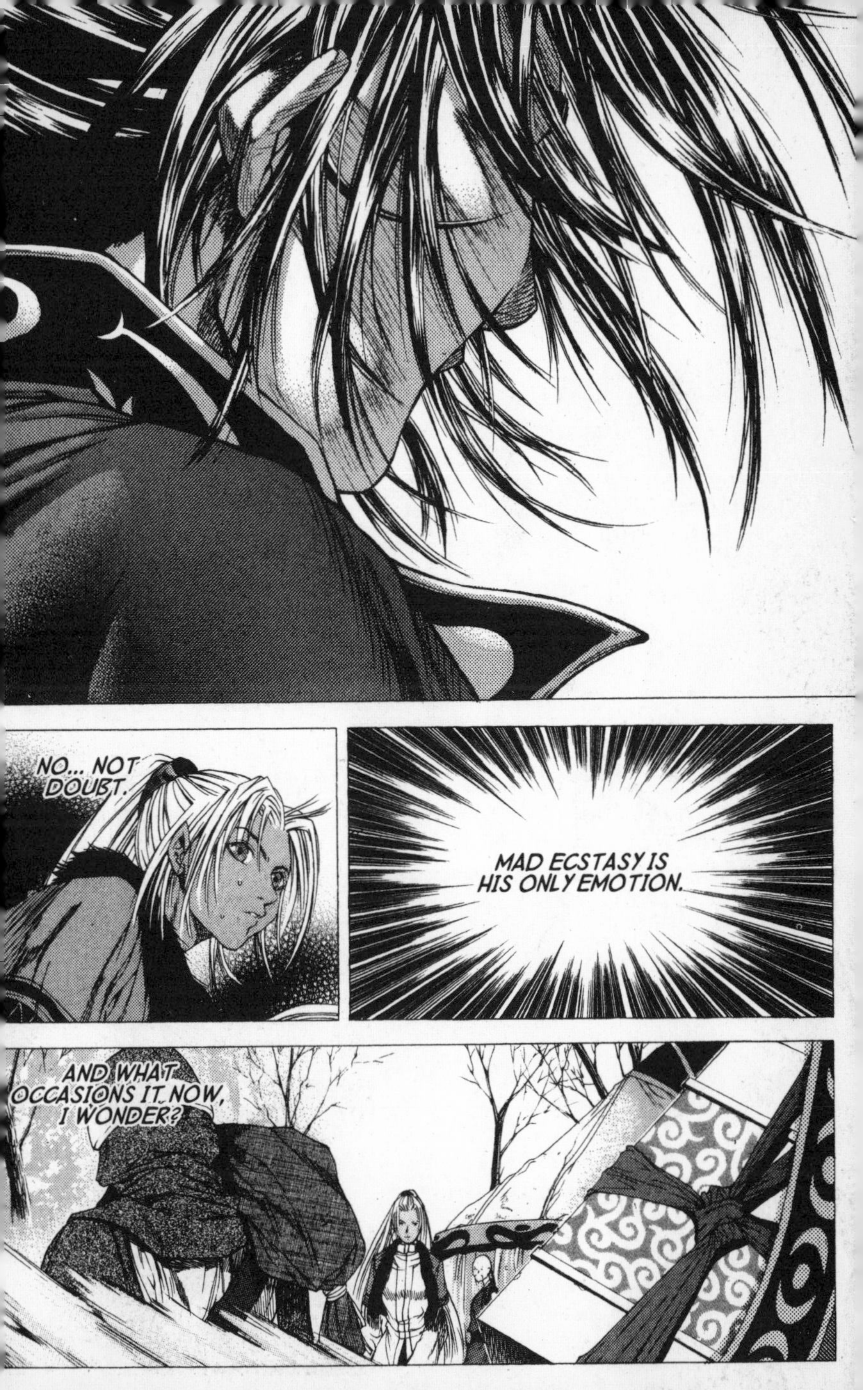
NO... NOT DOUBT.
MAD ECSTASY IS HIS ONLY EMOTION.
AND WHAT OCCASIONS IT NOW, I WONDER?

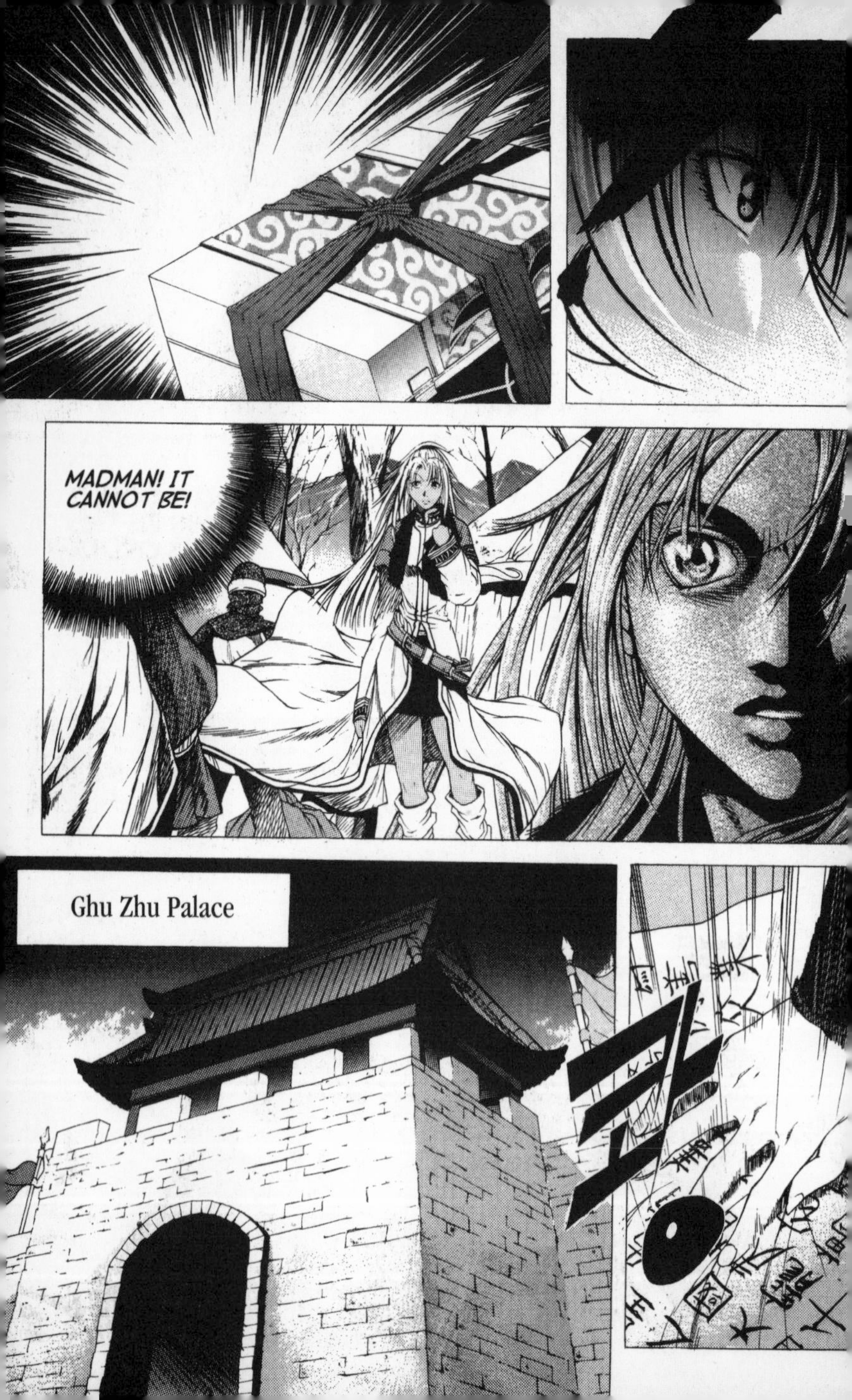
MADMAN! IT CANNOT BE!
Ghu Zhu Palace

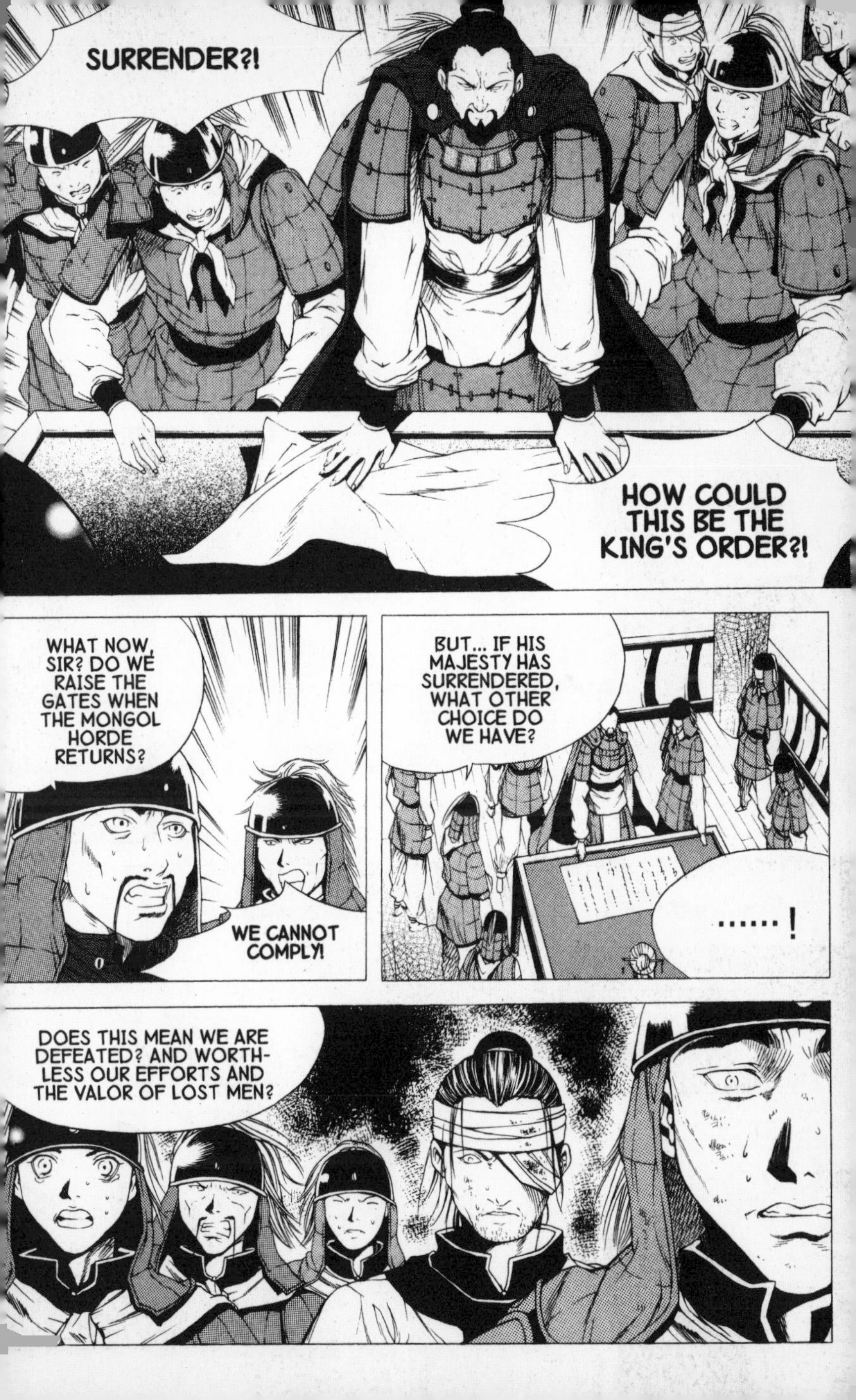
SURRENDER?!
HOW COULD THIS BE THE KING'S ORDER?!
WHAT NOW, SIR? DO WE RAISE THE GATES WHEN THE MONGOL HORDE RETURNS?
WE CANNOT COMPLY!
BUT... IF HIS MAJESTY HAS SURRENDERED, WHAT OTHER CHOICE DO WE HAVE?
......!
DOES THIS MEAN WE ARE DEFEATED? AND WORTHLESS OUR EFFORTS AND THE VALOR OF LOST MEN?

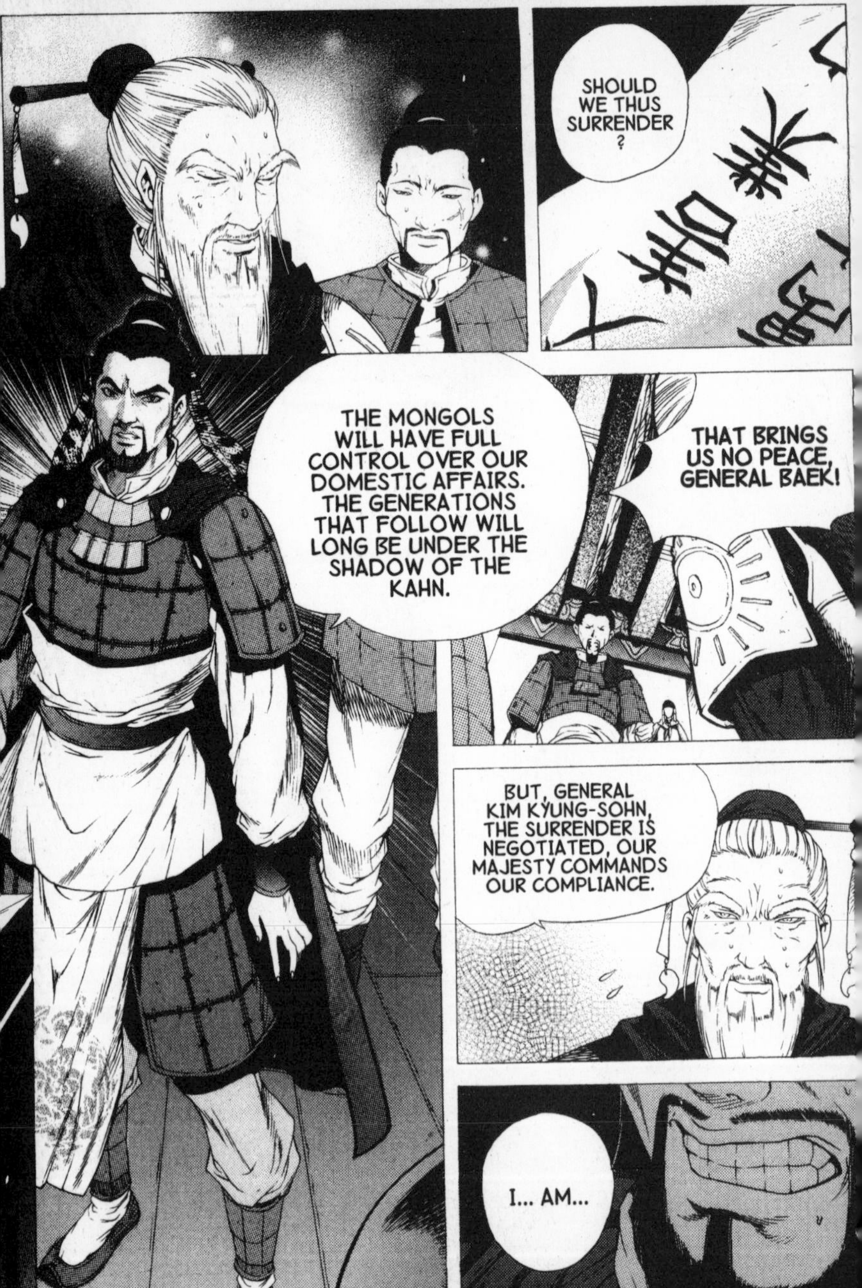
SHOULD WE THUS SURRENDER?
THE MONGOLS WILL HAVE FULL CONTROL OVER OUR DOMESTIC AFFAIRS. THE GENERATIONS THAT FOLLOW WILL LONG BE UNDER THE SHADOW OF THE KAHN.
THAT BRINGS US NO PEACE, GENERAL BAEK!
BUT, GENERAL KIM KYUNG-SOHN, THE SURRENDER IS NEGOTIATED, OUR MAJESTY COMMANDS OUR COMPLIANCE.
I... AM...

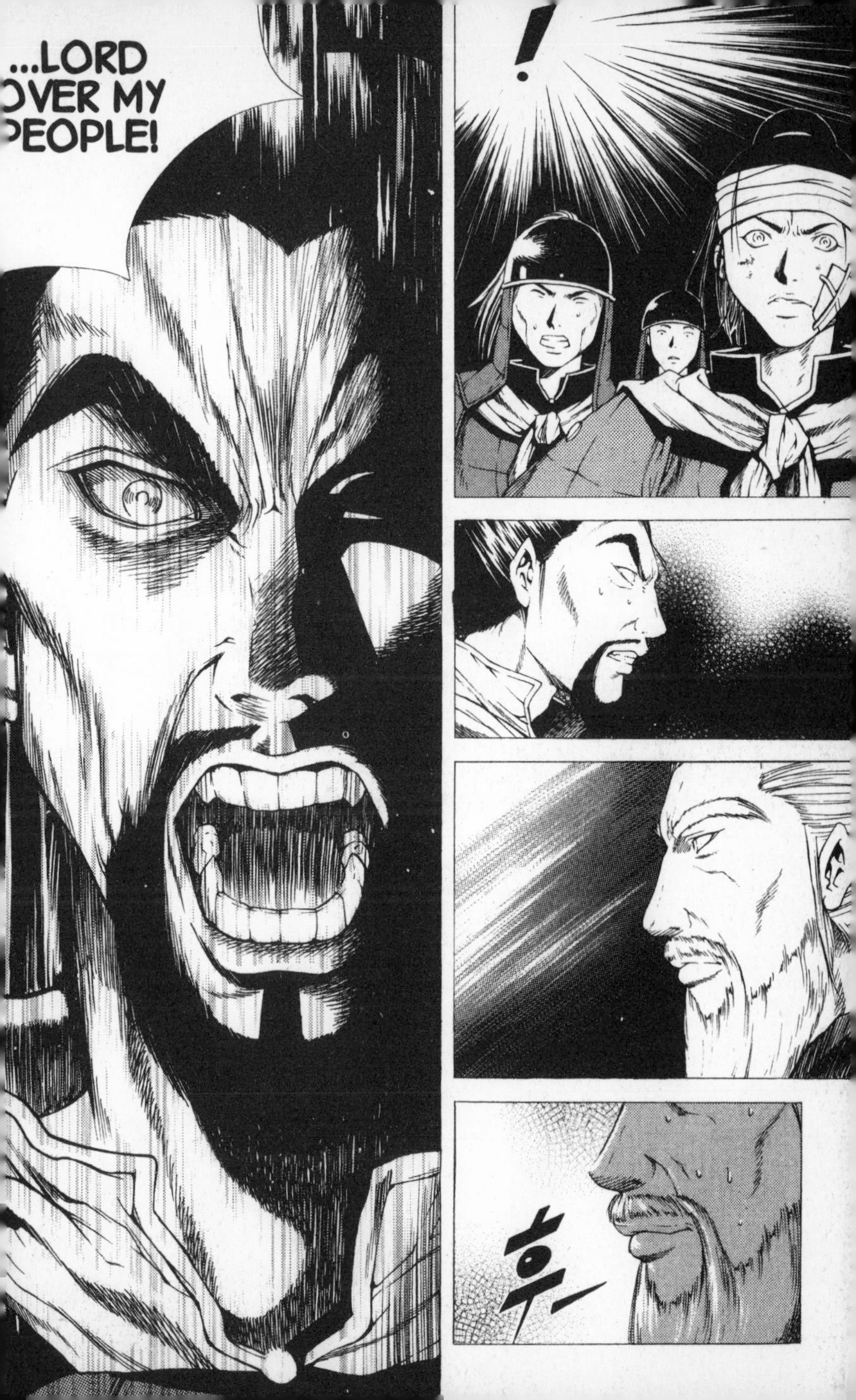
...LORD OVER MY PEOPLE!
!

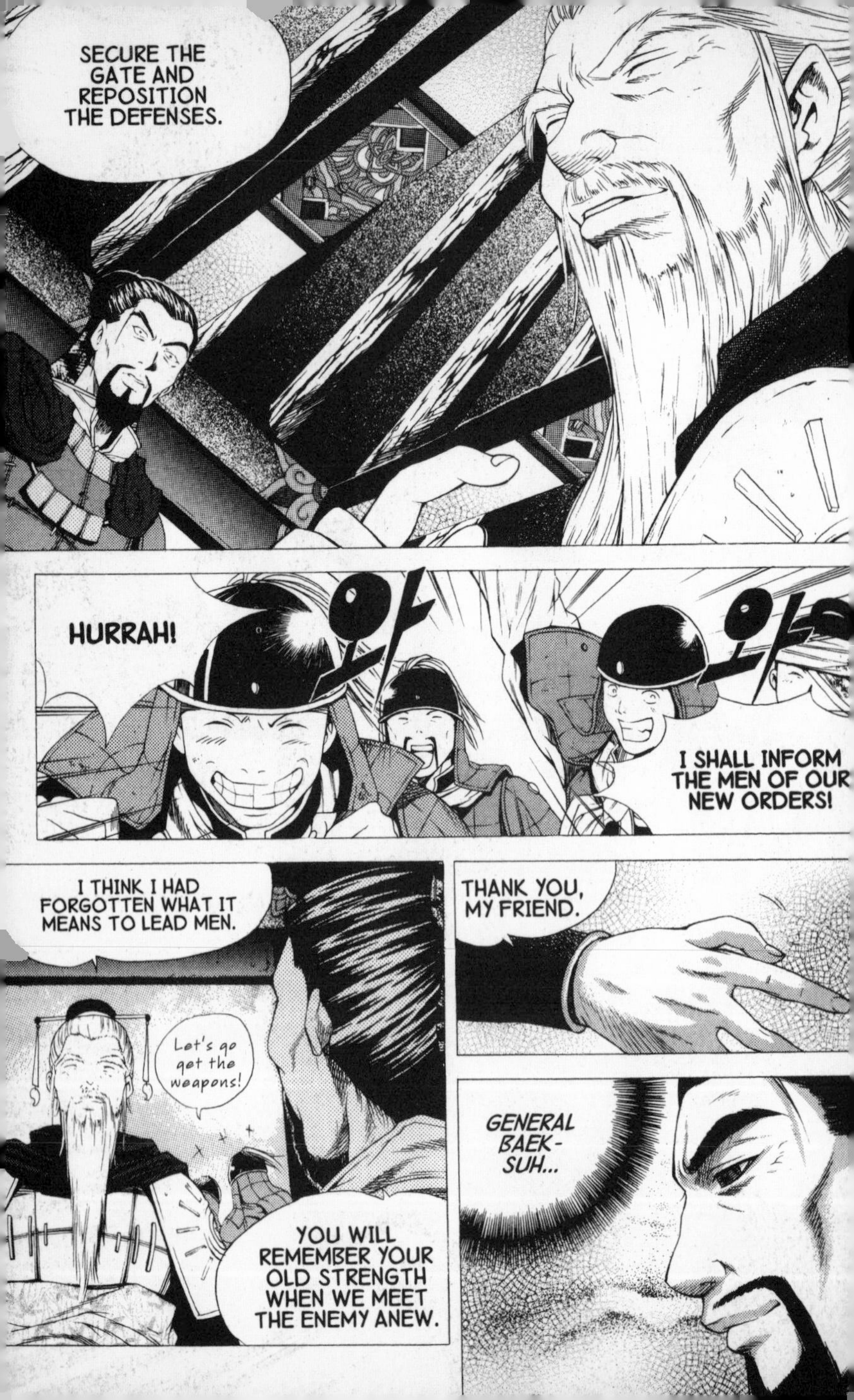
SECURE THE GATE AND REPOSITION THE DEFENSES.
HURRAH!
I SHALL INFORM THE MEN OF OUR NEW ORDERS!
I THINK I HAD FORGOTTEN WHAT IT MEANS TO LEAD MEN.
Let's go get the weapons!
YOU WILL REMEMBER YOUR OLD STRENGTH WHEN WE MEET THE ENEMY ANEW.
THANK YOU, MY FRIEND.
GENERAL BAEK-SUH...

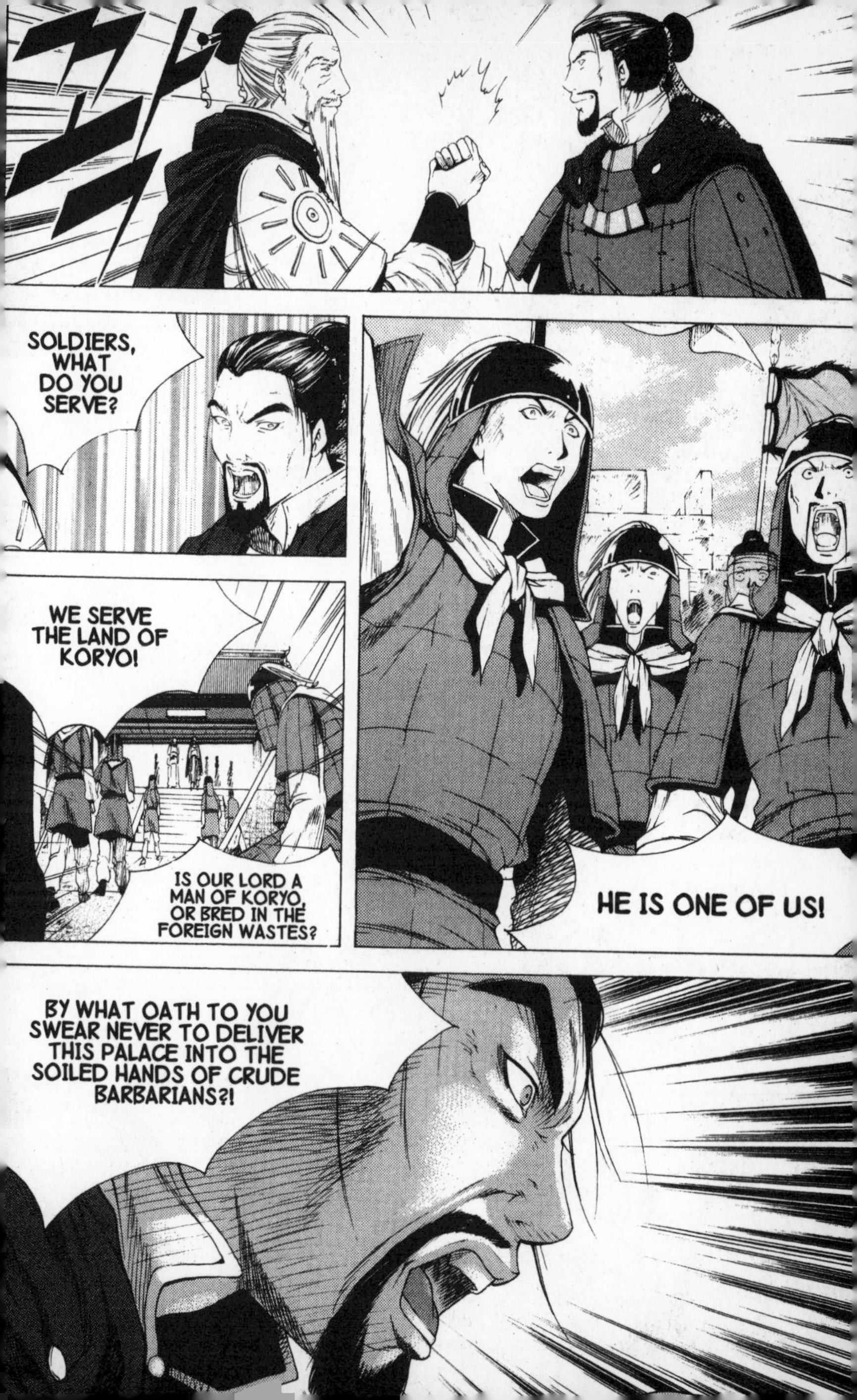
SOLDIERS, WHAT DO YOU SERVE?
WE SERVE THE LAND OF KORYO!
IS OUR LORD A MAN OF KORYO, OR BRED IN THE FOREIGN WASTES?
HE IS ONE OF US!
BY WHAT OATH TO YOU SWEAR NEVER TO DELIVER THIS PALACE INTO THE SOILED HANDS OF CRUDE BARBARIANS?!

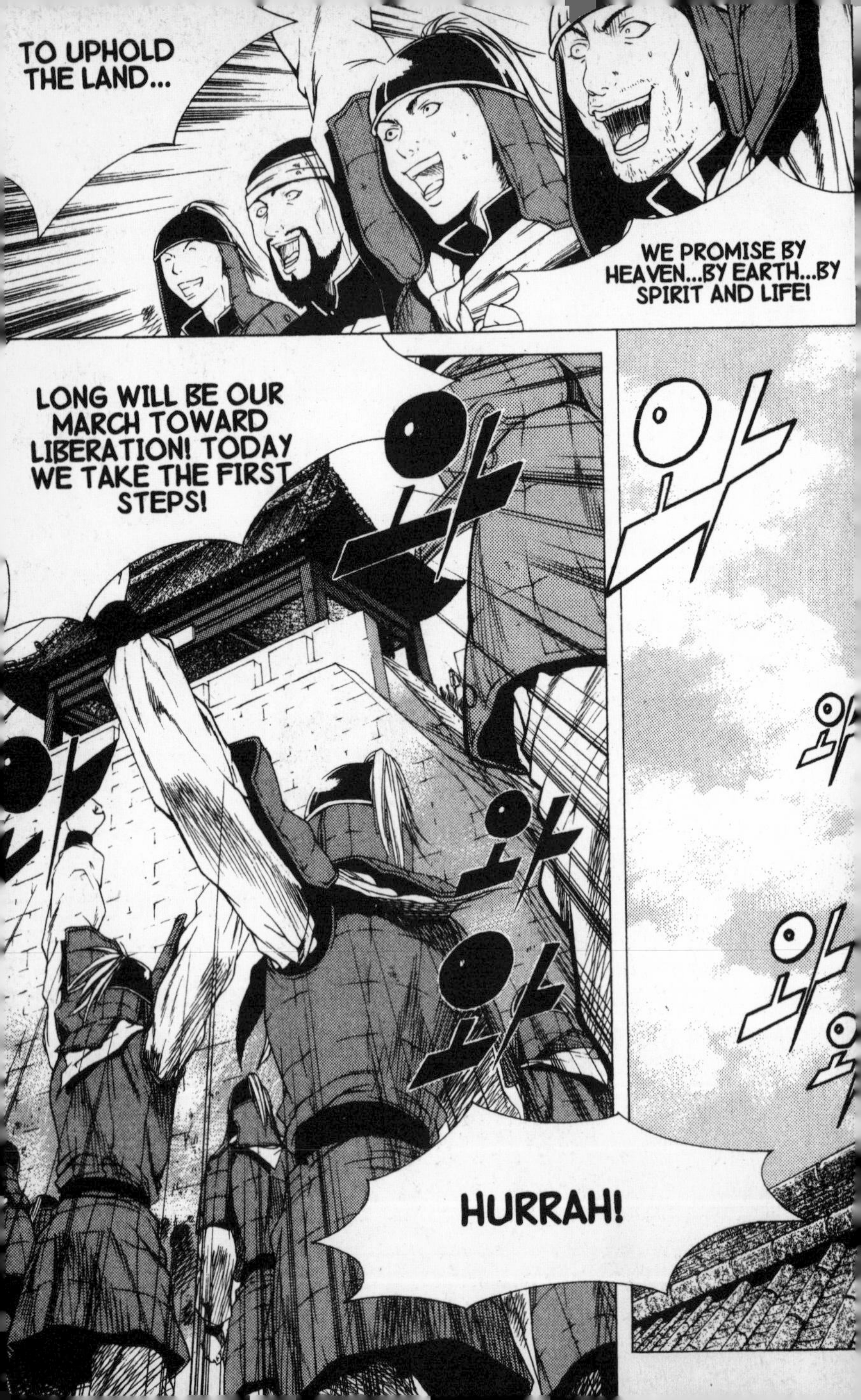
TO UPHOLD THE LAND...
WE PROMISE BY HEAVEN...BY EARTH...BY SPIRIT AND LIFE!
LONG WILL BE OUR MARCH TOWARD LIBERATION! TODAY WE TAKE THE FIRST STEPS!
HURRAH!

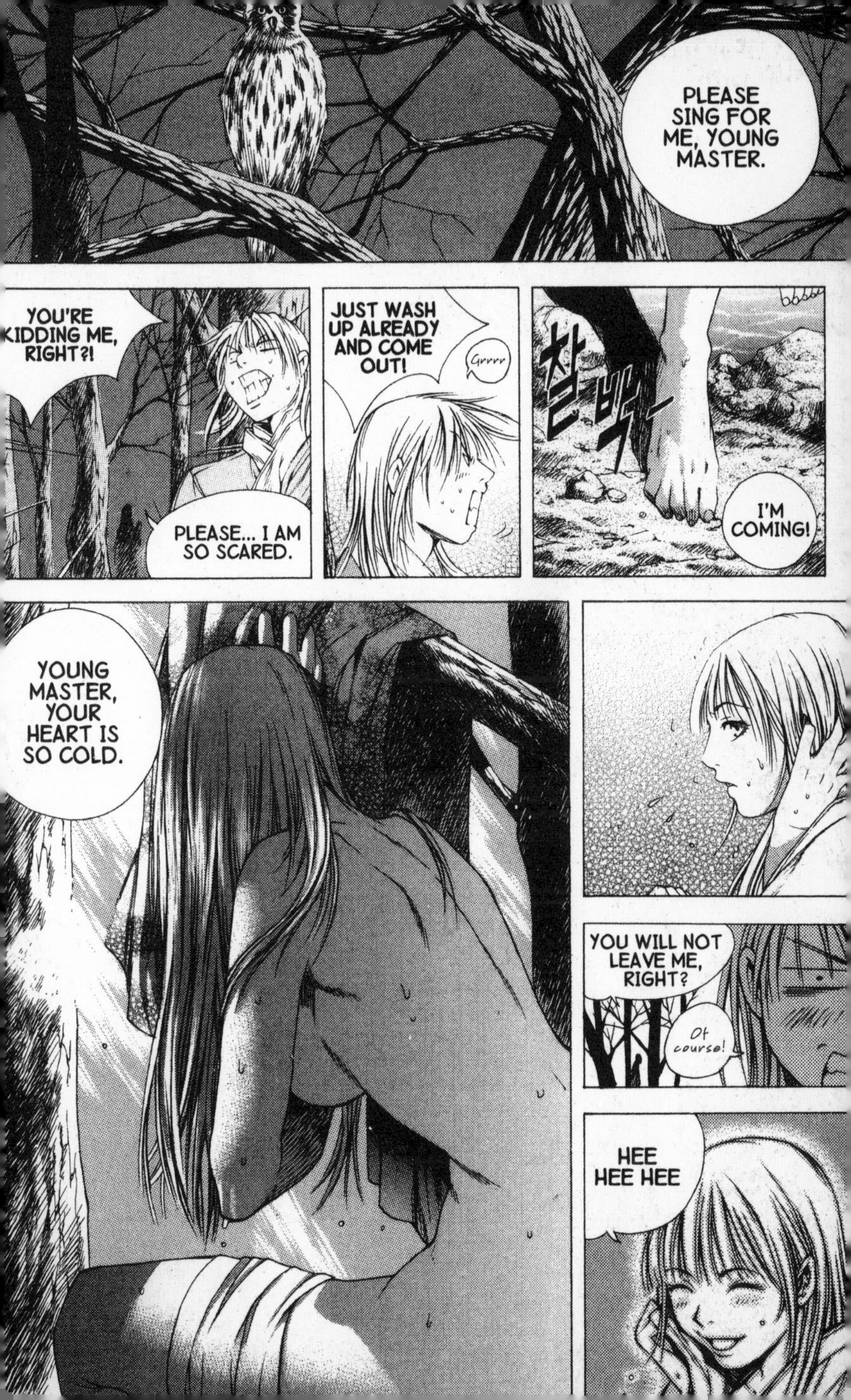
PLEASE SING FOR ME, YOUNG MASTER.
YOU'RE KIDDING ME, RIGHT?!
PLEASE... I AM SO SCARED.
JUST WASH UP ALREADY AND COME OUT!
Grrrr
찰박
I'M COMING!
YOUNG MASTER, YOUR HEART IS SO COLD.
YOU WILL NOT LEAVE ME, RIGHT?
Of course!
HEE HEE HEE

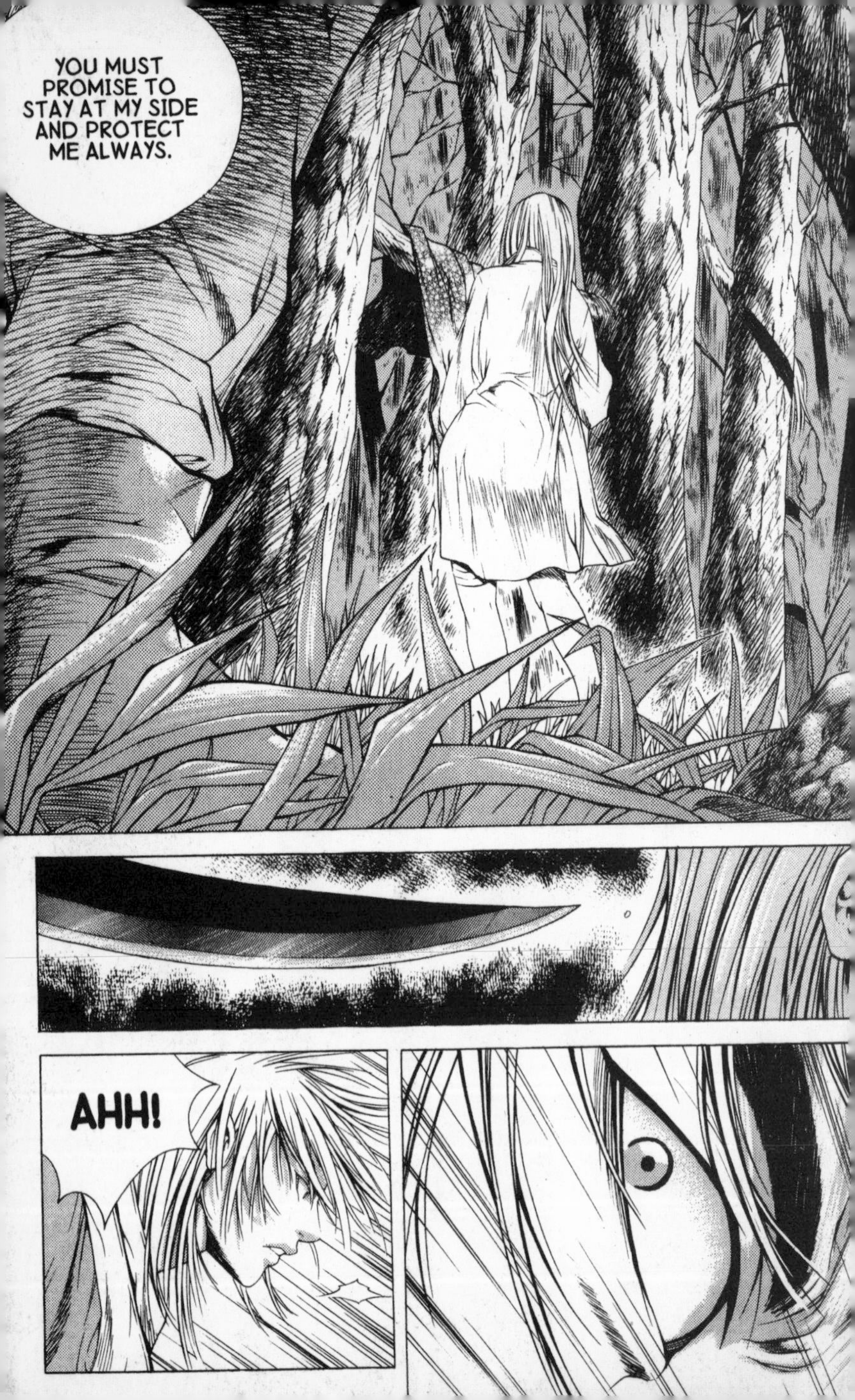
YOU MUST PROMISE TO STAY AT MY SIDE AND PROTECT ME ALWAYS.
AHH!

CHUNG-WAR! WHA-- WHAT HAPPENED?

YOUNG MASTER...

sniff

I AM SORRY, YOUNG MASTER... THEY TOOK ME BY SURPRISE.

YOUR ESCAPE ENDS HERE, RUNT.

HEH HEH.

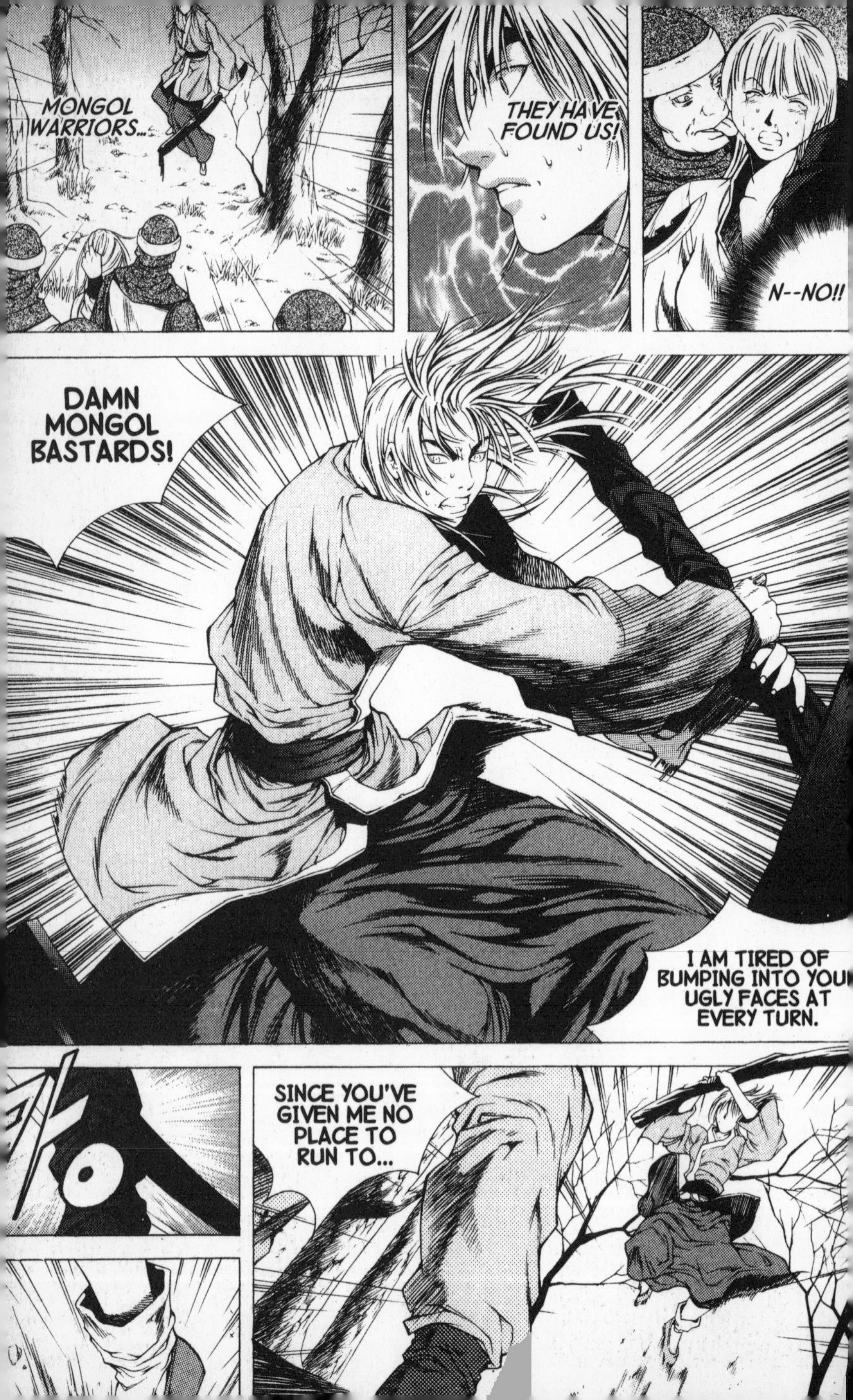
MONGOL WARRIORS...
THEY HAVE FOUND US!
N--NO!!
DAMN MONGOL BASTARDS!
I AM TIRED OF BUMPING INTO YOUR UGLY FACES AT EVERY TURN.
SINCE YOU'VE GIVEN ME NO PLACE TO RUN TO...

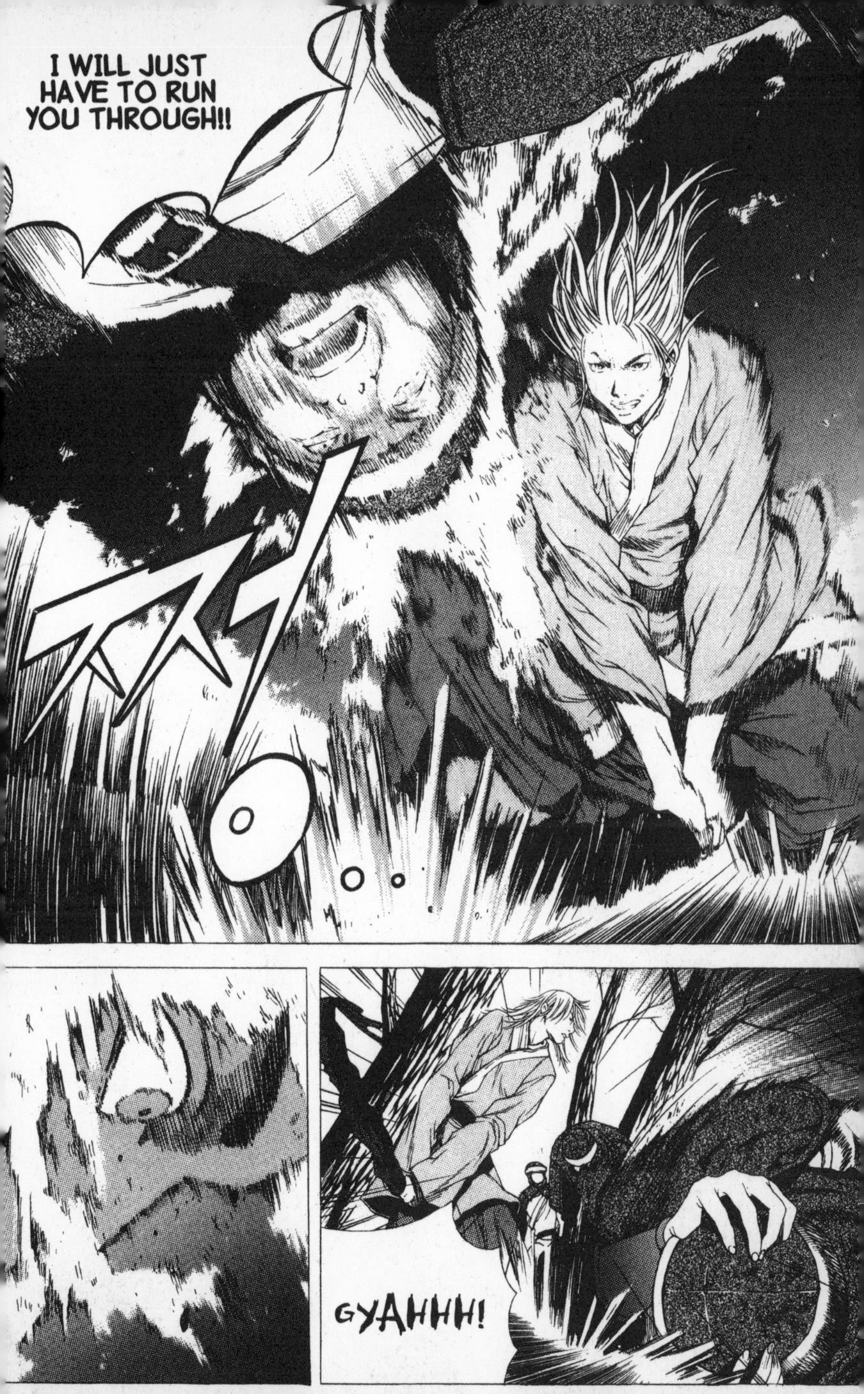
I WILL JUST HAVE TO RUN YOU THROUGH!!
GYAHHH!

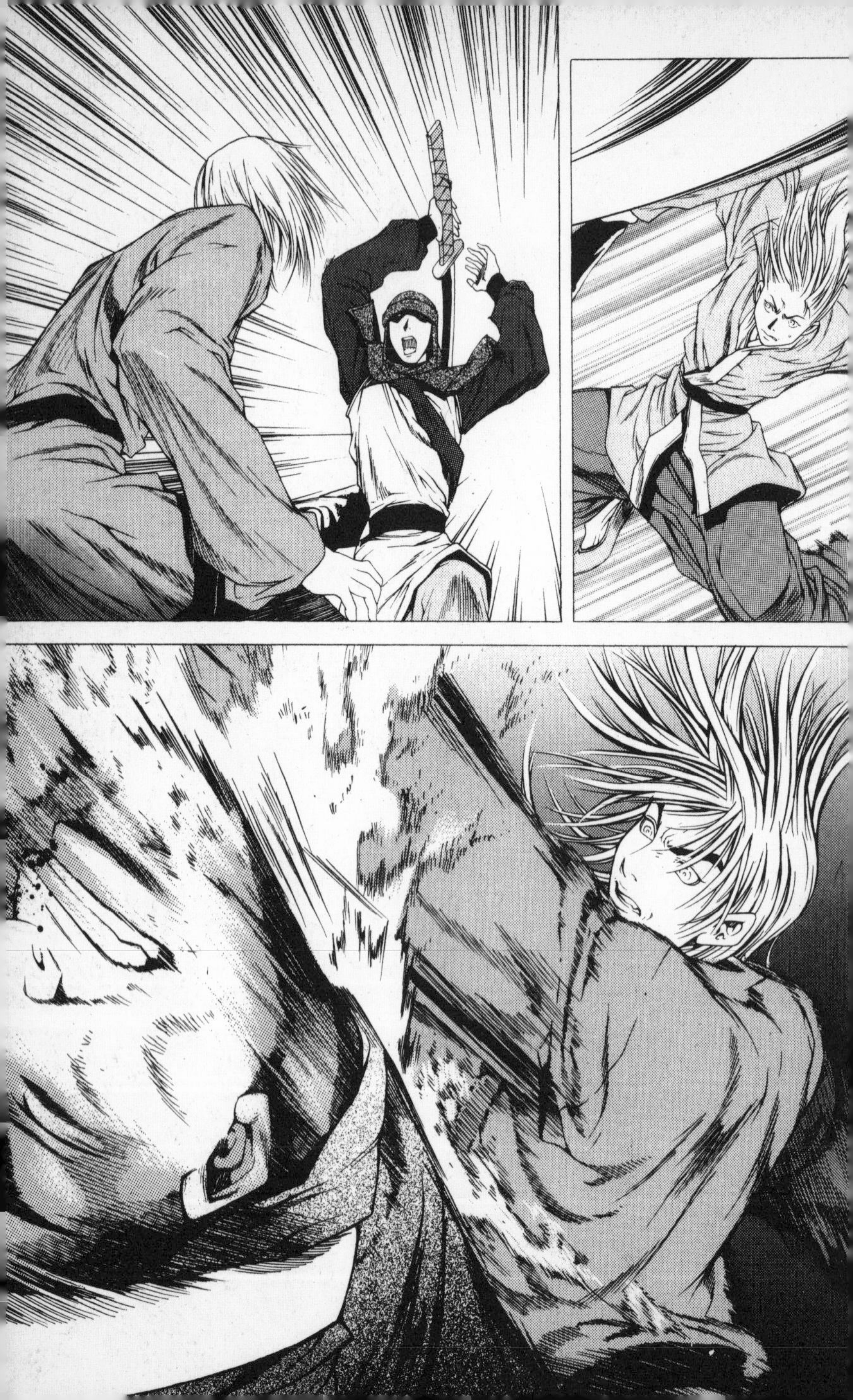

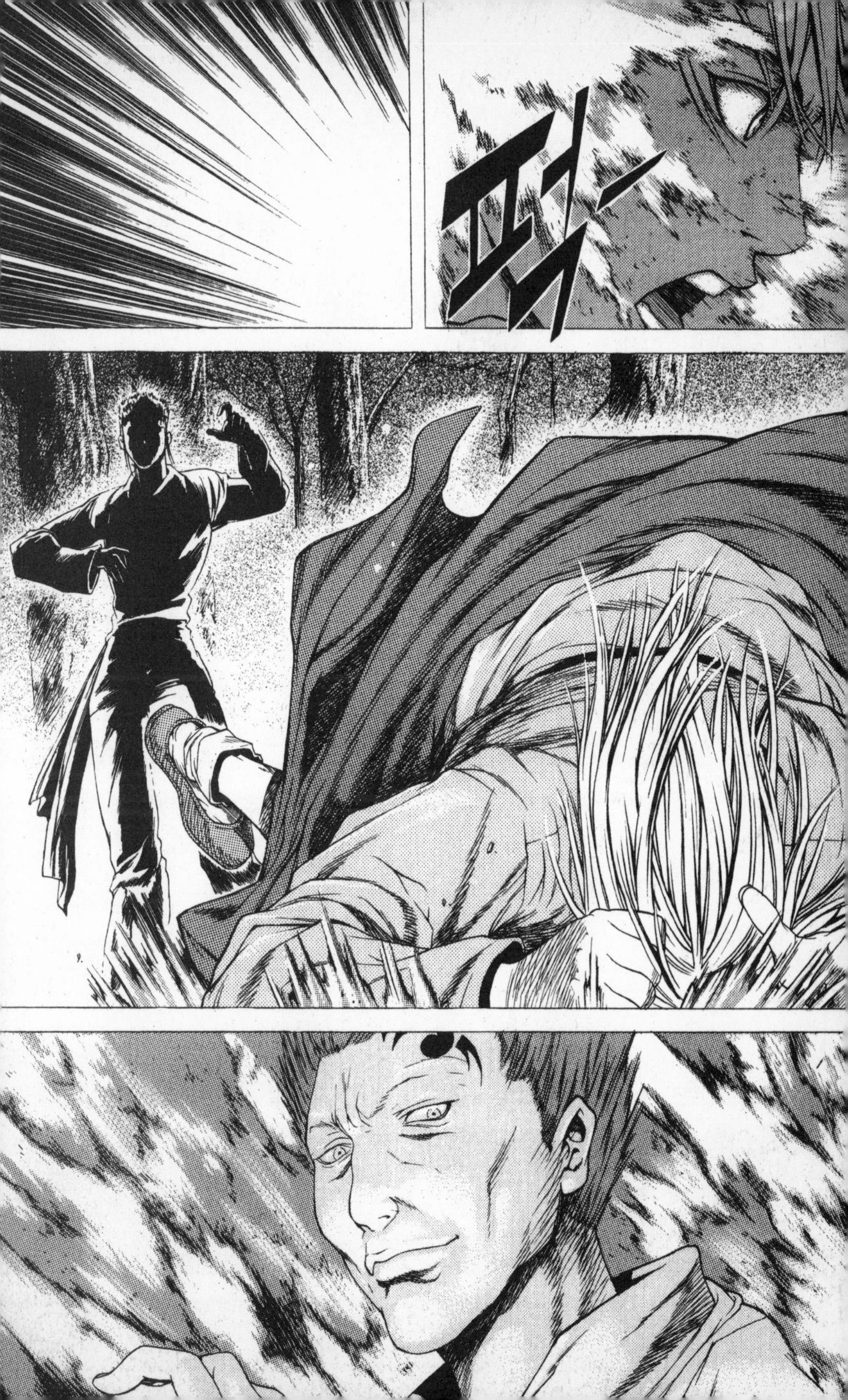

エイー

YOUNG MASTER!

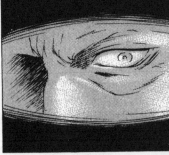

Chapter 23
Encounter

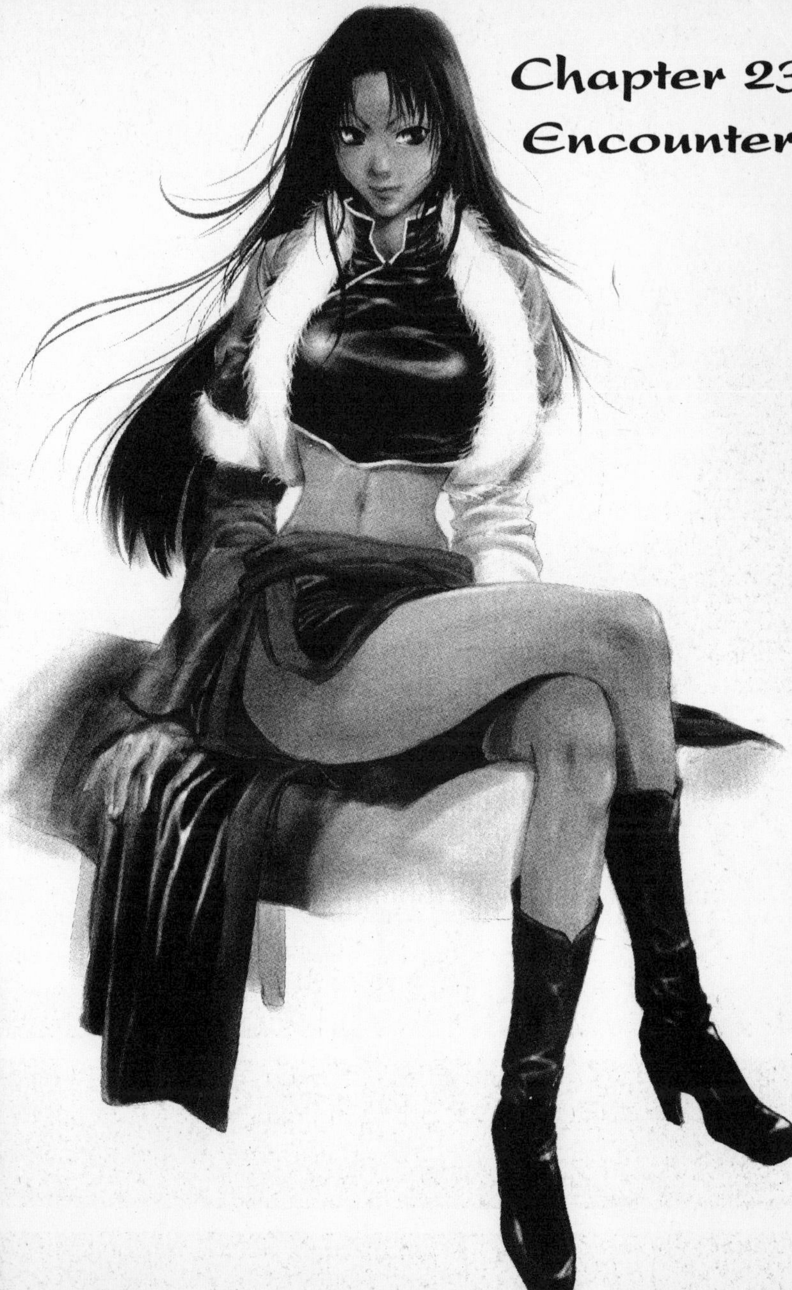

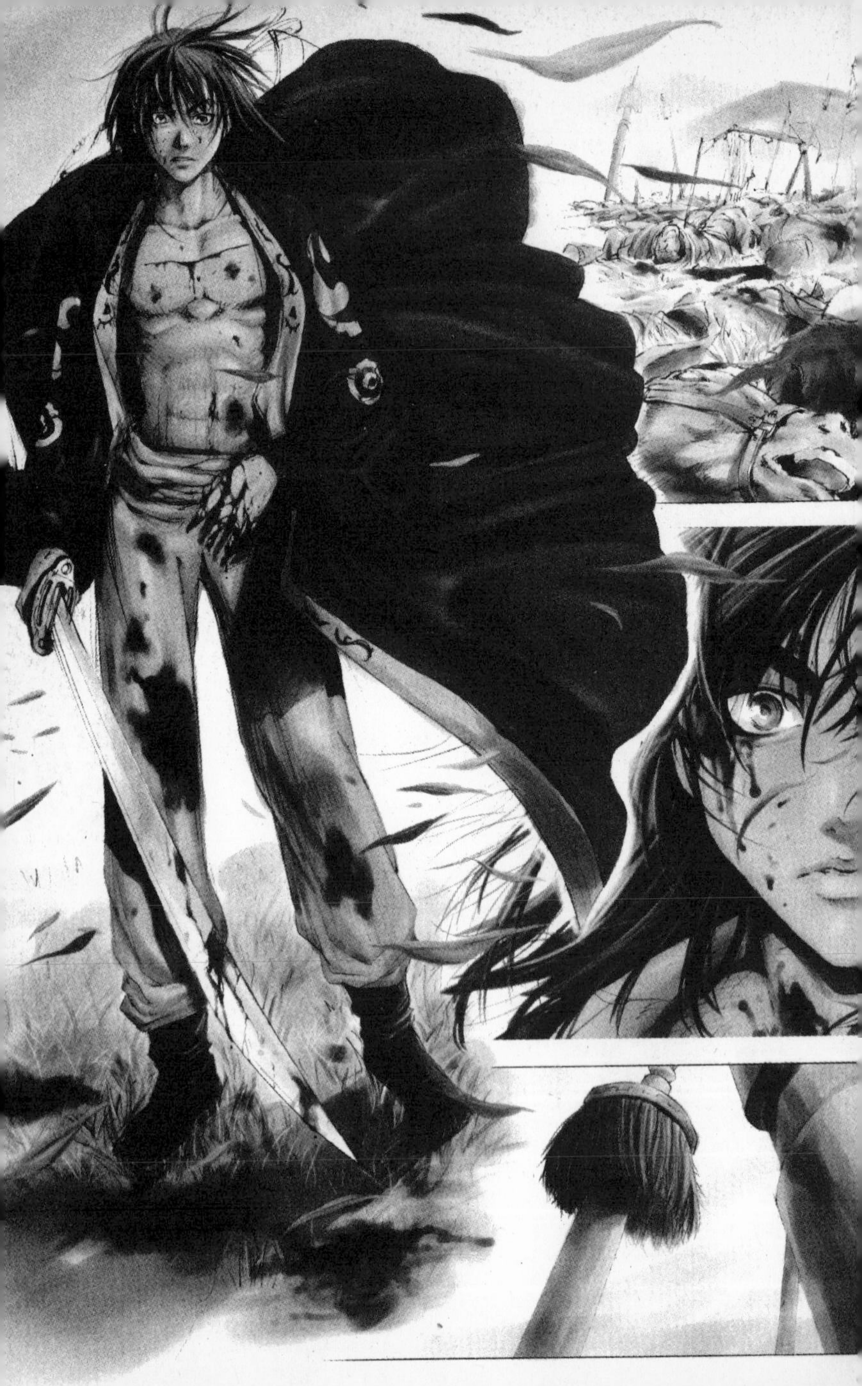

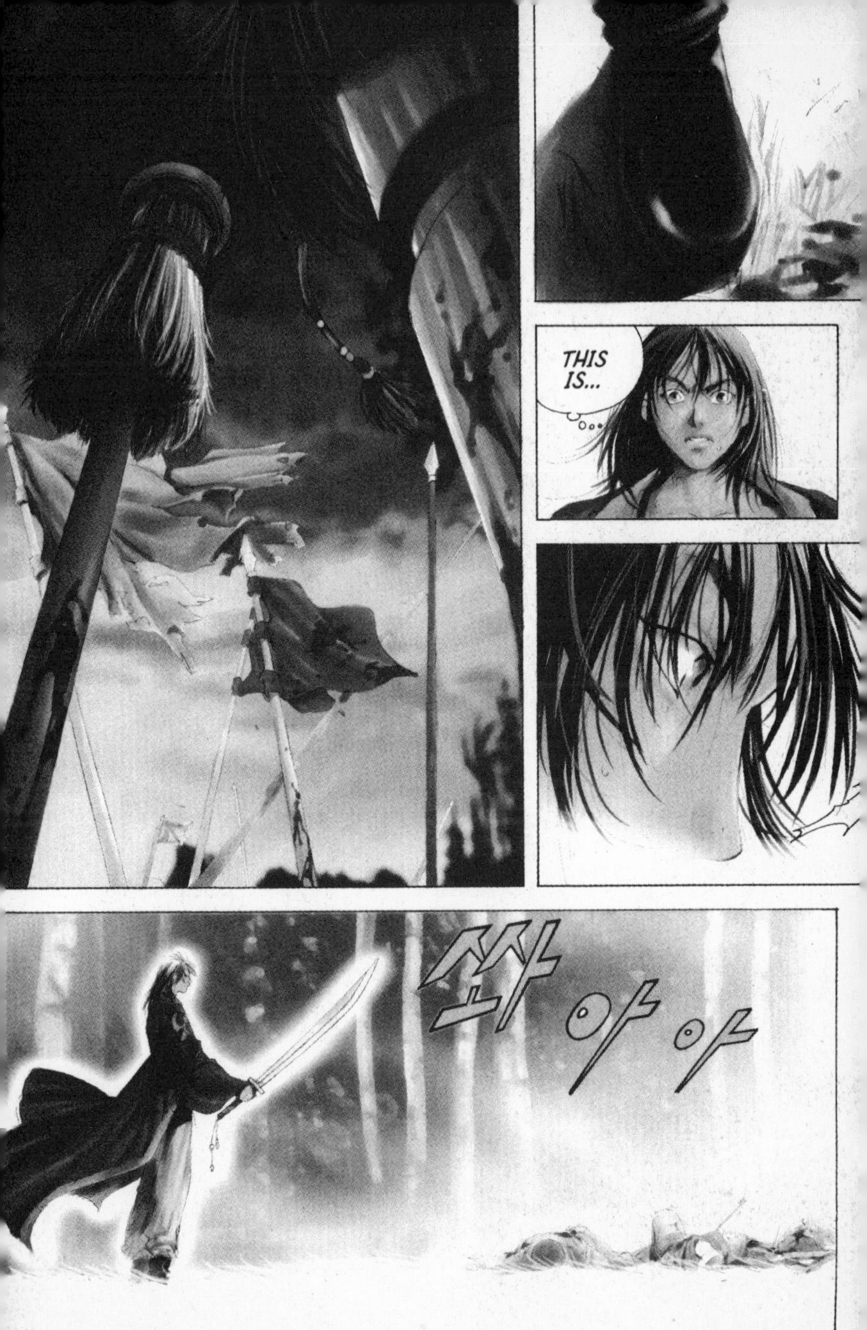
THIS IS...
쏴아아

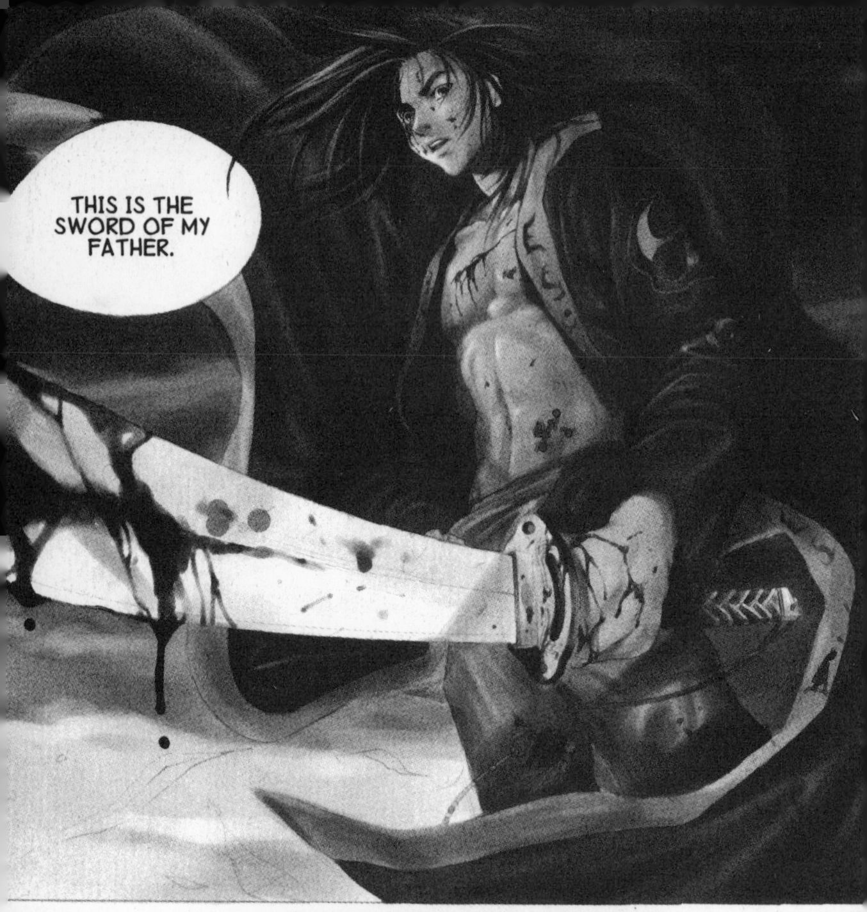
THIS IS THE SWORD OF MY FATHER.
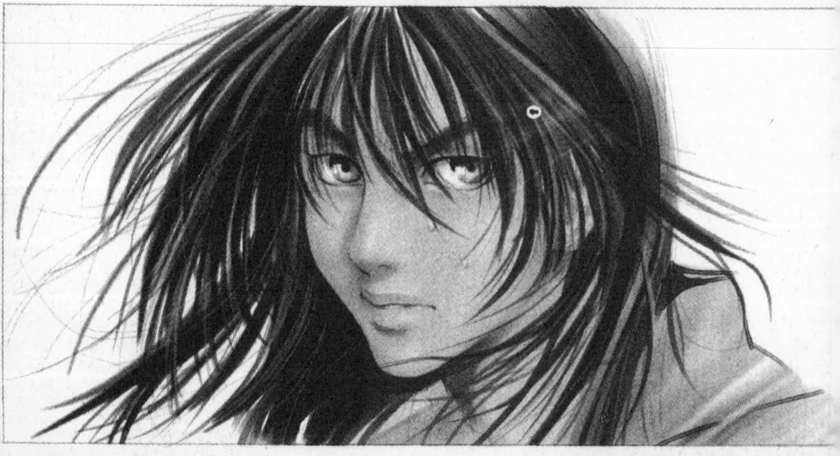

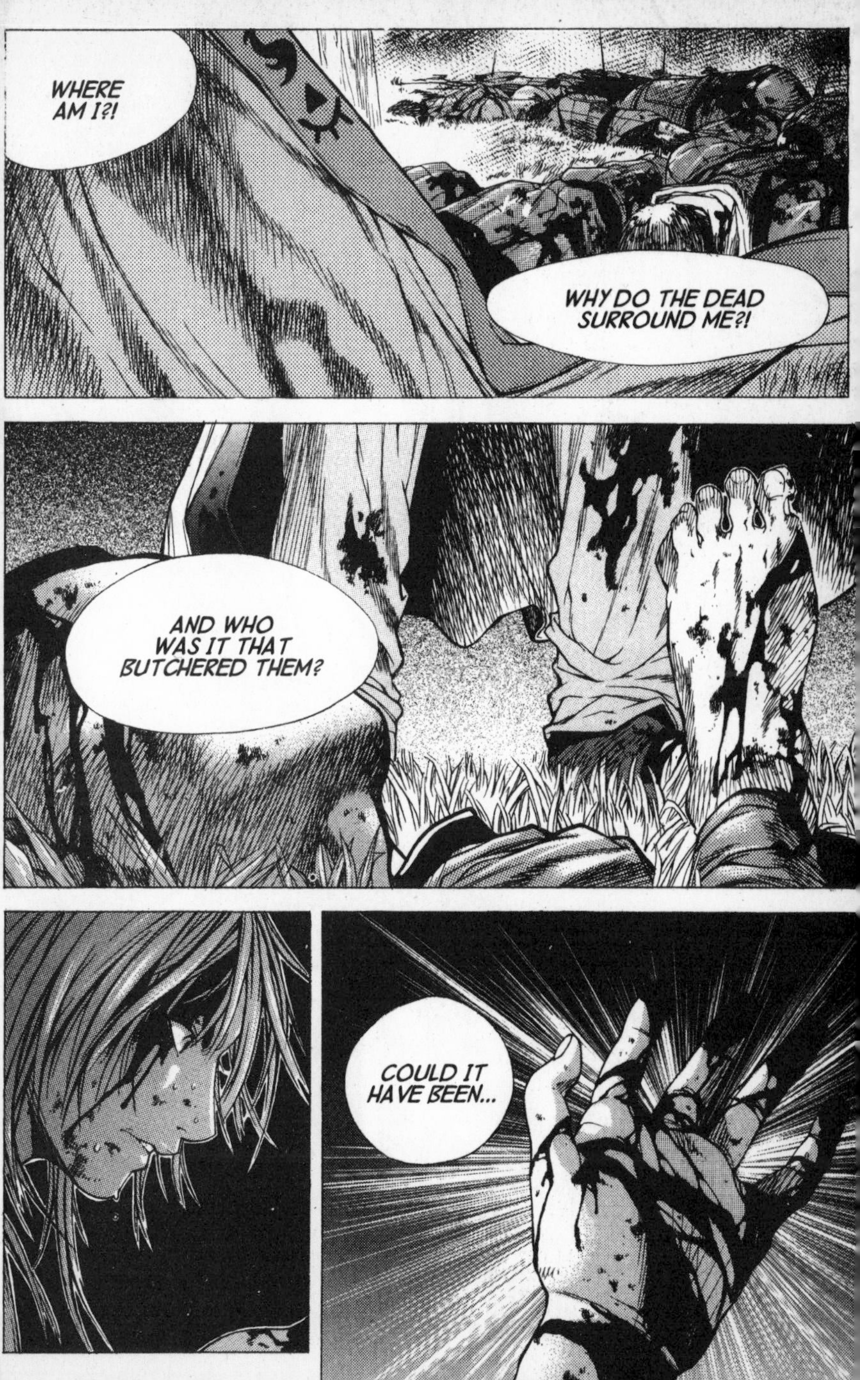
WHERE AM I?!
WHY DO THE DEAD SURROUND ME?!
AND WHO WAS IT THAT BUTCHERED THEM?
COULD IT HAVE BEEN...

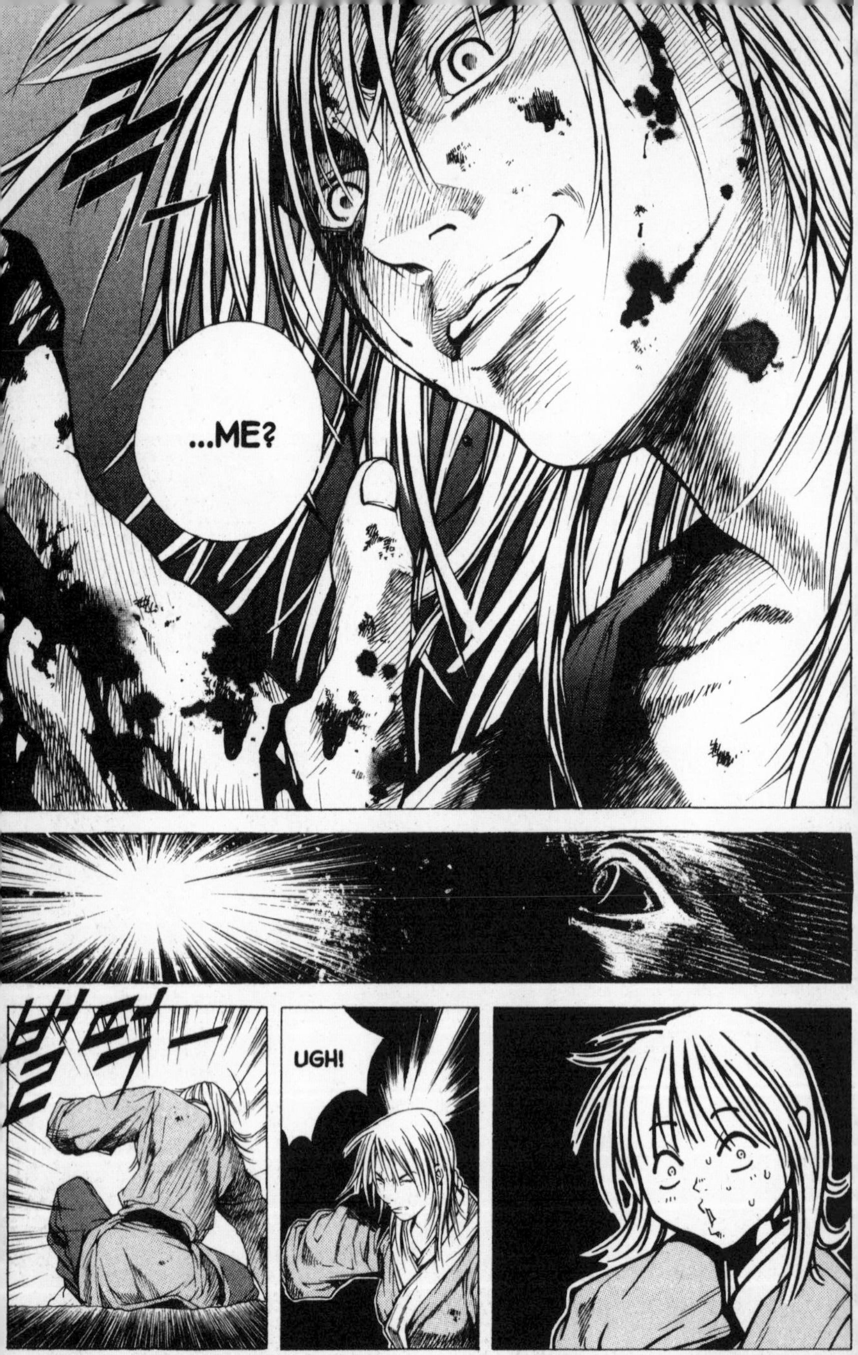
...ME?
벌떡
UGH!

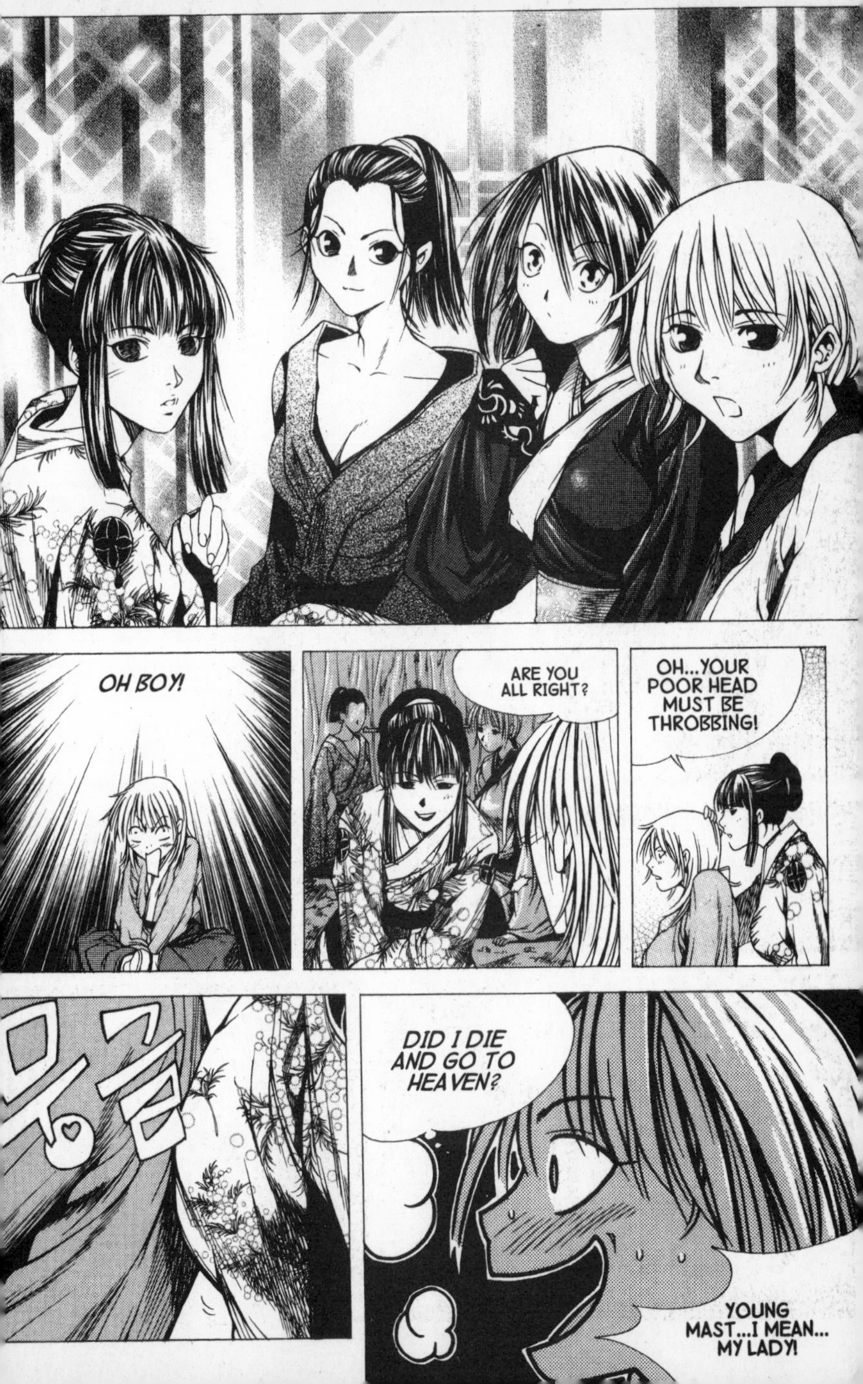
OH BOY!
ARE YOU ALL RIGHT?
OH...YOUR POOR HEAD MUST BE THROBBING!
DID I DIE AND GO TO HEAVEN?
YOUNG MAST...I MEAN... MY LADY!

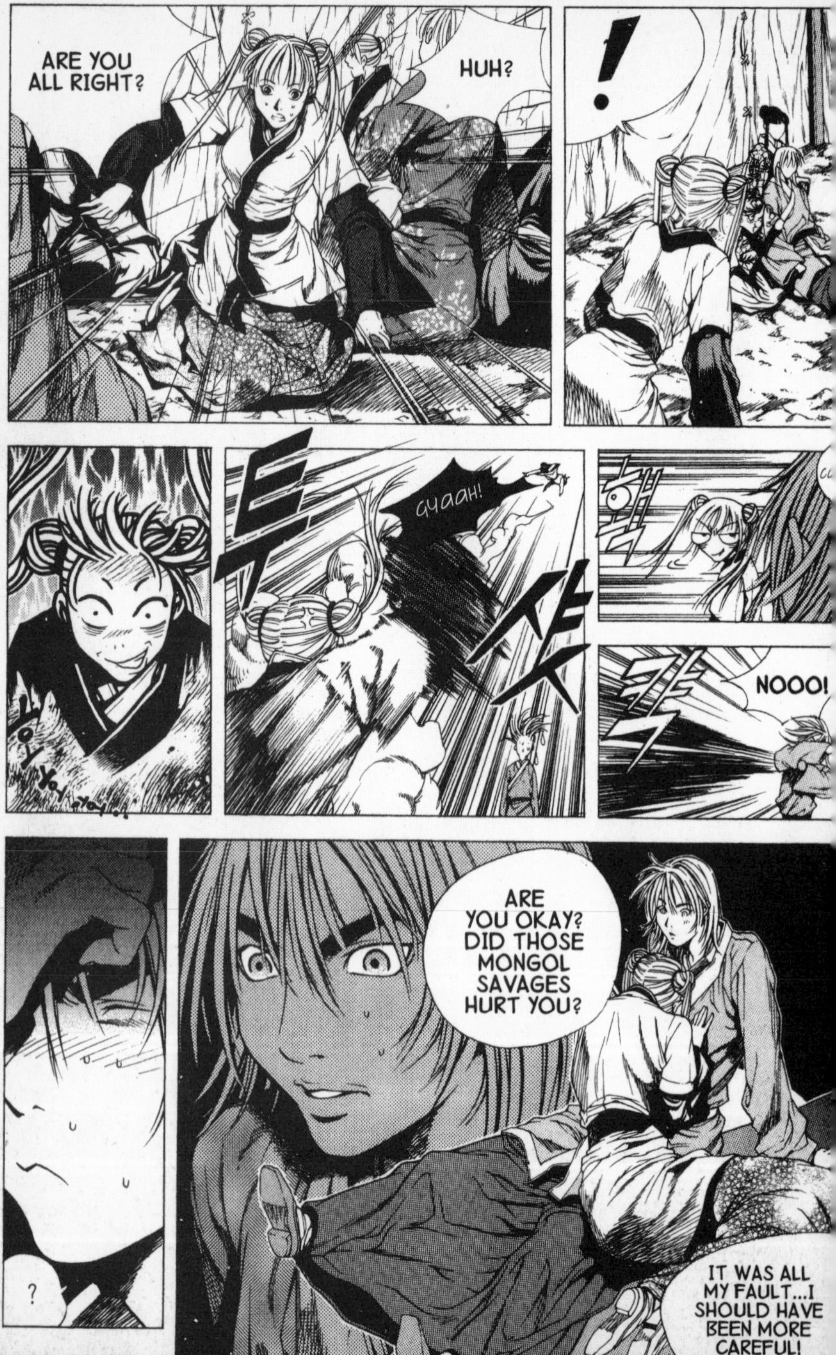
ARE YOU ALL RIGHT?
HUH?
!
GYAAH!
NOOO!
?
ARE YOU OKAY? DID THOSE MONGOL SAVAGES HURT YOU?
IT WAS ALL MY FAULT...I SHOULD HAVE BEEN MORE CAREFUL!

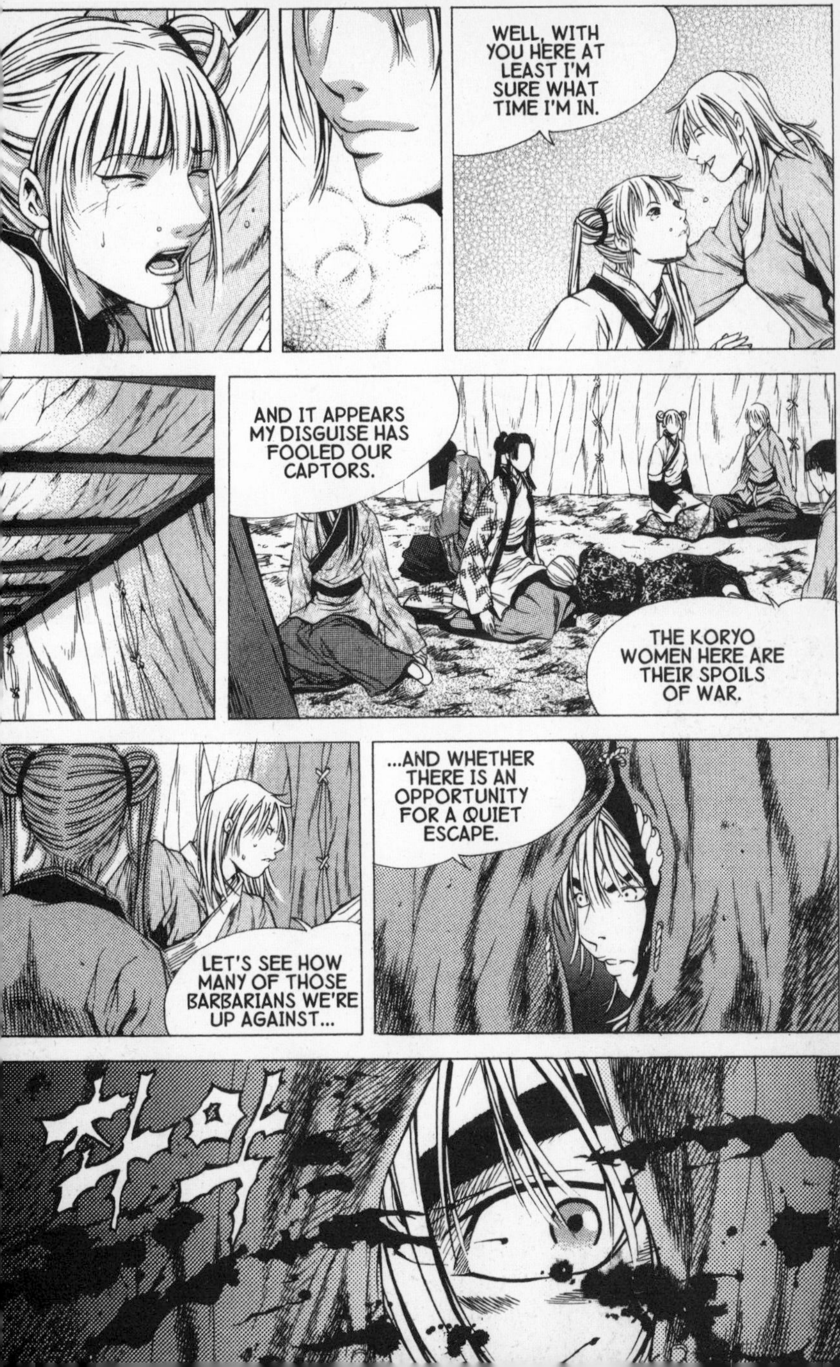
WELL, WITH YOU HERE AT LEAST I'M SURE WHAT TIME I'M IN.
AND IT APPEARS MY DISGUISE HAS FOOLED OUR CAPTORS.
THE KORYO WOMEN HERE ARE THEIR SPOILS OF WAR.
LET'S SEE HOW MANY OF THOSE BARBARIANS WE'RE UP AGAINST...
...AND WHETHER THERE IS AN OPPORTUNITY FOR A QUIET ESCAPE.

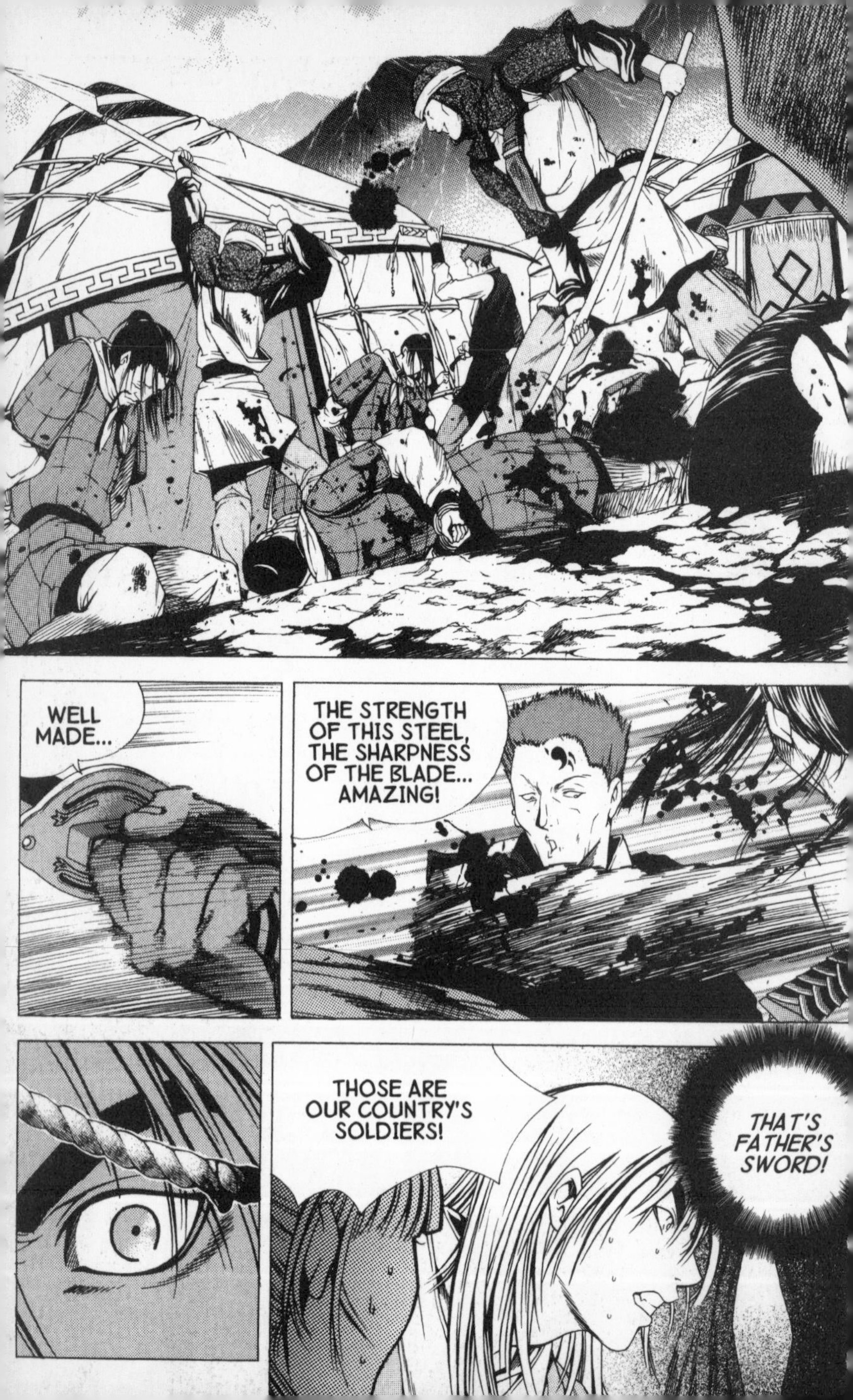
WELL MADE...
THE STRENGTH OF THIS STEEL, THE SHARPNESS OF THE BLADE... AMAZING!
THOSE ARE OUR COUNTRY'S SOLDIERS!
THAT'S FATHER'S SWORD!

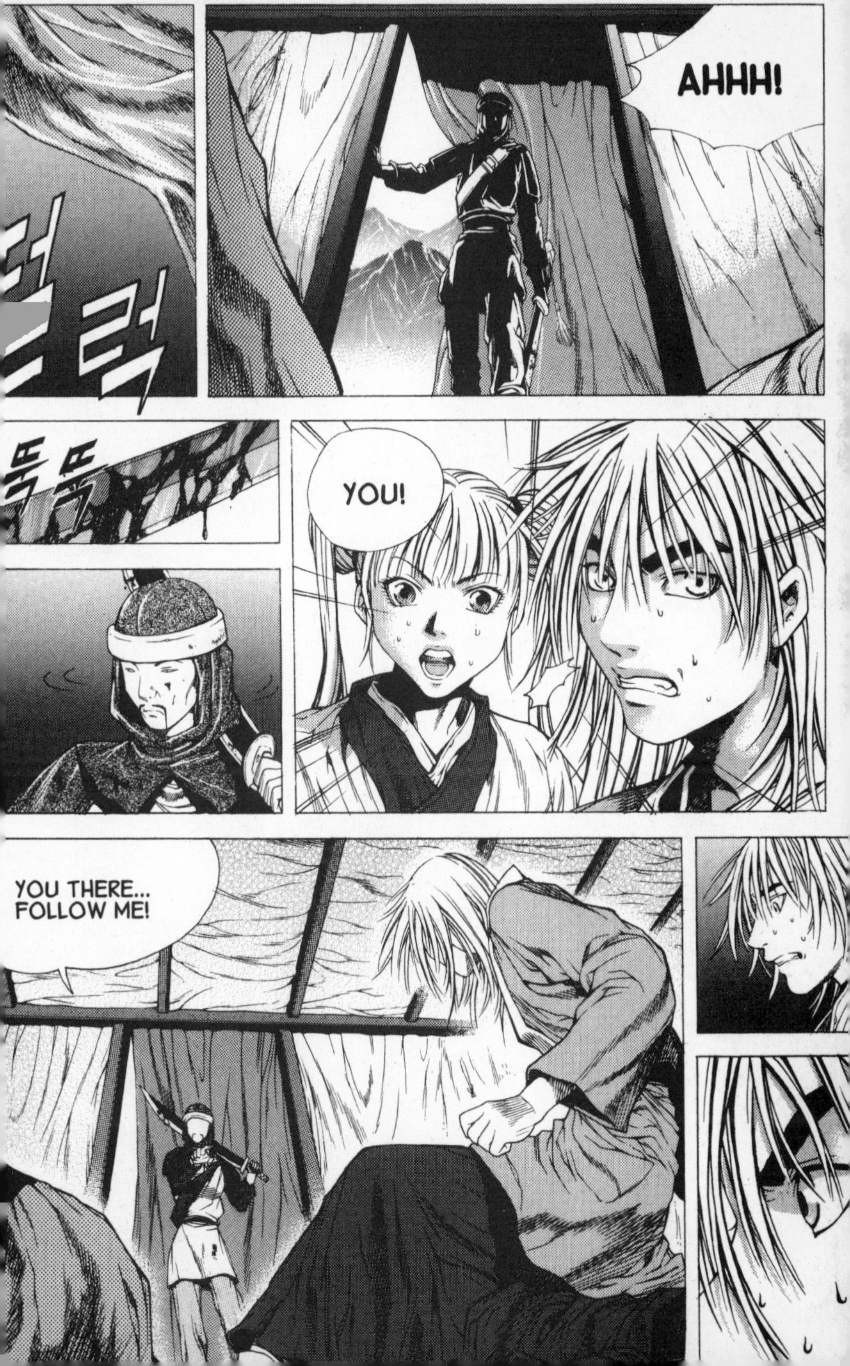
AHHH!
YOU!
YOU THERE... FOLLOW ME!

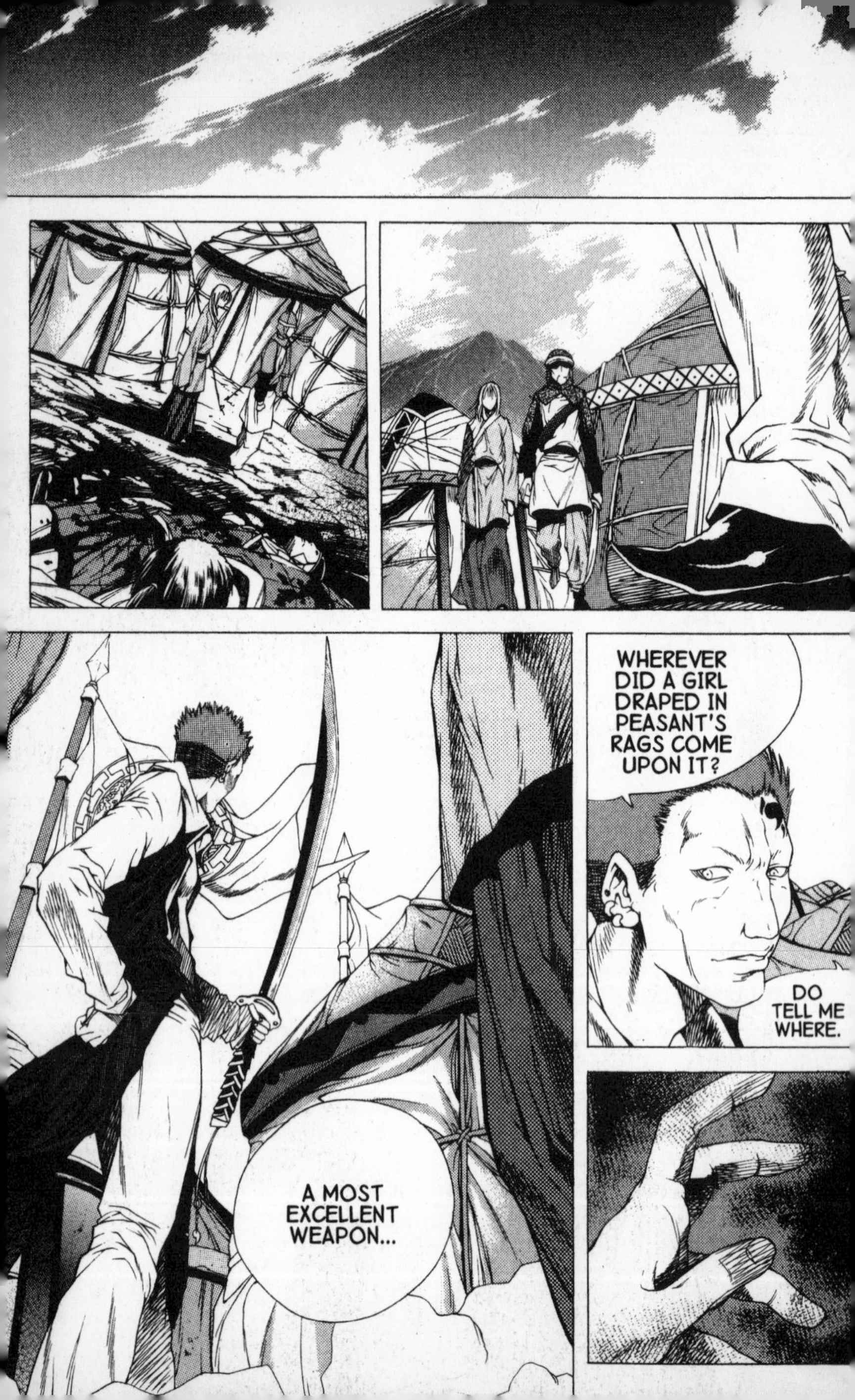
A MOST EXCELLENT WEAPON...
WHEREVER DID A GIRL DRAPED IN PEASANT'S RAGS COME UPON IT?
DO TELL ME WHERE.

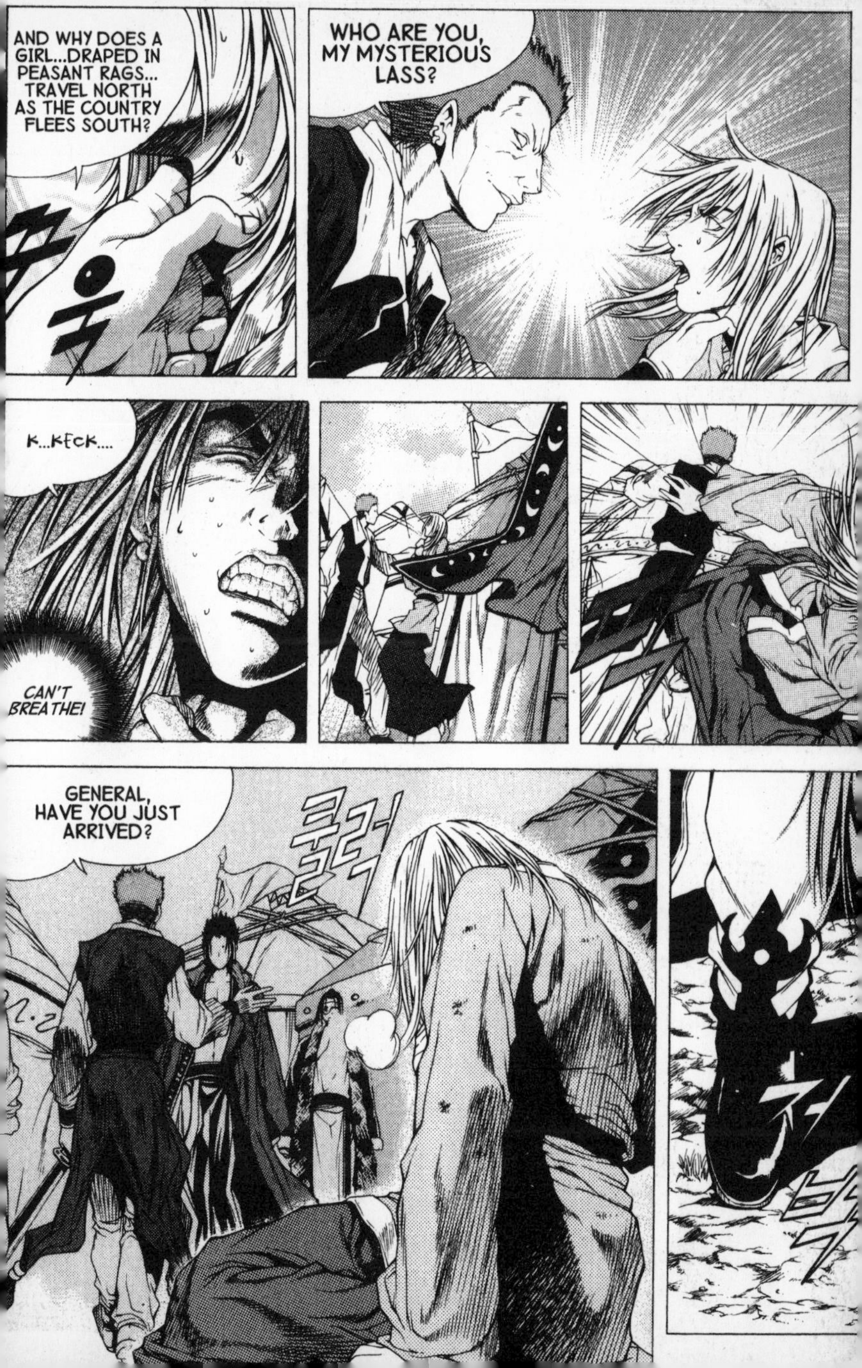
AND WHY DOES A GIRL...DRAPED IN PEASANT RAGS... TRAVEL NORTH AS THE COUNTRY FLEES SOUTH?
WHO ARE YOU, MY MYSTERIOUS LASS?
K...KECK....
CAN'T BREATHE!
GENERAL, HAVE YOU JUST ARRIVED?

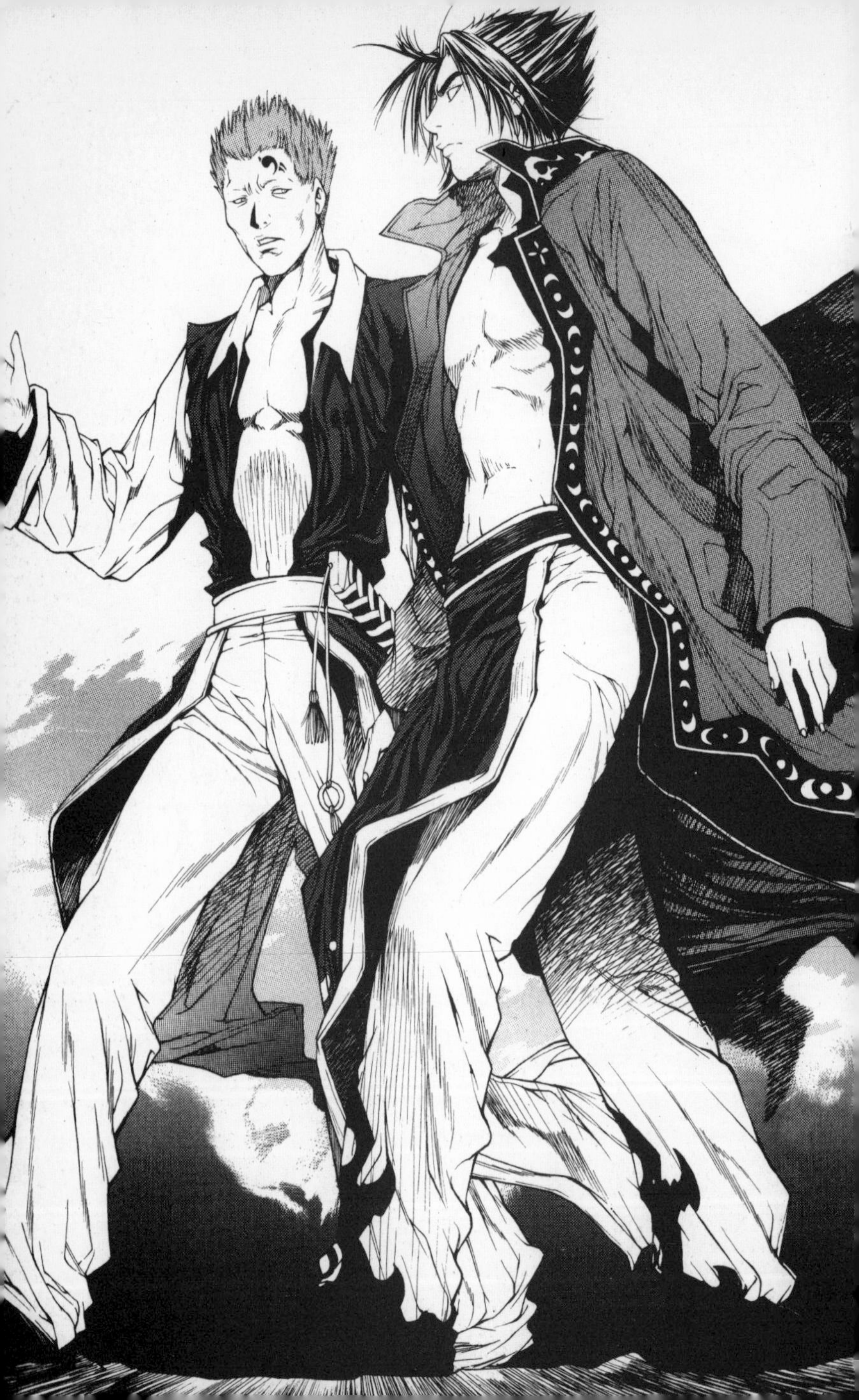

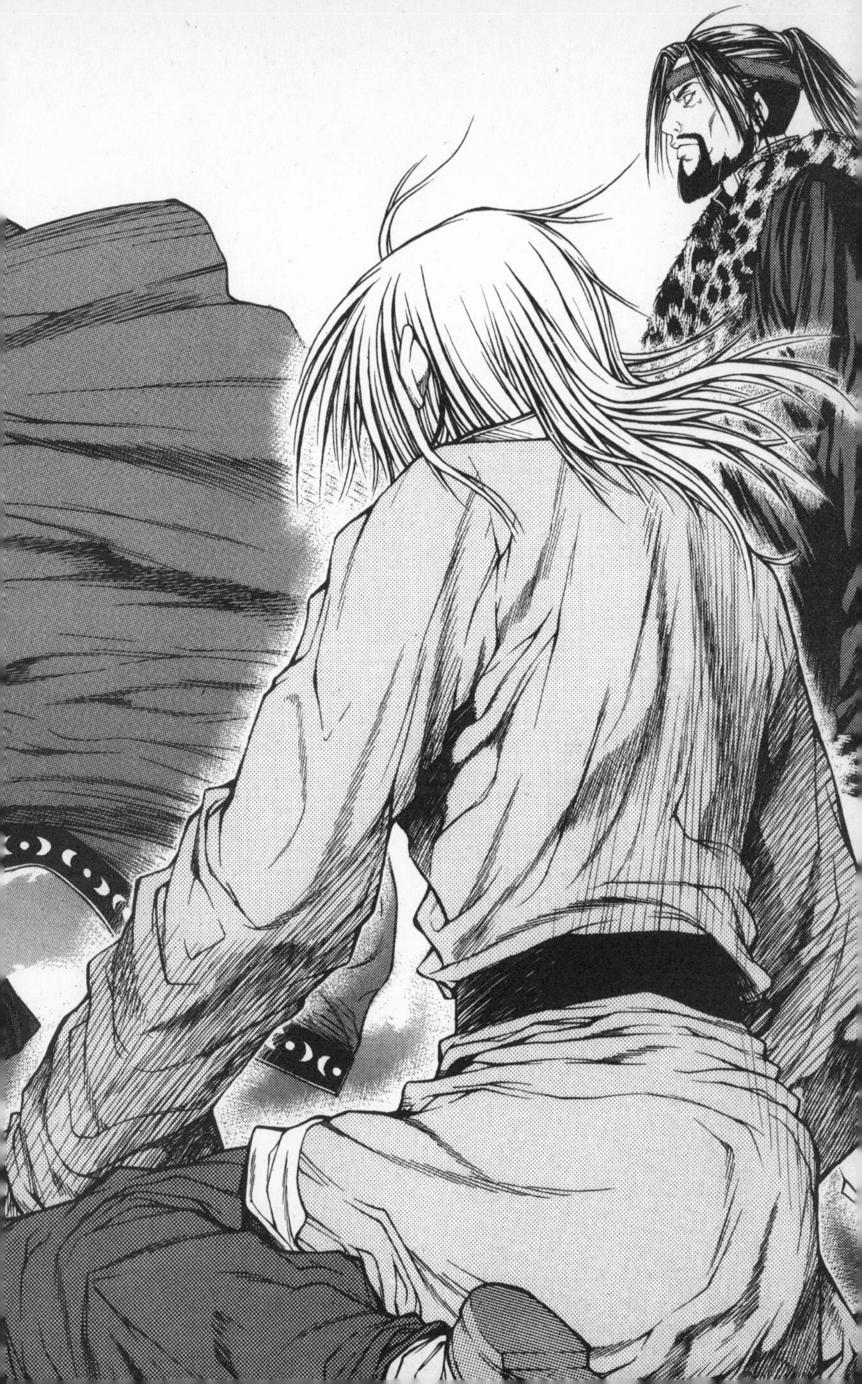

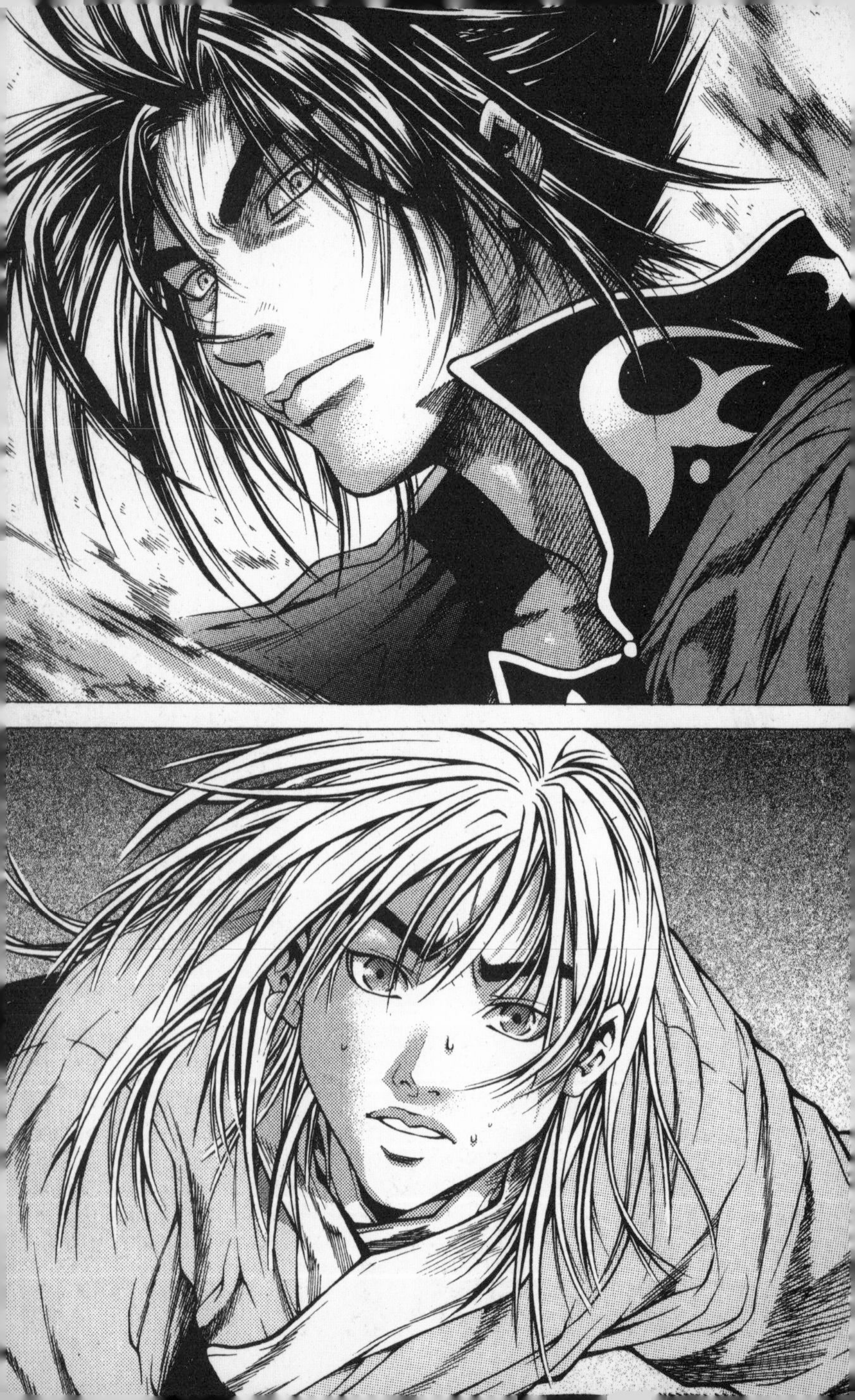

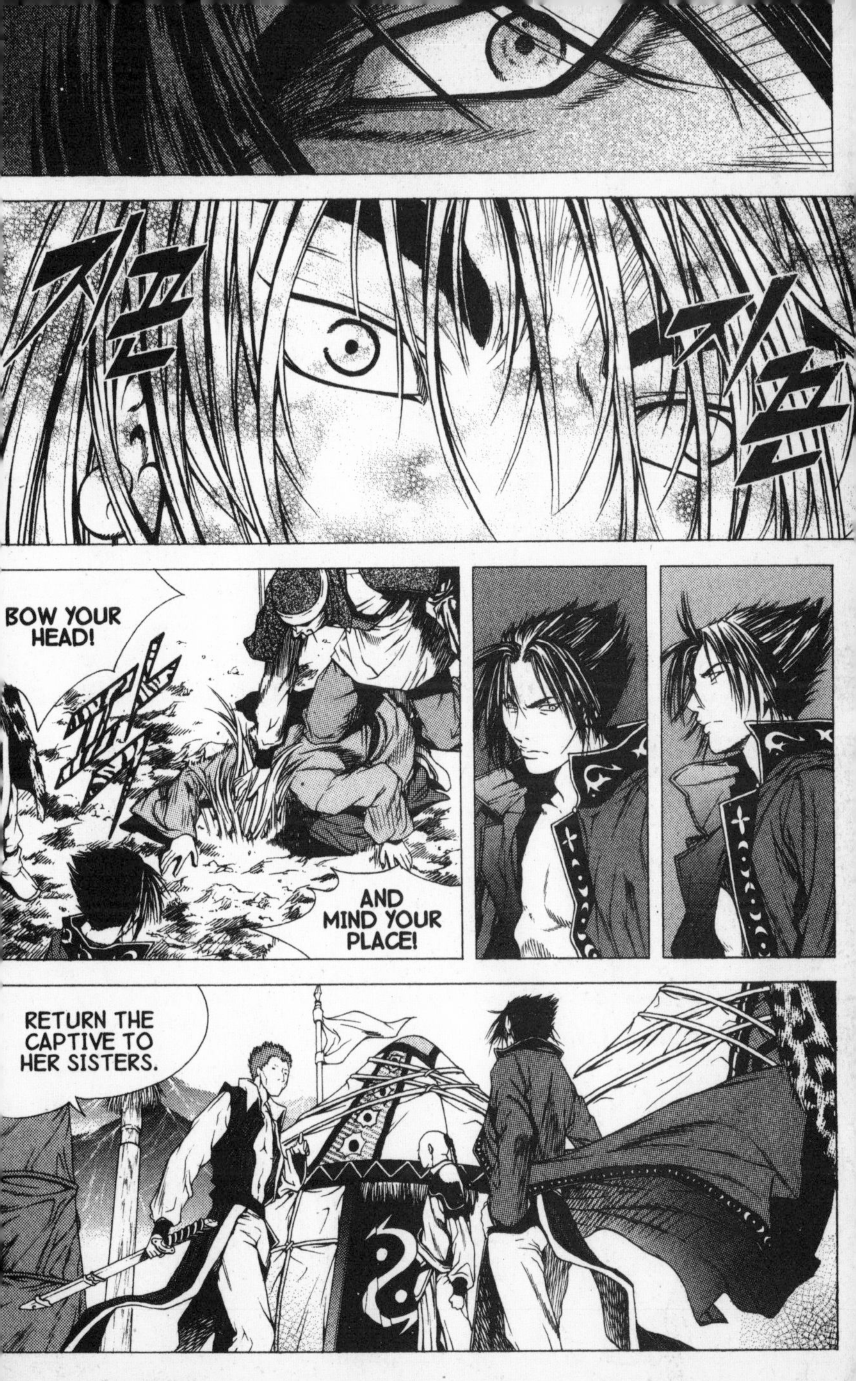
BOW YOUR HEAD!
AND MIND YOUR PLACE!
RETURN THE CAPTIVE TO HER SISTERS.

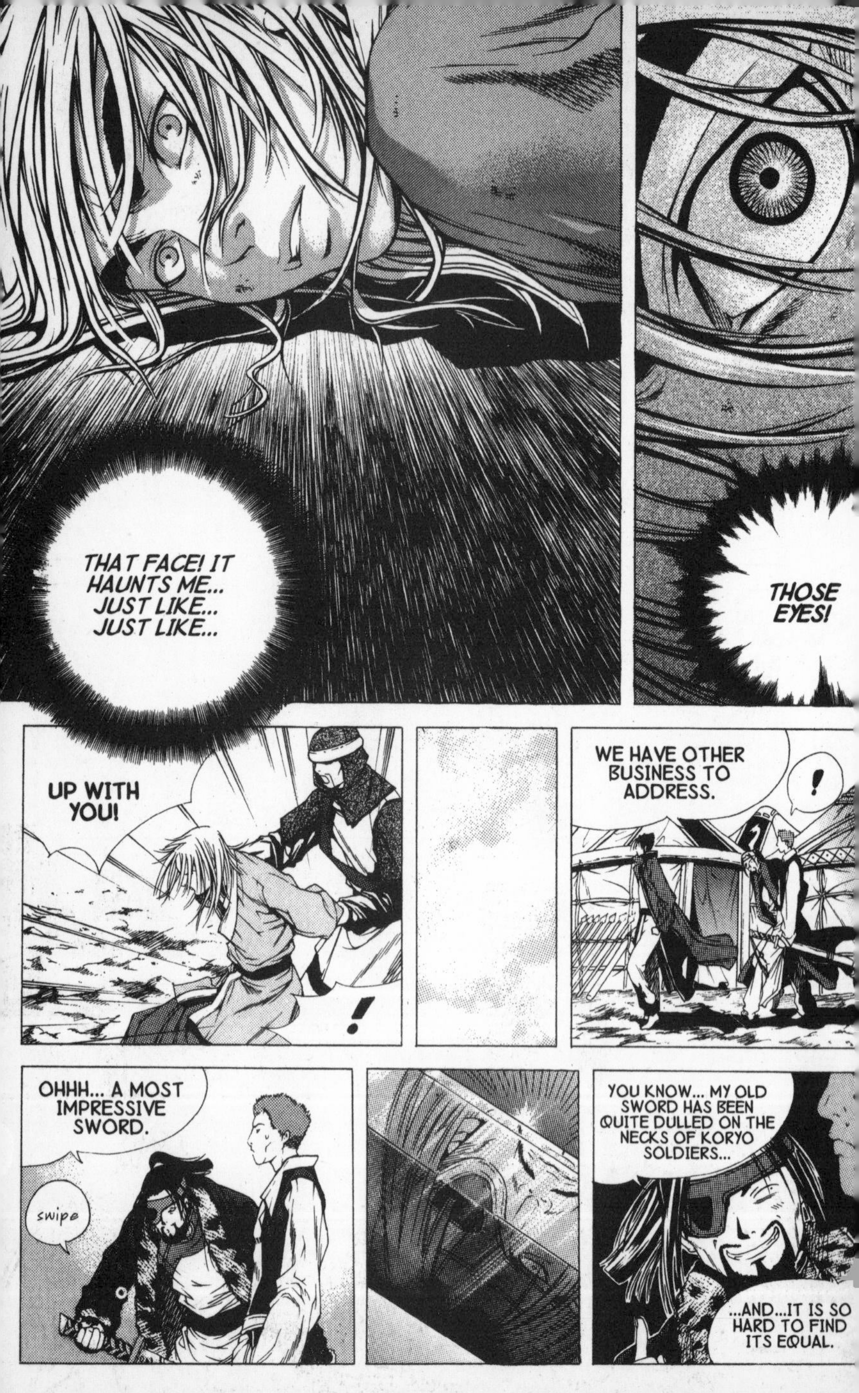
THAT FACE! IT HAUNTS ME... JUST LIKE... JUST LIKE...
THOSE EYES!
UP WITH YOU!
!
WE HAVE OTHER BUSINESS TO ADDRESS.
!
OHHH... A MOST IMPRESSIVE SWORD.
swipe
YOU KNOW... MY OLD SWORD HAS BEEN QUITE DULLED ON THE NECKS OF KORYO SOLDIERS...
...AND...IT IS SO HARD TO FIND ITS EQUAL.

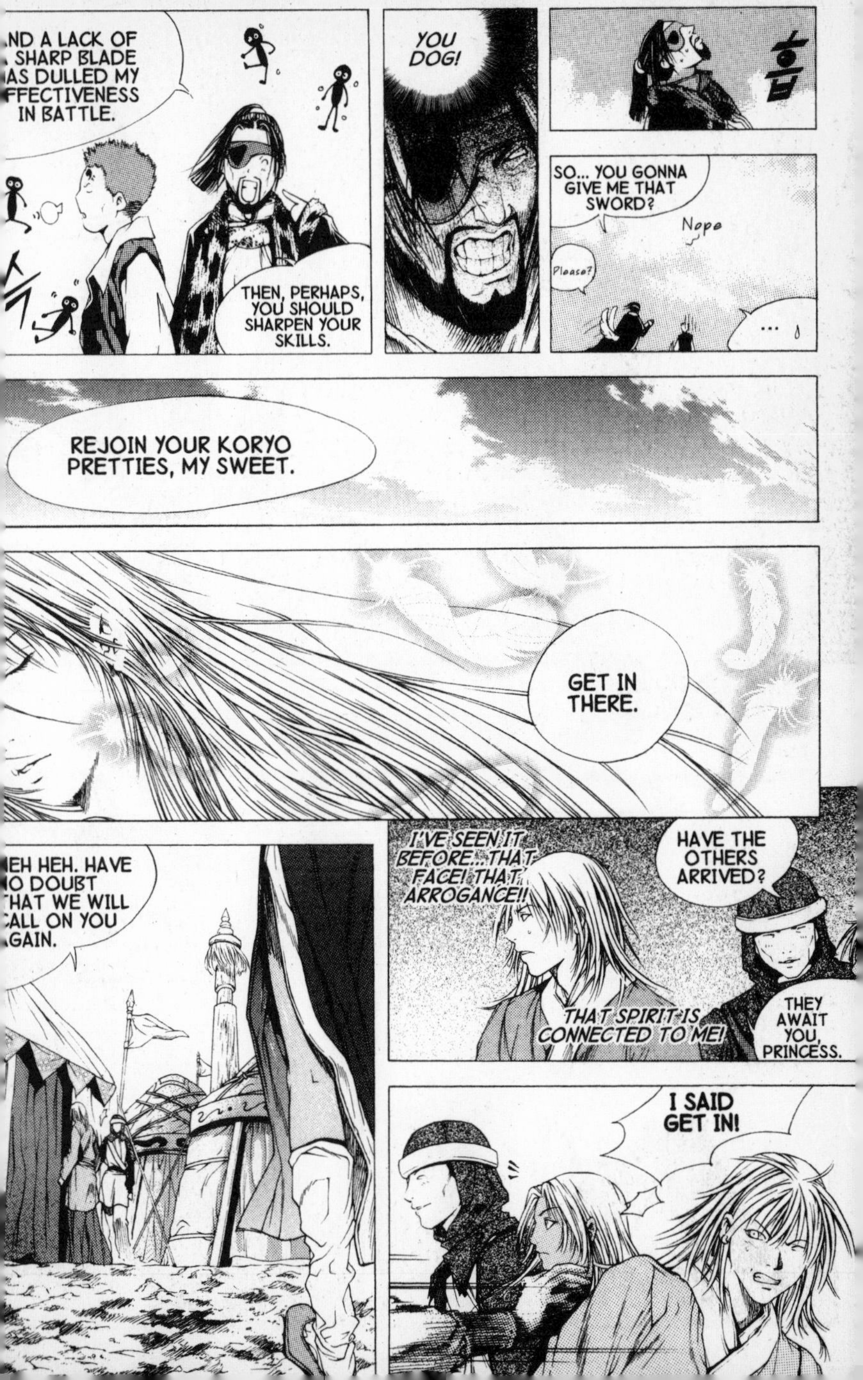
ND A LACK OF SHARP BLADE IAS DULLED MY FFECTIVENESS IN BATTLE.
THEN, PERHAPS, YOU SHOULD SHARPEN YOUR SKILLS.
YOU DOG!
SO... YOU GONNA GIVE ME THAT SWORD?
Nope
Please?
...
REJOIN YOUR KORYO PRETTIES, MY SWEET.
GET IN THERE.
EH HEH. HAVE O DOUBT HAT WE WILL ALL ON YOU GAIN.
I'VE SEEN IT BEFORE... THAT FACE! THAT ARROGANCE!!
HAVE THE OTHERS ARRIVED?
THAT SPIRIT IS CONNECTED TO ME!
THEY AWAIT YOU, PRINCESS.
I SAID GET IN!

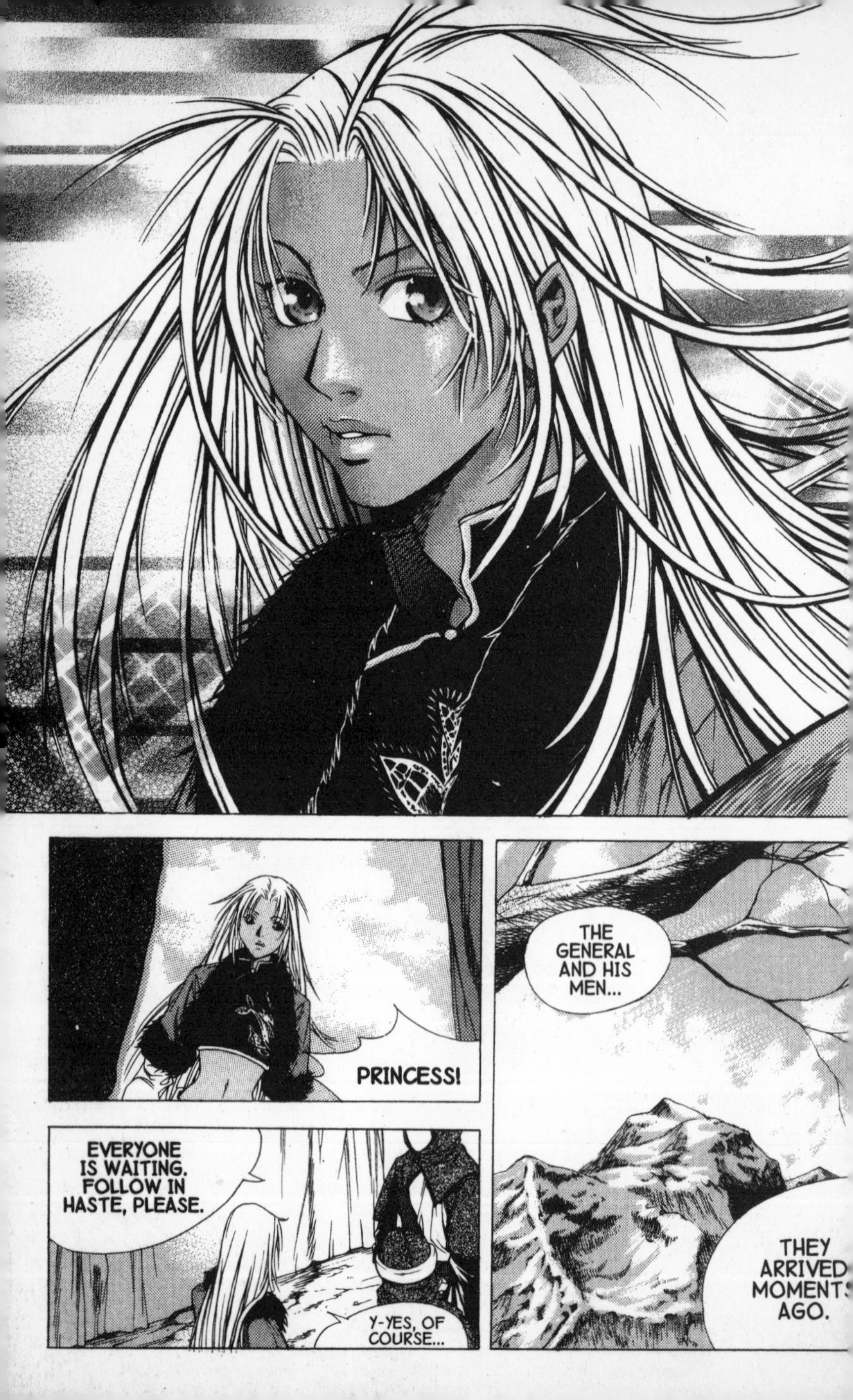
PRINCESS!
THE GENERAL AND HIS MEN...
THEY ARRIVED MOMENTS AGO.
EVERYONE IS WAITING. FOLLOW IN HASTE, PLEASE.
Y-YES, OF COURSE...

YOUNG
MAST--YOUNG
LADY! ANOTHER
SCAR ON YOUR
INNOCENT
FACE!

IT'S NOTHING.

BE STILL. I WILL
GO LOOK FOR
SOMETHING WITH
WHICH TO
TREAT IT.

*THE LOSS OF
MY FATHER'S
SWORD...*

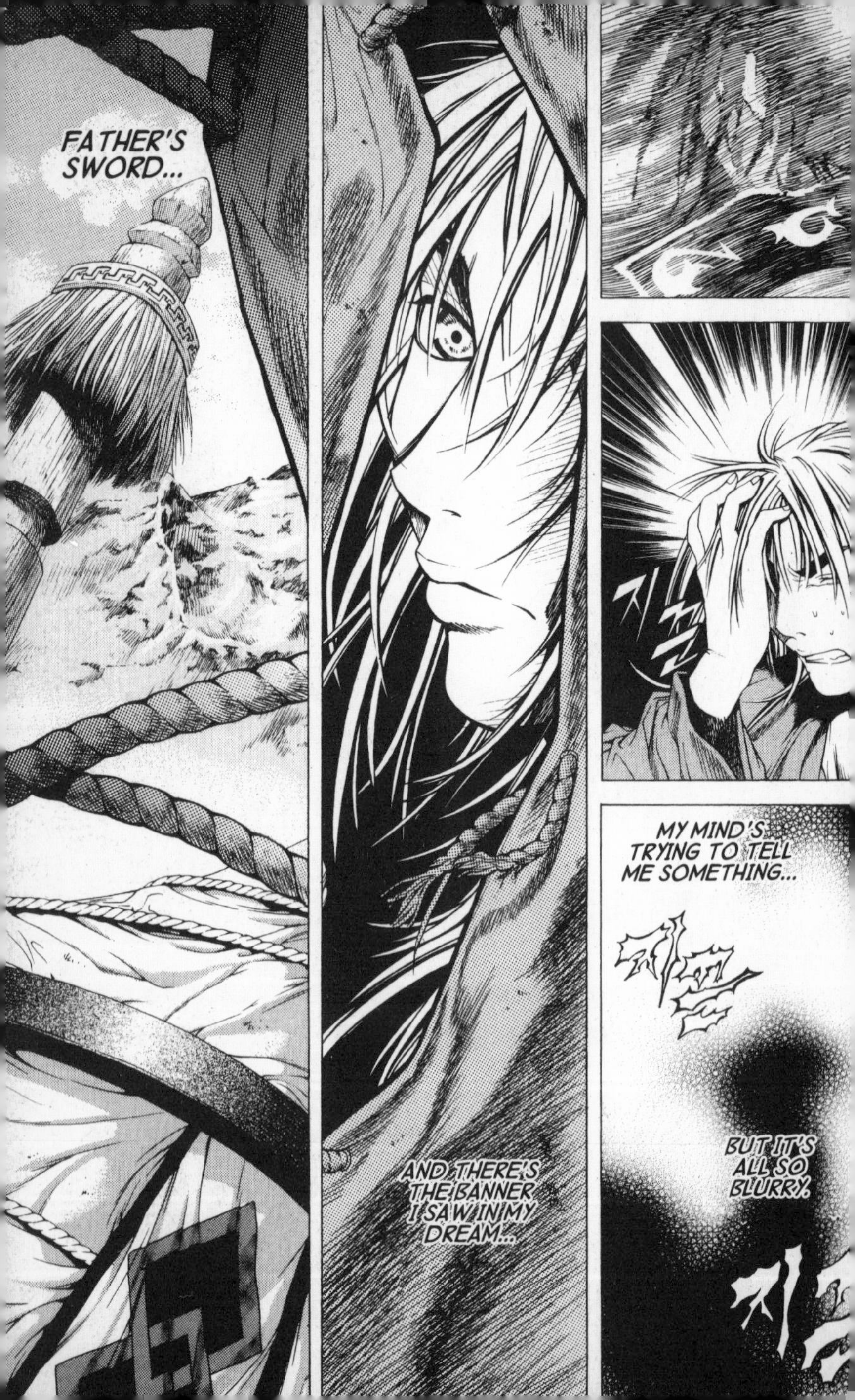
FATHER'S SWORD...
AND THERE'S THE BANNER I SAW IN MY DREAM...
MY MIND'S TRYING TO TELL ME SOMETHING...
BUT IT'S ALL SO BLURRY.

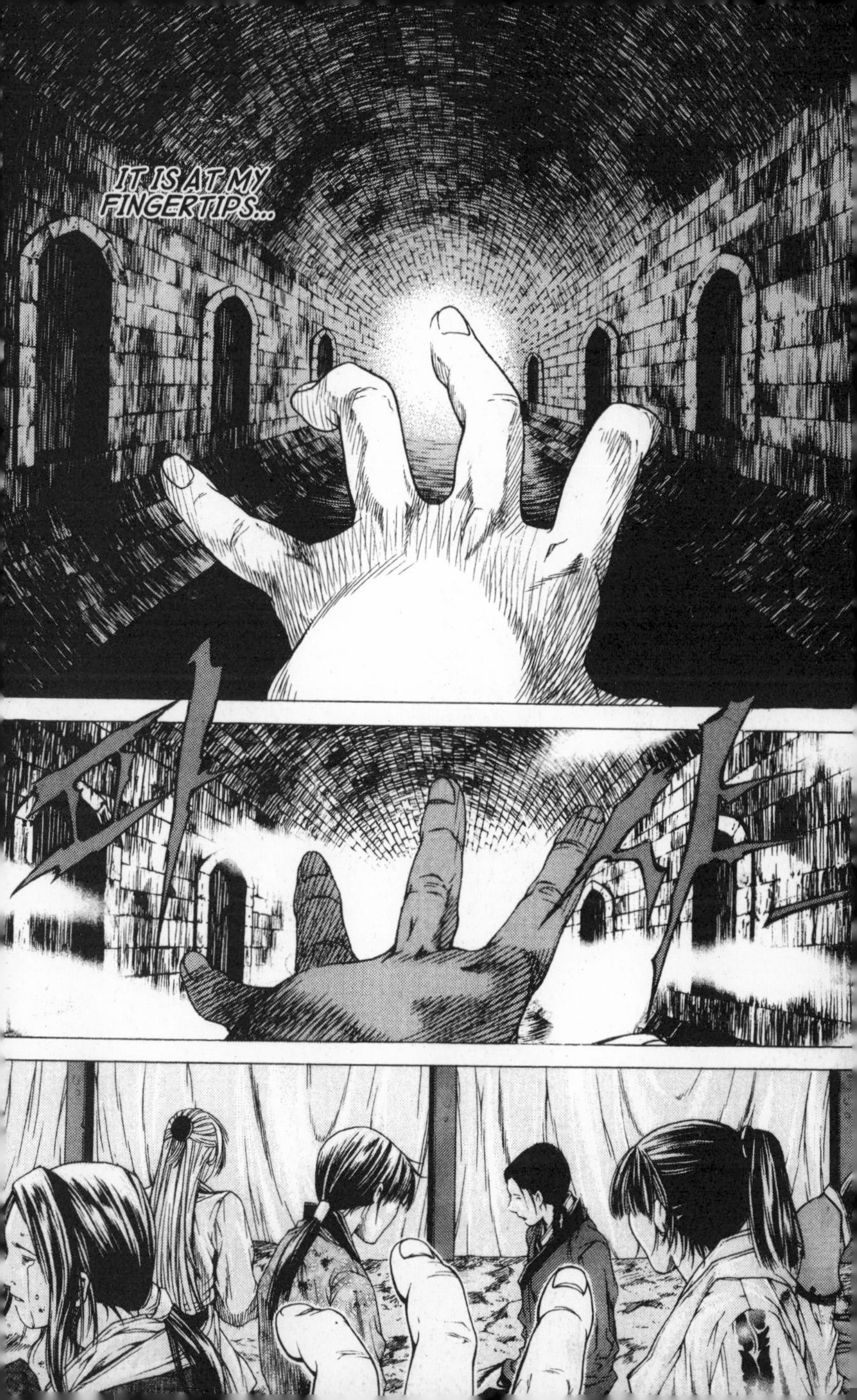
IT IS AT MY FINGERTIPS...

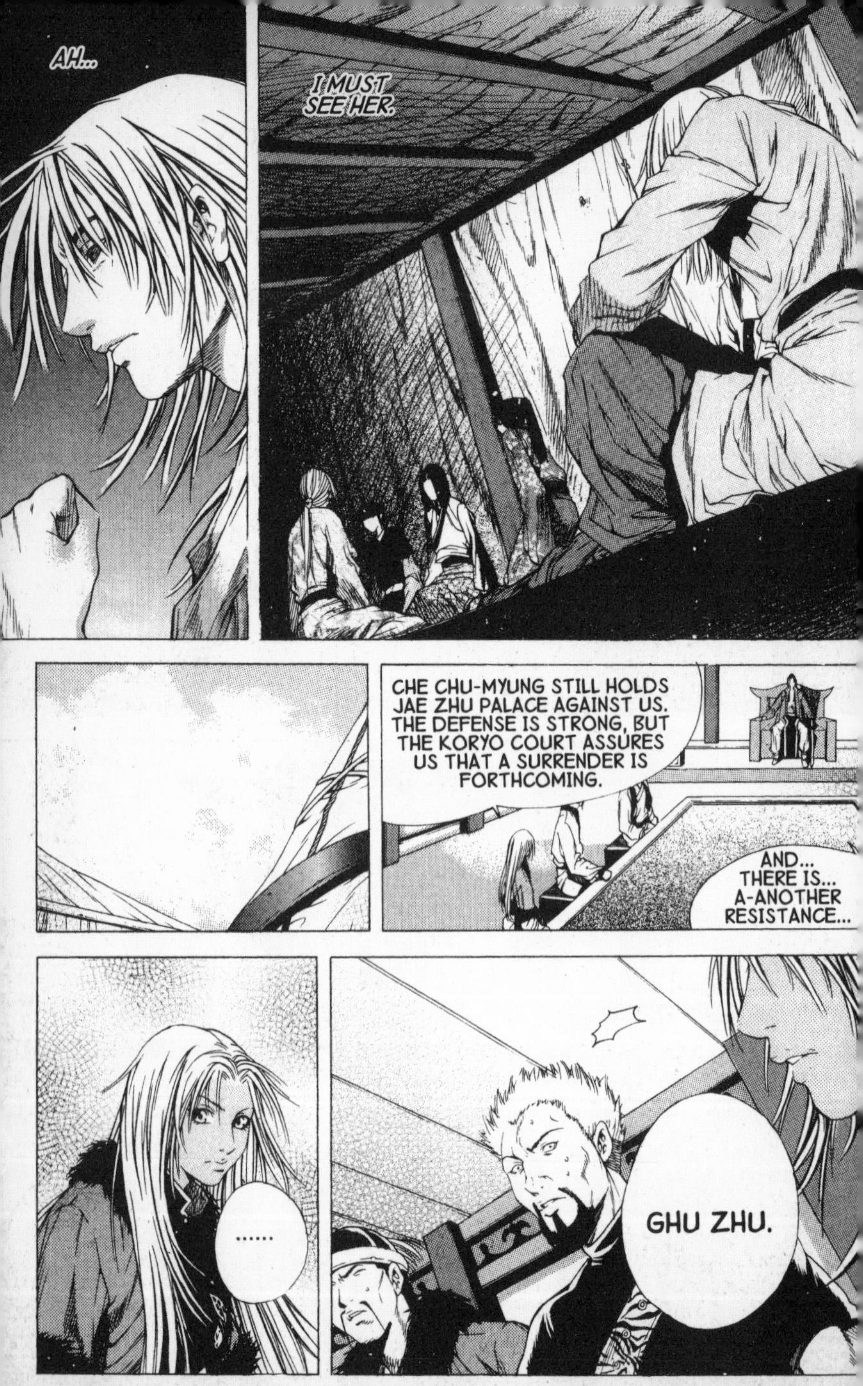
AH...
I MUST SEE HER.
CHE CHU-MYUNG STILL HOLDS JAE ZHU PALACE AGAINST US. THE DEFENSE IS STRONG, BUT THE KORYO COURT ASSURES US THAT A SURRENDER IS FORTHCOMING.
AND... THERE IS... A-ANOTHER RESISTANCE...
......
GHU ZHU.

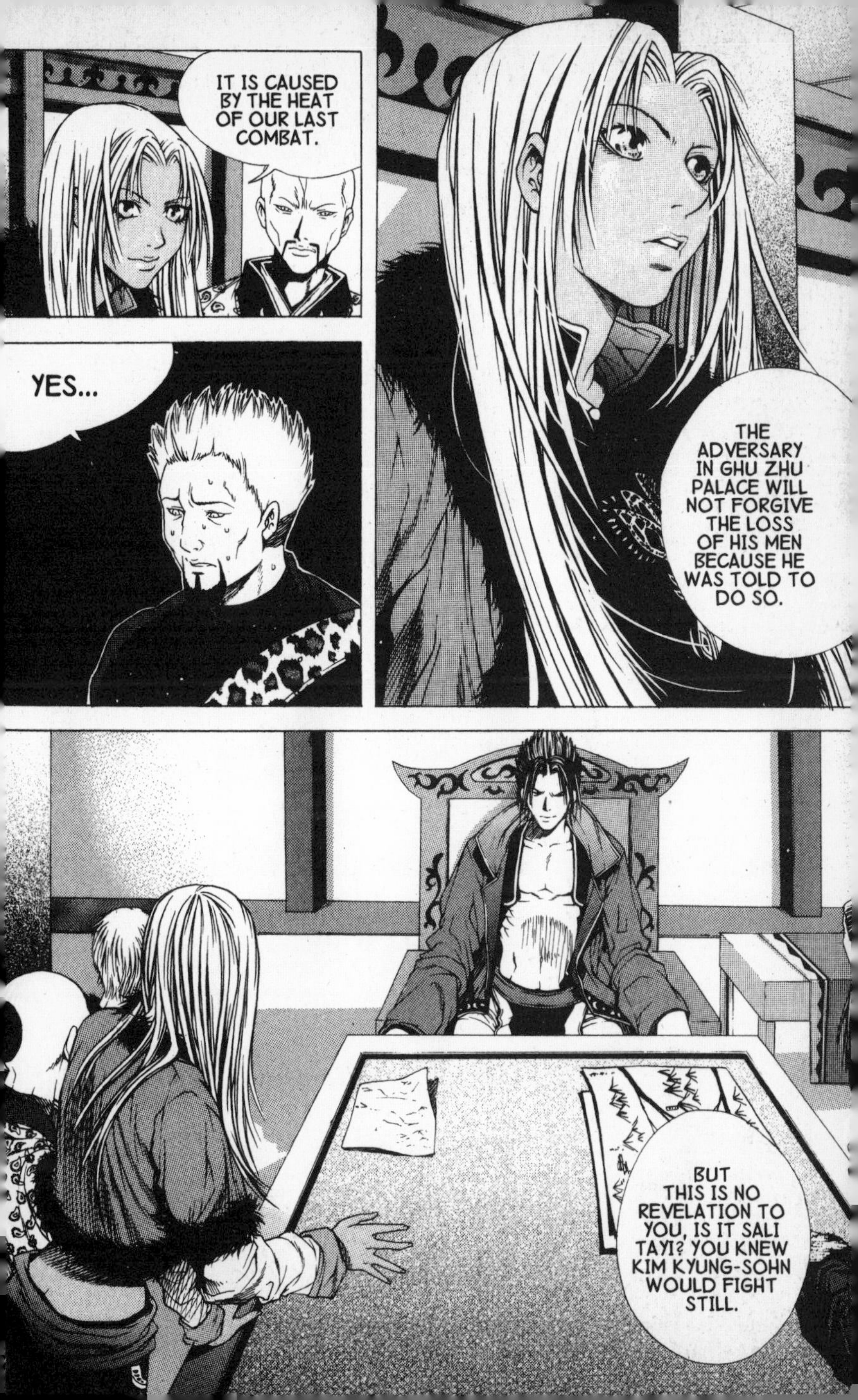
IT IS CAUSED BY THE HEAT OF OUR LAST COMBAT.
YES...
THE ADVERSARY IN GHU ZHU PALACE WILL NOT FORGIVE THE LOSS OF HIS MEN BECAUSE HE WAS TOLD TO DO SO.
BUT THIS IS NO REVELATION TO YOU, IS IT SALI TAYI? YOU KNEW KIM KYUNG-SOHN WOULD FIGHT STILL.

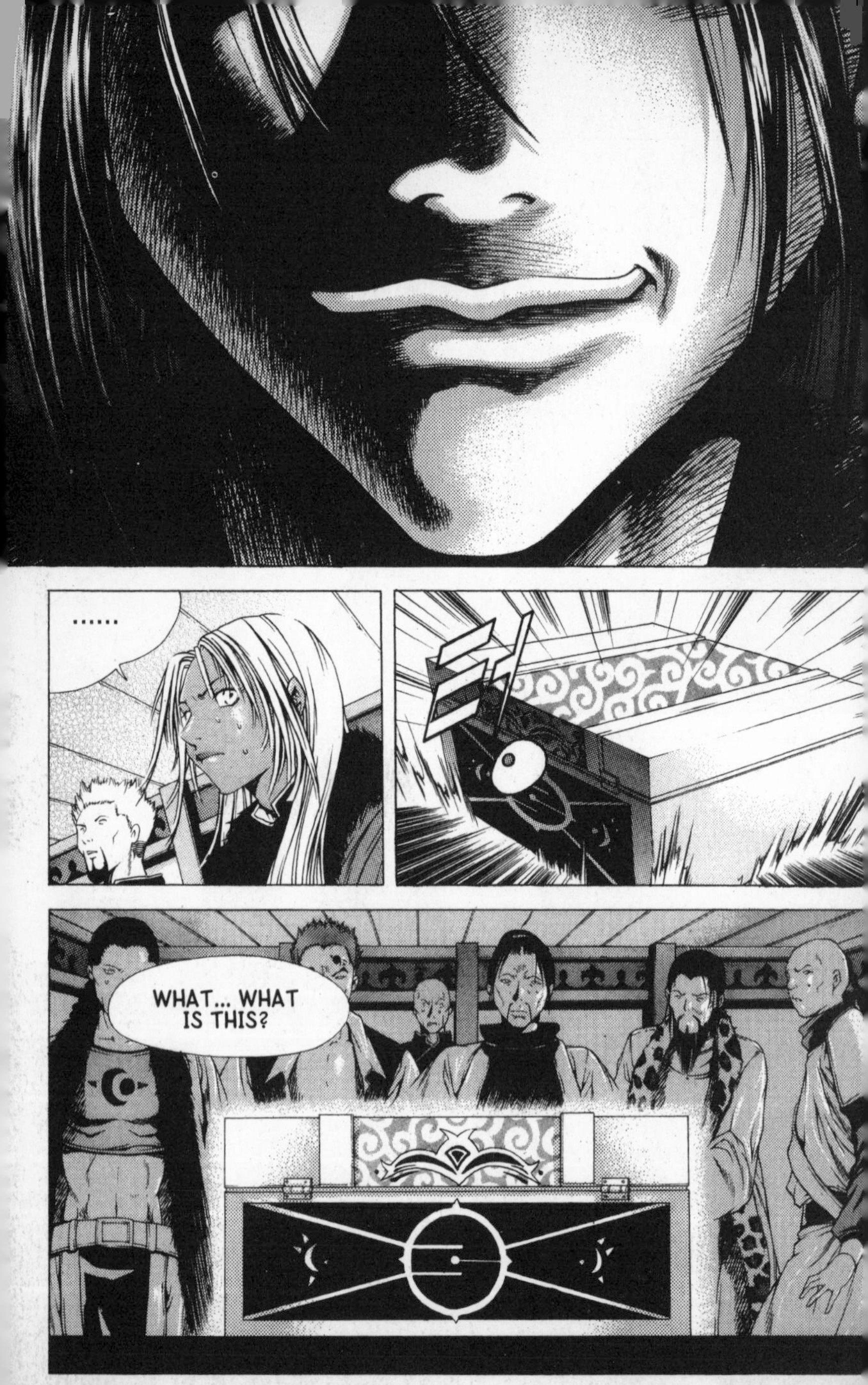
......
WHAT... WHAT IS THIS?

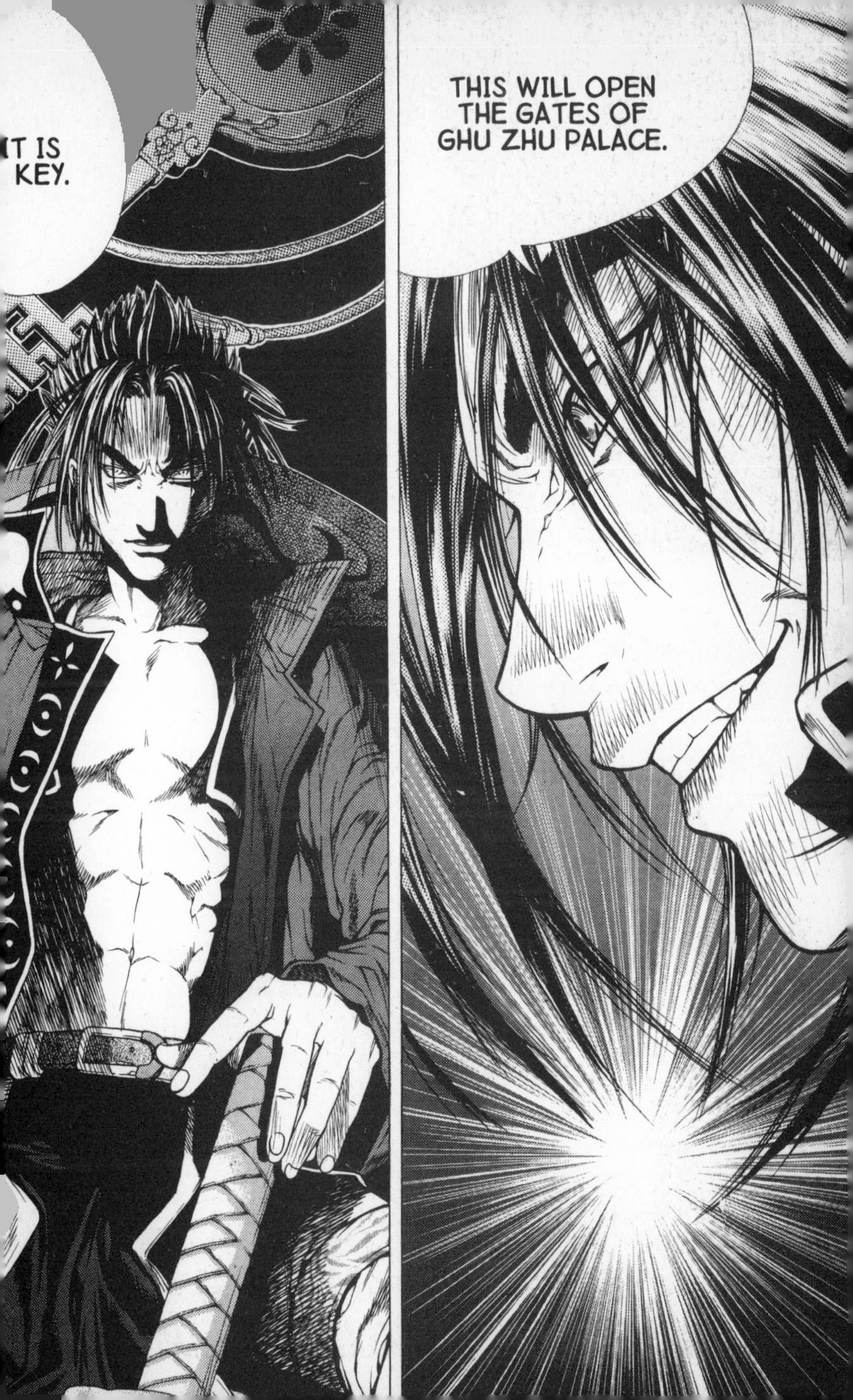

IT IS
KEY.
THIS WILL OPEN
THE GATES OF
GHU ZHU PALACE.

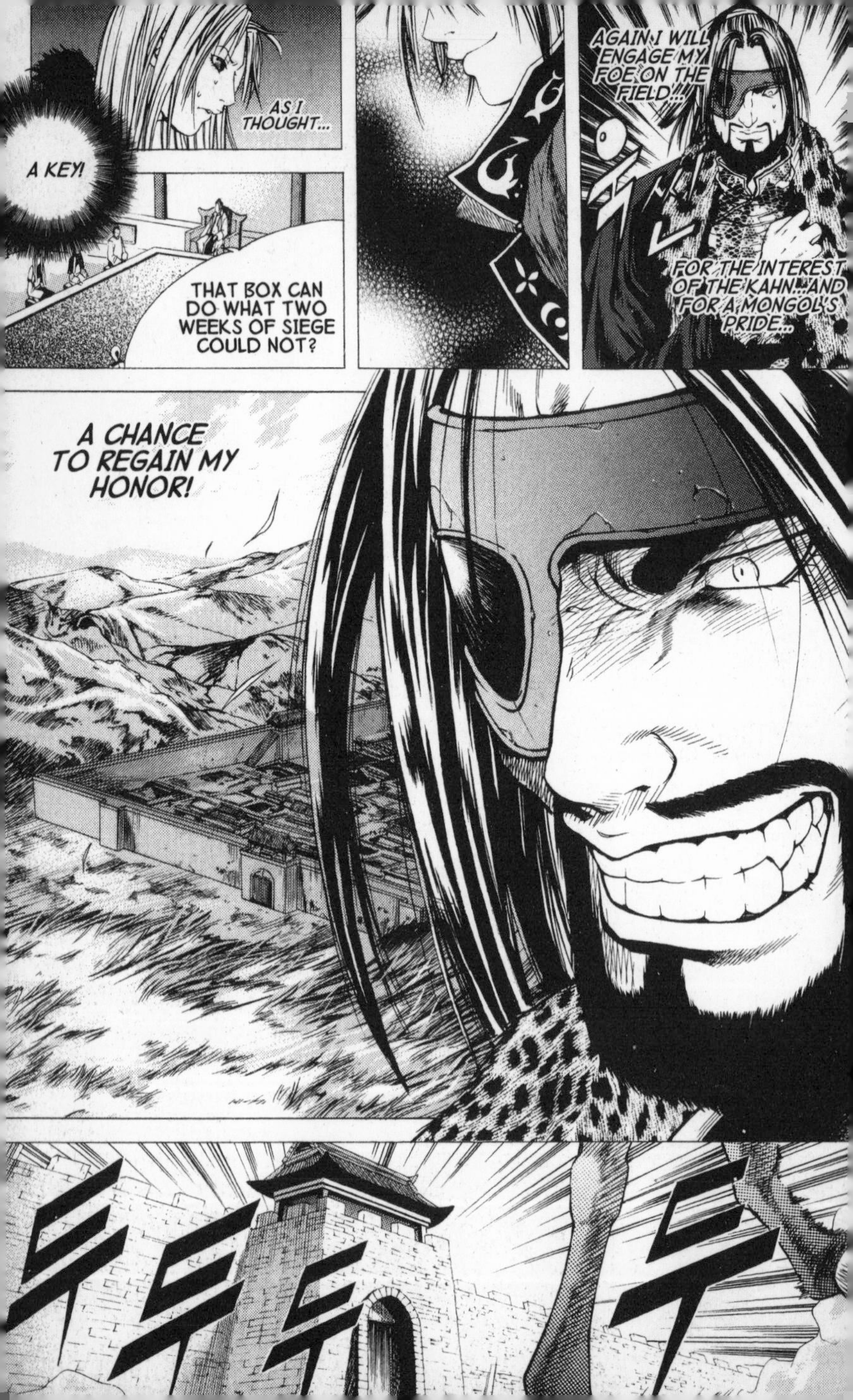
AS I THOUGHT...
A KEY!
THAT BOX CAN DO WHAT TWO WEEKS OF SIEGE COULD NOT?
AGAIN I WILL ENGAGE MY FOE ON THE FIELD...
FOR THE INTEREST OF THE KAHN...AND FOR A MONGOL'S PRIDE...
A CHANCE TO REGAIN MY HONOR!

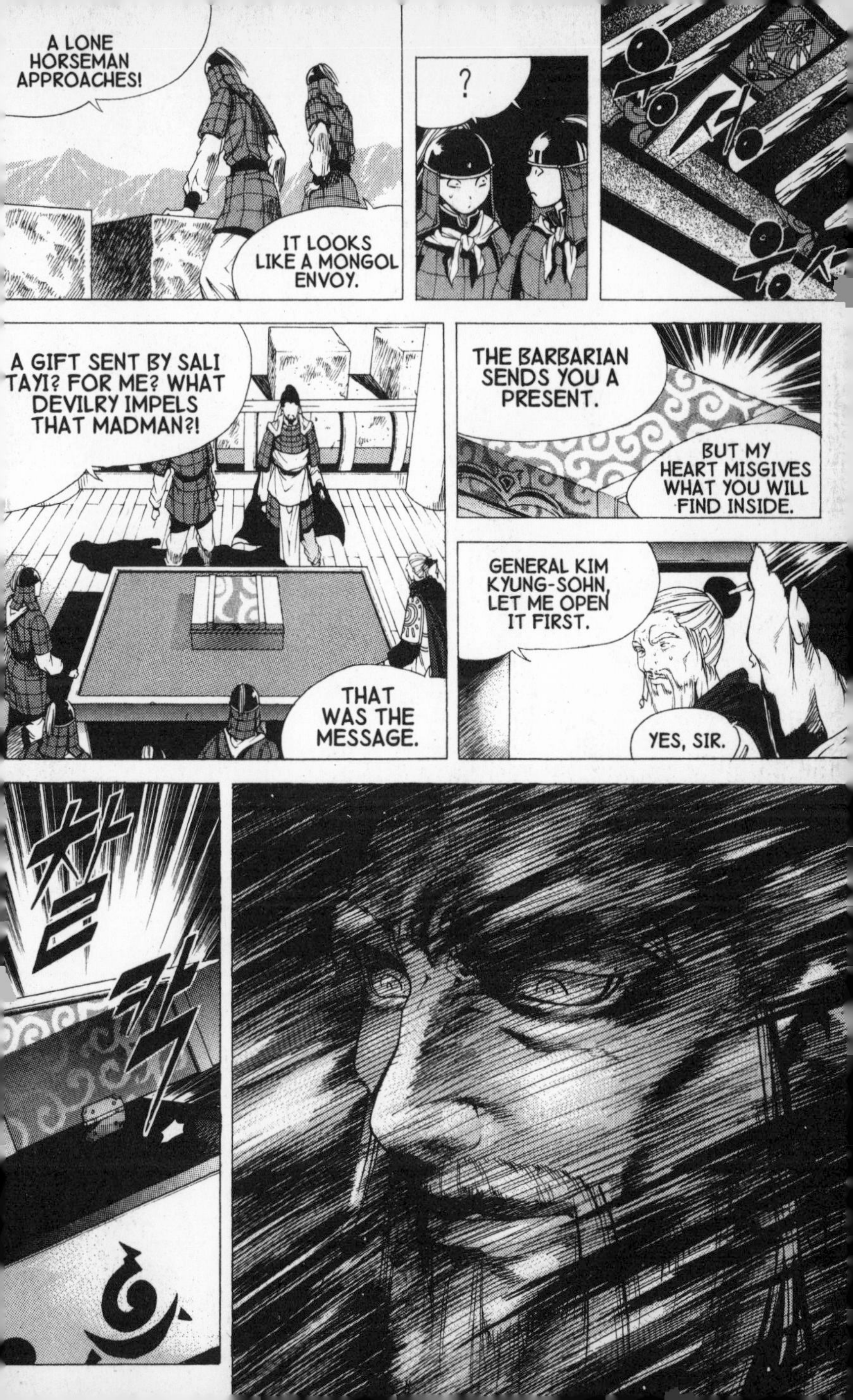
A LONE HORSEMAN APPROACHES!
IT LOOKS LIKE A MONGOL ENVOY.
?
A GIFT SENT BY SALI TAYI? FOR ME? WHAT DEVILRY IMPELS THAT MADMAN?!
THAT WAS THE MESSAGE.
THE BARBARIAN SENDS YOU A PRESENT.
BUT MY HEART MISGIVES WHAT YOU WILL FIND INSIDE.
GENERAL KIM KYUNG-SOHN, LET ME OPEN IT FIRST.
YES, SIR.

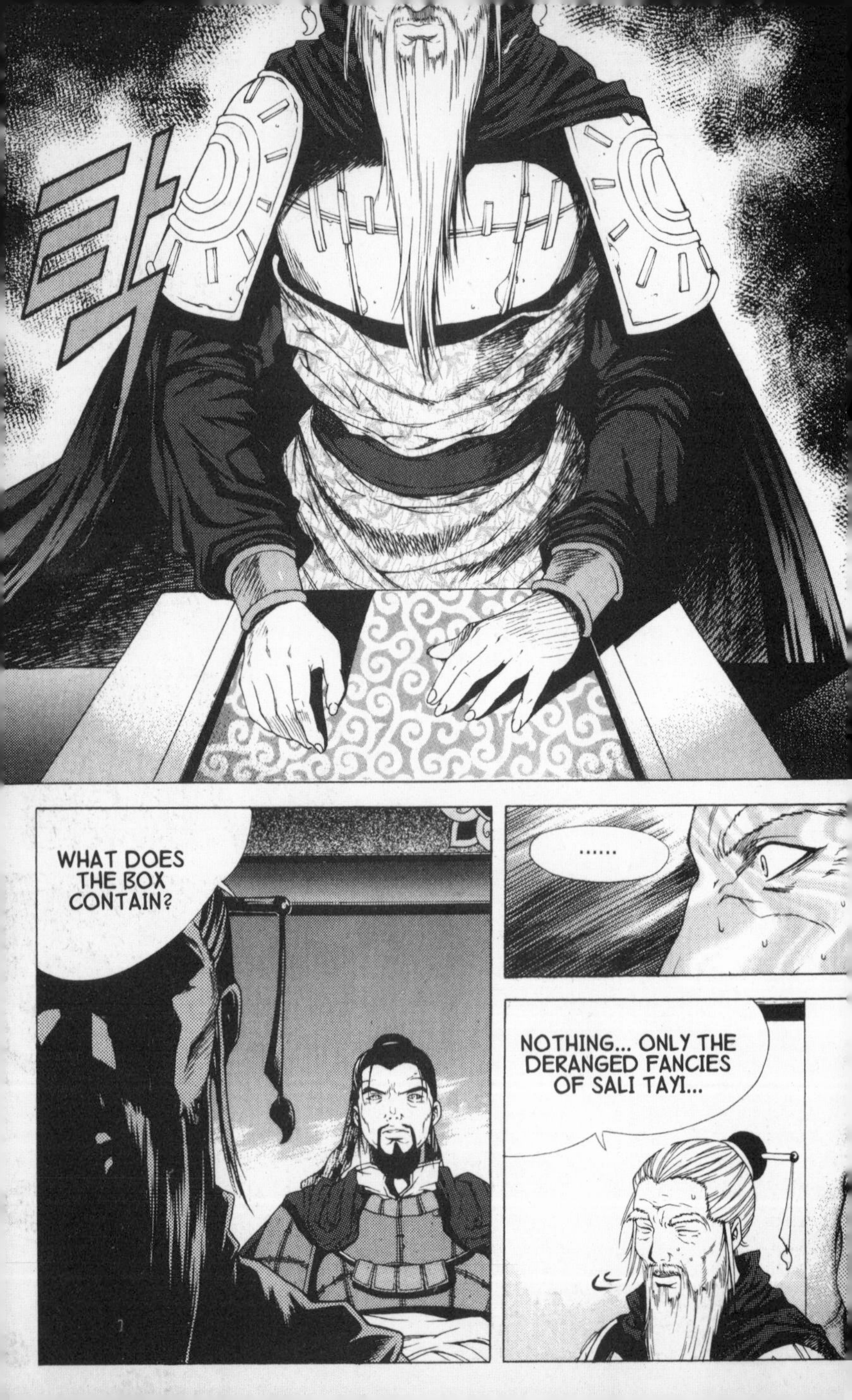
WHAT DOES THE BOX CONTAIN?
......
NOTHING... ONLY THE DERANGED FANCIES OF SALI TAYI...

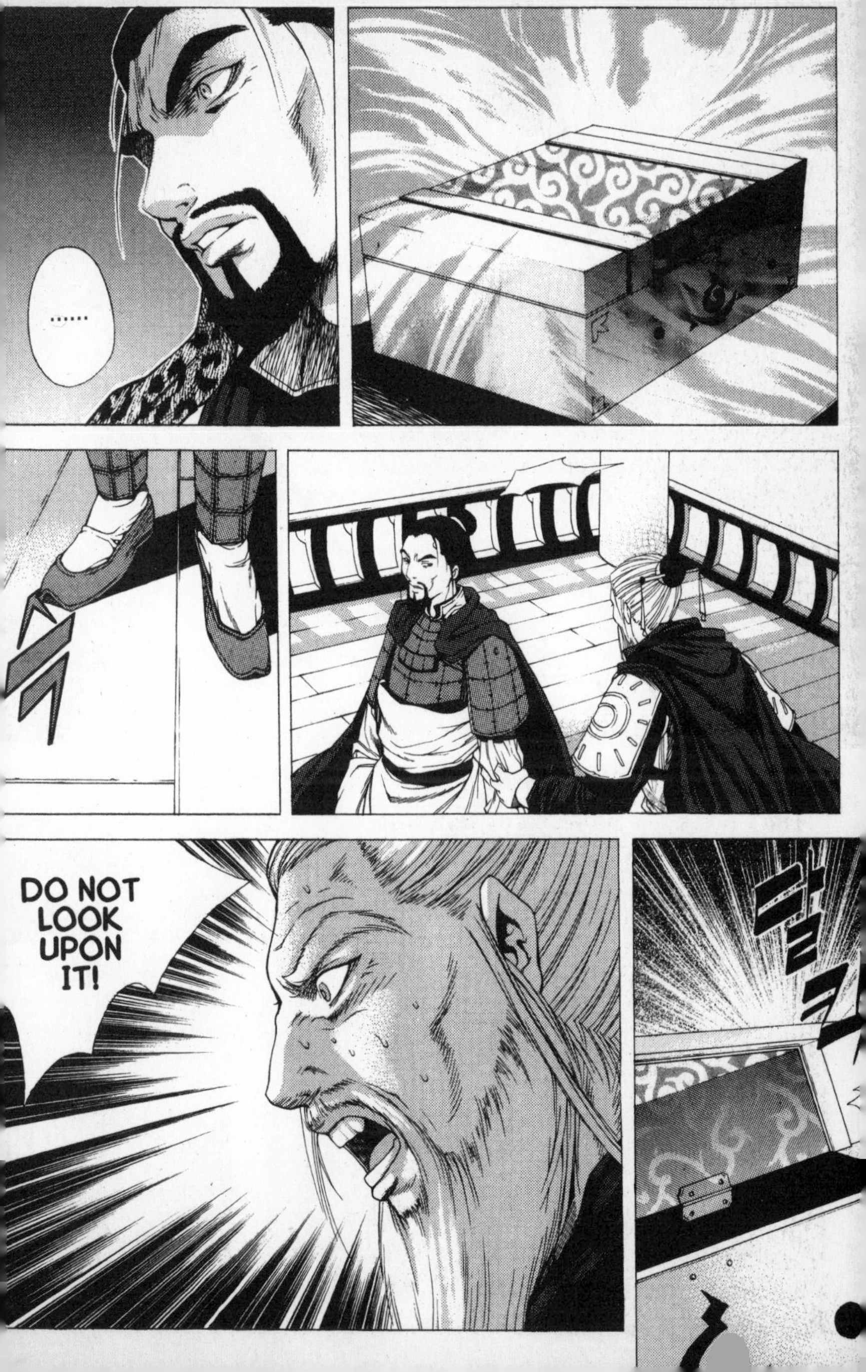
......
DO NOT LOOK UPON IT!

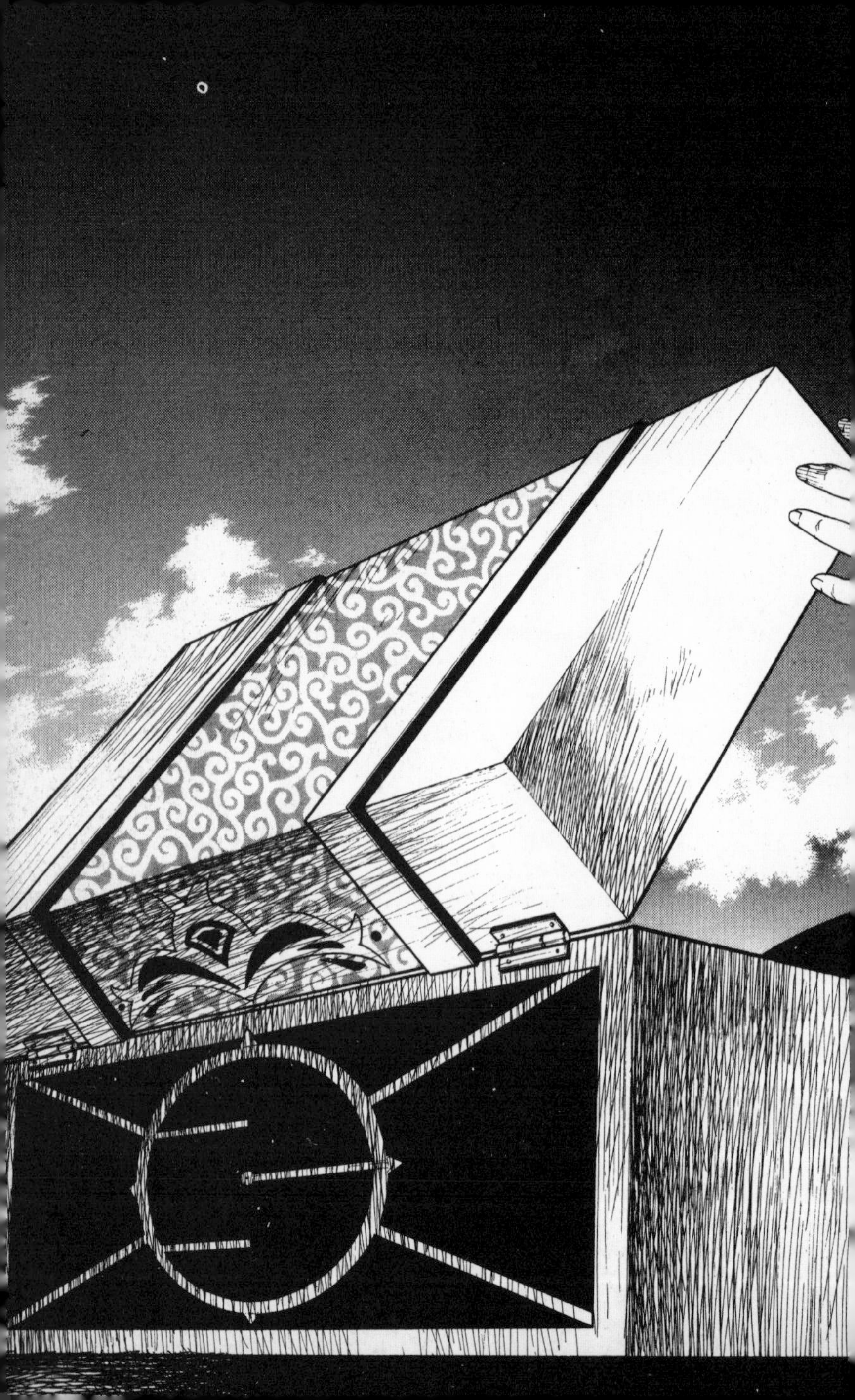

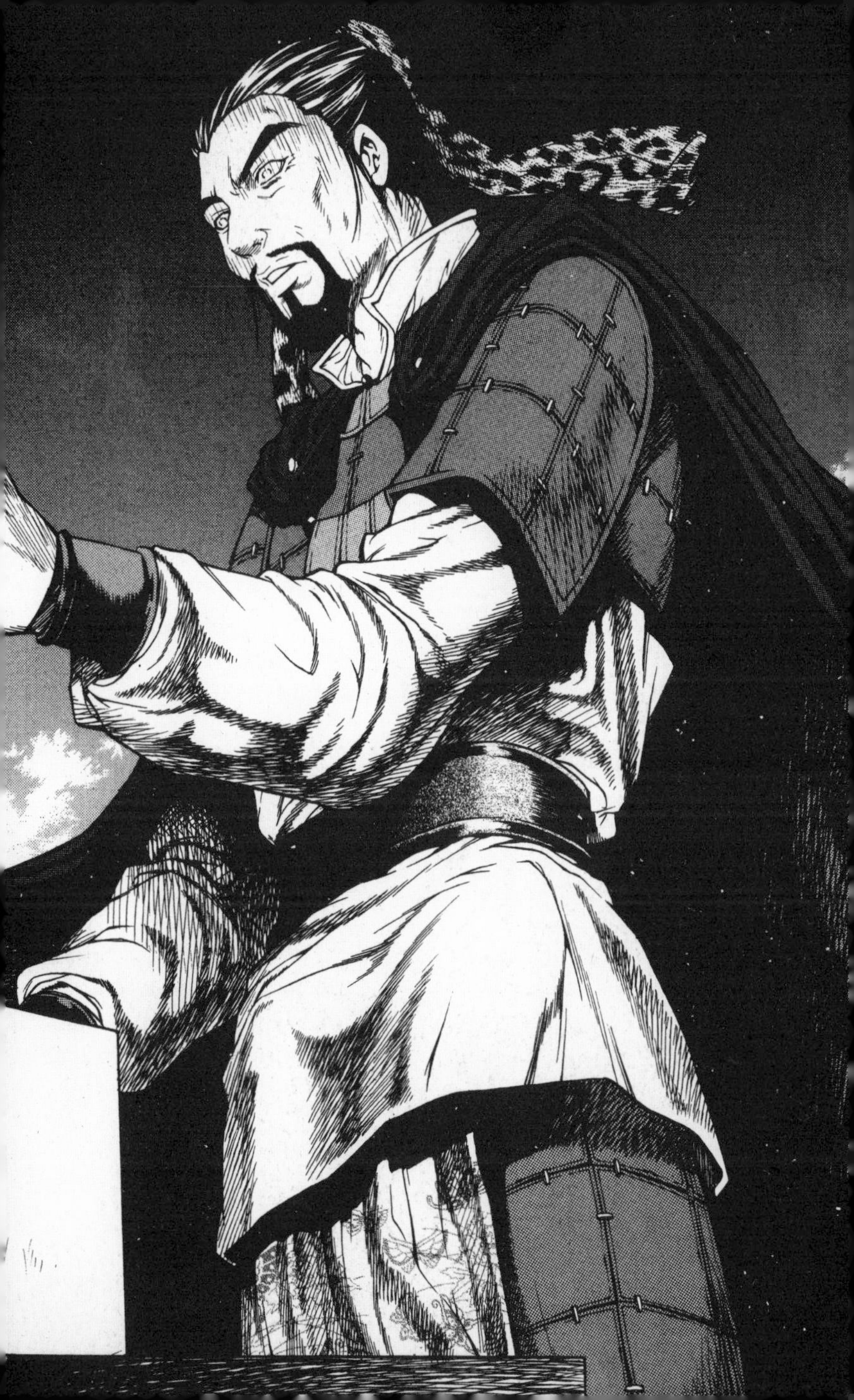

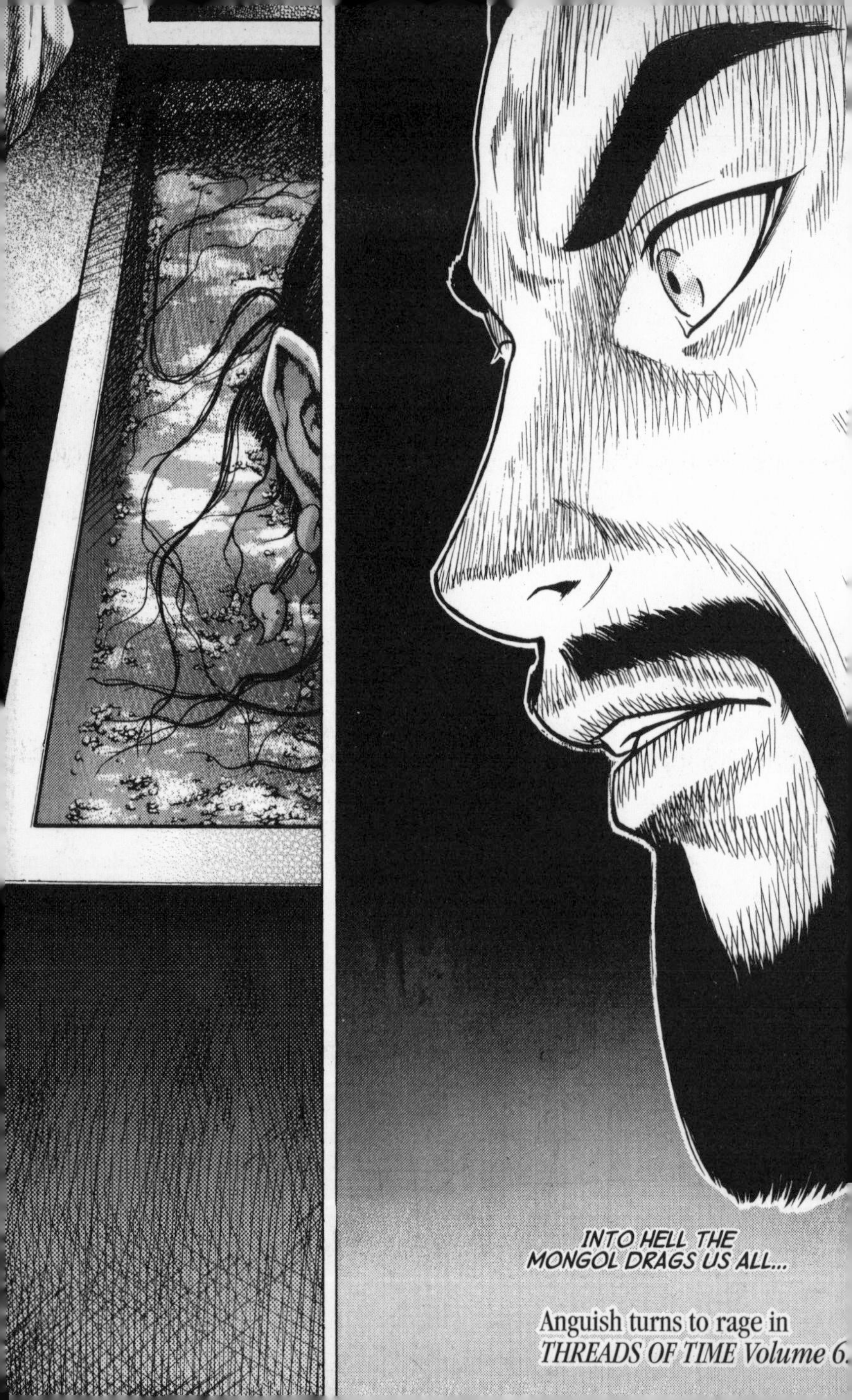
INTO HELL THE MONGOL DRAGS US ALL...
Anguish turns to rage in THREADS OF TIME Volume 6.

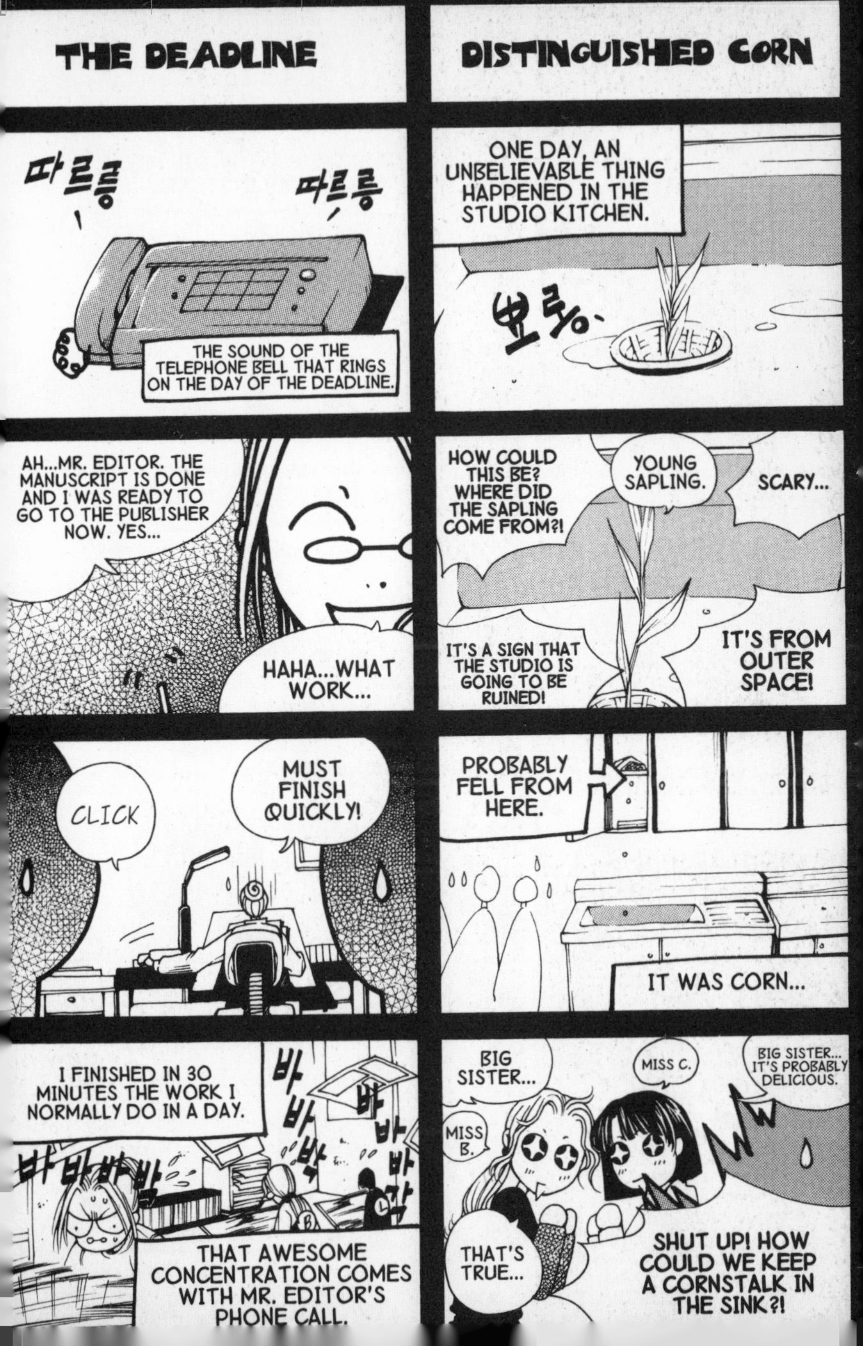
THE DEADLINE
따르릉
따르릉
THE SOUND OF THE TELEPHONE BELL THAT RINGS ON THE DAY OF THE DEADLINE.
AH...MR. EDITOR. THE MANUSCRIPT IS DONE AND I WAS READY TO GO TO THE PUBLISHER NOW. YES...
HAHA...WHAT WORK...
CLICK
MUST FINISH QUICKLY!
I FINISHED IN 30 MINUTES THE WORK I NORMALLY DO IN A DAY.
THAT AWESOME CONCENTRATION COMES WITH MR. EDITOR'S PHONE CALL.
DISTINGUISHED CORN
ONE DAY, AN UNBELIEVABLE THING HAPPENED IN THE STUDIO KITCHEN.
HOW COULD THIS BE? WHERE DID THE SAPLING COME FROM?!
YOUNG SAPLING.
SCARY...
IT'S A SIGN THAT THE STUDIO IS GOING TO BE RUINED!
IT'S FROM OUTER SPACE!
PROBABLY FELL FROM HERE.
IT WAS CORN...
BIG SISTER...
MISS C.
BIG SISTER... IT'S PROBABLY DELICIOUS.
MISS B.
THAT'S TRUE...
SHUT UP! HOW COULD WE KEEP A CORNSTALK IN THE SINK?!

STRESSED LADIES

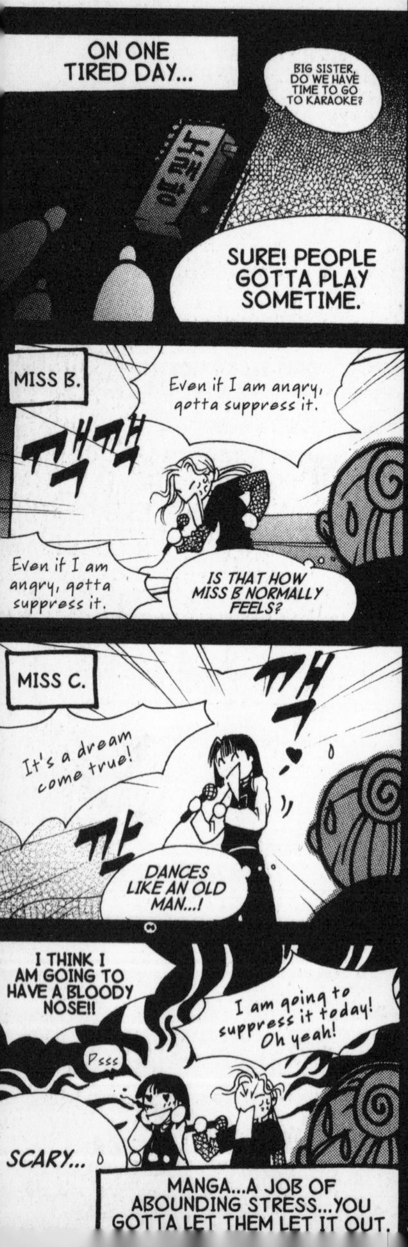

ON ONE TIRED DAY...
BIG SISTER, DO WE HAVE TIME TO GO TO KARAOKE?
노래방
SURE! PEOPLE GOTTA PLAY SOMETIME.
MISS B.
Even if I am angry, gotta suppress it.
Even if I am angry, gotta suppress it.
IS THAT HOW MISS B NORMALLY FEELS?
MISS C.
It's a dream come true!
DANCES LIKE AN OLD MAN...!
I THINK I AM GOING TO HAVE A BLOODY NOSE!!
I am going to suppress it today! Oh yeah!
Psss
SCARY...
MANGA...A JOB OF ABOUNDING STRESS...YOU GOTTA LET THEM LET IT OUT.

ATAN HADAS

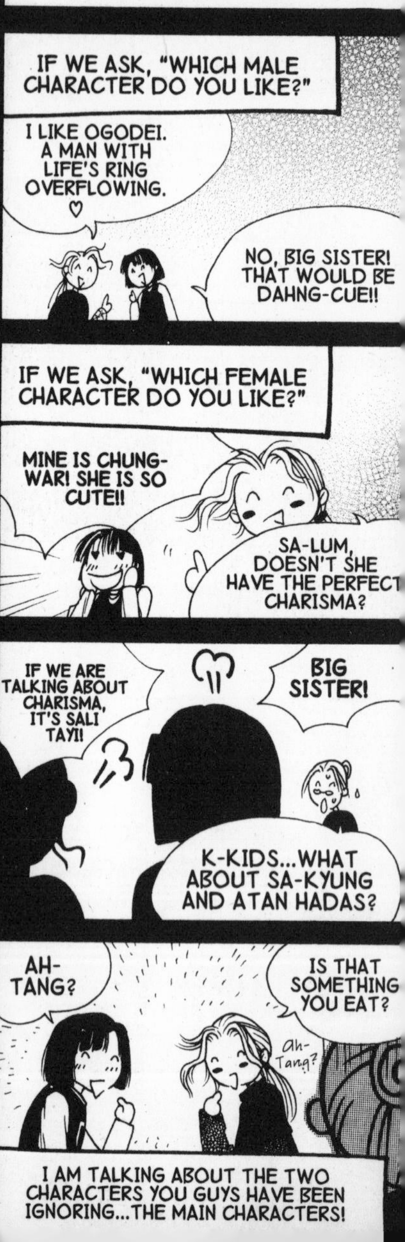

IF WE ASK, "WHICH MALE CHARACTER DO YOU LIKE?"
I LIKE OGODEI. A MAN WITH LIFE'S RING OVERFLOWING. ♡
NO, BIG SISTER! THAT WOULD BE DAHNG-CUE!!
IF WE ASK, "WHICH FEMALE CHARACTER DO YOU LIKE?"
MINE IS CHUNG-WAR! SHE IS SO CUTE!!
SA-LUM, DOESN'T SHE HAVE THE PERFECT CHARISMA?
IF WE ARE TALKING ABOUT CHARISMA, IT'S SALI TAYI!
BIG SISTER!
K-KIDS...WHAT ABOUT SA-KYUNG AND ATAN HADAS?
AH-TANG?
IS THAT SOMETHING YOU EAT?
Ah-Tang?
I AM TALKING ABOUT THE TWO CHARACTERS YOU GUYS HAVE BEEN IGNORING...THE MAIN CHARACTERS!

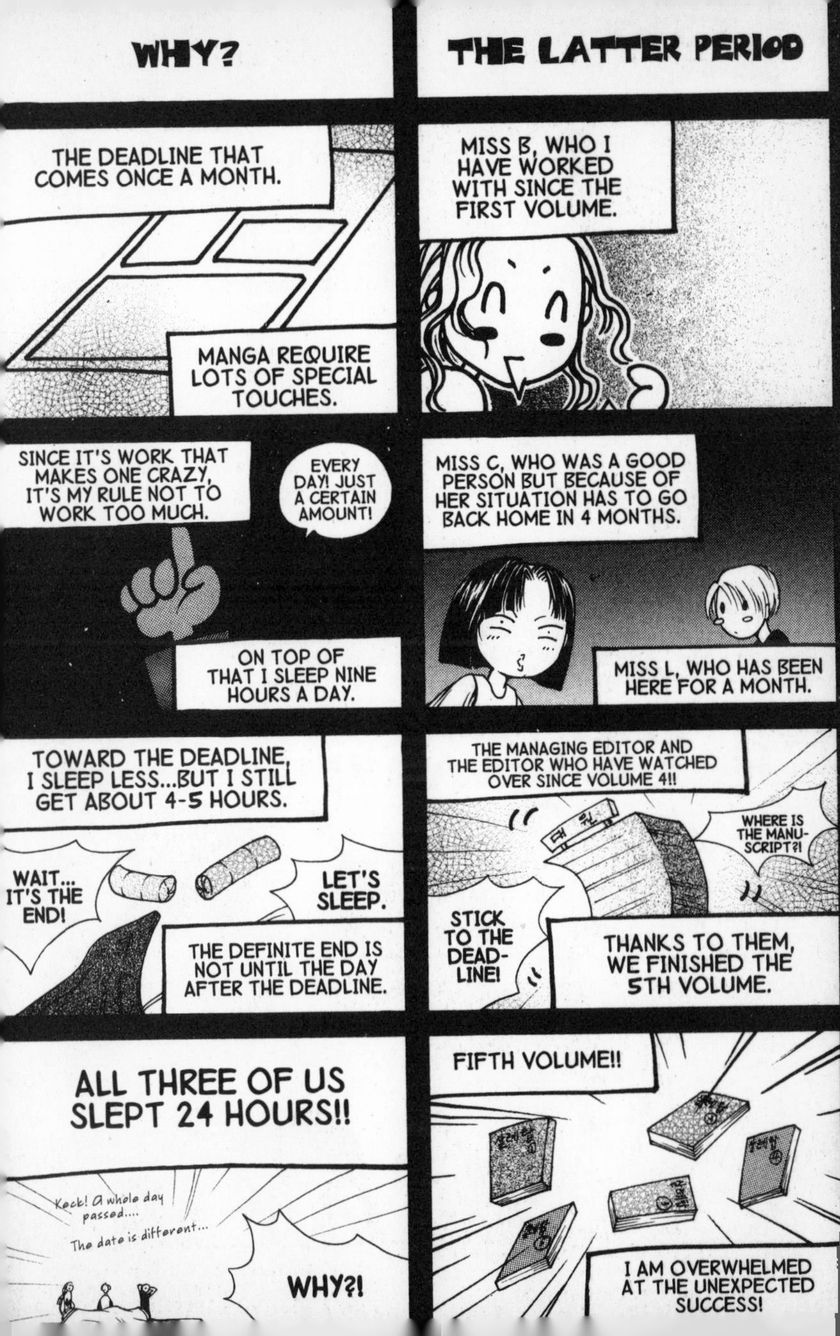
WHY?
THE DEADLINE THAT COMES ONCE A MONTH.
MANGA REQUIRE LOTS OF SPECIAL TOUCHES.
SINCE IT'S WORK THAT MAKES ONE CRAZY, IT'S MY RULE NOT TO WORK TOO MUCH.
EVERY DAY! JUST A CERTAIN AMOUNT!
ON TOP OF THAT I SLEEP NINE HOURS A DAY.
TOWARD THE DEADLINE, I SLEEP LESS...BUT I STILL GET ABOUT 4-5 HOURS.
WAIT... IT'S THE END!
LET'S SLEEP.
THE DEFINITE END IS NOT UNTIL THE DAY AFTER THE DEADLINE.
ALL THREE OF US SLEPT 24 HOURS!!
Keck! A whole day passed....
The date is different...
WHY?!
THE LATTER PERIOD
MISS B, WHO I HAVE WORKED WITH SINCE THE FIRST VOLUME.
MISS C, WHO WAS A GOOD PERSON BUT BECAUSE OF HER SITUATION HAS TO GO BACK HOME IN 4 MONTHS.
MISS L, WHO HAS BEEN HERE FOR A MONTH.
THE MANAGING EDITOR AND THE EDITOR WHO HAVE WATCHED OVER SINCE VOLUME 4!!
WHERE IS THE MANU-SCRIPT?!
STICK TO THE DEAD-LINE!
THANKS TO THEM, WE FINISHED THE 5TH VOLUME.
FIFTH VOLUME!!
I AM OVERWHELMED AT THE UNEXPECTED SUCCESS!

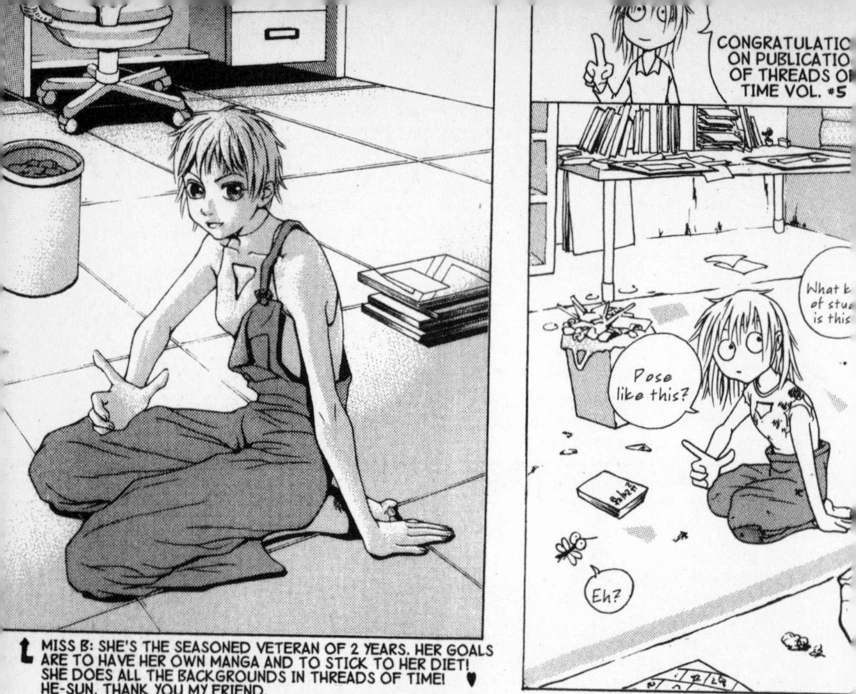
CONGRATULATIO
ON PUBLICATIO
OF THREADS O
TIME VOL. #5
What k
of stud
is this
Pose like this?
Eh?

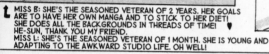

MISS B: SHE'S THE SEASONED VETERAN OF 2 YEARS. HER GOALS ARE TO HAVE HER OWN MANGA AND TO STICK TO HER DIET! SHE DOES ALL THE BACKGROUNDS IN THREADS OF TIME! ♥ HE-SUN, THANK YOU MY FRIEND.
MISS L: SHE'S THE SEASONED VETERAN OF 1 MONTH. SHE IS YOUNG AND ADAPTING TO THE AWKWARD STUDIO LIFE. OH WELL! ♥

SALI TAYI: HE'S SO DREAMY!

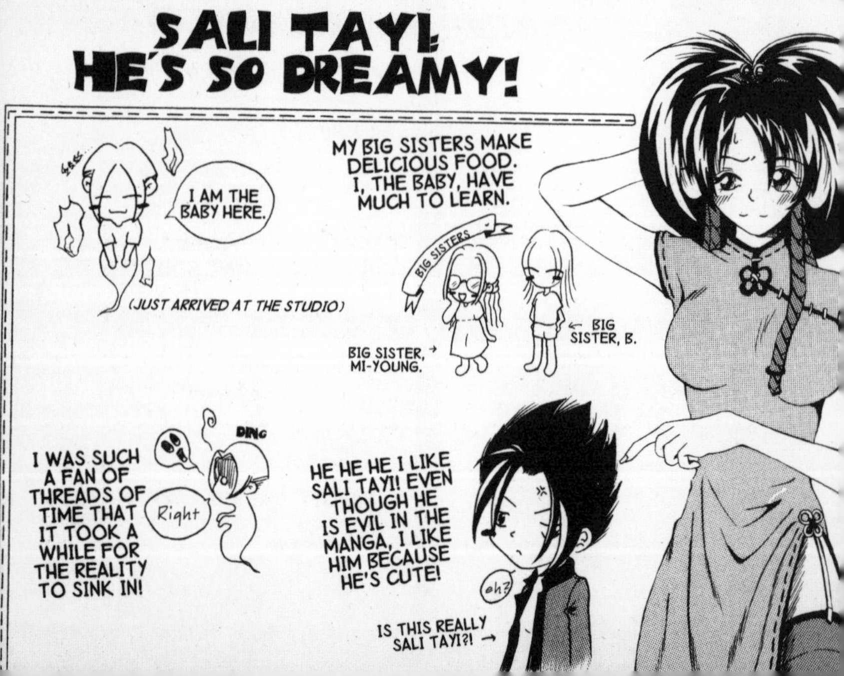
I AM THE BABY HERE.
(JUST ARRIVED AT THE STUDIO)
MY BIG SISTERS MAKE DELICIOUS FOOD. I, THE BABY, HAVE MUCH TO LEARN.
BIG SISTERS
BIG SISTER, MI-YOUNG.
BIG SISTER, B.
I WAS SUCH A FAN OF THREADS OF TIME THAT IT TOOK A WHILE FOR THE REALITY TO SINK IN!
DING
Right
HE HE HE I LIKE SALI TAYI! EVEN THOUGH HE IS EVIL IN THE MANGA, I LIKE HIM BECAUSE HE'S CUTE!
eh?
IS THIS REALLY SALI TAYI?!

Threads of Time

撤神塔

In Volume 6

The Mongol gift to General Kyung-Sohn Kim
is answered with a cry for vengeful insanity.
And when the Mongol troops eventually march
on Ghu-Zhu Palace, they are met with a lone
warrior, thirsty for the blood of the savages
who destroyed his family. But lurking among
the women prisoners, Moon-Bin can do
nothing but look on as the enemy of his people
dismantles the new home that he has only
recently chosen to adopt.

Koryo Soldier Profile:

The warriors of Koryo were renowned for both their martial prowess and indomitable spirit. During the later years of the dynasty and amidst the Mongol invasions, historical accounts on both sides of the conflict praised their remarkable valor and effectiveness on the battlefield. After the Koryo leadership negotiated a vassalage status, the Mongol overlords conscripted tens-of-thousands of soldiers and several prominent generals from the Koryo ranks to bolster the Khan's ambitions of empire throughout the Far East.

고려
KORYO

전사
soldier

TOKYOPOP
presents a special
and continuing
supplement to
Threads of Time...

The
Chronicles
of Koryo

Mongol Soldier Profile:

As the Mongol empire expanded to challenge the whole of the known world, their numbers were augmented by an endless variety of foreign mercenaries and tributary forces. The Mongols themselves, however, were mustered from small tribal clans united under the legendary Genghis Kahn. Honoring his namesake of "Universal Ruler," Genghis Khan's dominance resulted from a revolutionary tactical mind, a brutal standard of discipline and endurance for his soldiers, and a highly mobile army inspired by the nomadic history of his people.

몽고

MONGOL

전사

soldier

Art by
Jose Macasocol, Jr.
Written by
Brandon Montclare

TOKYOPOP SHOP

WWW.TOKYOPOP.COM/SHOP

HOT NEWS!
Check out the
TOKYOPOP SHOP!
The world's best
collection of manga in
English is now available
online in one place!

RG VEDA

VISITOR

Van Von Hunter
and other hot
titles are availab
at the store that
never closes!

VAN VON HUNTER

- • LOOK FOR SPECIAL OFFERS
- • PRE-ORDER UPCOMING RELEASES!
- • COMPLETE YOUR COLLECTIONS

BLAZIN' BARRELS

Sting may look harmless and naïve, but he's really an excellent fighter and a wannabe bounty hunter in the futuristic Wild West. When he comes across a notice that advertises a reward for the criminal outfit named Gold Romany, he decides that capturing the all-girl gang of bad guys is his ticket to fame and fortune!

MIN-SEO PARK HAS CREATED ONE WILD TUMBLEWEED TALE FILLED WITH ADVENTURE GALORE AND PLENTY OF SHOTGUN ACTION!

© MIN-SEO PARK, DAIWON C.I. Inc.

FOR MORE INFORMATION VISIT: WWW.TOKYOPOP.COM

Y YOUTH AGE 10+

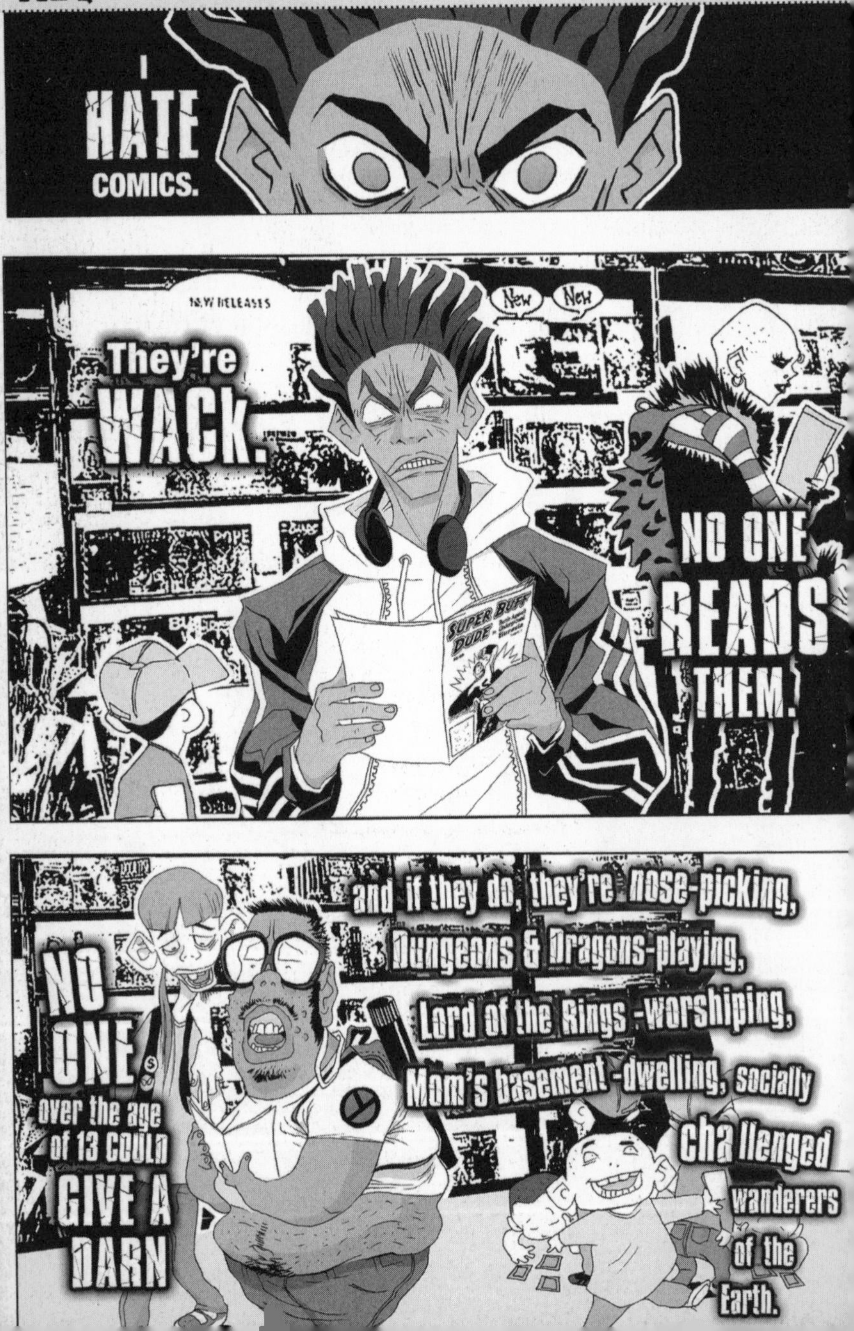
I HATE COMICS.
New
New
They're WACK.
SUPER BUFF DUDE
NO ONE READS THEM.
NO ONE over the age of 13 COULD GIVE A DARN
and if they do, they're nose-picking, Dungeons & Dragons-playing, Lord of the Rings -worshiping, Mom's basement -dwelling, socially challenged wanderers of the Earth.

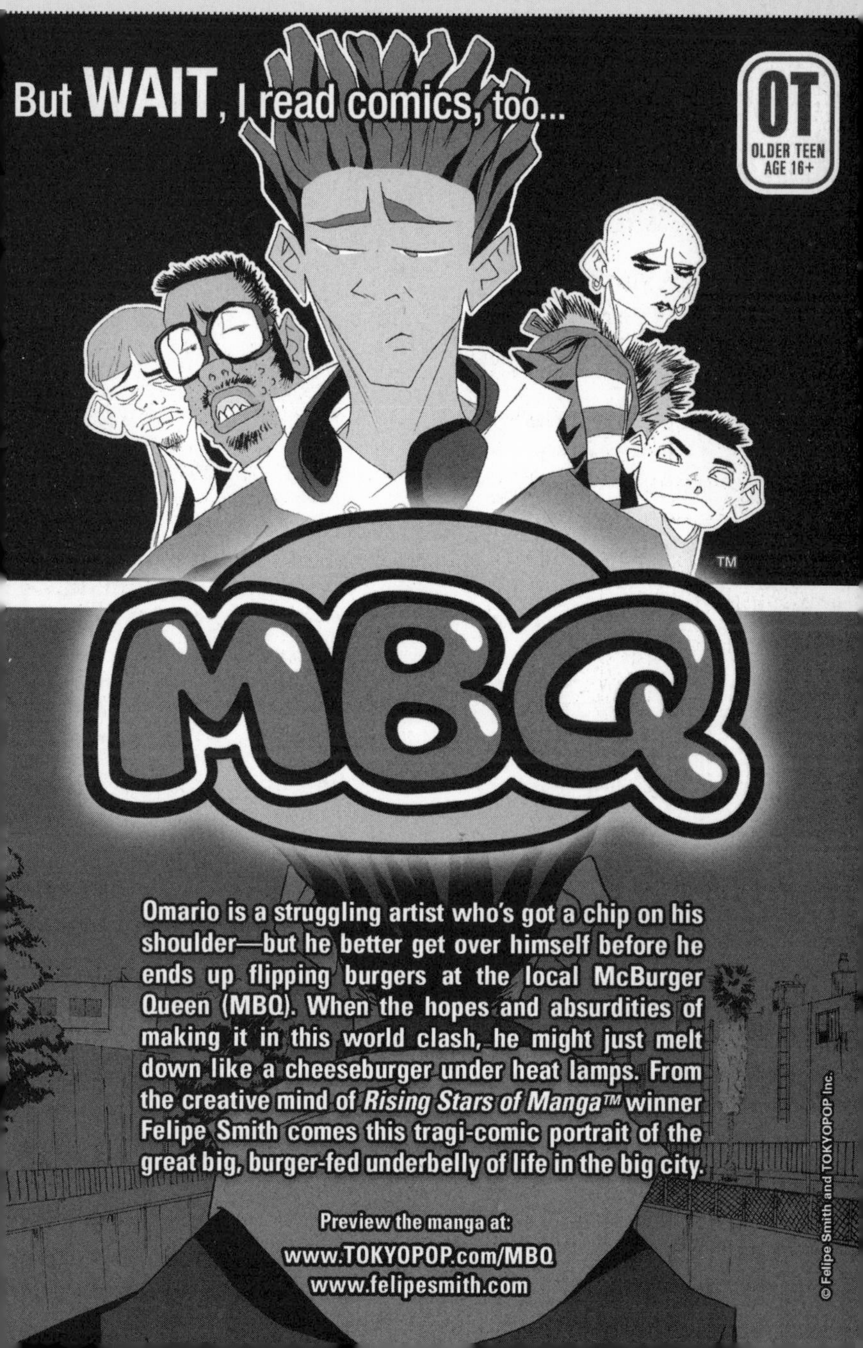
But WAIT, I read comics, too...
OT
OLDER TEEN AGE 16+
MBQ™
Omario is a struggling artist who's got a chip on his shoulder—but he better get over himself before he ends up flipping burgers at the local McBurger Queen (MBQ). When the hopes and absurdities of making it in this world clash, he might just melt down like a cheeseburger under heat lamps. From the creative mind of *Rising Stars of Manga™* winner Felipe Smith comes this tragi-comic portrait of the great big, burger-fed underbelly of life in the big city.
Preview the manga at:
www.TOKYOPOP.com/MBQ
www.felipesmith.com
© Felipe Smith and TOKYOPOP Inc.

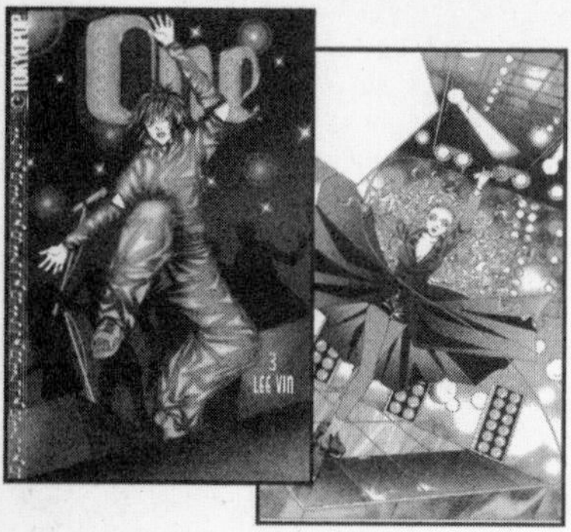
One
TOKYOPOP
3
LEE VIN

BY LEE VIN

ONE

Like American Idol? Then you'll love *One*, an energetic manga that gives you a sneak peek into the pop music industry. Lee Vin, who also created *Crazy Love Story*, is an amazingly accomplished artist! The story centers on the boy band One, a powerhouse of good looks, hot moves, and raw talent. It also features Jenny You, a Britney-Avril hybrid who's shooting straight for the top. But fame always comes at a price—and their path to stardom is full of speed bumps and roadblocks. But no matter what happens, they keep on rockin'—and so does this manga!

~Julie Taylor, Sr. Editor

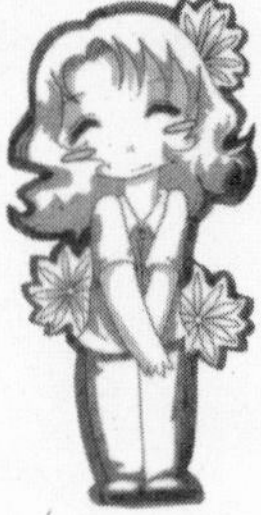

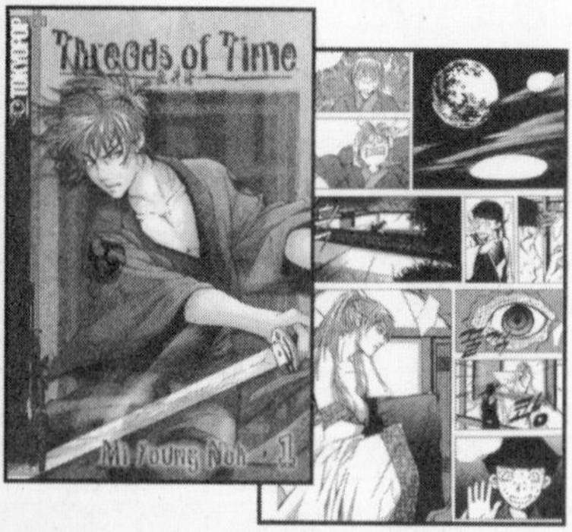
Threads of Time
TOKYOPOP
Mi Young Noh 1

BY MI-YOUNG NOH

THREADS OF TIME

The best thing about *Threads of Time* is its richly dramatic depiction of Korea's struggle to push back the Mongol Hordes in the 13th century. The plot focuses on a 20th century boy who ends up back in time. However, this science fiction conceit retreats to the background of this thrilling adventure in war-torn ancient Korea. Imagine a Korean general riding into battle with a battery of twelve men against two hundred Mongol warriors! Imagine back-stabbing politicians murdered in the clear of night. Imagine an entire village raped and slaughtered by Mongol hounds only to be avenged by a boy who just failed his high school science test.

~Luis Reyes, Editor

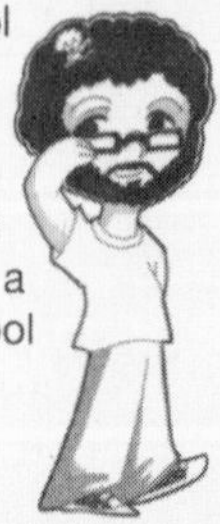

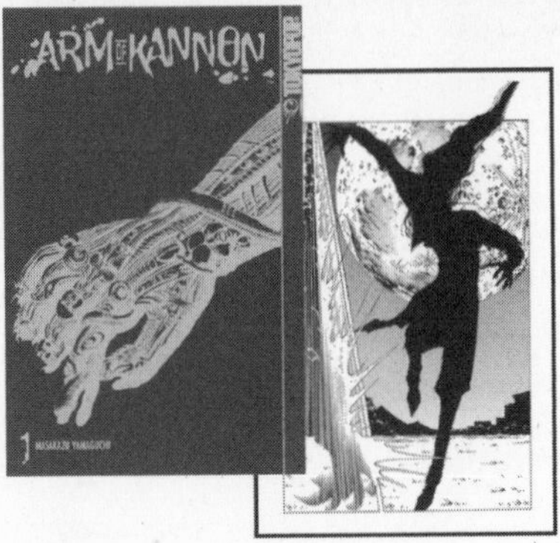
ARM OF KANNON

BY MASAKAZU YAMAGUCHI

ARM OF KANNON

Good and evil race to find the mysterious Arm of Kannon—an ancient Buddhist relic that has the power to bring about the end of humanity. The relic has been locked in a sacred temple for thousands of years. However, it is released and its demonic form soon takes over the will of a young boy, Mao, who must now flee from the evil forces that hunt the arm for control of its awesome power. This sexually charged action/horror story, traversing a vast landscape of demons, swordsmen, magicians, street gangs and government super-soldiers, will make the hairs on the back of your neck stand on edge.

~Rob Valois, Editor

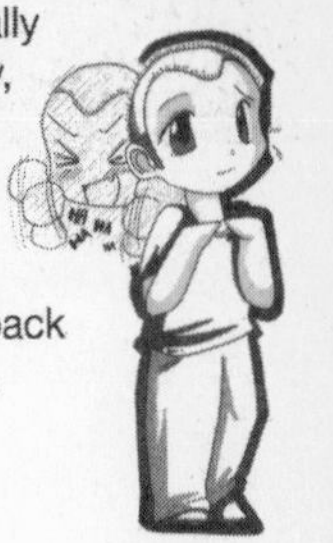

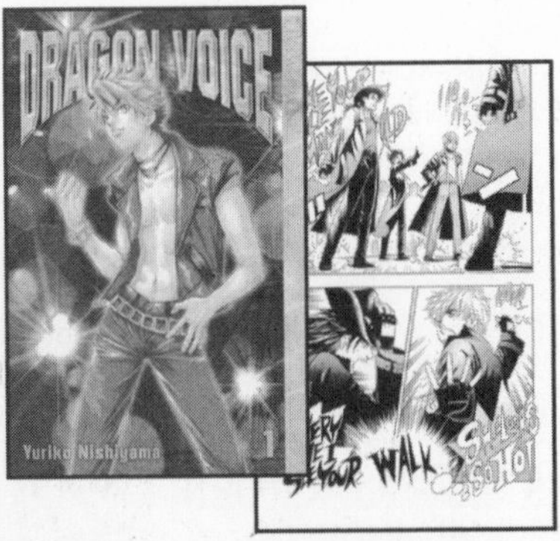
DRAGON VOICE
Yuriko Nishiyama
WALK

BY YURIKO NISHIYAMA

DRAGON VOICE

I have to admit that Yuriko Nishiyama's *Dragon Voice* was not at all what I was expecting. As more a fan of action/adventure stories like *Samurai Deeper Kyo*, the singing and dancing hijinks of a Japanese boy-band seemed hardly like my cup of tea. But upon proofreading Volume 3 for fellow editor Lillian Diaz-Przybyl, I found *Dragon Voice* to be one of my favorites! Rin and his fellow Beatmen dazzle their way past all obstacles—rival boy-band Privee, theme-park prima donnas, or TV production pitfalls—and do it with style! This book is one of the most fun reads I've had in a long time!

~Aaron Suhr, Sr. Editor

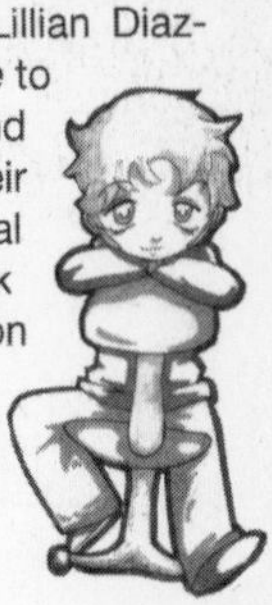

SORCERER HUNTERS
BY RAY OMISHI & SATORU AKAHORI

On the Spooner Continent, powerless commoners spend each day terrorized by merciless evil sorcerers. Big Mama has had enough, and she sends out an elite group of warriors—the Sorcerer Hunters: Carrot, Chocolat, Tira Misu, Gateau, and Marron.

The manga that inspired the hit anime!

OT OLDER TEEN AGE 16+

© Satoru Akahori/Ray Omishi

iD_eNTITY
BY HEE-JOON SON & YOON-KYUNG KIM

From Hee-Joon Son, creator of TOKYOPOP's *PhD: Phantasy Degree!*

Roto, Boromid and Ah-dol are a fellowship of friends who are terrific gamers. When Roto finds an ID card for the LostSaga online game with "Yureka" printed on it, he hacks into the game using "Yureka" as his identity. The trouble is, Yureka already has an identity all her own...

T TEEN AGE 13+

© Hee-Joon Son & Yoon-Kyung Kim, HAKSAN PUBLISHING CO., LTD.

From the creator of *Vampire Princess Miyu!*

SHAOLIN SISTERS: REBORN
BY TOSHIKI HIRANO & NARUMI KAKINOUCHI

Beginning with *Juline* and followed in *Shaolin Sisters*, *Shaolin Sisters: Reborn* gives the epic saga of Juline and her two sisters a modern spin. When an enigmatic masked man saves Julin Misumi from a mysterious bird woman, she learns her dreams of an age martial arts point to one thing...

T TEEN AGE 13+

© Narumi Kakinouchi

WARCRAFT

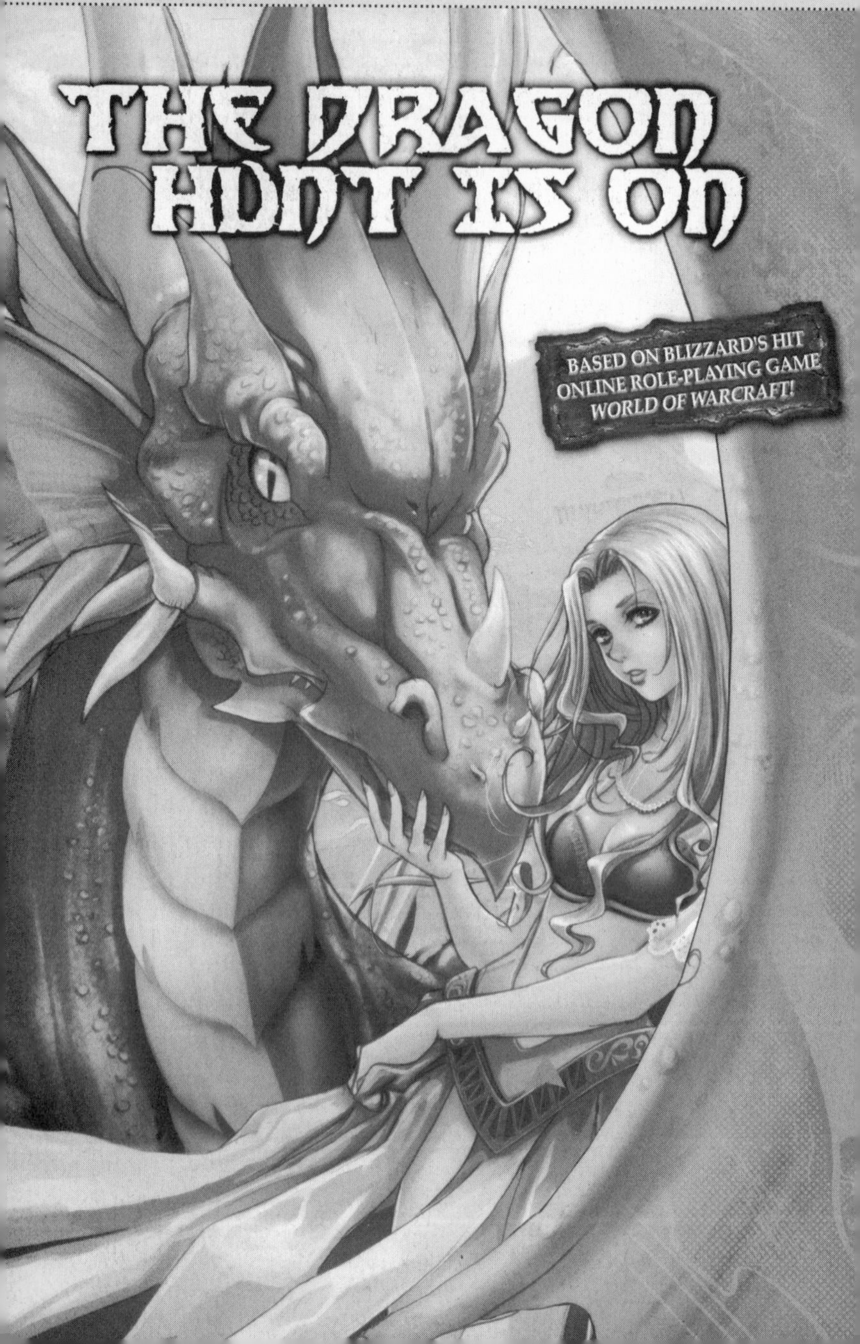
THE DRAGON HUNT IS ON
BASED ON BLIZZARD'S HIT ONLINE ROLE-PLAYING GAME *WORLD OF WARCRAFT!*